THE RISE OF CIVILIZATION
IN INDIA AND PAKISTAN

CAMBRIDGE WORLD ARCHAEOLOGY

THE RISE OF CIVILIZATION IN INDIA AND PAKISTAN

BRIDGET AND RAYMOND ALLCHIN

CAMBRIDGE
UNIVERSITY PRESS

Published by the Press Syndicate of the University of Cambridge
The Pitt Building, Trumpington Street, Cambridge CB2 1RP
40 West 20th Street, New York, NY 10011–4211, USA
10 Stamford Road, Oakleigh, Victoria, 3166, Australia

First published 1982
Reprinted 1985, 1988, 1993, 1996

Printed in Malta by Interprint Limited.

Library of Congress catalogue card number: 82–1262

British Library catalogue in publication data

Allchin, Raymond
The rise of civilization in India and Pakistan.
—(Cambridge world archaeology)
1. India—Civilization—To 1200
I. Title   II. Allchin, Bridget
934   DS425

ISBN-0-521-28550-X

CONTENTS

TABLES AND FIGURES

PREFACE

The process of gathering together material, planning and writing this book has been jointly undertaken by the two authors. As in the case of its predecessor, *The Birth of Indian Civilization*, they claim joint responsibility for its contents, its faults, and for any original contribution to the subject it may succeed in making.

Owing to the book's nature the authors have been dependent throughout upon the work of others. Those to whom they are indebted include: the great number of scholars whose published works they have read or whose lectures they have heard, a few of whom are included in the Bibliography, but a far greater number of whom are not; all the friends and colleagues who have conducted them round their Museums or their excavations, kindly allowed them to see unpublished material and spent many hours in discussion; more particularly there are those who kindly spent their time going through the earlier volume and suggested ways in which it could be changed, added to or improved; those who went through parts of the manuscript of the present book and made valuable comments and suggestions; lastly, there are all those people and institutions who supplied illustrative and other materials. The authors would like to express their gratitude and appreciation to them all.

It is quite impossible even to list those in the first two categories, and equally impossible to give any order of precedence to those in the last three, therefore they are listed here in alphabetical order:

Dr Z. Ansari, Dr D. K. Chakrabarti, Professor G. Dales, Professor F. A. Durrani, Professor W. A. Fairservis, Professor C. von F. Haimendorf, Mr M. A. Halim, Professor K. T. M. Hegde, Drs C. and J.-F. Jarrige, Dr J. P. Joshi, Professor R. V. Joshi, Professor B. B. Lal, Professor V. N. Misra, Dr M. S. Nagaraja Rao, Professor A. K. Narain, Dr S. R. Rao, Dr H. Rendell, Professor H. D. Sankalia, Dr A. Sarcina, Professor G. R. Sharma, Professor T. C. Sharma, Professor G. Stacul, Dr Suraj-Bhan, Dr B. K. Thapar.

Among Institutions and their Directors the authors wish to acknowledge: Director General of Archaeology in India; Director of Archaeology, Government of Pakistan; Director of Archaeology, Bihar; Deccan College, Pune; Jodhpur Museum; Director of Archaeology, Government of Karnataka; Madras Government Museum; Prince of Wales Museum, Bombay.

The authors also wish to acknowledge the great help they have received from a number of their students or former students in the preparation of the text, in editing it, and in the preparation of the index. These include Mr Piers Baker, Mr Richard Blurton and Miss Rima Hooja. Mr Peter Wright has been of great assistance in the preparation of illustrations, and Mrs Miriam Sidell was responsible for the final typescript.

To anyone they have inadvertently omitted the authors extend their apologies as well as their thanks. Finally, they would like to thank Dr Robin Derricourt, Miss Katharine Owen, Mr Robert Seal and others at the Cambridge University Press who produced the book with such efficiency and speed, so that its appearance might coincide with the British Festival of India in the summer of 1982.

Postscript

For the reprinting of this volume the opportunity has been taken of correcting minor errors and including references to some major new discoveries. It is hoped that full discussion of such discoveries, as well as the resulting reinterpretation, will appear in a subsequent second edition.

Bridget and Raymond Allchin

Cambridge, 1988

CHAPTER I

ARCHAEOLOGY IN SOUTH ASIA

This book is the lineal descendant of the *Birth of Indian Civilization* which came out in 1968. Since then so much new material has come to light, and ideas and approaches have so greatly changed, that a completely new framework is called for. It is now possible to write a more integrated and dynamic account of the rise of civilization in India and Pakistan: this is what we have attempted to do. The overall pattern of South Asian subcontinental cultural development has come much more clearly into focus. In some areas a great deal of work has been done, but in others there has been comparatively little or no advance during the past fourteen years. The reasons for this are various, but whatever they may be, as a result, certain passages from the *Birth of Indian Civilization* stand with only slight modification. Some of these have been carried over into the new book. Similarly, some of the illustrations still make their point better or as well as other available material could do. Here too we have not hesitated to re-use material from the earlier book. In spite of these borrowings the *Rise of Civilization in India and Pakistan* is to all intents and purposes a new book, and has been completely reorganized and almost entirely rewritten.

During the past fifteen years the increasing volume of fieldwork and research in all parts of South Asia has led to a growing spate of publications. Among these one notes with particular satisfaction the appearance of several new periodicals or serials. From India, where the official publication *Indian Archaeology – A Review* has recently seen the publication of its twenty-fifth number (1977–8), two important new arrivals on the scene are the journals *Puratattva*, the bulletin of the Indian Archaeological Society, of which eight numbers have so far appeared, and *Man and Environment*, the journal of the Indian Society for Prehistoric and Quaternary Studies, with five numbers to date. *Pakistan Archaeology* has continued to appear, though irregularly; and from Sri Lanka comes the welcome addition of a new journal *Ancient Ceylon*, of which we have so far received only two numbers. Outside South Asia a welcome innovation of the 1970s has been the appearance of *South Asian Archaeology*, the proceedings of the biennial conference of South Asian Archaeologists in Western Europe, of which five volumes have so far been published. These publications together provide useful sources of information regarding primary research and fieldwork in the several countries involved. In addition there are numerous volumes carrying the proceedings of seminars and conferences in various countries, both within South Asia and outside. Notable among these is Agrawal and Ghosh,

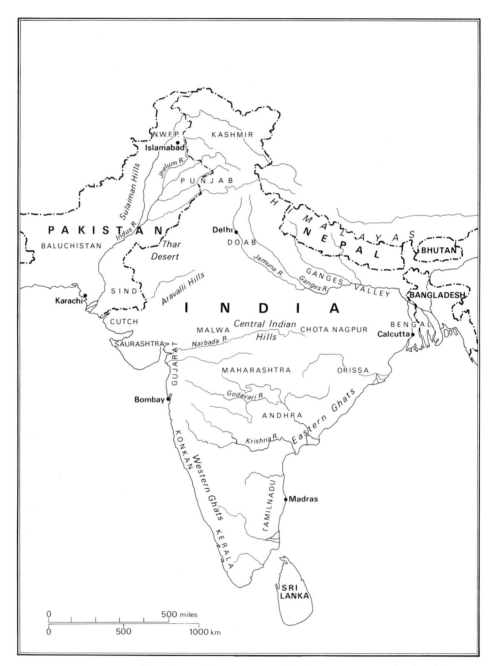

1.1 Map of South Asia showing principal political frontiers and cultural regions

Radiocarbon and Indian Archaeology (Bombay, 1973). There has also been a welcome growth in the number of monographs devoted to specific problems or periods of South Asian archaeology. Many are referred to in the Bibliography. These works have provided additional data, and with so much new data the need has become increasingly felt for synthetic works, offering more comprehensive accounts of the whole or significant parts of the subject. Among these are W. A. Fairservis's *Roots of Ancient India*, appearing in 1971; the second edition of Sankalia's monumental *Prehistory and Protohistory of India and Pakistan* was published in 1974, to be followed by the same author's shorter and more digested *Prehistory of India* (1977), perhaps the finest book of its kind so far.

During the 1970s the pace of archaeological research has been maintained, even if the number of excavations has not been as great as it was during the 1950s and 1960s. This is due in part to changing economic circumstances and in part to changing methods and approaches. Before discussing these innovations it is worth noting that a number of excavations, even major excavations from the earlier period, are as yet unpublished, or only partly published. Outstanding among these are the excavations at Lothal (now partly published) and Kaliban-gan, and the two seasons' work at Mohenjo-daro, first by Sir Mortimer Wheeler in 1950 and second by Dales in 1965 (both now in course of publication by Professor Dales). Many smaller excavations, some of crucial interest from one point of view or another, remain unpublished, and some – one fears – may never see the light of day.

Changing approaches

During the last two decades South Asian prehistory has moved into a new phase. Previously the majority of prehistorians working in the subcontinent were concerned with artefact typology and technology, its development through time, and the sequential and regional relationships of assemblages of stone and ceramic artefacts. Recently, owing both to new approaches beginning to be adopted by prehistorians working in the subcontinent and to advances in related fields, particularly geomorphology, palaeontology, palaeobotany and palaeocli-matology, throughout the world, there has been an increasing swing towards considering past cultures in their totality. This means finding out as much as possible about the ecological relationship between a human community or group and its environmental context. As a result artefacts are seen as only one aspect, although an important one, of any culture. This approach necessitates taking into consideration many other categories of evidence including the study of all animal, plant and other organic remains in associated cultural or geological deposits, thus giving an insight into the character of the immediate physical environment, and the way in which it was utilized. Complementary to this is the relationship of objects including both artefacts and organic remains to one another at living sites and factory areas. The distribution of sites in relation to the topography of an area or region, is another important line of enquiry, and allied to it is the evidence for widespread change in the environment that such topographic or geomorphologic studies provide. This in turn leads to the even more fundamental question of major climatic and environmental change which gave many regions of the world a totally different character in the past from that we see today.

Advances in earth sciences generally, and in the geomorphology of arid and tropical zones of the world, in particular, are two of the main factors that have made possible the change of emphasis in South Asian prehistoric studies. Palaeobotany, which has played such an important role in understanding past climatic conditions in northern temperate regions, has proved less rewarding in South Asia for a number of reasons. Geomorphology, the analysis of topographic features has, however, been more helpful. Examination of the present landscape shows many features, such as abandoned river courses, glacial moraines, buried soils, fossil desert dunes, and dead drainage systems, that are residual from earlier periods, having been formed under conditions different from those prevailing today. Analysis of such features can often indicate what these conditions were. Cultural remains found related to them, as for example when a working or living site is associated with a buried soil, can then be given an environmental context.

There is an increasing awareness of the need to study sites of all kinds, including open air factory floors, living sites and larger settlements in relation to environmental factors, and this is beginning to lead to a more careful and systematic approach. Coupled with this is a more realistic understanding on the part of prehistorians of the nature of the South Asian environment, present and past; and of the ways in which it differs, often radically, from the environment of temperate regions where methods and approaches to prehistory were initially developed. For example, in much of Europe or North America soil tends to form fairly rapidly on all but the steepest slopes, engulfing objects and remains of buildings, etc., and obscuring them from view without necessarily burying them deeply. In most parts of South Asia, where erosion is predominant, objects tend to remain exposed indefinitely in any rocky or hilly situation, with the result that in considerable areas of India and Pakistan structures and artefacts are to be found on the surface, unless disturbed by subsequent human activity. The corollary of erosion, aggradation or the deposition of silt, gravel, etc., produces the opposite effect, and in valleys and plains structures and objects become buried in a relatively short space of time. For example, a single flood may lay down five or ten centimetres of silt over many square kilometres in the valley of the lower Narbada and other major rivers. This does not happen every year but may take place several times in a decade.

Other aspects of the changing approach to the study of human cultures relate more specifically to the problems posed by later archaeological periods and contexts. Here too there has been a general shift away from the older approach to artefacts or categories of artefacts viewed in isolation, towards a more integrated view of cultures as functioning wholes, viewing cultural change as far as possible in much the same way as its modern counterpart in terms of dynamic processes, rather than as mere sequences of artefacts, traits or assemblages. These changes have been relatively slow in reaching South Asia, where it is still not uncommon to come across the either explicit or implicit view that changes in style of pottery or some other artefacts necessarily reflect more profound changes, such as the arrival of immigrants, rather than mere changes in style or fashion, occurring in much the same way as they still do today.

There has been considerable use (or abuse?) of the availability of language-historical, literary or quasi-historical data to augment archaeological evidence; but here – one feels – there is still a great need for consideration of the most suitable methodology for interrelating the data supplied by these subjects.

Above all, there appears to be a need for a clearer consensus of the main requirements of planned research for all periods. This, we believe, must be linked to a more problem-oriented approach. There are still some glaring lacunae in South Asian prehistory and later archaeology. For instance, there is still an almost complete absence of fossil hominids to compare with the many examples known from other parts of the world; our knowledge of the development of cities in North India and Pakistan during the first millennium B.C. is as yet rudimentary; and many regions of the subcontinent still lack clear and structured evidence for whole periods. Not the least of the advantages of a problem-oriented approach lies in the relative ease of publication, if only in the form of preliminary reports, as research progresses. All too often in the past it appears to have been the increasingly daunting and insoluble problem of total publication of the proceeds of large scale excavations which has proved the stumbling-block to final publication of any significant account of some of these costly operations. New methods of data processing, storage and presentation must be looked for as the older methods become impracticable.

It is interesting to consider the contrast presented by the progress of research in the several countries of South Asia. In India the Government's policy, pursued since the 1950s, of including at least some teaching of archaeology at every university, with full departments at several, and now of Advanced Centres at two, is beginning to pay dividends both in terms of the level of training and number of qualified students being produced, and of the volume and quality of research of all kinds. This development probably lies behind the appearance of learned societies such as those we noticed above, as well as contributing to the growing awareness among educated people of the urgent need for conservation of both the natural and cultural heritage in India. In Pakistan the development of university archaeology has been slower to emerge, but there are now several universities teaching the subject.

A feature of special interest is the encouragement by the Government of Pakistan of foreign archaeological missions: over the past years this has contributed markedly to the progress of research. There are currently French, Italian, British and West German missions operating, as well as several independent American and other expeditions. These serve an important role in providing a forum for the exchange of ideas and practical experience between local and visiting scholars. In India by contrast there have been surprisingly few foreign expeditions, and little fieldwork by individual foreign scholars. This has perhaps helped to contribute to the relative isolation of Indian archaeological thinking. There have been a small number of significant examples of collaboration between Indian and foreign teams (the Cambridge–Baroda Universities project in the 1970s was one, and the more recent collaboration between Berkeley and the new Centre of Advanced Study at Allahabad is another).

In Sri Lanka prehistoric and protohistoric archaeology have made little progress, with the result that in many of the chapters of this book it has been necessary to point to the complete, or almost complete, absence of firm data relating to some of the main prehistoric periods. Perhaps the most outstanding example is the apparent absence of any cultural remains prior to the Mesolithic with the exception of a single hand axe. The lack of information regarding early agricultural settlements comparable to those now known in almost every other part of the subcontinent, and the paucity of knowledge concerning the archaeological remains of the people of Sri Lanka in the centuries prior to the arrival of North Indian colonizers in the middle of the first millennium B.C., are equally glaring lacunae.

About the book

One or two features call for comment. Throughout the text we have quoted simple B.C. dates wherever possible. These are in all cases derived from available radiocarbon dates, calculated according to the MASCA calibration (wherever applicable), and giving a single medial date, discounting the plus or minus factor. In some cases the date is an approximation based on the various dates available, and markedly eccentric dates have generally been neglected (unless occasionally they are specially commented on). After much thought we have not included a table of actual radiocarbon dates with their laboratory and sample numbers. We are aware that these dates are essential for any serious study of problems and chronology, but they are, after all, all published or in process of publication in the annual volumes of *Radiocarbon*, and the Indian dates (from the Tata Institute of Fundamental Research, Bombay, and latterly the National Physical Research Laboratory, Ahmedabad) are also published in *Current Science*. Therefore in the interests of brevity we have not repeated here what must be now a long catalogue. Many relevant dates are included in Agrawal and Kusumgar's *Prehistoric Chronology and Radiocarbon Dating in India*, 1974. This invaluable little book certainly deserves a new and enlarged edition, bringing it up to date and correcting occasional misprints.

The text does not include references, but there is a select general bibliography at the end, with a series of suggestions for further reading for each chapter or group of chapters. In preparing these we have tried as far as possible to give references to other synthetic works, as these in many cases include their own often extensive bibliographies.

PART I

CONSTITUENT ELEMENTS

CHAPTER 2

PREHISTORIC ENVIRONMENTS

The second chapter of the *Birth of Indian Civilization*, 'The Geographical and Human Background', gave a fairly comprehensive outline of the basic physical and human geography of South Asia as it appeared at that time. As a statement of facts and an overall summary of the relationship between environmental and cultural distinctions this still stands. It emphasizes the role played by the cultural and linguistic regions of the subcontinent throughout historic and later prehistoric times, and the way in which the roots of regional character extend back into the early Stone Age. The close relationship of the environmental potential of any region and its developing regional character from the Palaeolithic right through to modern times was already apparent. Since 1967 this has become even clearer, as the following chapters aim to show.

Our approach to many questions of South Asian prehistory is still, as it was in the 1950s and 1960s, basically a geographical one. This is something which new methods and approaches have altered but have not changed fundamentally for it plays an essential part in understanding the regional character of South Asian culture and its fundamental quality of diversity within overall unity. The character of South Asian culture as a whole is as distinct as that of Europe, for example, or China. Like Europe or China it comprises a number of cultural and linguistic entities. One of the distinctive features of South Asian culture in historic and recent times is the way in which it has encapsulated communities at many different cultural and technological levels, allowing them, to a large extent, to retain their identity and establish intercommunity relationships. Early Indian literature makes it clear that this was a feature of north-west Indian society during the first millennium B.C. It seems highly probable that its roots, like those of the cultural regions, extend back much further. Both these characteristics help to give South Asian culture a peculiar flexibility and adaptability of its own. They ensure that in changing circumstances it has within itself the means, and the intellectual and practical reserves, to deal with the often catastrophic problems that arise in the rich and varied but unpredictable environment of the subcontinent. When one means of survival becomes impossible there is always another.

Floods, droughts, earthquakes and changes in the courses of major rivers are and have been part of the South Asian environment. References to them occur throughout history, from the Rigveda to eyewitness accounts in the publications of the Geological Survey of India of the late nineteenth and early twentieth centuries. That the Himalayas are geologically relatively young mountains; and that the Siwaliks and the Salt range are even younger, consisting as they do of folded Pliocene and early Pleistocene sediments, are generally accepted. The dramatically distorted folding of strata revealed by torrents cutting through the Salt range, and the curious phenomenon of walls of residual hardened Siwalik sediments, lifted from the horizontal to the perpendicular by intense folding, and now protruding from the surface of the Potwar plateau – both bear eloquent witness to the force of recent tectonic activity.

The general recognition during the last fifteen years of the important part played by plate tectonics (Continental Drift) in the formation of the major mountain ranges of the world has brought home the direct relationship between such observation and the earthquakes and unstable shifting river channels of modern times. One of the fundamental causes of these events is the active thrusting of the plate of ancient rock of Peninsular India into the main Asian land mass. The opinion was recently expressed in a letter to *Nature* by a group of earth scientists visiting China that within the last twenty thousand years the rains of the South-west Monsoon were reaching the now desert region of Chinese Turkestan. This means that the Himalayas must have been significantly lower then than they are today in order to allow the rain-bearing Monsoon winds to cross them. The implications of this suggestion in terms of the Indian subcontinent are many and various, and require much careful consideration, intelligent observation and research in the field and in the laboratory before they can begin to be fully appreciated. But one thing is clear from the outset: the environment of Palaeolithic man in South Asia and the landscape of his world must have been fundamentally different from that we see today. Indeed, a number of fairly radical changes in the morphology of the landscape and drainage patterns of North and North-west India, Pakistan and Bangladesh may well have taken place since the beginning of settled agriculture, now considered to have taken place some seven millennia before the present time in the north-western tributary valleys of the lower Indus.

One further aspect of South Asian prehistory that has come more sharply into focus since 1967 is its north-west/south-east axis. The predominant direction of outside influences appears to have been to the north-west. At times, however, the east and south-east have also played a significant role, and this has probably been predominant at certain times, as for example in the late Pleistocene, during periods of low sea level and greatly increased aridity. Again, at later periods when physical conditions or periods of military and political turmoil in Western and Central Asia made trade and other peaceful contacts in that direction virtually impossible, land and sea connections with South-east Asia and the Far East must have taken on increased importance. Many aspects of the art, culture and life-style of eastern Peninsular India and Sri Lanka bear witness to this process. At the level of village life and agricultural practice there are many culture traits that show a continuum from Eastern India and Bangladesh into

Assam, Burma and beyond. This is also indicated by the somewhat scanty archaeological record of these regions from Neolithic times forward.

The north-west/south-east axis is another of the strengths of South Asian culture. Like all the major enduring cultures of the world it draws upon the resources and the genius of contrasting but complementary regions. In this case it is that of two already highly complex regions. One is the world of oases linked by nomads of the arid regions to the north-west. The other is the tropical world, much of it potentially capable of carrying dense populations based on intensive agriculture of the east and south-east. By successfully encompassing these two aspects South Asia has added a further dimension to itself: the further reserves of intellectual and practical knowledge which have enabled the complex totality to survive. It survives not as a monolith – such cultures quickly pass into fossilized obscurity – but as a highly sophisticated structure maintained by many balances and counterbalances, and capable of lending itself to revival, additions and adaptation. Perhaps a complex living organism would be a better analogy, but this would lead one into too much controversy at the present time.

In the foregoing paragraphs we have briefly indicated some of the salient features of South Asian geography, and the part they have played in the formation and development of South Asian culture as a whole. The importance and antiquity of cultural regions, and their relationship to the varying physical environment have also been stressed. We shall now attempt to outline the available evidence regarding the nature of past climates and environments in the major regions of the subcontinent, and the extent to which this may be used to reconstruct the ecology of ancient societies. First there are a few further general observations that should be made about present and past climatic patterns.

The southern part of the Peninsula and Central India lie in the tropics; North India and Pakistan, outside. By analogy with Africa or Australia, where the world pattern of climatic belts is relatively uninterrupted, one would expect the subcontinent from the northern Deccan northward to have an arid, semi-desert or desert climate. In fact, owing to the juxtaposition of the mountain ranges of the Peninsula and the Himalayas, and the surrounding oceans, much of South Asia enjoys a sufficiently high monsoonal rainfall to support forests, grass land and long established traditional systems of fairly intensive agriculture. Consequently, what we see today is a complex pattern of regions of higher and lower rainfall. Two of the main areas of higher rainfall, the western coastal belt and the Ganges–Jamuna plain, coincide with areas of rich alluvial soil. A major area of lower rainfall extends from Central India down the interior of the Peninsula and across to the east coast. The greater part of Pakistan and Western India, with the exception of a broad belt along the Himalayan foothills and the plains of the northern Punjab, virtually forms an extension of the western Asiatic and Iranian desert lying to the west and north-west, from which it is divided by the rich but narrow belt inundated by the river Indus. In terms of human environments this presents a pattern of regions of arid conditions, not unlike those of Western Asia, interdigitating with more luxuriant environments having much in common with the tropical conditions of South-east Asia.

The Himalayas

Evidence that the Himalayan glaciers had formerly descended several hundred feet below their present termini was noted over a century ago. Subsequent studies of the Pleistocene geology of certain regions, such as that of the Kashmir valley by de Terra and Paterson and the Swat valley by Porter, for example, have shown in each case a series of old terminal moraines, below the present confines of the glaciers, related to terrace systems within their respective valleys. These appear to indicate major climatic changes generally comparable to those that took place in Europe and North America. This does not mean that they can be taken as representing a precisely corresponding sequence of events, as the climatic history of every major region of the world has been affected by many factors; and even where the same factors are at work some may be more pronounced in one region and others in another. The whole question of interpretation of the South Asian evidence is complicated by rapid uplift of the Himalayas, Tibetan plateau, Pamirs and other mountain ranges. Recent research on earth sciences has shown that this was still taking place during Palaeolithic times. As already indicated, the rapidity, scale and relatively recent date of this activity has only become apparent since the role of plate tectonics or 'Continental Drift' as a major factor in the shaping of these regions has been recognized. The relationship of past climates to such major tectonic activity is highly complex. At present all that can be said is that these changes must have had profound and far reaching effects not only upon the mountain regions but upon the whole subcontinent, and particularly upon the piedmont regions adjacent to the mountains, of which the Potwar plateau forms part.

The Potwar plateau, situated between the Indus and the Jhelum in the northern Punjab, offers a great deal of evidence of past environments that differed in many respects from that we see today. The problem for the archaeologist is to read this evidence correctly in terms of the association of stone industries and climatic episodes represented in the geological record, and then to try to work out and assess the ecology of each cultural phase as far as the evidence will allow. All this has to be done on an interdisciplinary basis in collaboration with experts in other fields, particularly geology, in this case.

Recent field research in the Potwar plateau has made it abundantly clear that the picture of the late Pleistocene and early Holocene sequence put forward by de Terra and Paterson in the 1930s requires radical revision. This is especially important as their work has formed the basis of much discussion and of fieldwork on the geomorphology and Pleistocene geology of the subcontinent

Table 2.1. *Relative chronology of the Pleistocene deposits of the Potwar plateau, according to de Terra and Paterson, 1939*

4th glaciation	T4	pink loam, silt, gravel	fluvial sedimentation
3rd interglacial	T3	thin loam	erosion/warping
3rd glaciation	T2	Potwar loessic silt and gravel	aeolian, fluvial, lacustrine
2nd interglacial	T1	upper terrace gravel	
		――――――――― erosion/tilting/folding ――――――――――	
2nd glaciation		Boulder Conglomerate	fluvial and fluvioglacial sedimentation
1st interglacial		―――――――― erosion/tilting/folding ―――――――	
		Pinjor Beds conglomerates, sands, clays	
1st glaciation		Tatrot Beds conglomerates and sands	

Table 2.2. *Modified relative chronology of the Siwalik and Pleistocene deposits of the Middle Soan valley, after H. Rendell, 1982*

		Tentative dates
	――――――― erosion/deposition ―――――――	
	Loess deposition	
	―――――――― erosion/warping ――――――――	– Middle Palaeolithic
	Lei Conglomerate Complex (valley fill) includes deposition of loess/uplift partly contemporaneous	(c. 40,000 yrs)
	――――― uplift/folding/start of erosion ―――――	– 0.7–0.5 million years ago
	Upper Siwalik Conglomerates	– 1.9 mya
Soan Formation	Pinjor Beds	– 2.5 mya
	Tatrot Beds	
	――――――― diconformity ―――――――	
Dhok Pathan Formation		
Nagri Formation		
Chinji Formation		

SIWALIK GROUP {

ever since, although recently more and more called in question. Revision is particularly necessary from the archaeological point of view as Paterson's discussion of the stone artefacts, found there in such abundance, claimed to show that there is a general correspondence between their physical condition, typology and technology, and their position in the terrace sequence. From this he postulated a number of minor sub-divisions, or stages for the Soan industries, in addition to a major cultural division into Early and Late Soan. The nature of such terraces as there are in the valleys of the Soan and other rivers that cross the Potwar plateau has been shown by surveys made by the British Archaeological Mission to Pakistan in 1980 and 1981 to have little direct relationship to those of the Himalayan valleys. Some of the lower terraces in de Terra's sequence postdate the Palaeolithic cultures; while the so-called upper terraces seem to be due to other causes, and associated with the formation of the plateau. Thus the Palaeolithic sites too must be seen in relation to the building of the plateau as a whole. Therefore both the geological and the archaeological sequences constructed by de Terra and Paterson must be set aside, and other means found for working out sequential relationships and dating individual sites and cultural phases.

Briefly, in summary form, it can now be shown that the Potwar plateau has been created by a number of processes acting simultaneously, all more or less closely associated with the uplift of the Himalayas (Fig. 2.1). As pointed out in the previous chapter, this has been caused by the pressure of the plate of relatively stable ancient rocks which make up Peninsular India upon the southern edge of the Asian plate. At times of intense pressure the process of folding appears to have been rapid, in geological terms, and to have resulted in the erosion of a great deal of material ranging from boulders to fine silts which has been carried by rivers, streams and torrents out of the mountains into the plains, and deposited there in approximately horizontal layers. Further episodes of intense pressure have caused the horizontal layers, of relatively recent, partially consolidated material, in turn to be folded to such an extent that in places they have been forced into a perpendicular or near perpendicular position. Erosion and weathering have swept away, or planed off, the tops of the folds of relatively soft material. At the same time new deposits have been laid down on top and in the interstices between the more resistant uptilted layers.

The most widespread of the new horizontal layers is the Lei Conglomerate, a massive layer of pebbles, cobbles and boulders, chiefly of limestone. It offers considerable resistance to erosion, and the down cutting of rivers in the plateau, and therefore tends to appear as residual shelves or benches on the valley slopes. This is probably what de Terra and Paterson took to represent one or more of their upper terraces. The surface of the Lei Conglomerate is that with which the majority of the Stone Age sites in the region are associated, although the quartzite cobbles, etc. used in tool making are derived from the underlying Siwaliks. Overall the last series of deposits takes the form of a blanket of loess of fine, mainly windblown silts. There are several phases of loess depositions, interspersed by minor, apparently local deposits of waterborne silts and gravels. The result is a gently sloping plateau crossed by ranges of low hills formed of the more resistant gravels, etc., and what appear to be natural walls of rock which are residual perpendicular folds poking up through the later deposits. The Soan

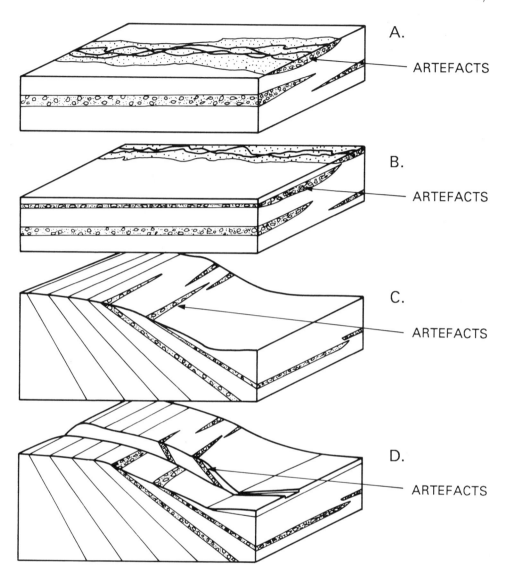

2.1 Diagram illustrating the incorporation of artefacts into the Siwalik deposits (courtesy H. Rendell).
Key
A. Braided river environment; B. Burial by river deposits; C. Folding and erosion; D. Incision.

and other rivers have cut their valleys through these deposits, some of which have proved more resistant than others.

The majority of Palaeolithic sites in the Potwar plateau are associated with the surface of the Lei Conglomerate. They consist of spreads of artefacts and factory debris covering areas of varying extent, some covering several square kilometres. Recent observations show that most of this material falls within the Middle Palaeolithic bracket of the subcontinent as a whole in terms of typology and technology, and it also appears to include significant Upper Palaeolithic elements. Artefacts also occur in the loess, above the Lei Conglomerate, but only in very limited numbers. Nearly all the artefacts and related material recorded on and above the surface of the Lei Conglomerate are in a relatively fresh, unrolled and unweathered state, indicating that they were covered by loess shortly after being made. Exceptions to this are a very limited number of hand axes and other pieces that appear to belong typologically to the Lower Palaeolithic, and are heavily rolled. These appear to come from within the underlying Siwalik beds, and therefore relate to a time prior to their upfolding and to derive from some distance upstream, possibly within the Himalayan foothills. Since the appearance of the 1982 edition of this book, a number of physical dates have been obtained for the Lower Palaeolithic of the Potwar plateau, northern Pakistan, the earliest being c. two million. This is comparable to dates obtained in East Africa and necessitates some fundamental rethinking

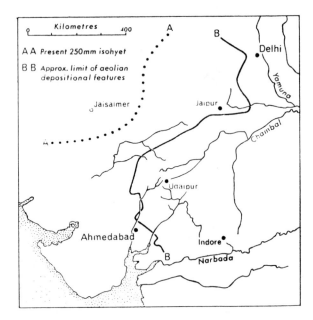

2.2 Map of Western India showing present approximate limits of actively moving sand (line AA) and approximate limit of actively moving sand during Late Pleistocene arid phases (line BB)

with regard to the antiquity of man and his immediate ancestors in the Indian sub-continent.

Arid and humid phases of the Thar desert and the Dry Zone

The Thar or Great Indian desert, and especially the Dry Zone that forms an arc all along its southern and eastern margins, has provided geomorphological evidence of past climates and environments of another kind. The Dry Zone, being a marginal area, is sensitive to changes in rainfall which would not have a marked effect on an area receiving, for example, 100 cm per annum or more, nor one of extreme aridity such as the central parts of the desert today. A consistent reduction in average annual rainfall could make the Dry Zone part of the desert, with actively moving dunes (Fig. 2.2). Conversely, a consistent increase in rainfall, or lowering of temperature and the resulting reduction in evaporation, could make it a savannah steppe region with good grass coverage and perhaps even woodland. This would result in the formation of soil which in turn would increase water retention and humidity. Today there is just enough vegetation in most of the Dry Zone to prevent large scale wind erosion and movement of sand, but not enough to form a significant depth of soil. Geomorphic studies in north Gujarat, Kathiawar and Rajasthan made during the last decade demonstrate that fossil dunes (i.e. dunes of characteristic form which have become fixed owing to the growth of vegetation, and sometimes also gullied by rain following an increase in rainfall) extend 200 to 400 km beyond the present limits of moving sand. Further, both within the fossil dunes and elsewhere, a buried red soil has been observed with a fully developed soil profile of much greater depth than any soil forming today.

The buried red soil is formed upon an earlier sand sheet, and overlain by a second layer of aeolian sand which includes considerably more kankar, or lime concretion formed since its deposition, than the first (see Fig. 2.3). When the balance of forces that maintain the upper sand layer in position is thrown out by exceptional natural conditions such as the three successive drought years of the early 1970s, combined with increasing human activity, ranging from overgrazing to road building, the upper sand layer tends to be blown off in patches, leaving exposed the surface of the buried soil which is compact and firm and offers great resistance to erosion of all kinds. On surfaces so exposed, and in sections cut through fossil dunes, Middle and Upper Palaeolithic working and living floors have been found at a number of sites throughout the Dry Zone, and notably in the Pushkar locality, near Ajmer in Rajasthan. The nature of the buried red soil shows that it must have carried a substantial vegetation cover throughout the year, and therefore have been formed under conditions of greater humidity (i.e. possibly heavier rainfall, or, more likely, of a different annual rainfall regime and a reduced rate of evaporation in relation to rainfall) than the present. This in turn implies an ample supply of surface water and game in areas where both are scarce today, making the Dry Zone and much of the desert an ideal habitat for hunters.

The climatic implications of the buried soil in the Dry Zone are corroborated by 'dead' drainage systems in the desert itself. These are not to be confused with abandoned channels of rivers that have changed their courses owing to river capture or other causes, but are the dried up channels of rivers and their tributaries forming complete, mature drainage systems, in which little or no water flows today. Many are blocked by sand dunes and when, following a rare downpour in the desert, water flows for a few hours in part of such a system it tends to pond up behind the dune, either becoming lost in the sand or forming a shallow lake or pan for a time until it evaporates. In this way salt and gypsum deposits are formed in the desert today, and many such lakes are now saline or

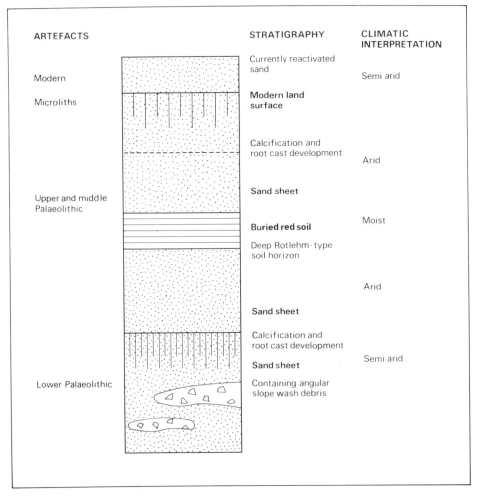

2.3 Schematic diagram of Late Pleistocene stratigraphic and cultural sequence at Pushkar (*after* Allchin, Goudie and Hegde)

brackish. Middle Palaeolithic artefacts are associated widely with 'dead' rivers and streams in the desert, and so to a lesser extent are those of the Upper Palaeolithic. Both Middle and Upper Palaeolithic artefacts are also found at the rare outcrops of rock suitable for tool making that occur in the arid regions, notably the Rohri hills and Jerruk in Sind, Mogara in south Rajasthan, and Nagri and Baridhani in central Rajasthan. The distribution of Middle Palaeolithic artefacts extends to the arid region west of the Indus, where they have been recorded in the Bugti hills and Las Bela district.

Since the appearance of this book in 1982, when Lower Palaeolithic material was thought to be sparsely distributed in the Desert and Dry Zone, rich Lower Palaeolithic sites have been located beneath later deposits in the Didwana area, Central Rajasthan. The quantity and situation of the artefacts, and other factors, combine to suggest that conditions were then less arid, and the tools were made, used and discarded on the banks of shallow lakes. Overlying deposits contained Middle Palaeolithic artefacts. These discoveries were made by Misra, Rajaguru and others, and are published in *Man and Environment.*

Mesolithic sites are found in profusion in the Dry Zone, with the apparent exception of the extreme north, where they have not been recorded at all, and the Kathiawar peninsula where they are comparatively rare. They become progressively more sparsely distributed as one moves into the desert, but small sites continue to occur even in the most arid regions. In the Dry Zone they are frequently found on the crests of fossil dunes, showing that they were occupied only after the dunes had ceased to move.

The most complete sequence of geomorphic and archaeological evidence is found in the Pushkar locality, already mentioned above, in the vicinity of a group of rare fresh water lakes. Mesolithic living sites are found on the surface of the most recent sand deposit, on the crests of dunes surrounding Budha Pushkar lake. Upper Palaeolithic living and working floors are found on recently exposed areas of buried red soil in the same basin and adjacent basins to the south-west and west. Some Middle Palaeolithic material is also found on the same horizon at Budha Pushkar, and there is an extensive Middle Palaeolithic working floor, again recently exposed, on the buried red soil, in the Hokra basin to the north-east. Lower Palaeolithic artefacts occur stratified directly below in scree from the hills bordering the Hokra basin.

Thus the evidence from the Pushkar locality shows that Lower Palaeolithic artefacts are associated with the beginning of the earlier of the two arid phases, or with the preceding period, but no artefacts appear to be associated with the height of the earlier arid phase. The Middle Palaeolithic is decisively associated with the humid phase represented by the buried red soil, and the Upper Palaeolithic too is associated with this phase, and probably continues through the succeeding final arid phase, forming a local cultural and technological continuum of which the Mesolithic industries of the locality are the final expression. Every part of this combined archaeological and geomorphic sequence is represented at other sites in the Dry Zone, but nowhere else has the complete dual sequence been found to be demonstrated in its entirety.

The presence of the makers of Upper Palaeolithic artefacts in the Dry Zone during the course of the last arid phase is indicated at another sand dune site, Visadi in Gujarat, where a factory site has been exposed by farmers levelling land for irrigation. It is recorded as being contained within the body of the dune, and not associated with the buried red soil which is also recorded in the locality. Whether this means that the last arid phase was less severe than the earlier one, or that its intensity varied, allowing Upper Palaeolithic hunters to move into the Dry Zone from time to time, or whether the Upper Palaeolithic hunters were more mobile and better equipped to survive in an arid environment than their predecessors is not yet clear. The first and second possibilities are supported by evidence from river valleys in Gujarat and Central India, while evidence of Upper Palaeolithic activity at factory sites in the heart of the desert inclines towards the last. Probably all are true to some extent.

The most notable factory sites in the Arid Zone are undoubtedly the complex in the Rohri hills in Sind. Not only does the preponderance of Middle Palaeolithic material argue forcefully in favour of this cultural phase coinciding with a period of more humid conditions, but the presence of Upper Palaeolithic artefacts on the same working floors as those of the Middle Palaeolithic, and apparently made from the same material, by identical processes, argues equally strongly for the development of a blade and burin based industry being established within the desert region before the end of the humid phase. This argument is further strengthened by the apparent sparsity of evidence for human occupation during the late Middle and early Upper Palaeolithic in the Hindu Kush region to the north. We shall return to this question of the role of the desert in the prehistory of the subcontinent during the latter part of the Pleistocene.

Rivers

The major rivers of the subcontinent as seen today play an important role in its economic life, religion and folk traditions and for our purposes can be divided into three groups. The rivers of the arid regions tend to build up their beds with material they have not the strength to carry, and are subject to seasonal or flash flooding and frequent lateral movement of their channels. Those in regions of somewhat higher, more regular rainfall in North and Central India are more stable, flowing in firmly incised channels, and tending throughout the major part of their courses to cut down rather than build up their beds. In the extreme south the major rivers appear to have scoured their valleys, and therefore are not incised into old valley fill, but are none the less comparatively stable. The most noteworthy river of the subcontinent, the one from which it takes its name, is the Indus. Rising in Tibet and flowing for a great part of its length in the Himalayas, it then emerges into the plains of the Punjab, and flows through them and the desert region of southern Punjab and Sind, for approximately a thousand miles, to the sea. The rate of accumulation of Indus alluvium in Sind has been estimated at approximately two metres per millennium during the last five thousand years. Today the channel of the lower Indus is shallow, and sometimes braided, and owing to its very shallow gradient it deposits large quantities of alluvial material in its channel throughout this part of its course. Thus it raises its bed above the level of the surrounding plain, and during floods or inundations it regularly breaks out from its banks and precipitates layers of fine silt over large areas of the plain, making it highly fertile. As the channel is not incised into the plain like those of rivers in other parts of the subcontinent, the Indus has a tendency to change its course from time to time. In all these respects it gives some indication of what the rivers of North and Central India and the Deccan may have been like during arid phases in the past. At such times they would be building up the plains and filling their valleys with the alluvial material seen today in terraces and sections exposed by their more recent down-cutting into earlier deposits.

As pointed out at the beginning of this chapter, implementiferous deposits laid down by the major rivers of Central India and the Deccan during the latter part of the Pleistocene provide a framework that has allowed the Palaeolithic industries of those regions to be seen in chronological order. During the Holocene there has been a tendency for the rivers to cut down into the Pleistocene deposits, throughout the greater part of their courses, incising their channels, and exposing sections cutting through the layers of silts, gravels, etc., that tend to fill the valleys (Fig. 2.4). Slight lateral movements of the rivers from time to time undercut the cliffs so formed, providing clean sections. Geologists and prehistorians have recorded their observations in almost every part of the region in the course of the last century and more. Their accounts are too

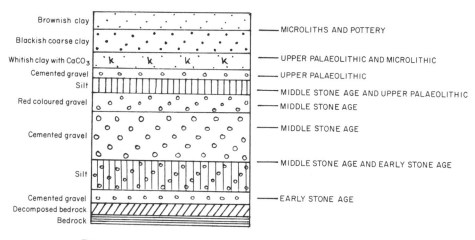

2.4 Diagrammatic section of the Belan river, Uttar Pradesh (*after* Majumdar and Rajguru)

numerous to list here, but certain points of particular interest and relevance to the relationship of Palaeolithic cultures and environments emerge.

Regarding the technological development of the industries, R. V. Joshi and others have demonstrated that the Lower and Middle Palaeolithic of the peninsular region represent a continuous process of development, which may or may not have been subject to influence from elsewhere, and shows no major break or innovation. This is in contrast to the situation noted in the arid regions north-west of the Aravalli range where there appears to be a dearth of cultural remains, although probably not a complete break, corresponding with the arid phase between the Lower and Middle Palaeolithic. De Terra and Paterson (in a note following their account of Kashmir and the Potwar region), and most sub-sequent writers, all note two major phases of aggradation interrupted by a major break or disconformity, on rivers in Gujarat, Central India and the Godavari system of the northern Deccan. Most authorities also agree that Lower Palaeolithic industries are widely associated with gravel deposits occurring at the bottom of the valley alluvium, on or near bed rock, and Middle Palaeolithic artefacts with gravels following the break in aggradation. This does not mean, of course, that there are no other gravel layers in the sections: there are many, and they provide the evidence of continuity noted above. Most authorities also consider that the cycles of aggradation represent changes in climate, with deposition of silt representing somewhat more arid conditions than at present, and the break or disconformity representing similar or somewhat more humid, cooler conditions. But there are difficulties in interpreting the various phases precisely, and again somewhat differing views are held on the relationship of arid and pluvial (or humid) phases in the tropics, to glacial periods in higher latitudes and in the Himalayas. Zeuner was perhaps the first to point out that in the Sabarmati valley, in north Gujarat, Lower Palaeolithic tools associated with the lower gravels in the sequence were rolled, and therefore derived, indicating that they were older than the gravels; and further that fragments of laterite, also rolled and derived from upstream in what is today the Dry Zone, were included in the gravels. Laterite only forms in humid conditions and its presence indicates a period of high humidity, and probably high rainfall, at a time prior to the two cycles of aggradation and the arid conditions they imply. Thus all the evidence suggests that before the deposition of the lower gravels the valleys of the region under discussion must have been virtually scoured of earlier alluvial material.

Middle Palaeolithic artefact assemblages recovered from the river sections and from surface sites in these regions, together with those found in South India, have a distinctive character which differentiates them from the Middle Palaeolithic north-west of the Aravallis, which we shall discuss further in the next chapter. This distinction tends to strengthen the case for the desert having formed a barrier between Peninsular India and Western Asia during an arid phase, and a highway during a humid one.

A number of prehistorians and others have noted indications of a third cycle of aggradation, following the two main cycles in Peninsular and Eastern India. Sometimes this is associated with a blade and burin (i.e. Upper Palaeolithic) or 'non-geometric microlithic' artefact assemblage. A third gravel layer has been observed in the Belan river valley and elsewhere in central North India. It has been dated by radiocarbon to approximately 17,000 B.P., and is definitely associated with Upper Palaeolithic material. On the lower Narbada and other rivers in the plain of central and north Gujarat a major break in the aggradation deposits of which the plain is built has been observed, and on the Narbada no less than three further buried soils have been observed in places, and dated by radiocarbon to between 17,000 and 24,000 B.P.

The character and chronological position of the Upper Palaeolithic in Central India has also been demonstrated in the Belan river valley and surrounding areas above and below the Vindhyan escarpment. The Belan is a southern tributary of the Jamuna and thence of the Ganges. Rising in Central India, it flows down from the plateau via a narrow valley with a series of gorges and rapids, to emerge into the plains south of Allahabad. For approximately 30 km it flows across the southern margin of the plain where some 20 m of alluvium overlie a shelf of old Vindhyan sandstone. Its present channel is cut down to bed rock, exposing along the greater part of this distance the vertical section illustrated (see Fig. 2.4). The two lower gravels are both heavily indurated (i.e. impregnated and held together by a natural lime concretion not unlike lime mortar), but differ from one another in size, colouring and condition. The lowest contains Lower Palaeolithic artefacts exclusively, while the upper contains artefacts of the Middle Palaeolithic as well as a small proportion of Lower Palaeolithic material. All the artefacts in both layers appear to be heavily rolled and stained by weathering, and both gravels are remarkable for the quantity of large fossil animal bones they contain. The third, uppermost gravel forms a much thinner layer than either of the other two. The gravel is of smaller size, is neither heavily stained nor cemented in a lime matrix, and grades off into the silts above and below, indicating that it was laid down under different conditions from the two earlier gravels. The Upper Palaeolithic artefacts it contains are less heavily rolled than those in preceding groups, and therefore probably not derived from sites upstream or from sites distant from the present river course, but more likely dropped near the river where perhaps they were also made. Like the associated gravel, they are dispersed in the silts above and below, forming a continuum upward to the Mesolithic artefacts found in the topsoil and scattered generally on the surface of this part of the plain. The relationship of Upper Palaeolithic artefacts in the silt to those of the Middle Palaeolithic in the upper of the two indurated gravels is not so clear. A technological and probably also a cultural overlap of Middle and Upper Palaeolithic is suggested by the distribution of surface factory sites in the region.

Surface sites of all periods have been recorded both above and below the

Vindhyan escarpment. Middle and Upper Palaeolithic artefacts are sometimes found closely associated on rocky spurs or promontories overlooking a valley, or at the foot of the escarpment overlooking the plain. Lower Palaeolithic sites tend to be found higher up, on larger hillocks or spurs, and Mesolithic sites again tend to occupy different locales, but they too are sometimes closely associated with Upper Palaeolithic sites, as at Birbhanpur.

Exposures of indurated gravel in the terraces of the Belan, the central stretch of the Narbada, and the upper Godavari system have all been found to contain rich faunal remains in the form of fossil bones and teeth of a number of species of animal, together with stone artefacts indicating the presence of man. Little attempt has been made to study the fossil remains, beyond identifying the species from a few sites, and no systematic search has been made for human skeletal remains. A thoughtful approach to the study of the fauna, beginning with a comparison between assemblages from different levels and different situations, could lend a new dimension to our understanding of past environments, and to the ecology of the tool makers. Any human skeletal remains from a Late Pleistocene context would be of prime interest, as at present no evidence whatsoever is available as to what type of man inhabited the subcontinent during the Palaeolithic prior to Mesolithic times. *Ramapithecus*, a type of early hominid found in Pliocene deposits in the Siwaliks, precedes the Lower Palaeolithic cultures discussed here by many thousands of years.

Eastern India

The lands of Eastern India are largely *terrae incognitae* as far as past climates are concerned. The river valleys of Orissa appear to have a sequence of implementiferous alluvial deposits similar to those further west, and to exhibit a closely comparable sequence of stone industries. Of the extreme east, including Bhutan and Sikkim, virtually nothing can be said as yet. Being a region of high rainfall it is not likely to register climatic change in the same ways as regions of lower rainfall. The Lower Gangetic plain has so far yielded little indication of its climatic past. Mesolithic sites at Sarai-Nahar-Rai, and elsewhere upon the surface of the old alluvium, on the Middle Ganges north of Allahabad, indicate that this part of the plain at any rate has remained in a state of equilibrium since their occupation, suggesting that this may also have been the case further east. The main period of deposition, when the immense quantities of silt (of which the plain is built) were laid down, must have come to a halt by that time. This is in marked contrast to the Indus which has continued to build up its plain throughout later prehistoric and historic times. There is evidence from the Mesolithic site of Birbhanpur in the Damodar valley, West Bengal, that the climate prior to, during and after the period of occupation was somewhat different. But the interpretation of these differences and the chronology of the site, particularly the relationship of the underlying deposit to the period of occupation, are not clear.

The South and Sri Lanka

In South India and Sri Lanka (Ceylon) there is, as yet, little positive evidence as to the nature of past climates and environments. At Attirampakkam, near Madras, near the place where Bruce Foote discovered his first hand axes in 1863, Lower and Middle Palaeolithic artefacts were found in stratified deposits in the locality of a small stream and described by Krishnaswami. In the Eastern Ghats Cammiade and Burkitt described finds of Lower and Middle Palaeolithic arte- facts in geologically stratified contexts, followed by an extremely sparsely represented Upper Palaeolithic blade and burin industry, and then by micro- lithic industries associated with the present topsoil. Both of these discoveries were made in the 1930s, and have been regarded as landmarks in the study of Indian prehistory like those of de Terra and Paterson in the north. More re- cently, during the 1960s, it has been demonstrated by Murty and others that Upper Palaeolithic industries are stratified below the modern soil and within the topmost layers of alluvium at several sites in the same region. All these examples point to the need for investigation of the climatic history of the extreme south of the subcontinent.

Another locality of interest is the group of what appear to be old coastal dunes, on the east coast near Cape Cormorin, commonly referred to by their local name as *teris*. They were first described in 1883 by Foote who found quartz artefacts associated with them, and noted that the sand was mixed with clay (due to formation of soil following the deposition of the sand) and that the clay con- tained particles of iron oxide. This last feature is responsible for giving the *teris* their strikingly vivid red colour. Today they are fixed by somewhat sparse vegetation, and show evidence of a complex geomorphic and archaeological history, aspects of which have been investigated and described by a number of geologists and prehistorians without, so far, producing any very positive cli- matic or cultural evidence. However, it appears that this locality may well provide a starting point in understanding some of the problems of past climates in the region. *Teris* have also been reported in Sri Lanka, where artefacts are again associated with them, and further north, on the east coast of India.

Typologically the Lower and Middle Palaeolithic industries of South India resemble those of the northern peninsula, and this suggests a similar continuity of development, although as yet we have no direct evidence of this. There is also a marked continuity of Middle Palaeolithic technology into the Mesolithic industries of South India and Sri Lanka, indicating that the change to the Upper Palaeolithic technique of blade production was less universal than was the case in Western and Central India. This will be discussed in more detail below, but it should be noted here as it indicates a technological and cultural continuity in the south which, in turn, is probably indicative of less radical changes of climate and environment than is evidenced in the north.

Environmental change during the Holocene

Environmental change during the Holocene must be thought of in a rather different way from the kind of changes we have been considering that took place during the Pleistocene. During the latter part of the Pleistocene the pattern of climatic change in South Asia was on a scale and of a nature to leave a consistent, recognizable pattern upon the landscape throughout extensive regions of the subcontinent. Dead drainage systems have been recorded throughout much of the Thar desert between the Indus and the Aravalli hills, indicating a widespread increase in humidity. Fossil dunes can be seen along the eastern margins of the desert from the Arabian Sea almost to Delhi – a distance of approximately a thousand miles. The pattern of rivers building up plains and filling valleys, and subsequently incising their channels into these deposits is more or less consistent from the Ganges–Jamuna Doab to Gujarat, and throughout western Central India and the Deccan. Further, these changes can be associated with comparable phenomena in other arid regions of the northern and southern hemispheres. They can therefore be attributed primarily to world-wide causes, modified by tectonic events, also part of a world pattern, but of a particular continental character in their effects, as indicated at the beginning of this chapter.

It is possible that by the end of the Pleistocene human groups were bringing about changes in their environment, consciously or unconsciously, by such means as burning off forest and grassland by accident or design; reducing certain species by excessive hunting or overkill, and thus altering the natural balance of wild life and the environment in general; and protecting and increasing the number or range, or both, of other species. But it is probable that at this stage the effect of man upon his environment was marginal, only effective in particularly sensitive areas. In general man was still largely at the mercy of his environment. The changes in the environment that took place at the end of the Pleistocene undoubtedly stimulated more resourceful human groups to advance and diversify their methods of winning a livelihood from the resources of different environments.

With the establishment at the beginning of the Holocene of conditions much like those of the present, some groups who had moved to new territory, or changed their life-style with changing conditions, and become conditioned to the idea of change, were in a position to exploit new opportunities as they arose. This is the stage at which there can be little doubt that man not only began to affect his environment, but also to attempt to control it to an increasing extent. Any attempt to assess the nature of environmental change during the Holocene must take this into account. The control and movement of herds of sheep and goats and other animals outside their natural habitat and beyond the confines of the natural territory of a herd; the building of huts and establishment of settlements, with all that this entails in terms of collection of fuel and fodder; clearance of land – probably often by burning off trees, bushes and coarse grass far beyond the area required – and the cultivation of selected cereals and other crops – all these things and many others, and their collective secondary effects upon the countryside, can bring about change without any more general or widespread natural agency.

There is evidence of fairly widespread climatic fluctuations of a minor kind during the Holocene from many parts of the world, and there can be little doubt that, like the more marked variations of the Pleistocene, some of these were part of world-wide patterns. In some cases, regional factors have proved stronger and dominated the world-wide pattern, at any rate in terms of the surviving evidence. In others there is evidence of quite marked regional or local change apparently unrelated to wider patterns. Regional and local fluctuations of climate, and some of a more widespread nature, have taken place during historical and recent times in many parts of the world, including South Asia, as witness the drought in the Sahel region of West Africa, and the succession of drought years during the 1970s in Western India. In marginal regions such as the Thar, where rainfall is very uncertain and variable at the best of times, there have also been droughts of a more localized kind. In all these cases the causes are complex, and human activities have to be taken into account as contributory factors. How effective, and indeed drastic, these can be is all too clear today: the areas of bare ground that surround villages on the margins of the Thar desert, where protected areas carry a considerable coverage of grass, low growing bushes and small acacia and other trees; the obviously rapid extension of gullying and sheet erosion in many areas of the North West Frontier, east and west Punjab, Haryana, Rajasthan and north Gujarat where, owing to population pressure, land has been increasingly more heavily exploited during the last century and a half – these and many other examples amply demonstrate.

There is a considerable amount of evidence from a variety of sources that the amelioration of the arid conditions at the beginning of the Holocene was a time of slightly greater humidity than the present in Western India generally. This would appear to be followed by a period when conditions were much like those of the present. A further slight ameloration seems to coincide approximately with the Mature Indus phase and to have been followed by a swing back to slightly more arid conditions that have continued, subject to local variations, to the present day. The impression of rapidly increasing aridity at the present time, frequently referred to in current literature, is considered by most more informed sources and authorities on climate and agriculture to be due to human activity. This is borne out by the notable increase in humidity, and in some cases actual rainfall, where irrigation and tree planting have taken place on a large scale, such as the Delhi region in North India and the area affected by the Tungabhadra project in the south. It seems quite possible that, as suggested by Fairservis, a similar process of over-exploitation may have brought about a series of local imbalances, which, combined with a more general deterioration, contributed to the collapse of the Harappan cities, particularly Mohenjo-daro. How far such imbalances are of a temporary nature and what the recovery period was in any particular case is an interesting question. In some cases there appears to be a permanent deleterious effect on the immediate surroundings of an ancient settlement. In noting these changes, and in order to understand them, three main groups or kinds of causality must be taken into account. The first is the more general climatic one. The second is that of major tectonic and seismic events to which South Asia as a whole, and the Himalayas and areas adjacent to them in particular, have been subject. These were the underlying causes of some of the more dramatic changes of environment during later prehistoric times, such as the diversion of the waters of the Saraswati and changes in the courses of other major tributaries of the Indus; and perhaps they also contributed to changes or switches in the course of the Lower Indus and the Hakra which may have profoundly affected Mohenjo-daro and other urban sites (see chapter 8). The third group is that of human activity.

Other sources of evidence

There is some evidence for changes in the relative levels of land and sea around the coast of India and Pakistan. For example, the *teris* mentioned earlier appear to have been at least partly formed at a time when the shoreline in the extreme south was rather lower than at present. There is evidence of sea levels both higher and lower than at present during the latter part of the Pleistocene and the early Holocene, at a number of places along the west coast from Ratnagiri south of Bombay to the Makran coast of Baluchistan. The problems involved in relating these changes precisely to climatic phases registered in the geomorphic features of the inland river valleys, or in the arid regions, are complex on account of the uncertainty of the causes of sea level changes. Not only do world-wide changes in sea level have to be taken into account, but also regional and local tectonic movements causing the continental mass as a whole, or sections of it, to rise or sink from time to time. Only by the systematic accumulation of more data of all kinds and of a series of C14 dates on the lines of those already obtained on the west coast, as in the work of Agrawal and Guzder, can this be clarified.

Caves and rock shelters are another potential source of evidence of past climates and environments, but those few in the subcontinent that have cultural deposits and have been systematically excavated, have scarcely been studied at all from this point of view. We shall discuss the cultural material from some of these excavations in the next chapter.

Summary

The evidence for climatic and environmental conditions during the latter part of the Pleistocene in various parts of the subcontinent, briefly indicated in this chapter, leaves no doubt that the North-west, North and Central regions underwent a series of major changes. The sequence of climatic phases and related Stone Age cultures recorded in the desert and Dry Zone are shown above in Fig. 2.3 This shows two arid phases separated by a humid phase of considerable duration, together occupying a period of time that probably corresponds very approximately to that of the last major glacial period in northern temperate latitudes. Recent radiocarbon dates indicate, as we have pointed out, that the final advance of the Himalayan glaciers in Kashmir was already over and in retreat before the end of the final arid phase. The Lower Palaeolithic is associated with the climatic phase preceding those just described and about which little is known except that it was probably a time of conditions fully as wet as those of the present, and possibly more so. The Lower Palaeolithic industries of this and earlier periods have much in common with those further west, and such evidence as we have indicates a continuous distribution from Peninsular India through Gujarat and southern Sind into Iran and Western Asia. This too is indicative of rather less severe arid conditions than we see today in the Thar and the Iranian desert.

The extension and intensification of desert conditions that took place during the arid phase that followed the Lower Palaeolithic must have resulted in those parts of India that remained habitable being effectively cut off from contact with the north and west. Thus the penultimate Pleistocene arid phase contributed to the independent development from Lower to Middle Palaeolithic technology in the peninsula; and this and the subsequent humid phase must also have contributed to the clear distinction noted between the Middle Palaeolithic industries of Central and Peninsular India on the one hand and those of the arid north-western region on the other. Further, the world-wide lowering of sea levels during the last glacial period must have tended to facilitate contact between Eastern India and South-east Asia, with its very different stone tool making traditions. It is not surprising therefore that this complements the change of emphasis noted in the Middle Palaeolithic industries of the subcontinent south and east of the Aravalli range.

When the desert and Dry Zone became habitable once more during the humid phase, the industries of the people who occupied it had a regional character, which had more in common with the Middle Palaeolithic of Afghanistan and Western Asia than with that of Central India, suggesting that their makers moved in from the north-west to fill the new hunting grounds, perhaps induced to do so by the increasing cold of the Hindu Kush mountain region during a period of colder conditions. The apparent scarcity of later Middle Palaeolithic and Upper Palaeolithic remains in the sequence of stone industries from the

Hindu Kush, and the mountains of Afghanistan generally, have been taken by archaeologists working there to indicate an exodus of population due to extreme cold. It seems quite possible that as a result there was a shift of population into the Indus plains and the region between the Indus and the Aravalli hills. Whether there was at the same time a movement of the animals that formed part of the regular diet of the Middle Palaeolithic inhabitants of Afghanistan, notably sheep and goats, is an interesting question for future research.

There is some evidence that Upper Palaeolithic techniques developed locally from those of the Middle Palaeolithic in the desert region towards the end of the humid phase. Whether this development also took place in Central India, or whether the desert region acted as a centre of dispersal is another question for the future. At present the homogeneous character of the South Asian Upper Palaeolithic tends to suggest the latter. Following the final arid phase, the Mesolithic industries, which apparently developed from the Upper Palaeolithic in Central and Peninsular India, flourished and expanded in the Dry Zone around the south and east of the desert.

During the Holocene all the evidence points to general climatic stability, but there are indications that significant minor fluctuations of climate took place. A number of factors indicate an amelioration of the arid climate during the early Holocene, and again at a time coinciding with the period of the Mature Indus civilization. It is never certain how far the kind of changes noted may be due in part to human activity, nor, even if a minor change is unequivocally demonstrated to have taken place in one region, how far it extends. These are questions, therefore, that need precise examination on a wider basis. Undoubtedly, fluctuations of climate have occurred during the Holocene, but the pattern and intensity of change in the subcontinent as a whole is not yet clear.

The actual evidence for climatic and environmental change during the Holocene includes a limited amount of palaeobotanical material from cores taken from saline lakes in central Rajasthan, analysis of soils from below Neolithic sites in the Deccan, changes in the distribution patterns of settlement sites of all periods, and other things. Each of these examples and categories of evidence is indicative rather than conclusive, and it is by the accumulation of examples and the extent to which different categories of evidence are found to support one another that the full story of South Asian Holocene climates and environments is likely to be worked out in the future, rather than by any dramatic discovery or single set of factors.

CHAPTER 3

THE EARLIEST SOUTH ASIANS

South Asia is rich in remains of the Stone Age. This is more evident in some regions than in others, but there is no major region that is without Stone Age sites of several periods, and in some they are found in a profusion that is almost overwhelming. As in Europe, Western Asia and Africa, the Palaeolithic industries of the Pleistocene can be divided into three major groups, on the basis of ths shape, size and methods of manufacture of the principal artefact types. The Lower Palaeolithic is characterized by hand axes, cleavers, chopping tools, and related artefact forms. Middle Palaeolithic industries are characterized by smaller, lighter tools based upon flakes struck from cores, which in some cases are carefully shaped and prepared in advance; the Upper Palaeolithic by yet lighter artefacts, and parallel-sided blades and burins. Each group is broadly comparable to its counterparts in the west, but at the same time has definite regional characteristics which distinguish it from them. The distinction between the South Asian stone working tradition as a whole and that of East and South-east Asia is a more profound and complex one.

The sequential order of the three main groups, the continuous process of technological development that they represent, and their regional divisions within the subcontinent are all demonstrated by assemblages of artefacts incorporated in a series of geologically stratified deposits, the majority laid down by rivers and streams in many parts of Central and Peninsular India. Noted and studied by a small band of geologists and prehistorians for well over a century, they provide the framework or skeleton of early South Asian prehistory. A number of advances have taken place in the last two decades, perhaps the most significant being independent physical dates obtained for various phases of the Palaeolithic. More important, the skeleton is gradually becoming articulated, and clothed with flesh, as other aspects of Palaeolithic cultures and of their environmental setting come into focus. The development of Environmental Studies in India and Pakistan, as in other parts of the world, is probably the most important advance in approach and in interpretation that has taken place since the appearance of the *Birth of Indian Civilization* in 1968.

The Mesolithic and other stone industries of the Holocene in the subcontinent represent a further continuation of the developmental processes of the Palaeolithic; and in the same way as in the Palaeolithic much of their technology approximately parallels that of the Mesolithic of Western Asia, Europe

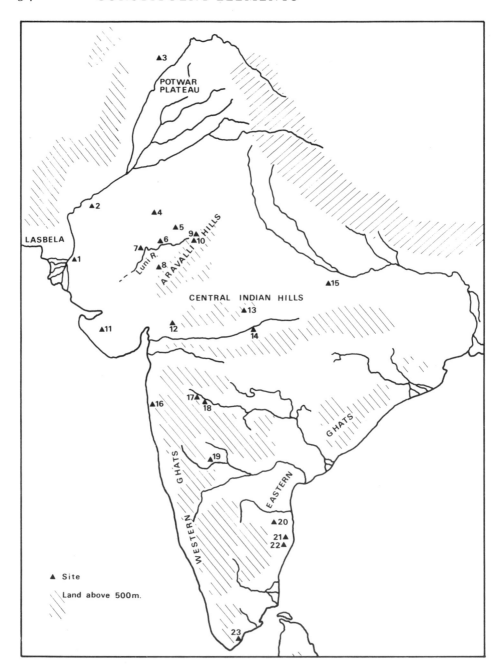

3.1 Map of principal sites mentioned in chapter 3

Key

1. Jerruk   2. Rohri hills   3. Sanghao   4. Baridhani   5. Nagri   6. Mogara   7. Thob   8. Jalor   9. Hokra
10. Pushkar   11. Rojadi   12. Pavagarh hill   13. Bhimbetka   14. Adamgarh   15. Belan river sites
16. Bombay   17. Nevasa   18. Chirki   19. Hunsgi   20. Renigunta   21. Attirampakkam   22. Gudiyam
cave   23. Teri sites

and parts of Africa. In the wider cultural sense, too, the Mesolithic appears to parallel its counterparts to the west, in that while its beginnings probably preceded the earliest settlements, Mesolithic communities of hunters, fishers, gatherers and pastoralists co-existed with settled communities in some regions for many millennia. The term Mesolithic in South Asia covers the life-styles of a wide range of predominately stone using communities from the beginning of the Holocene, *c.* 9000 B.C., to the beginning of the Iron Age in approximately 1000 B.C., and in places even later. Among archaeologists of South Asia at the present time 'Mesolithic' is commonly used in a wide and rather loose sense to cover hunters living in the hills and forests of Central India and elsewhere, fishing communities all round the coast, and nomadic herdsmen of many regions; and it grades, almost without a break, into the cultures of itinerant traders and animal breeders. Many such communities must have been in regular contact with the urban centres of the Indus region from the fourth millennium, and with settled communities of various kinds from a much earlier date.

The relationship of Mesolithic communities to their Palaeolithic forebears in regard to stone technology and many other aspects of life, and their relationship, both ancestrally and contemporaneously, to settled communities, through economic interdependence and social intercourse of all kinds, are questions that Indian prehistory is now beginning to tackle. In the course of this and the following chapter we shall attempt to summarize the evidence available today for cultural development during the Palaeolithic and Mesolithic. We shall note some of the more important pieces of research and fieldwork contributing to this, both in the past and currently in progress, and indicate some outstanding problems and areas of future research. In view of the volume of work done during the last twenty years, it is not possible to make this an exhaustive account, and we shall endeavour to cover some of the omissions in this respect in the Bibliography, by listing a selection of books which cover some further aspects of this work, but it must be borne in mind that this too is selective and aims to be representative rather than comprehensive.

The techniques employed in working stone during Palaeolithic times in the Indian subcontinent are basically very similar to those found in Western Asia, Europe and Africa at corresponding periods. They consist essentially in chipping or flaking stone to certain more or less regular and often-repeated forms. Types of stone were chosen which would fracture in a predictable manner. By a steady, but extremely slow, refinement in the methods used to remove the flakes, an increasing variety of tools was made, and they also became smaller and more delicate. There are already many excellent accounts of the various methods of making stone tools, so we shall not describe them here. Because the first hand axes were discovered in South India, near Madras, by Bruce Foote in 1863 the hand axe industry of the peninsula came to be referred to as Madrasian (Fig. 3.2). The somewhat different industries found by de Terra and Paterson in the Punjab seventy years later in association with what they believed to be a sequence of river terraces, similar to those described from certain north European river valleys, were called Soan. The Soan industry, or sequence of industries, was considered by Paterson to include two elements, or traditions. One was the hand axe tradition, the other a chopper–chopping tool and flake tradition with parallels and perhaps direct links with the Lower Palaeolithic of Eastern Asia. Opinions have varied on these questions during the ensuing half century. Recently it has emerged, in the course of a revision of the Pleistocene geology and Palaeolithic industrial sequence of the northern Punjab, that much of the material considered by Paterson to be Lower Palaeolithic falls stratigraphically and in other respects into the Middle Palaeolithic bracket (see Figs. 3.3 and 3.4 and chapter 2, pp. 14–18). The whole question is in the process of radical revision at present. Therefore we shall not use the terms Soan and Madrasian in this context. The Middle Palaeolithic industries of that region are further discussed below.

The Lower Palaeolithic

Since this book first appeared in 1982, two significant dates for the Lower Palaeolithic in the Potwar plateau, northern Pakistan, have been obtained. Handaxes have been found in a geological context dated by the palaeomagnetic method to c. 500,000 years. The relationship of the handaxes to the deposit indicates that they are approximately contemporary with it, and certainly not younger. In 1983 a group of quartzite artefacts and flakes were found near Rawalpindi, in a recently exposed deposit in a deep gully, beneath 65 metres of silts and conglomerates, which was subsequently dated by the palaeomagnetic and fission track methods to c. two million years. Of 23 specimens found, five show indications of deliberate flaking, and one, a core tool made on a pebble, has had seven flakes removed from three directions (3.2). Its position in the matrix in which it was found, with the flaked edges embedded, means that the flaking could not have taken place by natural means at the time of exposure. There can be little doubt that it is an artefact, and therefore it must have been made by an early hominid ancestor of man. As yet no skeletal remains have been found to show what type of hominid this may have been, and the search continues. Rich deposits of animal fossils have been found in adjacent areas, and the Siwalik deposits, of which the Potwar plateau is built, provide a whole range of sources of environmental evidence covering the last two and a half million years. These discoveries have been made by the British Archaeological Mission to Pakistan and published in a range of archaeological journals.

Lower Palaeolithic sites in South Asia are of several kinds: habitation sites, either in rock shelters or in the open; factory sites associated with sources of raw material; sites that combine elements of both these functions; small concentrations of artefacts with or without an apparent specific character; open air sites in any of these categories subsequently covered by deposition of sand, silt, loess, etc., and seen in section or in process of re-exposure; derived material in geologically stratified deposits, either in river terraces or in buried scree or deposits of other detrital material; scatters or spreads of varying numbers of artefacts on old erosion surfaces; and isolated finds of single artefacts.

Sites where people lived, temporarily or more or less consistently over periods of time, are the most obviously interesting category and have the greatest potential for yielding internal cultural and ecological evidence. But a more

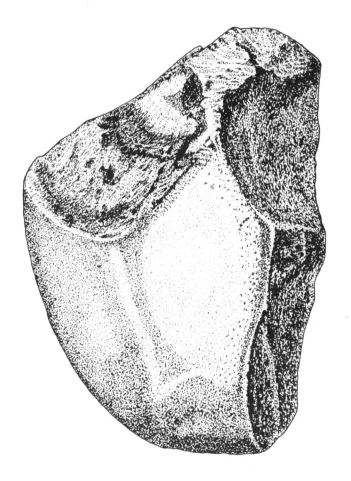

3.2 Core tool from which seven flakes have been removed, from a geological context dated to c. 2 million years, near Rawalpindi, northern Pakistan

complete picture can be built up by considering all types of site in a locality or a region, even if, in the first instance, their chronological relationships are not clear. By surveying all the available evidence one can begin to work out the relationships of different kinds of sites to each other and to the environmental setting, and to interpret what one finds.

An example of an Acheulean habitation site in a rock shelter has recently been excavated. It is one of a large group of rock shelters, many of which show evidence of habitation during the Stone Age, situated around Bhimbetka hill, in Central India, some 30 km north of Hoshangabad on the Narbada river. This rock shelter, named Bhimbetka III F-23 by its excavators, Wakankar and Misra, provides an area of over 100 sq. m protected from the weather, in which there is an occupation deposit varying in depth from one and a half to over three metres. Excavations to date show eight distinct layers, the lowest three (6, 7 and 8) all containing a late Acheulean lithic industry. Following the layers upwards, in

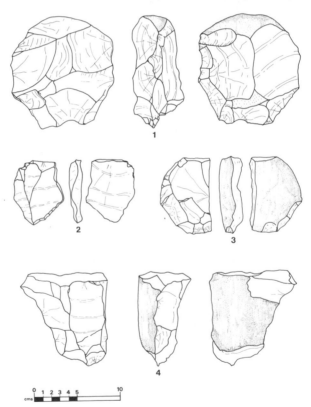

3.3 and 3.4 Potwar plateau, stone artefacts found in the course of the 1980 survey at sites stratified below the loess: 1 Kasala Kalan, discoidal core; 2, 4 and 7 Rawat, core and two flakes, part of a larger assemblage that fit together found within a small area; 9 cleaver made on a flake struck from a quartzite cobble; 3, 6 and 8, Aurangzeb, struck core, utilized blade and pebble segment; 5, Morgah, cleaver made on a flake struck from a quartzite cobble

reverse order, layer 5 contains an interesting Middle Palaeolithic assemblage; layer 4 a late Middle or Upper Palaeolithic industry; layer 3 a microlithic industry without pottery; and layers 2 and 1 a microlithic industry with pottery. The nature of the deposit in each layer is described as having a distinctive character. When all the deposits are analysed they should provide a very much fuller picture of the life and environment of the inhabitants of the shelter from late Acheulean times onward. Preliminary reports on the excavation provide much interesting information about each cultural phase, and we shall refer to layers 1 to 5 in the appropriate sections below. Here we are concerned with layers 6, 7 and 8.

Analysis of the artefacts from the lower levels at Bhimbetka, in terms of typology, average size of artefact types, and other factors, shows the industry to be substantially homogeneous throughout the three Acheulean layers. The small size of the artefacts and high standard of craftsmanship; the ratio of cleavers to hand axes, and range of variants of both these artefact types; the predominance of scrapers in the total assemblage – (28%) – all show this to

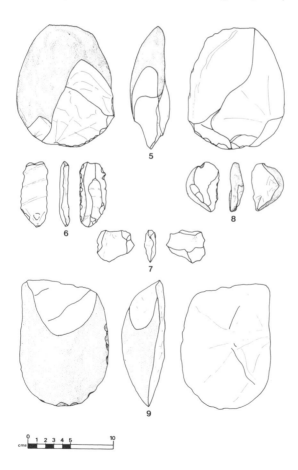

be a late Acheulean industry. Many of the artefacts, including hand axes and cleavers, are made from flakes. This is taken by the excavators as a probable further indication of the late Acheulean character of the industry, but it also seems possible that it may be due to the nature of the available raw material, which tends to occur in large blocks.

In the excavation of the late Acheulean occupation levels a series of five floors paved with flat stones was encountered at different depths. There were no indications of fire, and no organic remains, probably because the nature of the deposit was not conducive to their preservation. Use marks on the edges of many artefacts, and fragments broken in use, show that they must have been employed in the shelter for various types of work. The nature of the flakes and chips of stone further indicate that some artefacts, at any rate, were made there. A few exceptional pieces are made of chalcedony or chert, but the majority of the artefacts are derived from a yellowish quartzite available in abundance in and around the shelter. A minority, chiefly hand axes and cleavers, are made of a tougher purple or dark grey quartzite, less plentiful in the immediate neighbourhood and probably obtained at some distance from the shelter. Presumably harder rock was obtained for making tools that were used for the most demanding work. In the lowest layer (8) artefacts made from the local, partially metamorphosed rock were heavily weathered and tended to crumble into powder when handled, while those made of harder, more intensely metamorphosed rock had scarcely suffered any weathering. In layers 6 and 7 conditions for preservation appear to have been better, and all the artefacts looked fresh and unweathered.

These observations leave little doubt that Bhimbetka III F-23 was regularly inhabited, either seasonally or continuously throughout the year, for considerable periods during late Acheulean times, and that its inhabitants relied upon the locality for supplies of stone, and probably for all, or almost all their other needs. The excavators point out that today the surrounding countryside is well supplied with edible wild plants, still extensively used by local communities, who depend upon them for a significant part of their diet, and that within living memory it was rich in wild life. Larger game animals, such as antelope, are now rare, but fish are regularly caught in rivers and streams. There is no reason to presume that precisely the same resources were available during any period of the Stone Age, and indeed there is every reason to suppose that conditions varied considerably from one period to another, as pointed out in the previous chapter. However, these observations are interesting, although perhaps more relevant to Mesolithic ecological studies. The absence of surviving organic remains in the occupation deposits in the rock shelter emphasizes the importance of making a comprehensive investigation of all faunal and other organic remains in implementiferous deposits, such as those in the Narbada valley 25 km to the south; and of attempting to relate the cultural and climatic phases represented in the rock shelters to stratified alluvial deposits.

There appear to be a number of further occupied rock shelters in the Bhim-betka group. Three of them have been excavated, and shown to have varying quantities of Acheulean material, comparable to that from shelter III F-23 in the lower layer. It is not yet clear whether they show the same kind of evidence of continuous occupation and tool making, and therefore offer the same potential for reconstructing the ecosystems, or life-style and environmental relation-ships, of the communities inhabiting them. Many of the rock shelters of this extensive group are rich in rock art. This provides an extra potential dimension to understanding the culture of their inhabitants, but like rock art elsewhere it is extremely difficult to establish a sequence or relate it to the cultural sequence revealed in the excavation.

Another Central Indian site from which a sequence of Early and Middle Stone Age assemblages has been obtained is Adamgarh hill in the Narbada valley near Hoshangabad, excavated by R. V. Joshi in 1964. This is an isolated low hill, free from direct river action. The hill is composed of sandstones, quartzites and shales, and is partly covered by a derived laterite crust, which in turn is covered by fine gravel, and then by sands and red clay. The clay contains fragments of rock, some of which also overlie it, and Lower Palaeolithic tools make their appearance among these rock fragments. The assemblage near the bottom includes hand axes, chopping tools, ovates and a few cleavers. Higher up, the proportion of hand axes and chopping tools decreases, and cleavers become more numerous, varied and finely made. In the upper part there is a marked change to flake tools, including scrapers and pointed flakes.

Further investigation of intelligently selected localities may be expected to bring to light more rock shelters with Lower Palaeolithic occupation. Investiga-tions to date, however, make two points clear. The first is that a high proportion of the caves and rock shelters we now see in parts of the subcontinent show no evidence of human occupation prior to the Mesolithic, although the reasons for this are not altogether apparent. The second point is that a number of rock shelters show evidence of occasional or sporadic occupation by Palaeolithic man. Here again one can only speculate at present as to why this is so. An example of the latter is Gudiyam cave, a few miles from Madras, where a small excavation showed a sequence of Lower, Middle and Upper Palaeolithic arte-facts, but they were few in number, and other evidence of occupation was almost entirely absent – suggesting that the cave was not regularly inhabited. Today it contains the shrine of a local mother goddess.

In 1974 an Acheulean living floor was discovered by Paddayya in Gulbarga district, Karnataka, in the south-western Deccan. The site, Hunsgi, is on the bank of a stream of the same name, a tributary of the Krishna. Acheulean artefacts were found, at intervals, extending altogether for about 75 m along the course of the stream. Trial trenches at several points showed the level with which the artefacts were associated to be covered by approximately half a metre of alluvium. They were embedded in a layer 30 cm to 1 m thick, composed of limestone, granite detritus and disintegrating granite with some larger boulders. Neither the artefacts nor the rubble were rolled, nor did they show signs of having moved far from their source. At one point on a terrace about 5 m above the stream a living floor was encountered beneath about 75 cm of detrital material. On it were artefacts, and blocks and nodules of stone apparently imported from the nearest source, 3 km distant or more. Extensive excavations showed an area of rather over 40 sq. m enclosed by granite boulders.

The assemblage from the enclosed area included over 300 artefacts, of which finished tools, chiefly hand axes and cleavers, form one third, the rest being factory debris, and hammer stones, etc., indicating that the site was a factory or working area as well as a living place. So far no organic remains have been found to give a fuller picture of the range of activities carried out there. Most of the artefacts are of limestone, which is readily available at the site, but some are of quartzite and other types of imported stone. As in the case of the Bhimbetka rock shelters, more detailed studies of the artefacts, the site and the whole locality may be expected to provide a fuller picture of the life of a late Acheulean community than anything so far known in the subcontinent.

At a number of other sites in Peninsular and Central India unrolled Acheulean assemblages have been excavated from beneath alluvial deposits in the proximity of streams and rivers. In all these cases the state of the artefacts indicates that they are *in situ*, or nearly so, in contrast to the derived artefacts found in many terrace gravels which may have been transported many kilometres from the sites where they were made or used. The presence of a number of fresh unrolled tools does not in itself represent an Acheulean living or working floor, but it undoubtedly demonstrates the presence of man, and indicates a locality where the potential for such a find is high. Examples of such localities are Anagawadi on a small tributary of the Ghataprabha river in Karnataka; Chirki, near Nevasa on the Pravara river in Maharashtra; Lalitpur situated on a small stream in Uttar Pradesh; Mahadeo Piparia, on the banks of the Narbada in Narasimhapur district, Madhya Pradesh; and Kuliana, in Mayurbhanj district, Orissa. At the foot of Pavagarh hill in central Gujarat a Lower Palaeolithic factory site was found, exposed and partly destroyed by a stream. Many localities of this kind have been recorded in South India and elsewhere in both Pakistan and India, but few have so far been excavated. Acheulean assemblages have been recorded in detrital material stratified below later, aeolian deposits at several places such as Jalore and Pushkar in the Dry Zone on the margins of the Thar desert, usually in the vicinity of lakes or minor streams (Fig. 3.5). The evidence from all these sites shows that Lower Palaeolithic habitation sites were chosen by taking into account various factors, including water, raw materials, and no doubt all the other necessary elements of a hunting and gathering life. On typological grounds some of these assemblages form a group earlier in character than the Bhimbetka assemblage.

Lower Palaeolithic factory sites are associated with sources of top quality raw material, particularly fully metamorphosed quartzite, and primary chert nodules, as opposed to derived chert nodules from river gravels, which were also occasionally used, but not to the same extent as in later times. Some of the sources of good material were resorted to continuously or intermittently over long periods, and artefacts representing a wide range of technology are found there, while others were in use for more limited periods of time. For example, at Mogara hill, an isolated outcrop of rhyolite in the Dry Zone near Jodhpur, in Rajasthan, Lower, Middle and Upper Palaeolithic, as well as Mesolithic arte-facts were all found at different small working areas. Jerruk, a limestone hill capped by chert nodules, in Lower Sind, appears to have been frequented by Lower, Middle and Upper Palaeolithic tool makers, but not by those of later cultures. The vast expanses of chert in the Rohri hills, in Upper Sind, were extensively exploited in Middle and Upper Palaeolithic times and again by Chalcolithic entrepreneurs; but they appear to have been largely neglected during the Lower Palaeolithic and again during the Mesolithic, probably for climatic reasons. Extensive spreads of quartzite boulders, cobbles and pebbles in the Potwar region in the northern Punjab were used by Middle and Upper Palaeolithic tool makers. Many of the derived artefacts contained in stratified river terrace deposits must have come from similar sites that were destroyed when terraces were undercut or swept away by the rivers that earlier built them.

3.5 View of the Pushkar basin, Rajasthan

A feature of many factory sites of this kind is the way in which flakes or large pieces of rock were struck from boulders too large to be moved, or from outcrops of rock, and then worked into artefacts; or alternatively into cores from which further flakes were struck, which in turn were utilized or worked into hand axes, cleavers, scrapers and other tools.

There can be little doubt that large factory sites based on sources of good quality chert or quartzite served a wide area, but just how wide, in each case, is a matter for future research. In many cases it must have been very much more than the territory of a single group occupying a site or a locality such as Hunsgi or Bhimbetka, even if we allow that each of the occupation sites so far excavated was only one of a group, and that several such sites in any group or locality were in occupation simultaneously. Thus the sociological and economic implications of the large factory sites are profound. It appears that during Lower Palaeolithic times regular living sites were established both on the banks of rivers, in the open, and in rock shelters. The web of socio-economic relationships based on the use of large factory sites must have covered far more than the territory of a single extended family group or band of hunter-gatherers as this term is understood today. The provenance of stone types found in Lower Palaeolithic assemblages provides us with one of the few indicators of the economy of Lower Palaeolithic society. Even at this early stage the catchment area of a particular site is clearly complex and requires careful definition. However, it is also clear that – as exemplified at Bhimbetka and Hunsgi – most of the requirements of each group were met locally, whether stone for the production of tools, or animals or plants hunted or gathered for food.

In Central and Peninsular India, Lower Palaeolithic factory sites tend to be smaller than in the north-west, probably because more suitable rock was exposed and it was not necessary to go so far to obtain it. Acheulean factory sites in these regions tend to be on small hillocks or on the sides or spurs of larger hills and escarpments. They occur widely and are too numerous to be discussed individually. As in the case of the larger sites in the west and north, many of these sites have been known and visited by collectors for up to a century. As a result not only have many of the best artefacts been removed, but the relationships to each other of artefacts such as cores, hammer stones and factory debris have been lost in most cases. One can only regret this and emphasize the need for accurate recording of all these details in the case of future discoveries of surface sites as well as excavations. As a result of this and of other, largely geological factors smaller sites which must often record the scene of a single activity, such as cutting down a tree, making other artefacts of wood, bone, hide, etc., or killing and dismembering a large animal, can no longer be interpreted. Thus, like finds of individual artefacts, they must be regarded as of distributional rather than cultural significance. On the coastal plain of south-east India, near Madras, Lower Palaeolithic artefacts occur in places as continuous spreads over many square miles, mixed with pebbles and boulders of the same kinds of rock – chiefly quartzite. Finished tools such as hand axes and cleavers and recognizable factory debris form a surprisingly high proportion of these spreads. At present there seems to be no positive geological or cultural explanation of this phenomenon.

Acheulean sites of various kinds are very widely distributed throughout South Asia. Finds are so widespread that it is tempting to assume that in all regions where they have not been reported, such as large parts of north-eastern India, it is merely a question of searching systematically and they will be found. This is a strong probability, but it cannot be taken for granted, for, while it is unlikely that these areas were completely uninhabited throughout Lower Palaeolithic times, it is possible that they may have been the territory of a different technological tradition related to that of Eastern Asia. Again, in the high rainfall area of the Western Ghats and the narrow western coastal plain south of Bombay, the place of the characteristic Acheulean industries appears to be taken by somewhat formless chopping tools and flakes. The distribution of later Acheulean industries in South Asia, as far as it is recorded at present, suggests a climatic pattern much like that of today, with the main emphasis upon open woodland and savannah. There is evidence of limited human presence in the desert, and some indications of a different life-style in the areas of highest rainfall and of dense tropical forest. As yet there is virtually no positive evidence regarding the climate of the time, and it is only possible to make inferences from other factors. Regarding earlier stages of the Lower Palaeolithic the situation is even more speculative.

To summarize some aspects of the raw materials and technology of the South Asian Lower Palaeolithic cultures, we can say that the majority of Lower Palaeolithic artefacts recorded or collected in all parts of the subcontinent are made of quartzite. Sometimes quartzite pebbles were used, particularly for making the earlier and cruder hand axes, and for making chopping tools at all periods (Fig. 3.2, Nos. 2, 3 and 7). The other sources of quartzite were outcrops of rock and large boulders, and in these cases in order to make tools, large flakes or pieces of quartzite first had to be removed from the parent rock. It is not always clear whether this was done by striking the rock with another stone, an operation which would require great strength, or by fire-setting which meant lighting a fire against the rock and then cooling it suddenly by throwing water over it, and so causing large pieces to break away from the main body. Perhaps both methods were used. Some tools, usually cleavers, can be seen to have been made from flakes which had been struck off larger blocks of raw material (Fig. 3.2, No. 4). In the case of many such tools all traces of a primary flake surface or a bulb of percussion, if they were ever there, have been lost in the removal of further flakes, as the process of giving the tool its final form proceeded (Fig. 3.2, Nos. 7 and 8). A collection of early Acheulean tools from a surface site at Kibbanhalli, situated on a quartzite ridge in Mysore, illustrates this point. This assemblage includes cleavers made on large flakes and hand axes and other tools, also of quartzite, flaked all over, so that all traces of a primary flake surface have disappeared.

Quartzite is the material from which Lower Palaeolithic tools in river gravels and other geologically stratified deposits are most commonly made, although tools of other materials, such as vein quartz, volcanic rocks, and various types of crypto-crystalline silica are sometimes found. Where sufficiently large nodules of chert were available, as at Jerruk, and in the Rohri hills in Sind, these were used with varying degrees of preparation as cores. The flakes struck off sometimes served as tools with a minimal amount of reworking, or were made into specialized forms such as cleavers, hand axes, discoids, scrapers, and so on.

Large flakes lend themselves to the production of cleavers more readily than pebbles or nodules of rock, and therefore it seems probable that the increasing number of cleavers in later phases of the Acheulean may be related to changes in the sources of supply. Other core tools, more or less elliptical or circular in outline, made by the same flaking techniques as the hand axes and cleavers, are found in almost every assemblage (Fig. 3.2, No. 5). These generally show signs of use around the edge, but this is often concentrated in one or two areas. There is little doubt, therefore, that these tools were used for chopping and cutting, and also perhaps for digging, and for scraping hides. In most large collections they grade imperceptibly into the hand axe forms, and sometimes also into the cleavers. In the later stages of the Acheulean, as for example the Bhimbetka industry, they also grade into cores from which flakes were struck for use as tools. In this capacity they continue as a basic and essential part of the flake industries of the succeeding Middle Palaeolithic. Some archaeologists classify such artefacts arbitrarily as hand axes or cleavers, but others refer to them as discoids or ovoids, according to their form.

Flakes, whether as by-products of the manufacture of core tools or as the main objective of the tool makers, are an intrinsic part of the hand axe industries in India, as in many other parts of the world. Some collectors have overlooked them, but they are present at factory sites and in river gravels to be found by anyone who looks for them. Many flakes show signs of use, and the practice of striking flakes from specially prepared cores and using them as a basis for making the more delicate tools had already begun in the Lower Palaeolithic. This can be seen in all the collections we have discussed above.

As in corresponding periods in other parts of the world, the methods of flaking used to produce the tools became steadily more refined throughout the Lower Palaeolithic. At the beginning a flake was knocked off by a blow with another stone, leaving a markedly concave flake scar with a pronounced bulb of percussion. Gradually the maker's control over his material increased, and by using a more delicate hammer, probably a piece of hard wood or bone, in the later stages of making a tool, shallower and more regular flakes were taken off. By dint of these and other means, including step-flaking (Fig. 3.2, No. 3), it was possible to produce a small, light, regularly shaped hand axe, thin in section and with an approximately straight-cutting edge. Small, shapely hand axes are present among the assemblages of tools from all the sites in the group of late Acheulean industries of the Bhimbetka type in Central and Peninsular India, and in the industries from Sind. A tool of this kind must have taken considerable time and skill to produce, and alongside it will be found a great many less perfectly made, but none the less effective tools. Chopping tools, cores, flakes, and many objects that can only be described as utilized pieces of stone, will generally be found in profusion at a site which yields a few finely made hand axes or cleavers. This is demonstrated by collections from factory sites, and also from the earlier cemented gravels of most of the major rivers, including those we have mentioned.

The Middle Palaeolithic

Throughout Europe, Africa and those parts of Western Asia where research has been conducted on the Palaeolithic, the Middle Palaeolithic can be seen as a time of regional and local diversity both in terms of stone technology and artefact types; and also in terms of other aspects of culture insofar as these have been investigated. It is also a time of increasing adaptability, when, for example, during the last major glacial advance in Europe and West and Central Asia human communities maintained themselves in many regions in the face of severe reductions in temperature. South Asia appears to be no exception to this. There is a marked distinction between the Middle Palaeolithic industries of the Deccan and Central India, including the Kathiawar peninsula, on the one hand, and the desert region of the north-west, including the northern Punjab and the Indus plains, on the other. The middle Palaeolithic industries of the south have not been studied in so much detail, but, as in the case of those of the Lower Palaeolithic, appear to correspond fairly closely with the Central Indian and Deccan group. North-east India is again largely *terra incognita*.

The presence of flake industries, occupying an intermediate position, technologically and in terms of geological stratigraphy, between the Lower Palaeolithic and the Mesolithic, was recognized in the 1930s by Todd in the Bombay area and by Cammiade in the south. The character of these industries and their association with a break in the deposition of alluvial silts throughout Central and Eastern India, the Deccan and Kathiawar, was recorded by a number of prehistorians – in several cases working independently of each other – during the 1950s and early 1960s. The name Nevasan, after the type-site of Nevasa, in Maharashtra, was suggested by Sankalia. This seems eminently suitable for the industries of the region south-east of the Aravalli hills, particularly in view of the distinction between the Middle Palaeolithic industries of the peninsula, and those of the north-west that has emerged recently. So far little cultural information, beyond what can be deduced from the industries themselves and their distribution, has come to light. Apart from a brief discussion of a Middle Palaeolithic occupation layer at Bhimbetka, already referred to, and not yet studied or described in detail, no clear example of a Nevasan living site has been recorded. One phase of occupation at Chirki, near Nevasa, appears to represent a Middle Palaeolithic factory and living site, possibly somewhat disturbed anciently by the river.

We have already pointed out that the Middle Palaeolithic industries of Central India and the Deccan have been shown to have developed from those of the Lower Palaeolithic of the same region, with which they appear to form an unbroken continuum. The change takes the form, first of all, of a slightly altered distribution pattern. Surface sites are not found so consistently throughout what are today areas of moderate rainfall, as they were during the later phases of the Lower Palaeolithic. In some localities, such as the Belan river valley and the surrounding country in Central India, where the location of sites has been studied, a change in the choice of factory sites and working floors has been noted, those of the Middle Palaeolithic tending to be lower down on slopes and spurs overlooking valleys, and somewhat less exposed than those of the Lower Palaeolithic which tend to be on or near the summits of small hills and ridges. There are also marked changes in the choice of raw materials, artefact types and technology which we shall summarize below.

The materials from which the Nevasan artefacts were made are chiefly crypto-crystalline silica of various kinds such as agate, jasper, or chalcedony, all of which have a smoother and more regular concoidal fracture than the somewhat granular quartzites favoured in Lower Palaeolithic times. Most frequently the material appears to have been obtained in the form of river pebbles. These derive from nodules of silica formed in the volcanic trap rocks which are found in so much of Central India and the more northerly parts of the peninsula. Pebbles of the same kind are also found in river gravels outside the main trap regions, and here again were utilized. When quartzites were employed in Nevasan industries, as at Gundla-Brahmesvaram in the Eastern Ghats, they were always fine-grained, and therefore probably carefully chosen.

The flakes, which are the basis of these industries, vary considerably in shape, including round, rectangular and pointed forms, and long parallel-sided blade-flakes (Fig. 3.6, No. 3). They show pronounced bulbs of percussion, where these have not been removed, indicating that they were probably struck off the parent core with a hammer stone. Rounded and oval-shaped pebbles, battered at one or both ends, are found at Middle Palaeolithic factory sites in many parts of India and suggest that this was the means used. Some archaeologists consider that the more slender flakes could only be obtained by using a wooden hammer. With the flakes are found cores of the well-known 'tortoise' type (Fig. 3.6, Nos. 1, 4 and 5), and cores of another type, made by removing one or two flakes from a suitable pebble to provide a striking platform, from which thick but sometimes approximately parallel-sided blade-flakes were then struck off (Fig. 3.6, No. 7). A certain number of cores of both kinds show signs of subsequent use as chopping tools, which indeed the second type closely resemble. Occasional small, often cordiform, hand axes are found in the upper gravels, in association with the flake tools and cores.

With the exception of the small hand axes, bifacially worked points are seldom found in Nevasan industries. Pointed flakes, generally more or less leaf-shaped, and sometimes with fairly steep retouch or regular use marks along one or both edges, occur fairly commonly, and could have been used as scrapers, knives or spear heads. A feature noticed in many regions, including Kathiawar in the west, and Orissa in the east, as well as in the centre and south, is a pointed flake with a bulb of percussion which is considerably 'off centre'. Large borers or awls, worked with steep retouch on thick flakes, are also characteristic of

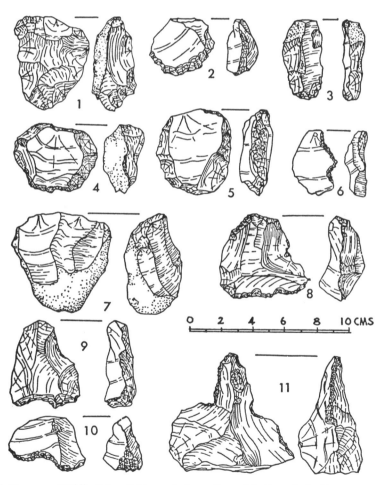

3.6 Nevasan: Middle Palaeolithic tools from Central India and the Deccan: 1 core unstruck; 2, 6, 8, 9, 10 and 11 scrapers of various types on flakes; 3 blade-flake; 4, 5 and 7 struck cores

Nevasan industries, particularly in Central and Peninsular India. Frequently they form part of a composite tool consisting of a 'beak' or borer-point and two hollow scrapers (Fig. 3.6, No. 11). Burins are generally rare and of a simple undifferentiated kind at this stage, but in certain of the later industries they are rather more common.

There is a wide variety of scrapers in the Nevasan industries, and they were undoubtedly the characteristic tool of these and indeed of the whole complex of South Asian Middle Palaeolithic industries. Concave, convex or straight scraper edges were worked, generally with steep retouch, on round, square or pointed flakes, only rarely with prepared striking platforms. Scrapers are sometimes also found worked on the long edges of blade-flakes. A characteristic form has the scraper edge worked on the distal end of a thick squarish flake, which has frequently been re-edged until a considerable proportion of the flake has been removed (Fig. 3.6, Nos. 8, 9 and 10). It has been suggested that these are the features indicative of a woodland industry, in which scrapers were used to make various tools from hard tropical woods. The absence of developed types of stone points suitable for missile points certainly suggests that these, if they were used, were made from other substances, presumably wood or perhaps bone. In Southeast Asia today arrowheads and knives are made from bamboo, and the latter serve for general cutting purposes, even when metal is available. It seems quite possible therefore that during Middle Palaeolithic times the same was true of much of tropical India.

Middle Palaeolithic industries from regions west of the Aravalli hills and north of the Kathiawar peninsula, while showing the basic technological fea-

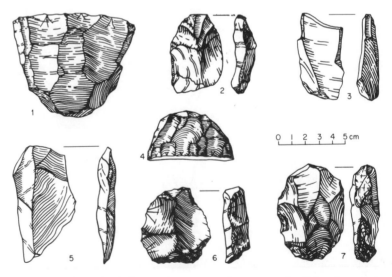

3.7 Hokra: Middle Palaeolithic artefacts: 1 struck core; 2 and 5 flakes from prepared cores; 3 burin; 4 carinated scraper; 6 scraper made on flake from prepared core; 7 unstruck core

tures common to both the Nevasan group of industries of India and the Mousterian of West and Central Asia, also have distinctive characteristics which differentiate them as a major regional group. They may be further sub-divided into lesser regional groups, and into what appear to be the outcome of a series of marked local traditions. Some of these outlive the Middle Palaeolithic, continuing into the succeeding Upper Palaeolithic and even the Mesolithic industries of the same localities, as in the case of several factory sites and habitable localities in the desert and the Dry Zone. The Pushkar locality, with its fresh water lakes, in the Dry Zone is an example of such a situation (see Figs. 3.5 and 3.10).

The first indication of the distinctive character of the western group of Middle Palaeolithic industries was demonstrated by de Terra and Paterson's brief description of what they termed the Late Soan, which appeared in their 1939 monograph, referred to in the previous chapter. Recent research in the Soan valley and Potwar plateau, of the northern Punjab, in Pakistan, has shown the large open air sites found there to belong primarily to the South Asian Middle Palaeolithic tradition in typological terms (see Figs. 3.3 and 3.4). There are also indications of the presence of Upper Palaeolithic artefacts at some sites. Further, certain of these sites show evidence of occupation as habitation areas as well as factories. This is partly demonstrated by the kind of artefacts and debris found there, and, more directly, by traces of structures associated with the Palaeolithic occupation. Field research taking place at the time of writing may be expected to provide a fuller picture of the culture and ecology of Middle and Upper Palaeolithic man in this region than has hitherto been available for any part of South Asia.

The excavation of Sanghao cave in the early 1960s, discussed at some length in the *Birth of Indian Civilization*, showed that in the extreme north-west of the subcontinent there was another Middle Palaeolithic tradition with pronounced regional character. Situated in a sheltered valley, near the source of a mountain stream, the cave (perhaps more accurately described as a large rock shelter), was found to contain three metres or more of occupation deposit, including a great deal of cultural and organic material such as hearths, bones (certainly animal and possibly also human), and quantities of artefacts and factory debris (Fig. 3.8). Unfortunately, its early date and its importance in these respects was not recognized by the first excavators, and almost all this valuable material was discarded. Four periods of occupation were distinguished, the first three grading into one another apparently without any break in continuity. Throughout, the tools are made entirely of quartz, of which there is a prominent outcrop, not much more than 100 metres from the cave. Quartz tends to fracture irregularly on account of its crystalline structure, and it is therefore a difficult material to work. For the same reason it is difficult to recognize tools made of quartz, as their outlines tend to be obscured by its irregular fracture. The industry of period I in particular testifies to a remarkable degree of control over this awkward material (Fig. 3.9). In the absence of any comprehensive published classification or enumeration of the tools, which must run into some thousands, we shall endeavour to give some account of the industry in general terms, on the basis of the material which the excavators retained.

The tools were made from flakes struck from prepared cores, which were generally round, oval or elliptical in outline (Fig. 3.9, Nos. 1, 2 and 5). No flakes with prepared striking platforms were recorded, and only a few with any regular secondary work. There are a small number of hollow scrapers (Fig. 3.9, No. 7), but scrapers of every other kind, and trimmed or reworked points are re- markable by their absence. One small hand axe was recorded (Fig. 3.9, No. 6). Cores and flakes of triangular outline are seen in small numbers (Fig. 3.9, No. 8), and parallel-sided blade-flakes are more numerous. The bulbs of percussion on both flakes and blade-flakes are pronounced, as in the Indian Middle Palaeolithic industries, suggesting direction percussion with a robust hammer, probably of stone.

One of the most interesting features of the industry is the burins, of which there are a considerable number (Fig. 3.9, Nos. 3 and 4). They are made from convenient fragments of tabular quartz, frequently using one of its natural facets as a striking platform, and many show signs of heavy use on the burin edge. A number of unretouched pointed flakes appear to have been used for

3.8 Sanghao: view of rock shelter and excavation

piercing and boring, and a few flakes and quartz fragments have been carefully worked to a point and can be classified as awls.

In period II there is a slight decline in the number of the tools and also in their size and in the quality of the quartz. In period III this decline is more marked, but the quantity of tools and quartz debris increases. Burins continue, though reduced in size; blade-flakes disappear, but a few fine microlithic blades and blade cores make their appearance. The top layer is somewhat disturbed and the artefacts are mixed with pottery and other debris of the Gandharan period, presumably associated with the Buddhist remains of this period lower down the valley.

All that can be said on the basis of the present recorded evidence is that Sanghao cave was a place of regular habitation where quartz tools were made and used for a very considerable period of time during the Middle Palaeolithic, and also to some extent during the Upper Palaeolithic and perhaps the Mesolithic. The proximity of the Mousterian site and Neanderthal burial at Teshik-Tash in Soviet Tajikistan, on the other side of the mountains to the north, makes the prospect of future investigation of Sanghao cave an exciting one.

It was pointed out by Misra in 1961, that the geographical frontier formed by the Aravalli range divided the Nevasan Middle Palaeolithic industries of Central

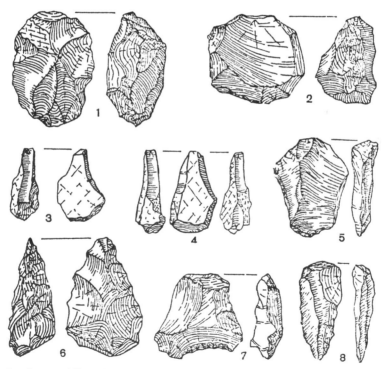

3.9 Sanghao: Middle and Upper Palaeolithic artefacts from the excavation: 1 unstruck discoidal core; 2 struck core; 3 and 4 burins; 5 flake struck from prepared core; 6 hand axe; 7 hollow scraper made on flake; 8 pointed flake struck from prepared core

and Peninsular India from an industry of a rather different kind in the arid region immediately to the north-west. He made two further highly significant observations. First, that while the Nevasan industries to the east of the range were preceded by and developed from a well-represented Lower Palaeolithic tradition, the industry to the west appeared to have no such direct local antecedents. Secondly, he suggested that the most fundamental distinction between the two groups of industries was in the quantity of reworked flakes. In the Nevasan of south-eastern Rajasthan the percentage of reworked flakes, including all those made into scrapers and other artefacts, is no more than 5% to 7% of the total artefact assemblage, while at sites in the Luni basin west of the Aravallis it ranges from 21% to 45%. The western group also include a wider range of artefacts of specific, predetermined forms, in contrast to the preponderance of amorphous, utilized flakes in the eastern group.

Misra called the western group of artefacts the Luni industry, after the almost extinct river Luni with which most of his finds were associated. Subsequent finds of Middle Palaeolithic material in the Luni catchment area as a whole, and much of Rajasthan, have proved remarkably consistent with these observations, in terms of the total range, proportional representation and average size of artefact types, making this an appropriate term for the Middle Palaeolithic of the whole region.

The tool kit of the Luni Middle Palaeolithic is more varied and richer in developed forms than the Nevasan, but convex and concavo-convex scrapers made on flakes are again the basic, universal artefact type. It should be noted that the character of the collections from Rojadi in Kathiawar and Thob in south Rajasthan are closer to the Nevasan type of assemblage. Although strictly west of the Aravalli range, both are in the extreme south-west of the Arid Zone in positions readily accessible from Central India.

In addition to the convex and concavo-convex scrapers, industries of the Luni group include finely worked carinated scrapers, points of various types, burins, side choppers, hand axes, cleavers and adze blades (see Fig. 3.7). They are not all present in every collection, but all have a wide distribution throughout the region. Points are similar to those in Nevasan collections described above, but tend to conform to a rather more regular, limited range of types. The commonest is a pointed flake, struck from a prepared core of appropriate shape, and subsequently reworked along one or both edges. Burins, like those in Nevasan collections, tend to be simple and made as flakes, or fragments of debris. Hand axes and cleavers are small in comparison to those in Lower Palaeolithic collections, and finely worked. Cleavers tend to be made on flakes, and the larger ones sit easily in the hand, while the smaller ones grade into adze blades. The latter have a similar working edge and a smaller body, sometimes deliberately thinned at the butt end by the removal of flakes. This is probably an indication that they were intended to be hafted, as were similar tools made and used by the Aborigines of Australia until the beginning of this century.

Assemblages of artefacts of the Luni industry have been found at two principal types of site in the Dry Zone and the desert. The first is on extensive working floors, such as Hokra or Baridhani, both of which are close to what appear to be former lakes, now dry. The second type of site is a small concentration of artefacts associated with the gravels of dead water courses. Both emphasize the association of the Luni industry with the last humid phase of the Pleistocene, when there must have been considerably more potable surface water in the Thar region than there is today. Hokra and Baridhani are both in situations where water and a supply of raw material appear to have been readily available. There are other sites, such as Mogara south of Jodhpur, several miles from the course of the Luni, and Nagri, between Jodhpur and Bikaner, many miles from any apparent source of water, both of which centre around isolated outcrops of rhyolite. Rhyolite is one of the materials most commonly used for tool making, where quartzite is not available, in the desert and Dry Zone, and occurs in various forms. In addition quartzite, quartz and other stones were all used in the Luni industries, and the industry of each locality tends to have its own distinct character, which is related to the available raw materials. The distance between sources of material helps further to emphasize these differences.

The Middle Palaeolithic sites of the Thar region, like those of Central and Peninsular India, do not give many direct indications of the way of life of those who inhabited or used them, but it is possible to make a number of inferences, both from individual sites and from their relation to the topography of the region. Today the desert offers an exposed environment, with little shade from the heat of the summer sun, or shelter from the cold winds and low night temperatures of winter. During Middle Palaeolithic times cooler, damper conditions prevailed, and grass, trees and bushes must have provided a certain amount of shelter, although in most of the region the terrain would offer little protection from wind. It seems highly probable that in such an environment the makers of the Luni industries built huts or wind breaks of some kind, at certain seasons of the year. That they were often on the move is indicated by the many small concentrations of tools they left on the banks and gravel terraces of the old river systems. Sites of this kind, where the artefacts are made from the materials immediately available, suggest that as far as possible tools were made where and when they were needed, and not carried for long distances. On the other hand, the larger sites associated with isolated or particularly good sources of raw material show that, for certain purposes, people were prepared to make stone artefacts at these places, and carry them away with them for use elsewhere. This parallels the situation already noted in Lower Palaeolithic times in Central and Peninsular India, where some artefacts were made from materials locally available, while others were brought to habitation sites from sources some miles distant. So far no caves or rock shelters have been found in the Thar region, so there are no occupation deposits to provide more detailed evidence of the culture and ecology of Middle Palaeolithic communities, and there is also as yet no suitable material for C14 dating. Consideration of the dates available for the Nevasan industries, and those for the buried soils of Gujarat mentioned earlier, together with the dates of Mousterian industries in caves in Afghanistan to the north, and the Zagros Mountains to the far west, suggest that the Luni industry occupies a period extending, very approximately, from 45,000 to 25,000 B.P., and probably continuing somewhat later.

Perhaps the most remarkable group of Middle Palaeolithic sites in the sub-continent are those in the Rohri hills of Upper Sind. The industry is based upon the large nodules of chert that cap this group of flat topped limestone hills. In terms of technological detail and of the proportion of certain artefact types, this industry differs somewhat from those of the Luni group, and for this reason it has been separately named as the Rohri industry. Its distinguishing characteristics are the somewhat larger size of certain artefact types, and the tendency to use suitable nodules of chert as cores with little or no preparation. In some cases a succession of flakes has been struck off an unprepared nodule one after another, rather like slices of bread. The remarkable feature of the sites is their extent: many acres of the flat hill tops are covered with factory debris and broken or discarded Middle Palaeolithic artefacts. The social and economic implications of this concentration of sites are profound, for they far exceed all the other recorded sites in the arid regions of India and Pakistan (with the possible exception of those on the Potwar Plateau) in terms of quantity of artefacts and factory debris, and therefore they must have served a wide area, as well as being in use for a long period of time. Today the region is extremely arid, and almost entirely dependent upon the Indus for water. Even allowing for rather more hospitable conditions in Middle Palaeolithic times and for a certain concentration of population near the river, the products of such extensive working floors must have been shared by many different groups and communities. This in turn indicates a complex and far reaching system of social and economic relationships between the groups concerned on a scale seldom envisaged for Middle Palaeolithic man. This group of sites is of particular interest for another reason, namely that at one of them, Chancha Baluch, there is some evidence for the local development and emergence of the basic stone technology of the Upper Palaeolithic.

The same limitations regarding cultural information and dating apply to the Rohri industry as to the Luni group, but there is a reasonable hope of finding caves or rock shelters in the Rohri hills which may help to remedy this in due course. A site in a similar situation on a limestone hill at Jerruk, near Hyderabad in Lower Sind, mentioned earlier in discussing the Lower Palaeolithic, also appears to have extensive Middle Palaeolithic working floors. So far it has not been possible to study this industry in great detail, but it appears to resemble the Luni–Rohri group of industries rather than the Nevasan. Further Middle Palaeolithic industries have been reported from the Las Bela district of southern Baluchistan, but so far only a summary mention of what appear to be very

interesting collections from a large number of sites has been published. Particular interest attaches to these collections on account of their being the most
westerly in the subcontinent, and providing a link with the Persian Gulf, Arabia
and Africa.

The Upper Palaeolithic

Wherever Upper Palaeolithic industries have been found they have been recognized primarily as a technological entity. They represent a marked and fairly
consistent change in methods of making stone tools, and therefore also probably
in some of the underlying concepts relating to their use. These changes may also
reflect changes in associated crafts such as those of working wood, bone, leather,
etc. Whether they are also related to changes in hunting methods, or to a more
general shift in the utilization of resources, or are in any sense a response to
environmental change, are in most instances questions for further and more
wide ranging investigation and discussion. Some of these questions have been
more or less fully answered in the case of individual sites or localities, in
Western Asia and elsewhere outside the subcontinent, but by and large they
appear to have no complete or simple solutions.

The basic technological innovation of the Upper Palaeolithic is the method of
producing parallel-sided blades from a carefully prepared core, a specialized
development of the unidirectional type of Middle Palaeolithic core (see
Fig. 3.10, Nos. 10 and 11). One good core of this kind, once prepared, can
yield many parallel-sided blades with little or no further preparation. In this
respect it is an advance on the Middle Palaeolithic method – a process of core
preparation aimed at obtaining one flake of predetermined shape, and demonstrated by material illustrated from Central India and Sanghao (Figs. 3.6 and 3.9).
The whole or a large part of the process usually had to be repeated in order to
produce further flakes. The technique of making parallel-sided blades is an
essential basic element of all Upper Palaeolithic industries of the subcontinent,
and of many of its later Mesolithic industries. Neolithic and early Chalcolithic
settlements almost always yield large numbers of blades, made by the same
method, and blades of this kind appear to have been an essential element of
equipment until the beginning of the Iron Age.

Upper Palaeolithic industries make their appearance in the arid regions of
Pakistan and Western India towards the end of the late Pleistocene humid
phase. Recent evidence suggests that Upper Palaeolithic techniques developed
in the region as an element of the Middle Palaeolithic industries of the Rohri and
Luni groups, and became a dominant part of the stone working tradition wherever this region remained habitable during the final Pleistocene arid phase.
Further east, in the Ganges valley and Central India, Upper Palaeolithic techniques are associated with the final phases of alluvial deposition in the river
valleys, and therefore here too are probably contemporary with the final arid

phase. The level containing the main concentration of Upper Palaeolithic tools in the geological sequence of the Belan river valley in southern Uttar Pradesh has been dated by radiocarbon to approximately 18,000 to 17,000 B.P. Upper Palaeolithic artefacts were found in the alluvium above and below this layer, forming a continuum from the Middle Palaeolithic material, in the upper of two indurated gravels, to the Mesolithic material on and just below the top soil. In the Belan valley and the Central Indian hills, immediately to the south, Upper Palaeolithic working floors are found closely associated with those of the Middle Palaeolithic, and Upper Palaeolithic occupation deposits sometimes appear to underlie those of Mesolithic cultures in rock shelters and at least at one open site. Thus there is every indication of continuity. The same is true of certain limited localities in the Dry Zone, such as Pushkar, where sites ranging from Middle Palaeolithic to Mesolithic cluster around the lakes, and again appear to represent a continuous local cultural and technological tradition.

The characteristics of the Thar Upper Palaeolithic industries have been shown to be fairly consistent throughout, and thus seem to justify their designation as a regional entity (see Fig. 3.10). No detailed analysis of the Belan valley material has so far appeared, so the two groups cannot be closely compared, but the Belan material appears to share many of the characteristics of the Thar Upper Palaeolithic. The Thar Upper Palaeolithic is based primarily upon the production of parallel-sided blades made from prepared unidirectional cores (Fig. 3.10, Nos. 10 to 12). Middle Palaeolithic techniques of core and flake production are not lost, but continue alongside the new methods, on a reduced scale both numerically and in terms of average size. Burins become a rather more prominent feature, and are increasingly made from milky, partially crystalline quartz where this is available. Whether made of quartz or other materials, they tend to be of the South Asian kind noted at Hokra, Sanghao and elsewhere. The majority are simple angle burins, the burin edge made by the removal of a single flake or burin spall, by means of a carefully controlled blow, using as a striking platform a facet provided by the natural tendency of quartz to fracture into rectangular pieces (e.g. Fig. 3.10, Nos. 1 and 6). Alternatively, the broken edge of a flake or blade, or any other available piece of quartzite or other raw material of suitable thickness was sometimes used (e.g. Fig. 3.10, No. 2). Scrapers of various kinds, including carinated scrapers (Fig. 3.10, Nos. 4 and 5), continue to be made from both flakes and blades, but are not such a major part of the assemblage as in Middle Palaeolithic industries. Hammer stones continue to be found on working floors, as in the Middle Palaeolithic. Small palette stones of a kind found henceforward at sites of every period up to and including Mature Indus urban settlements are found at some Upper Palaeolithic sites. The artefacts of earlier Thar Upper Palaeolithic industries show bulbs of percussion as pronounced as those of the Middle Palaeolithic, but as time goes on the technique of making parallel-sided blades is continually refined, the bulbs of percussion become less predominant, and the blades more slender, straight and regular.

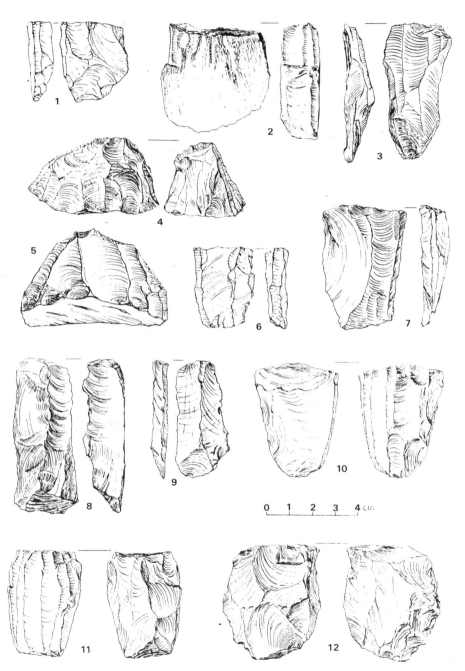

3.10 Pushkar: Upper Palaeolithic artefacts: 1, 2, 6 and 7 burins; 3, 8 and 9 blades; 4 and 5 carinated scrapers; 10 and 11 blade cores; 12 unstruck blade core

The whole tool kit of the Thar Upper Palaeolithic, as represented by surviving artefacts of stone and (rarely) bone, is markedly on a smaller scale, and, perhaps more significantly, lighter, than that of the Middle Palaeolithic of the same region. It is eminently suitable for people constantly on the move, and carrying their equipment with them. It is tempting to interpret the change as a response to increasingly arid conditions in the region at the end of the Pleistocene, but at present there is little or no supporting evidence for this. Upper Palaeolithic sites are more sparsely distributed in the Thar region than those of the Middle Palaeolithic, as might be expected in view of the climatic sequence. As in the case of the Middle Palaeolithic, little can be said as yet about the social and economic life of Upper Palaeolithic times in any part of the subcontinent.

Since this book appeared in 1982, an Upper Palaeolithic site has been excavated near Rawalpindi, in northern Pakistan, and a survey of the locality made noting changes that have taken place in the environment since the site was occupied. An important feature is the widespread deposition of loess, covering the site and much of the surrounding landscape. The loess immediately over the site has been dated by the TL method to c. 40,000 years. Upper Palaeolithic artefacts and debitage in a fresh and unweathered state indicate that the loess deposition must have taken place during and immediately after the site was occupied.

Sangao cave in the North-west Frontier Province, which was excavated some years ago, has a deep occupation deposit which yielded Upper Palaeolithic tools of milky quartz, but these have not so far been fully described or dated.

In both Central and Western India the change from Upper Palaeolithic to Mesolithic appears to have been a steady process of development involving in each case a change in the choice of raw materials – in some cases complete, but in others merely a change in emphasis. This change is accompanied by a partial change in the range of artefact types and a reduction in the average size of artefacts common to industries of both periods. Parallel-sided blades continue to form the basis of the Mesolithic industries, as in the Upper Palaeolithic, and the techniques of the Middle Palaeolithic continue as a minor part of the Mesolithic tradition of the region, producing smaller artefacts, and thus making them commensurate in size with other microlithic artefacts (see e.g. Fig. 4.18, No. 4). The overall difference in average size of all artefacts as between Upper Palaeolithic and Mesolithic industries is apparent when one looks at assemblages of both periods. In the Thar region this has been quantified by measuring many of the collections from geologically stratified sites, and shown to be remarkably constant. No measurements are available for collections from Uttar Pradesh, Central India or the south, but a similar reduction in scale from Upper Palaeolithic to Mesolithic is observable.

Upper Palaeolithic industries have been reported from parts of South India, while industries with certain Upper Palaeolithic features are known from central Gujarat and north-western Kathiawar. In each case they raise a number of questions concerning the relationship of Middle and Upper Palaeolithic traditions. A collection from Visadi in central Gujarat, which was found in a stabilized dune of the last arid phase, appears to represent a blend of the Upper Palaeolithic and Nevasan Middle Palaeolithic traditions, as do finds from stratified river gravels in Kathiawar. In South India the situation is somewhat different. On the one hand there appear to be a number of industries in which microlithic tool making methods are directly superimposed upon Middle Palaeolithic traditions, and others in which an Upper Palaeolithic blade technology is more fully developed, as in the north.

An Upper Palaeolithic blade and burin industry from a group of sites near Renigunta in Chittoor district, Andhra Pradesh was found by Murty during the 1960s and discussed by him in some detail. The group includes some surface sites, and others stratified beneath the uppermost alluvial deposits in the valley of the Rallakgava river, a tributary of the Swarnamukhi. No precise dating evidence is available for the industry, and we agree with Murty that its character and stratigraphical position combine to show it to be between the Middle Palaeolithic and the Mesolithic in the regional cultural sequence. It may date from the late Pleistocene or perhaps even the early Holocene. A number of artefact types are common to this and to the Mesolithic industries of the region, and Murty has demonstrated that there is a consistent difference in average size, similar to that noted in the Thar region and in North India. He also notes the choice of raw material which is predominantly quartzite in the Upper Palaeolithic, in contrast to Mesolithic industries which tend to be made predominantly in quartz and various kinds of semi-precious stones (cryptocrystalline silica) as in the north. The technology and range of artefact types in the Renigunta group of Upper Palaeolithic industries also appear to correspond closely to those of the north-west and north, especially the burins, which show the same distinctive South Asian character. Murty considered the Renigunta industries to represent a local centre of development of Upper Palaeolithic techniques from a common Middle Palaeolithic basis, and in this also we are inclined to agree. At the same time neither this group of industries, nor the Thar group discussed earlier, should be looked upon as developing in total isolation, any more or any less than other stone industry with distinctive regional characteristics of Palaeolithic or later times. In both cases a great deal more information is needed regarding the cultures of intervening regions, including their chronology, before these questions can even be discussed.

CHAPTER 4

HUNTER-GATHERERS AND NOMADIC PASTORALISTS

We must recall that in the Indian subcontinent distinct, self-contained social groups, at different levels of cultural and technological development, survived right into this century. They include hunting and collecting tribes, pastoral nomads, shifting cultivators, traditional settled agriculturalists, modern 'developed' agriculturalists and several levels of urban industrial society, all co-existing and economically interdependent. This provides us with a basic model for past developments. When settled agricultural communities began to appear in South Asia, they cannot have done so in a vacuum. Already in almost every region there were existing populations of hunters, fishers and collectors, among whom adaptations of local food grains or other plants, or the domestication of local species of birds or animals must have taken place, more or less independently of movements of peoples or ideas from outside. Thus we may expect more than one pattern of local adaptation to the environment, including some emphasizing pastoralism and others horticulture or agriculture. When we consider the first settlements in any area, we must remember that they fit into such a broader pattern, with various groups adapting differently, and in different stages of transition from hunting and collecting to pastoralism and agriculture. This tendency to variation is further emphasized by the widely divergent climatic and environmental conditions pertaining in different parts of the subcontinent which at all times have contributed to the peculiar character of South Asian life-styles.

Thus in the Indian context, there emerges a broad overlap in the chronology of the so-called Mesolithic cultures and the earliest agricultural settlements now coming to light in the Indus basin. Microlithic industries associated with what appear to be the cultures of hunting people, fishermen, pastoralists or people practising some form of agriculture, have been found widely throughout the subcontinent. Many have been recorded with little or no cultural evidence other than that provided by the stone industry itself. In distribution they range from the north-western borderlands, to Central India, north Karnataka and Sri Lanka (see Fig. 4.1). Some of the most notable of these microlithic assemblages come from large factory sites, each of which must have served a wide area, and perhaps also been used by communities of many different kinds and sizes. The means of distribution of this high quality raw material must have been either through many people visiting the site or by those living near it having a system of exchange with people from other groups. There are examples of trade or exchange from many early settlements, which overlap in time with Mesolithic communities. Bagor is one such example (see below); Mehrgarh too provides ample evidence of trade in a variety of items with distant regions from the pre-ceramic period forward (see chapter 5, pp. 106–7).

Dancing scenes in the caves of Central India depict gatherings which must have included quite a number of families or bands. Occasions such as these are known to have provided hunter-gatherers in many parts of the world, including groups in Central India, South African Bushmen and the Australian Aborigines, with the means of exchanging objects of interest and value, and also of strengthening wider social ties, beyond the immediate family or local group. Therefore it seems highly probable that they did so in the case of the Stone Age inhabitants of many parts of India. Such gatherings would also facilitate the passing on of stone working and other techniques. As we have seen in the foregoing chapter, large factory sites of earlier periods indicate that such practices may long antedate the Mesolithic period in South Asia.

Because of the quantity and variety of these Indian microlithic industries, we propose to summarize the evidence regarding them rather as we have done in the case of the Palaeolithic, describing briefly those sites or localities in each major region that provide an insight into broader aspects of life. We have drawn a somewhat arbitrary line, necessary in view of the quantity of material, between these microlithic industries and those associated with settlements in or near the main stream of cultural development, which are dealt with in the following chapter.

Throughout the Indus system virtually all microlithic industries so far recorded are associated with what appear to be permanent settlements. These include urban settlements of the Early Indus period as well as settlements of earlier periods with a less developed urban character which, on the basis of their size and relationship to later cultures, must be regarded as being within the mainstream of development of settled agriculture and urban life. Lithic assemblages from such sites will be discussed in chapter 6. Blade industries, an essential element of the Indus civilization and of other urban cultures up to the beginning of the Iron Age, will be discussed in appropriate chapters. Microlithic sites have been found in the Las Bela district of south Baluchistan, but as with material of earlier periods, these have only been published in the briefest manner. A considerable amount of microlithic material has been recorded from the arid Thar region of Western India and Pakistan to the south-east of the Indus, particularly in the Dry Zone on the south-eastern margins of the desert. With a few notable exceptions all the material so far put on record comes from surface sites, and appears to be ancestral to the present predominantly semi-nomadic, pastoral cultures of the region.

As we have pointed out in the previous chapter, much of the Thar region must have become virtually uninhabitable during the final Pleistocene arid phase, but there is evidence of a continuous process of technological development from

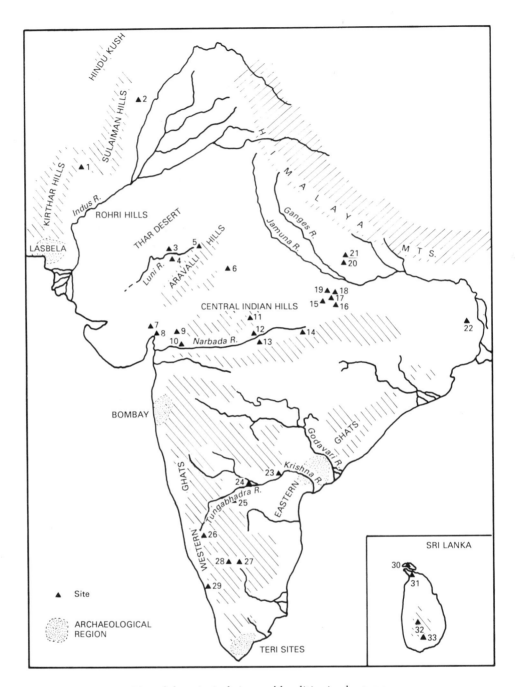

4.1 Map of the principal sites and localities in chapter 4

Key
India & Pakistan
1. Mehrgarh 2. Lewan 3. Mogara 4. Khairla hill 5. Pushkar 6. Bagor 7. Langhnaj 8. Mitli
9. Pavagarh hill 10. Visadi 11. Bhimbetka 12. Adamgarh 13. Pachmari 14. Barasimla 15. Morhana Pahar 16. Lekhahia 17. Chopani Mando 18. Barakaccha 19. Siddhpur 20. Sarai-Nahar-Rai
21. Mahadaha 22. Birbhanpur 23. Nagarjunakonda 24. Krishna Bridge 25. Sanganakallu 26. Barapedi cave 27. Jalahalli 28. Kibbanhalli 29. Calicut

Sri Lanka
30. Jaffna 31. Teri site (Sri Lanka) 32. Bandarawela 33. Batadombalena

Upper Palaeolithic to Mesolithic industries on its eastern margins, as in the Pushkar locality with its exceptionally good supply of fresh water (see Fig. 3.5). Other examples are known from similarly favoured places. The arid phase, by providing a break between two horizons (that of the buried soil formed during the preceding humid phase and that of the modern soil), helps to emphasize the distinction between Upper Palaeolithic and Mesolithic cultures. The difference between the industries of the two horizons has been quantified on the basis of average measurements of artefacts common to both, from sites widely distributed throughout the region. This demonstrates the consistent reduction in the size of artefacts of well-established types. The process of change is further demonstrated by the proportional difference in the representation of various artefact types in the two groups of industries, and by the changing choice of raw material within sub-regions. Tables 4.1 and 4.2 illustrate this with reference to the Pushkar locality in Rajasthan, and to sites in the central Gujarat region.

Table 4.2 also shows how these changes continue during the Holocene, with a progressive reduction in size, a decreasing proportion of burins, an increasing trend towards the production of geometric microliths or composite points and barbs, and a declining use of quartz in the central Gujarat sub-region. In the Pushkar locality a comparable change in raw materials was noted.

Whether and how far these changes relate to the minor fluctuations of climate during the Holocene mentioned earlier is a matter than can only be discussed when further research has been done. The distribution of microlithic sites in the arid regions as a whole emphasizes their association with the return of more hospitable conditions at the beginning of the Holocene. In central Gujarat and much of Rajasthan where Upper Palaeolithic material appears to be largely confined to favoured localities, microlithic industries, by contrast, are found widely distributed. Usually they are situated on fossil dunes and on spurs and slopes of hills, particularly where these overlook permanent or seasonal water sources. Such sites vary in extent and appear to represent temporary or semi-permanent seasonal camping places of families or somewhat larger groups. There are also examples of factory sites associated with sources of raw material, such as Mogara near Jodhpur, and sites where analysis of the material indicates a combination of both these functions, such as Khairla hill a little further south, across the Luni river.

Around the fresh water lake at Budha Pushkar there is a concentration of sites with microlithic industries showing a range of variation comparable to those of Gujarat. Analysis of the finds indicates that these are primarily living or camping sites. Pottery, showing general affinities with such Chalcolithic sites as Ahar and Bagor, has been found at several of these sites, and at one of them a copper fish-hook was also found (see Figs. 4.2 and 4.3). While these cannot be positively proved to have been contemporary with the microlithic industries, their presence strongly suggests an overlap in time between the microlithic and certain semi-urban Chalcolithic cultures, thus supporting the evidence from

Table 4.1. *Average measurements (in cm) and percentage of the total artefact collection formed by selected artefact types, from Upper Palaeolithic and Mesolithic horizons at Budha Pushkar*

	Blade cores				Concavo-convex scrapers				Flake cores				Burins				
	L.	B.	T.	% of total	L.	B.	T.	% of total	L.	B.	T.	% of total	L.	B.	T.	Facet	% of total
Pushkar Upper Palaeolithic	3.26	2.73	2.15	23.80	3.25	3.35	1.48	4.76	6.74	7.05	3.80	7.13	3.24	2.42	–	0.65	13.49
Pushkar Mesolithic	2.61	2.04	1.76	29.08	2.27	1.59	0.96	3.55	3.43	2.88	2.13	9.93	2.35	1.46	–	0.60	11.35

Key: L. = length; B. = breadth; T. = thickness
Source: After Allchin, Goudie and Hegde, 1978

Table 4.2. *Percentage of total artefact collection formed by and average measurements (in cm) of selected artefact types, and the percentage of quartz used as a raw material, at representative Upper Palaeolithic and Mesolithic sites in central Gujarat*

	Blade cores				Burins					Composite points and barbs	% of total no. of artefacts made of quartz
	L.	B.	T.	% of total	L.	B.	T.	Facet	% of total	% of total	
Visadi (Upper Palaeolithic)	3.81	3.49	2.50	10.99	2.82	2.07	0.95	0.51	12.11	–	100
Pavagarh (Larger Mesolithic)	2.05	1.41	0.90	3.02	2.27	1.38	0.85	?	10.88	1.02	49.74
Mitli (Smaller Mesolithic)	1.88	1.42	0.94	3.91	2.00	0.95	0.50	0.25	1.56	14.06	8.59

Key: L. = length; B. = breadth; T. = thickness
Source: After Allchin, Goudie and Hegde, 1978

excavated sites discussed below. Today, and throughout historical times, Push-kar has been regarded as a place of exceptional holiness and as one of the most important places of pilgrimage in India. A large cattle fair, which also has a long tradition, is held in the neighbourhood every year. Thus there are a number of indications that the importance of this unique place may extend back without a break to prehistoric times, as far back as the Middle Palaeolithic and perhaps further. This in turn suggests the archaeological potential of other sites with these characteristics.

The Mesolithic site of Bagor, also in Rajasthan, but in an area of somewhat higher rainfall east of the Aravalli range, was excavated by V. N. Misra during the 1960s, and is the most completely investigated and best documented Meso-lithic site in the subcontinent. It is a small settlement, situated on a dune on the bank of a seasonal stream, a tributary of the Chambal river, and also associated with an old lake basin. Summarizing, Misra writes:

The total thickness of habitation deposit in various trenches is about 1.50 m. It reveals a regular occupation of the site over a period of five millennia immediately before Christ. During this period a culture based on stone technology and hunting–pastoral economy underwent continuous evolution as evidenced by the appearance of new material traits and the decline or disappearance of others. The most abundant material which continued all through the occupation was the very distinctive microlithic industry. No strati-

4.2 View of Budha Pushkar lake with Microlithic working floor and campsite at which a copper fish-hook and pottery were found in the foreground

graphical break was seen at any stage in the occupation, at least not by the excavation techniques we adopted, but on the basis of changes in material culture three phases of Bagor culture can be recognized. [See Fig. 4.4.]

Three radiocarbon dates were obtained for phase I, and two for phase II, while the last phase, III, is dated by objects in the deposit. Bones, some of them charred, of both wild and domestic animals were found throughout, but declined somewhat in quantity in phase III. A distinctive microlithic industry, at its height in phase I, declines progressively in phases II and III. Burials were found on the site, associated with all three phases. In phase I, dated by C14 to c. 5000 to 2800 B.C., there is evidence of huts with paved floors. Animal bones include domestic sheep and goat, cattle (probably some wild and some domestic), several species of deer, wild boar, jackal, rat, monitor lizard, river turtle and fish. In phase II, dated c. 2800 to 600 B.C., pottery and copper objects, including three arrowheads make their appearance (Fig. 4.5). The pottery is associated with the burials of this period, and is a coarse, gritty ware, sometimes with a red slip, having craft affinities with pottery from other Chalcolithic sites in the region, such as Ahar (see p. 263). The copper arrowheads have affinities with those from Harappan sites in north Rajasthan and Sind. In phase III (c. 600 B.C. to A.D. 200) the area of occupation is restricted to the central part of the site. Not

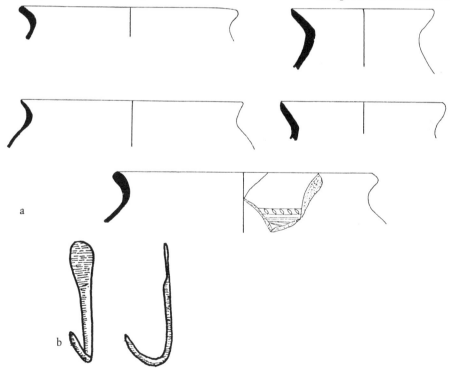

4·3 (a) Pottery (1:4) and (b) copper fish-hook (1:1) from a Microlithic working floor and looking Budha Pushkar lake

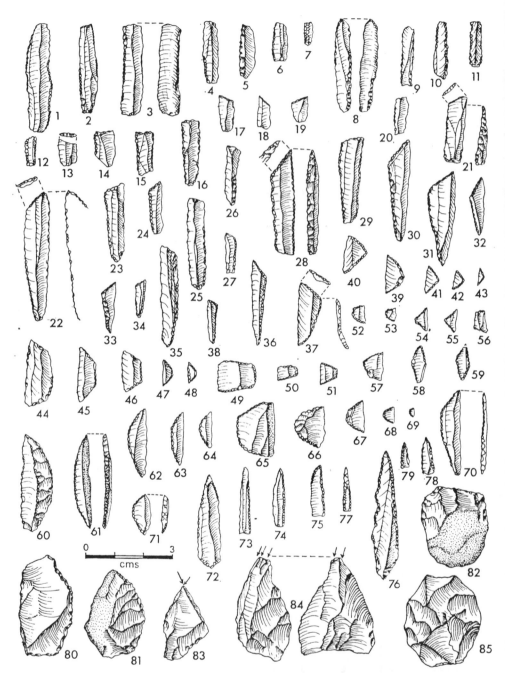

4.4 Bagor: Mesolithic artefacts: 1–12 retouched blades; 13–29 truncated blades; 30–43 triangles; 44–48 and 52–57 trapezes; 49–51 transverse arrowheads; 58–59 rhomboids; 60–71 lunates; 72–79 trimmed points; 80–82 scrapers on flakes; 83 and 84 burins; 85 unstruck discoidal core (*after* V. N. Misra)

only do animal bones and microliths decrease, but iron tools, glass beads, bricks, tiles and wheel-made pottery appear, all indicating an increasing reliance upon crop based agriculture.

The microlithic industry of Bagor has a distinctive character throughout. The excavator estimates that 'several hundred thousand worked pieces' together with debris of manufacture were recovered in the course of the excavation. The majority of the finished tools were of chert, but a higher proportion of the waste material was of locally available quartz. The published account indicates no marked typological change between levels, only a progressive decline in quantity. The significant features of the industry are that it is based predominantly upon blades; that there is a great variety of reworked artefact types, including many so-called geometric forms; and that many of the artefacts are of extremely small size, recalling the smaller microlithic industries of the Thar region to the west, but of a standard of craftmanship only seen otherwise in the Mesolithic industries of western Central India. The stone objects found also included ring stones (Fig. 4.6).

Langhnaj in Gujarat, excavated some years earlier by H. D. Sankalia and others, shows a somewhat similar cultural sequence, and has the distinction of being the first site discovered in the Arid Zone to demonstrate the development of a Mesolithic culture, parallel in time to the urban cultures of the Indus system and other more favoured regions.

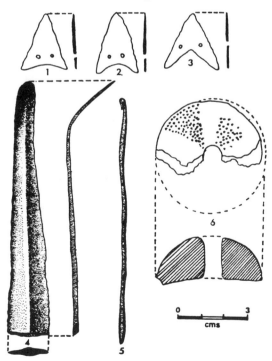

4.5 Bagor: metal tools, and terracotta spindle whorl, phase II (*after* V. N. Misra)

At both Bagor and Langhnaj, where there was moderate or low rainfall, hunting must have continued to be of importance alongside other means of subsistence. The presence of bones of wild and domestic animals suggests that the economy of the hunters was augmented by pastoralism, or perhaps by trading with settled neighbours, or preying upon their herds.

North and Central India form another major region where the continuity of development from the Upper Palaeolithic industries of the late Pleistocene to the Microlithic blade industries of the Holocene can be clearly perceived in the archaeological record, although it has not been quantified. The hill region of Central India, today still relatively undeveloped agriculturally, is as rich in Mesolithic sites as is central Gujarat. As on the margins of the Thar desert, numerous sites are located on small hills or rising ground, commanding a view of the surrounding country. Most of these yield a range of artefacts and waste materials which indicate that they were the camping places or temporary living sites of small groups or families. Such sites are still favoured by local people as temporary or semi-permanent camping places to which they return from time to time. There are a number of much larger factory sites, some of which cover an acre or more of ground, which in certain cases appear to have served other communities both before and after the microlith makers of the Holocene. These large factory sites are also suggestive of external trade. Barasimla, near Jabalpur, is not many miles from the Chalcolithic site of Tripuri. Barkaccha and Siddhpur, two further large stone factories, at the former of which a butt of a ground stone axe was found, are both on the edge of the Ganges plains where they meet the hills of Central India. This, along with other factors, suggests some contact between the peoples of the plains and the Late Stone Age hunters of the hills. The archaeological evidence is further enhanced by modern ethno-

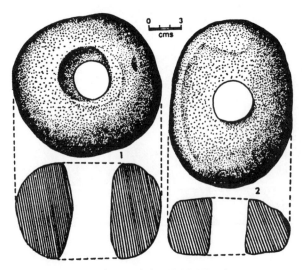

4.6 Bagor: ring stone, phase II (*after* V. N. Misra)

graphic evidence. In Central India, communities with very different standards of living have for long co-existed at very close quarters, and depended upon one another economically, as we have already had occasion to point out.

As well as factory sites and minor camp sites in the North/Central Indian region there are what appear to be more permanent living sites such as Sarai-Nahar-Rai in Uttar Pradesh, and Birbanpur in Bengal, which are discussed below. Finally, there are numerous rock shelters which contain occupation debris in the form of massive quantities of stone tools and waste material, varying amounts of bone and charcoal, and other cultural remains. Many of these contain only shallow deposits consisting of little more than a few inches of dust and microliths disturbed by the feet of sheltering herdboys and their animals. Baghai Khor (Fig. 4.7) is one of this kind. Some, however, have been found to contain a greater depth of occupation.

Of the smaller sites, little more can be said in the absence of a systematic survey. The same applies to the large factory sites, except to repeat what we have said previously about large sites of earlier periods in Sind and elsewhere – namely that the extent of the working floors and the volume of material in themselves indicate that each such site must have served a very wide area. Thus they must have formed part of a fairly extensive socio-economic system. Such

4.7 Baghai Khor, Central India: a rock shelter containing Mesolithic cultural debris and rock art

major sites may further have been in use for a considerable time. Any studies that have been made of the material from these sites tend to bear out this contention indicating that they were in use throughout more than one major cultural phase. Again, factory sites such as Barkaccha and Siddhpur are located on the frontier between the Vindhya hills, a region well supplied with suitable stone for tool making, and the alluvial plains of the middle Ganges–Jamuna valley where virtually no stone is available. Therefore it is reasonable to assume that one of their functions must have been to supply material for the inhabitants of the plains, and this is turn indicates a pattern of relationships between two geographically different regions.

Throughout Central India, both north and south of the Narbada rift, the general character of the industries appears to be consistent, allowing for a certain amount of variation in the quality and nature of the raw material. This includes a whole range of jasper, agate and other kinds of chalcedonic silica often referred to as semi-precious stones, usually obtained in the form of pebbles from river gravels, and a certain amount of exceptionally fine-grained quartzite which appears to have been quarried, although no quarries have yet been reported. As in the Thar region burins are often made from quartz, even when the rest of the industry is largely made from other materials. The microlithic industries of this region are based upon parallel-sided blades struck from carefully prepared cores. Like those further west, they appear to have inherited this technique from Upper Palaeolithic predecessors in the same region together with certain elements of Middle Palaeolithic technology, all on a reduced scale and practised with increasing finesse during the Mesolithic. In western Central India the quality of both material and workmanship is very high. The technical skill and perfection of form of many of the artefacts seems quite beyond that required for practical purposes. Many of the semi-precious stones, such as agates, used for making microliths are still employed today by jewellers and bead-makers, who obtain some of their best material from the gravels of the Narbada and other rivers – the same sources which supplied the Mesolithic hunters. The Adamgarh industry illustrated here (Fig. 4.8) is of this kind, and the site is close to the Narbada.

In recent years Mesolithic sites have been discovered on the old alluvium of the Gangetic plain. Artefacts collected from a group of such sites north of the Ganges have been found to be made of the same materials as those from sites on the south side, including the factory sites mentioned in the previous paragraph. This must indicate that the raw material, or the finished artefacts, or both, were carried across the river, thus further extending the connection between hill and plains regions. Several groups of these sites, north of Benares and Allahabad, are associated with old ox-bow lakes formed by the cut-off meanders of the numerous minor northern tributaries of the Ganges. One site, Sarai-Nahar-Rai, was excavated by G. R. Sharma and the Department of Archaeology of Allahabad University. The locality, although intensively cultivated today, must then have been forested, like the Terai zone on the Nepalese frontier a little further north, where areas of forest can still be seen between the cultivated lands of villages, although these are being increasingly cleared as cultivation is extended. Sarai-Nahar-Rai is considered by the excavators to be a small settlement or semi-permanent camping place. Situated on the bank of one of the ox-bow lakes, the occupation deposit has been reduced by erosion of the surface. Features excavated include a number of small hearths, one large communal hearth or hut floor, and several burials. The skeletal remains are those of large boned, robust

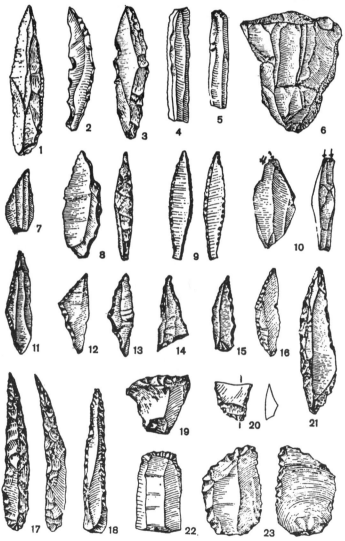

4.8 Adamgarh cave: Mesolithic artefacts: 1, 3 and 21 backed blades; 4 and 5 blades; 2, 8, 11 and 16 lunates; 6 blade core; 7 and 15 single trimmed points; 9 double trimmed point; 10 burin; 12–14 triangles; 17 and 18 borers; 19, 22 and 23 scrapers; 20 transverse arrowhead (1:1) (*after* R. V. Joshi)

4.9 Mahadaha: burial (*courtesy* G. R. Sharma)

people, buried in oblong graves with an east–west orientation. Microliths and lumps of burnt clay and charred bone from the hearths were found in the graves, and a point was found embedded in a rib bone of one of the male skeletons. Other microlithic points were found in positions which strongly suggest that they had pierced the flesh of two further bodies.

In the course of the excavation of Sarai-Nahar-Rai no pottery was found, but there was a large number of microliths, a few bone tools, and a quantity of animal bones, many partially charred. The microlithic industry was evidently based upon parallel-sided blades and included triangles, points and backed blades of various kinds. The animal bones are said to have included those of cattle (*Bos indicus*), buffalo, sheep, goat, elephant and tortoise. The suggestion is made that while most of the cattle were probably wild, some may have been domesticated. This is a question that deserves further careful investigation.

One radiocarbon date of approximately 8000 B.C. has been obtained for Sarai-Nahar-Rai, but the excavator explains that being a single date based upon uncharred bones 'its credibility is not beyond question'. He points out that the microlithic sites in the alluvial plain north of the river Ganges show a pattern of progressive technological development, from the Upper Palaeolithic through several Mesolithic phases, with artefacts of decreasing size and changing type, to the advent of pottery. Sarai-Nahar-Rai falls somewhere near the middle of this sequence.

A second site, Mahadaha, similarly situated, also appears to be a Mesolithic campsite where bone artefacts were produced, evidenced by bones with cut marks indicating butchering and objects in process of manufacture. These included arrowheads and bone ornaments. Stone querns and mullers are recorded. The animal remains include a variety of bos, buffalo, elephant, rhinoceros, stag, pig, turtle and birds, with stag predominating. Here too a number of burials were excavated (Fig. 4.9). These include male and female skeletons and some double burials. Two male skeletons were wearing bone necklaces, and arrowheads and animal bones were also found associated with the burials. In both these sites the height and size of the skeletons is remarkable: the average height of the males at Mahadaha being 1.92 m, and the females 1.78 m. The physical types appear to be quite unlike those of North or Central India in any later period.

At Birbhanpur on the Damodar river in West Bengal, in the extreme eastern extension of the Central Indian hills, excavations were carried out by the Archaeological Survey of India at a group of microlithic sites which surface observation indicated cover approximately a square mile in all. The tools are made of quartz and other materials, and they occur in clusters upon an old land surface about a metre below the present surface, and also below this, in what are considered to have been fissures caused by the drying out of the soil. A number of holes were noticed which the excavator tentatively interprets as post-holes. This, and the character of the industry suggest that we have here a combined factory and living site upon which huts were erected by the microlith-makers. The climate during and immediately after the period of occupation is thought to have been somewhat drier than at present, and there is evidence of an earlier phase of heavier precipitation and higher humidity.

Birbhanpur did not yield such massive quantities of stone tools as sites in western Central India, and the industry is of a somewhat different character. This is partly due no doubt to the high proportion of quartz used: 68.7% of the stone tools and factory debris excavated are made of this somewhat intractable material. The blades and blade cores, whether in quartz or other materials, are not quite so fine, the points and the lunates are broader than in western Central India, and a significant proportion of the last two are made on flakes rather than blades. Of the whole assemblage excavated 6.8% are cores and 87.9% are flakes; the total number of finished tools (282) are only 5.1%. The excavator classifies the tools from the excavations, excluding surface finds, as follows:

Blades	Lunates	Points	Borers	Burins	Scrapers	Total
106	42	60	19	12	43	282
37.5%	14.8%	21.2%	6.6%	4.2%	15.3%	

These figures indicate that we are dealing with a factory site and living site combined. The absence of triangles and trapezoidal forms, and of crested guide flakes – a by-product of the manufacture of fine parallel-sided blades – all distinguish this industry from those from areas further to the west discussed earlier. Whether this distinction is one of time or regional character is not clear.

Those caves and rock shelters of Central India that have been excavated have yielded microlithic artefacts that appear to complement the assemblages from the factory sites both in character and volume. For example, collectively the trenches excavated at the Adamgarh group of rock shelters in the 1960s, discussed below, are said to have yielded approximately 25,000 microliths (see Fig. 4.8). Morhana Pahar, excavated by A. C. Carlleyle in the late nineteenth century but never published in full, must have yielded a collection of comparable size if we can judge from the quantity of material which has found its way into museums in many countries of the world. Sadly, the example set by Carlleyle of excavating a very rich site and failing to publish it in full, has been followed by many of those who have subsequently worked in Central India. As a result, much valuable evidence has been destroyed to no purpose. One of the reasons for this is undoubtedly the large quantity of microlithic artefacts and debris found in most such excavations, which renders a complete systematic study of the results virtually impossible in terms of available time and resources. This points to the need for new approaches which must include methods of sampling suited to the problem and the context.

Examples of excavations at least partially successful in terms of results put on record are two rock shelters near Pachmari, Jambudip and Dorothy Deep, excavated by an amateur archaeologist, G. R. Hunter, in the 1930s. Hunter was able to show that the microlithic occupation overlay bed rock in some places, and sterile earth in others, and was not preceded by occupation deposits of any other distinct cultural period. He also showed that an a-ceramic microlithic phase was followed, without a significant break, by one in which pottery was found with a reduced stone industry, and that some at least of the fragmentary burials encountered belong to the pre-pottery phase. Finally, he was able to indicate that there was a discernible sequential development in the stone industry of the pre-pottery phase. Another example is a group of rock shelters excavated at Lekhahia in Mirzapur district by the Department of Archaeology of Allahabad University during the 1960s. These yielded blade industries and microlithic artefacts throughout several feet of occupation deposit, and were shown to contain burials of the microlithic period, and to be associated with open sites nearby. A progressive change and development in the stone industry towards smaller, more delicately made and varied artefact types was noted, and briefly described. Pottery is recorded as making an initial appearance at a certain point in the sequence, and becoming more frequent towards the top. A C14 date of 1710 B.C., upon which some doubt has been cast, but which is none the less of interest, has been obtained for a bone sample from one of the burials.

In none of the excavations of Central Indian rock shelters so far recorded has a recognizable Upper Palaeolithic or a Middle Palaeolithic occupation deposit been found below the microlithic levels, enabling a relationship to be established. It appears, however, that the Bhimbetka group of rock shelters referred to earlier (pp. 38–9) is an exception in this respect, and detailed publication of the later cultural phases from this interesting site is eagerly awaited.

The site of Chopani-Mando at the foot of the Kaimur hills in southern Allahabad district, excavated by the Department of Archaeology of Allahabad University, provides a continuous sequence from late Upper Palaeolithic to late 'Mesolithic' with coarse handmade pottery, decorated with cord-impressed patterns (Fig. 4.10), recalling the Neolithic pottery of Mahagara and Koldihwa (see below, pp. 117–18). The 1.55 m deposit was seen to include four cultural phases, the first transitional in terms of lithic typology from the Upper Palaeolithic of the region to Mesolithic. The lithic blade industry showed a continuous development throughout towards smaller, more delicately made and varied artefact forms. In the second and third phases (Early Mesolithic A and B) round hut floors were found. One hut floor in the latter phase was paved with stone. In this phase lumps of burnt clay with reed and bamboo impressions, indicative of wattle and clay walls, were found; also hammer stones, anvil stones, stone sling balls and ring stones. All these features continued into the final (Late Mesolithic) phase, in which pottery made its appearance, both round and oval hut floors were found and the cultural remains were generally richer and more numerous. Fuller publication of this important site is eagerly awaited.

Rock shelters excavated at Adamgarh hill in the Narbada valley by R. V. Joshi present the clearest record of the finds from a Mesolithic site so far recorded. A few artefacts of earlier periods were found in and upon the surface of a stone deposit which in places underlay the Mesolithic occupation, but, as we have pointed out in an earlier chapter, these do not constitute the remains of regular Palaeolithic occupation. Microlithic artefacts, animal bones and pottery were found throughout a layer of black soil varying from 50 to 150 cm in depth, which in places lies upon the earlier deposits, and elsewhere upon bed rock. The excavator selected the finds for detailed analysis from one trench which he considered representative, and Table 4.3, taken from his published account of the excavation, summarizes his findings.

There were also broken mace heads, or ring stones, comparable to that illustrated from Bagor (see Fig. 4.6), and pebbles which appeared to have been used as hammer stones. The animal bones found in the excavation include the domestic dog, Indian humped cattle, water buffalo, goat, domestic sheep and pig. In addition there are remains of a number of species of wild animals including sambar, barasingha, spotted deer, hare, porcupine and monitor lizard. Wild and domestic animals are represented in approximately equal proportions, and a few of the bones of the cattle, pig and spotted deer are charred.

4.10   Chopani-Mando: cord-impressed pottery (*courtesy* G. R. Sharma)

Table 4.3. *Microliths and other antiquities from Adamgarh Trench 1*

Depth in cms	Points				Burins and awls	Blades			Scrapers		Burins	Triangles		Trapezes	Tranchets	Cores	Animal bones	Pottery	Charcoal	Glass bangles	Iron fragments	Haematite nodules
	On flakes	On retouched Blades	On unretouched Blades	Unclassified and broken		Retouched Crescentic	Retouched Others	Simple	On cores	On flakes and blades		Isosceles	Scalene									
10	29	111	7	13	3	6	18	17	1	1	–	–	–	–	4	3	–	–	–	–	–	–
20	–	38	5	107	3	20	64	85	20	9	1	6	25	1	4	67	–	–	–	–	–	–
30	21	51	24	163	3	13	114	263	54	9	3	10	45	6	4	118	–	–	–	–	–	–
40	42	319	33	259	5	67	324	315	52	6	2	10	27	2	5	64	–	–	–	–	–	–
50	11	135	22	233	6	28	210	281	63	11	–	14	25	2	2	47	–	–	–	–	–	–
60	10	184	27	125	3	26	121	113	57	7	–	6	13	1	–	44	–	–	–	–	–	–
70	2	45	3	1	–	8	16	73	9	–	3	–	1	–	–	–	–	–	–	–	–	–
80	–	8	1	9	–	8	–	16	2	3	–	3	1	–	–	–	–	–	–	–	–	–
Total	115	791	122	910	23	176	867	1,163	258	46	9	49	137	12	19	343	–	–	–	–	–	–

Source: After R. V. Joshi.

Shells found between 15 and 21 cms from the top have been dated by radiocarbon to approximately 5500 B.C. Although this date is based on a single sample, and the material, shell, is not universally regarded as a satisfactory medium for C14 dating, it is a factor to be taken into consideration.

The stone industry from Adamgarh is shown by analysis, description and illustration to be based almost exclusively upon parallel-sided blades, and to include a wide range of artefact forms, among which blades, points and triangles predominate (see Fig. 4.8). Scrapers of various kinds are the next most important element, and awls, borers and burins form a much smaller but significant element. Such an industry, in association with pottery, and domestic and wild animal remains, is of great interest and, if the mid-sixth millennium date provided by a single C14 sample is correct, its cultural implications are far reaching.

Nearly all the Central Indian rock shelters discussed, and many others as well, contain 'rock paintings', of a variety of subjects, chiefly of animals, or scenes including both people and animals (Fig. 4.11). These are discussed at the end of this chapter. The bow and arrow are shown in many of the hunting scenes, and one of the drawings from Morhana Pahar, the site excavated by

4.11 Morhana Pahar, Central India: rock painting of herd of animals, probably goats

Carlleyle, shows two chariots, one drawn by four horses and another by two, being waylaid by a group of men on foot armed with bows and arrows and spears (Fig. 4.12). The bow and arrow was very widely used for hunting, particularly in Central India and also in parts of Eastern and Peninsular India, in the first half of the present century, and it is still used in some remote areas. Although neither of these sources of evidence is conclusive, both strengthen the case for the association of microlithic artefacts with the use of the bow and arrow. More direct evidence is provided by the microlithic point embedded in a human rib bone at Sarai-Nahar-Rai mentioned earlier. Many of the wide range of points and geometric microliths found at Adamgarh and other sites were clearly intended for hafting as composite tools and weapons. There are analogies for this from many parts of the world. This method makes for economy in the quantity of stone needed, and for lightness, as much of the tool is made of wood, mastics, etc., which are lighter than stone. Stone is used only for points, barbs and cutting

4.12 Morhana Pahar, Central India: rock painting of chariots ambushed by men on foot

edges. It also allows for a great variety of tools to be built up from a limited range of forms, and it is particularly suitable for making arrowheads of all kinds, and composite sickle or knife blades. An example of this method, from Mehrgarh, Baluchistan, is illustrated in ch. 5 (Fig. 5.4). If the advent of the bow and arrow did not actually coincide with the advent of microliths, it must certainly have had its heyday in Mesolithic times.

Ring stones and hammer stones found in association with microlithic industries, both in occupation deposits as at Bagor and Adamgarh, and at open sites, are of the greatest interest, particularly in view of their widespread occurrence at early settlements in the Indus plains and in the foothills of the north-western borderlands (see Figs. 4.6 and 6.20). Stone axes have been widely reported and collected in all parts of Central India, and occasional specimens of all these artefacts have been found at microlithic factory sites. The conclusion that they formed part of the equipment of the Mesolithic cultures of the region seems inescapable.

In Peninsular India Mesolithic sites are found in a number of regions, each group tending to have its own character. A group of coastal microlithic sites around Bombay, situated chiefly on headlands and small rocky islands or on rising ground near the banks of streams, were described by another amateur archaeologist, K. R. U. Todd, in 1950. The industry has the basic characteristics of those we have already discussed, but with a certain admixture of larger tools such as scrapers and points – many of the former made on flakes. Blades and blade cores, and lunates and points made on both blades and flakes are the predominant forms. Burins are found, as elsewhere, in a limited variety of simple forms, and made on flakes and pieces of raw material, usually jasper. As at other Mesolithic sites there are also occasional ring stones, made by the technique of pecking also used in making stone axes. These probably served as mace heads or weights for digging sticks, and perhaps other purposes. Fragments of pottery found with the stone tools may well be contemporary. The situations chosen by these people show that they probably had boats of some kind, and relied on fish as a staple part of their diet. It is possible that these sites were the temporary or permanent homes of coastal fishing communities who subsequently lived alongside Neolithic, Chalcolithic and later peoples. The character and traditions of present day fishing communities around Bombay, and extending northward up the Gujarat coast support this view. The stone industry has a distinctive character of its own which quickly becomes modified as one moves inland.

Inland sites in Maharashtra yield somewhat impoverished microlithic assemblages without the fine finish of the Central Indian industries or the distinctive blend of Middle and Upper Palaeolithic traditions seen at the coastal sites. The same can be said of the assemblages from the western edge of the Deccan plateau, where the familiar pattern of sites upon small hillocks and ridges continues. This pattern is seen again in Andhra Pradesh, where a large number of microlithic sites were found more than forty years ago in the lower Godavari valley, and many more have since been found throughout the region. Chenchu groups of hunter-gatherers living in this region, recorded and photographed during the 1930s occupied rock shelters (Fig. 4.13) and semi-permanent settlements or camping places in this region (Fig. 4.14). The location of their

4.13 Group of Chenchu boys in a rock shelter (*courtesy* C. von Fürer-Haimendorf)

4.14 Chenchu settlement (*courtesy* C. von Fürer-Haimendorf)

settlements is very similar to that of certain types of microlithic sites throughout Central and Peninsular India. Therefore they are highly suggestive of the patterns of living of Mesolithic communities in the subcontinent.

Moving southwards from any of the regions we have just mentioned – Bombay, upland Maharashtra or northern Andhra – we approach a new region in terms of Mesolithic technology. The microlithic industries so far recorded in the southern part of the Indian peninsula are predominantly based upon milky quartz. This is in part due to the granite rocks underlying so much of the country, in which quartz veins and dykes are readily found. The jaspers and chalcedonies so common in the volcanic rocks farther north are in short supply, but they do occur in places and they are present in some river gravels. Both earlier and later peoples undoubtedly found these sources, but many of the southern microlithic assemblages are almost a hundred percent quartz. This was first noticed in Karnataka where the change takes place between the districts of Raichur and Bellary. In Raichur, Stone Age factory sites on the banks of the Krishna produce an industry comparable to those we have discussed from regions farther north, based largely upon pebbles of jasper taken from the river gravels. A late Middle Palaeolithic site lay in close proximity to one of these factory sites, and the source of supply was common to both. River pebbles of jasper and similar materials are the basis of the stone-blade industry found at Neolithic sites in the same region. Whether the Neolithic blades were made at the same factory sites and perhaps even by the same people as those used by the Mesolithic hunters is an interesting subject for research. If Mesolithic communities were already in the habit of exchanging objects with one another, the first settled agriculturalists or representatives of urban communities in the region cannot have had much difficulty in establishing economic links with them.

All the evidence suggests that in the south the same sources of stone were exploited more or less continuously from Middle Palaeolithic to Neolithic times. Mesolithic and Neolithic industries, because of the use of the same raw material and technique, can only be distinguished by comparing the proportions of different tool-types. The Mesolithic industries tend to include more re-worked tools, and those of the Neolithic more unretouched, utilized blades. This and a good deal of other evidence points to mutual exploitation of certain large factory sites by hunters and settlers alike. More probably in the light of Indian tradition, the hunters exchanged stone artefacts for other goods, perhaps food, pots or cloth with the Neolithic farmers. Such intercommunity exchanges would have occurred as and when agricultural settlements were established in any region. Baskets, honey, venison and Mohua flowers, which tribal people still barter with their village neighbours for food, metal tools and cloth, may also have begun to change hands at this early stage.

In contrast to these sites where jaspers and chalcedonies were exploited, further south, in the former Mysore state, and to the west, Mesolithic hunters seem to have preferred to make their tools of quartz. A group of sites at Jalahalli in the vicinity of Bangalore produced a distinctive quartz industry in which both the technique of striking flakes from small, carefully prepared discoidal cores, and that of making microlithic blades, are represented. The latter is rather poorly developed, probably on account of the intractable nature of quartz. The same range of tools is found as in the industries farther north, including scrapers of several kinds, burins, awls, lunates and points. This group of industries might in fact be described as the translation into quartz of all the elements seen in the microlithic industries we have mentioned from regions further north. One new feature makes its appearance, a 'D' shaped, transverse arrowhead. A closely similar assemblage was found at Kibbanhalli to the north-west of Bangalore, and further assemblages of quartz microliths have been recorded from Giddalur in the Eastern Ghats, Calicut in Malabar, on the west coast and elsewhere. A large number of sites yielding quartz tools of this and earlier periods have recently been found in Goa. Quartz tools have also been reported lying on top of ruined buildings in the Buddhist city of Nagarjunakonda in southern Andhra Pradesh. The implications of this are remarkable, and, although the city itself is now submerged beneath the waters of the Nagarjunasagar, the surrounding regions deserve investigation. In Belgaum district, at the top of the escarpment of the Western Ghats, a quartz industry is reported from Barapedi cave, and at Sanganakallu, a granite hill in Bellary district, quartz flakes were found below the lowest levels of Neolithic occupation.

On the east coast, south of Madras, a distinctive group of coastal sites has been discussed by several writers, associated with a group of old sand dunes. The dunes are locally known as *teri*, and hence the industry associated with them has come to be known as the *teri* industry. They were probably in the process of formation when the first hunters, or fishermen, camped among them. Later they became fixed, due to the growth of vegetation and the formation of soil, perhaps as the result of a slight increase in rainfall. The industry from the dunes is made up of approximately fifty percent quartz and fifty percent light brown chert. The flake tradition is more strongly represented here than in the Mysore quartz industries, and small discoidal cores and the flakes struck from them are characteristic, as are lunates, transverse arrowheads and points of various kinds. Blades and blade cores are represented, but they are a minor element in the industry as a whole. The majority of the finished tools is made either on flakes or on chips of raw material – it is often impossible to know which, as reworking has removed any indications there might have been. There are also scrapers, a few somewhat problematic burins, and numerous utilized flakes, cores and fragments of raw material. In addition there is a small proportion of very fine points, including both edge-trimmed and bifacial types. The latter are unlike anything found in Late Stone Age microlithic industries elsewhere in the subcontinent, with the exception of Sri Lanka, and they can only have been made by the very specialized technique of pressure flaking. A somewhat less developed flake industry, without microliths, has also been found among the dunes. There is of course no reason to suppose that the dunes were only inhabited at one period of the Stone Age. They provide a sheltered camping place, within reach of the sea, and near lagoons and estuaries suitable for fishing and fowling. Fishing communities on the coasts of India still live in similar situations, building their huts among sand dunes which are sometimes far from stable, in order to be near their fishing grounds. As in the case of the Bombay sites, there seems little doubt that this is the industry of a coastal Mesolithic fishing community.

The Mesolithic of Sri Lanka exemplifies all that we have said about this period of India. Our knowledge of earlier phases of the Stone Age here is limited to a single hand axe, but the Mesolithic has been exceptionally well recorded, first by the Sarasin brothers who visited Ceylon in 1907, by the Seligmans (1911), then by the excavations of C. Hartley in 1913 and 1914, and more recently by the researches of P. E. P. Deraniyagala. The Sarasins and the Seligmans each carried out small excavations in caves – the Seligmans in one which was actually occupied by a Vedda family (Fig. 4.15). They both found quartz microliths together with larger tools, such as pounders and hammers made of various kinds of stone, and there were animal bones and bone tools throughout, and pottery in increasing quantities in the upper layers (Fig. 4.16). Objects of iron were found in the topmost levels, where the quality of the stone industry tended to decline. A quartz industry of the same kind has been found in caves and at surface sites in southern Sri Lanka in the mountainous part of the island, and at one site in the north, near Jaffna, under about a metre of earth. This last is not far removed from the *teri* sites of southern India. Both the Sarasins and the Selig-

4.15 Veddas encamped in a rock shelter (*after* Seligman)

mans considered the Vedda tribes, who then inhabited the remoter parts of the southern mountains, where many of the caves and related surface sites were found, to be the direct descendants of the Palaeolithic inhabitants of the caves. Some doubt has since been cast on this, on account of the intermixture of later peoples, but there can be no doubt that the cave culture represents a continuous tradition of hunting, gathering and living for part of each year in the caves, which only finally gave way to the pressures of agriculture and industry at the beginning of this century. Ever since the beginning of the Iron Age, which probably antedates the arrival of settlers from North India that took place from the fifth century B.C. onward, the hunting tribes must have been steadily drawn into relations of an economic kind with more advanced communities, but like many such groups in India they managed to retain their own cultural identity.

Since the appearance of this book in 1982, the systematic examination of prehistoric sites, and in particular the excavation of a number of caves, has been carried on by S. U. Deraniyagala and others. In Batadombalena cave seven

4.16 Stone and bone artefacts from excavated rock shelters in Sri Lanka (*after* F. and P. Sarasin)

distinct layers containing microlithic artefacts were found. Charcoal samples from these layers gave C14 dates ranging from *c.* 28,000 B.P. (layer 7) to *c.* 9,000 B.P. (layer 4a). This gives microlithic technology a considerably greater antiquity than was previously assumed, and it will require careful consideration in terms of the sub-continent as a whole. Skeletons recovered from burials at Batadombalena and other caves are being examined, and these together with animal and plant remains should provide an insight into the development of

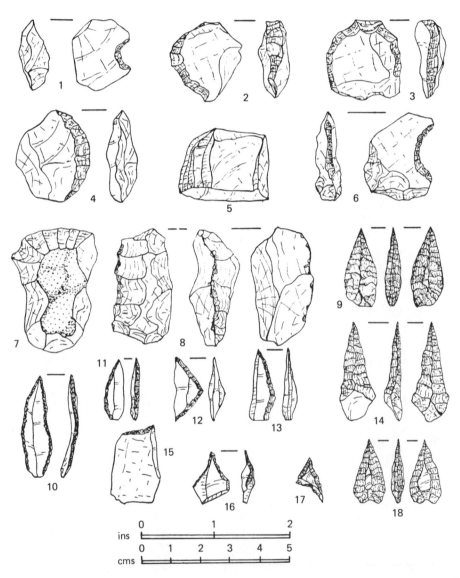

4.17 Bandarawela, Sri Lanka: Mesolithic artefacts: 1 and 6 hollow scrapers; 2, 3, 4 and 8 convex scrapers; 5 carinated scraper; 7 steep scraper; 9, 14 and 18 bifacial points; 10 and 13 trimmed points; 11 lunate; 12 triangle; 15 burin; 16 awl; 17 tanged point

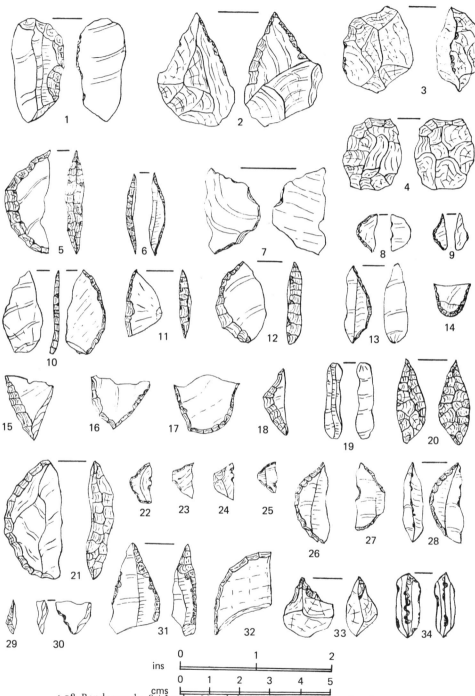

4.18 Bandarawela, Sri Lanka: Mesolithic artefacts: 1, 5, 7 and 21 large segments; 2, 31 and 32 scrapers; 3 flake from prepared core; 4 discoidal core; 6, 8 to 18 and 22 to 30 composite points and barbs and transverse arrow heads; 33 awl; 34 rock crystal; 19, blade; bifacial point

man in the tropical environment of Sri Lanka from 28,000 B.P. to the beginning of the Iron Age.

Excavation of the larger factory site of Bandarawela, which covers four small hillocks in the plateau country of southern Sri Lanka, showed only a few inches of soil above a gritty layer two to three inches deep containing tools, debris and charcoal. Below this was the decomposing gneiss of which the hills are formed. In the course of two short seasons of one month each 4,768 recognizable artefacts were recovered, together with a large but unspecified quantity of factory waste (see Figs. 4.17 and 4.18). All except three artefacts were of quartz.

Observations of collections in museums in Britain confirm that, as in the *teri* industry, blades and blade cores are comparatively rare, but their presence shows that the technique was known. Larger tools such as scrapers and utilized flakes, cores of all kinds and fragments of quartz are abundant, and both awls and burins are similar to those in Indian Upper Palaeolithic and Mesolithic industries. What is remarkable about this industry is the variety and perfection of the microliths. Lunates and transverse arrowheads predominate, ranging from four centimetres down to less than one centimetre in length. These groups grade into one another and also into smaller groups of trimmed points, and triangular and trapezoidal forms. Bifacial points (Hartley's arrowheads), like those in the *teri* industries, are also found in relatively small numbers, but show considerable variety of form. Discoidal cores prepared for the removal of flakes, similar cores already struck, and the flakes produced from them, are all present in some number. A proportion of the finest tools can be seen to be made from flakes of this kind and a proportion from blades – more often the former – but the majority have no bulb of percussion or other definite indication of how they were made. This can sometimes be accounted for by the removal of the bulb in process of making the tool, but it occurs so frequently as to suggest that there must be some other explanation. The charcoal found at Bandarawela is suggestive, especially in the light of the method of shattering quartz recorded in the Andaman Islands. The Andamanese practice was to heat pieces of quartz and then strike them with stones while they were still very hot. This caused the quartz to shatter into sharp fragments, the majority showing no bulbs of percussion. These they then used for shaving and general cutting purposes without further preparation. The adoption of such a method would explain the marked preference for quartz seen in Sri Lanka and much of South India. Once this method was established it must have been less tedious than the preparation of cores, and the removal of flakes or blades, one by one. The small fragments of quartz would be particularly suitable for incorporating in the composite tools of the Mesolithic. They could be trimmed into shape as easily as small flakes or blades.

Religion and art

Archaeology can still tell us little of the religion of non-literate stages of society, and in a real sense the history of Indian religion only begins with the Rigveda.

But religion has a prehistory, and archaeology can and does afford some evidence of its nature. As yet the remains of the earlier stages of the Stone Age are too shadowy to yield any information, but with the Mesolithic the first archaeological information becomes available. Ethnographic evidence provided by the recorded practices of hunting communities in isolated situations sometimes helps to interpret it. We find, for instance, inhabited caves in which the dead are buried, such as Lekhahia in Central India. Other caves which were either inhabited or frequented by Stone Age man are today associated with cults of folk deities. Discussing the rock art of Central India W. S. Wakankar writes, 'At the top of one of the hills stands a temple dedicated to the goddess Kankali. This is actually built over a huge rock shelter which has beautiful drawings of hunted deer.' Gudiyam cave near Madras, which we have already mentioned, contains the shrine of a local goddess, and recent excavations showed that it had been frequented, although not actually inhabited, by man throughout the Stone Age. Another clue is afforded by Stone Age factory sites which may sometimes coincide with modern cult spots: the late D. D. Kosambi reported instances of this kind in Maharashtra. An outstanding example of this is Pushkar, in Rajasthan, mentioned earlier, and traditionally a locality of great sanctity. Situated in the Dry Zone, on the edge of the desert, it includes a permanent fresh water lake, surrounded by sites of all periods of the Stone Age, and a temple of Śiva. On the banks of an artificial lake nearby is a celebrated temple of Brahmā, close to which a great annual cattle fair takes place. There is also an important Muslim place of pilgrimage in the city of Ajmer only a few kilometres distant.

All long surviving traditions of this kind require very careful consideration. The religion of modern hunting communities must have been invaded by and become closely integrated with that of neighbouring people at many different stages. Ethnographic accounts of hunting people such as the Veddas of Sri Lanka, or the Chenchu, who inhabit the Eastern Ghats in Peninsular India, indicate that it is to indigenous deities that they turn for success in hunting and the continuance and abundance of fruit, flowers, honey and other wild products of their forest environment. These deities include both male and female elements, sometimes with separate identities and sometimes combined. They also worship other deities, primarily associated with more advanced communities, to whom none the less indigenous elements may have accrued. The Veddas attach great importance to the spirits of ancestors, who merge with benevolent local deities. Both peoples bury their dead in the open with little ceremony, and the Veddas are also recorded as abandoning corpses in rock shelters which they avoid for some years thereafter. Ancient centres such as Pushkar require careful analysis in much more sophisticated terms, as the religious practices and prejudices of literate peoples belonging to more than one of the major religions of the world are involved. They need to be considered in the combined light of historical, theological and anthropological observation.

As implicitly suggested above, there must have been a close connection in prehistoric societies between their beliefs concerning religion and ideology, and their artistic expression. Whether people of Lower and Middle Palaeolithic times found any means of utilizing their aesthetic abilities other than in the making of fine tools, is unknown. However, in the Mesolithic, and perhaps also the preceding Upper Palaeolithic, there begins in Central India, in caves and rock shelters, a distinctive form of rock art. Such rock art occupies a singular position in our understanding of Stone Age society, as generally the art of prehistoric societies fails to survive at all. Rock art, if it is in a sufficiently well-protected situation, can survive for many thousands of years, and so to some extent do carvings in stone, bone or ivory, as can be seen in the European Stone Age. On the other hand, wood carving, and painting on wood, bark, or even on the bare ground, which form a major part of artistic expression among both hunter-gatherers and more advanced rural communities in many parts of the world including India, have little chance of survival. Hence the importance of the surviving examples of rock art in Central India. At present we have no means of knowing whether the Mesolithic peoples of other regions practised any comparable form of art which has been lost, except in Karnataka where, in Neolithic times, another type of rock art flourished (see pp. 293–4).

Many of the rock shelters which were inhabited during Mesolithic times in Central India and which have protected rock surfaces, have been decorated with single figures or scenes. Painting is perhaps a misnomer: crayoning might be more accurate. The pieces of haematite found among the occupation debris of some of these rock shelters, and the pictures themselves, demonstrate this. Animals are the most frequent subjects, either alone on a small flat area of rock, or in larger groups, where this is possible. They are shown as herds or in hunting scenes, such as the rhinoceros hunt from the Adamgarh group of rock shelters. They are drawn boldly in outline, and the bodies are sometimes filled in completely, or partially with cross-hatching. Examples of all three methods can be seen among the drawings of deer on the walls of the Morhana Pahar group of rock shelters near Mirzapur (see Fig. 4.11). The animals most frequently represented are deer or antelope, which are shown with rather bulky bodies and slender legs and horns. It is not always clear to what species they belong, but sometimes there are suggestive details. Other animals, including tigers and monkeys, are also shown, but not so frequently. In spite of the somewhat stylized representation, many of the figures are full of life and action. People are even more stylized than animals, but equally active and lively. They are shown with bows and arrows and spears, and also dancing in lines, this last being reminiscent of decorations on the Malwa ware pottery of the Chalcolithic period of Western India. Other subjects include animal-headed human figures; squares and oblongs partly filled in with hatched designs which may represent huts or enclosures; and what appear to be pictures of unusual events, such as the chariots waylaid by men armed with spears and bows and arrows at Morhana Pahar (see Fig. 4.12). The colours used range from purple, through crimson and vermilion to terracotta, light orange and brown. The many caves and rock shelters around Bhimbetka, near Bhopal, contain a splendid series of paintings. Wakankar has studied many sites in this area and has suggested a stylistic sequence, partly supported by content and other evidence, extending through into the historic period.

As already mentioned, the aesthetic feelings of Lower and Middle Palaeolithic man can today only be traced in their stone artefacts. This tradition of crafts-manship continued in the Upper Palaeolithic and also in the Mesolithic, along-side the new medium of rock painting. Again the sites of Central India are important in this respect, and have provided evidence of this overlapping tradi-tion. We encounter finely produced Mesolithic tools in many parts of the subcontinent, including particularly Sri Lanka. Especially in Central India and Sri Lanka there is a technical excellence and precision far surpassing that demanded for purely utilitarian purposes. In Central India great attention was given to the choice of material. The range of semi-precious stones – agate, carnelian, jasper, blood-stone, and so on – employed by Mesolithic tool makers were in common use continuously throughout Neolithic and Chalcolithic times. They are still used by the makers of beads and jewellery of all kinds. The traditions of making fine blade tools and making beads have overlapped in every sense since the Mesolithic period, if not earlier. The facets of extremely fine, regular blades produce an effect not unlike that achieved by faceting gem-stones today, causing the tools to reflect the light and to sparkle. It seems highly probable that the makers of these tools were guided by aesthetic as well as utilitarian considerations.

This chapter and the previous one have attempted to make clear the essentially continuous character of the development of human cultures within the Indian subcontinent throughout the Palaeolithic period. We have used the somewhat arbitrary divisions into chronological and technological phases and regional groupings that archaeologists have imposed upon their cultures as a means of studying them and attempting to interpret them. The Mesolithic cultures of the Holocene discussed in this chapter have particularly pronounced regional iden-tities. At the same time they overlap and interrelate with both older and newer cultures. All those discussed so far lie to the east and south of the Indus, and many can be shown or inferred to be contemporary with settled cultures of the Indus system, and the valleys and foothills of the mountains to the north-west. Some of them have regional characters that later develop into fully settled and regional cultures, and form the basis of further stages of urban development. Others, like the Mesolithic cultures of the arid Thar region, appear to be the ancestors of more sophisticated nomadic communities with widespread trade links in and beyond the subcontinent. Others again are ancestral to more specialized agricultural communities, or to groups who have remained as hun-ters or fishers, to be ultimately absorbed or to become part of more complex groupings. The variety and persistence of these Mesolithic adaptations to the wide range of environments offered by the subcontinent east of the Indus is probably the main reason for the apparent absence there of early cultures based upon settlements and agriculture of the kind known further west.

CHAPTER 5

THE FIRST AGRICULTURAL COMMUNITIES

At the end of the Pleistocene, approximately ten thousand years ago, climatic conditions more or less similar to those of today were established in West and South Asia. This provided the setting for man to make a number of important advances in his control of the environment, and set in train a series of events which led ultimately to the appearance of the first urban societies in both regions, some six thousand years ago. Perhaps the most fundamental advances were the domestication of several breeds of animals and plants. The present evidence suggests that in West Asia emmer wheat, einkhorn wheat and barley were already domesticated by *c.* 7000 B.C. The first domestication of sheep, goats and cattle may have been considerably earlier. As yet there is little evidence of comparable dates in South Asia, nor is it known whether the two innovations first appear there together, or singly. Evidence from the Indo-Iranian borderlands, however, from caves in the valleys of the Hindu Kush (notably Aq Kupruk) suggests that wild precursors of domesticated sheep, goat and cattle were already being exploited by man *c.* 16,000 years ago. The continuing presence of quantities of sheep and goat bones in the subsequent 'Non-ceramic Neolithic' of that area, dated to 7000–10,000 years ago, has been interpreted as an indication that sheep were already domesticated by this time.

The domestication of various species of animals produced the specialized pastoralists who appear to have continued through into modern times, to lead a nomadic or semi-nomadic life. On the other hand, the domestication, or successful exploitation, of various species of wild plants produced the shift towards sedentary settlement. This latter adaptation came to dominate the subsequent economic and cultural developments. The relationship of the two trends in their earliest stages is still not clear. Moreover, it must be repeated that in an area as great as South Asia, with its major divergences of climate and physical environment, it is most unlikely that a single pattern would be found throughout: different plants and hence crops may be expected to have been favoured in different regions. Indeed, in reviewing the evidence, it becomes clear that the ancient agriculture of the subcontinent can be divided up into distinct regions which were caused by climate, physical environment, presence of wild progenitors of domesticates, etc. These units are (i) the Indus system and its western borderland; (ii) Western India and the north Deccan; (iii) the Ganges valley; and (iv) the southern Deccan. The economy of all the earlier Neolithic cultures was apparently one of subsistence agriculture, including plant and animal

5.1 Map of principal sites mentioned in chapter 5

Key
1. Siah Damb   2. Anjira   3. Mehrgarh   4. Kili Ghul Muhammad   5. Rana Ghundai   6. Mundigak
7. Jalilpur   8. Gumla   9. Lewan   10. Ghaligai   11. Aligrama   12. Loebanr   13. Sarai Khola
14. Burzahom   15. Mahagara   16. Koldihwa   17. Chirand   18. Daojali Hading   19. Sarutaru   20. Kodekal
21. Utnur   22. Kupgal   23. Pallavoy

domesticates. In some cases, however, they also received stimuli from outside contacts and influence from neighbouring hunting communities. This formed an important part of their local character.

When man first started to cultivate crops and to herd his own domesticated animals, an increased interest in fertility and in magical means of promoting it appears to have become an almost universal aspect of culture. It may well be that this interest gave rise to some of the most important new concepts in the whole of religion, namely, belief in an afterlife, in resurrection after death, and belief in the transmigration of souls and the cycle of rebirth. Throughout the length and breadth of India there are found today, at the folk level, rites and festivals which are intimately associated with the changing seasons, the sowing and harvesting of crops and the breeding of cattle and other livestock. There is also a whole pantheon of local gods and goddesses some of whom remain unassimilated while others have been absorbed at different levels into the sanskritized hierarchy of gods of the 'great' or classical Indian tradition. There can be no doubt that a very large part of this modern folk religion is extremely ancient and contains traits which originated during the earliest periods of stock raising and agricultural settlement.

Also associated with permanent settlement were a series of new crafts involving important technological discoveries. Among these were the manufacture and use of pottery, in time to become ubiquitous as a trace of human occupation; and the discovery of the smelting of copper and its alloys, and their use in the manufacture of tools and weapons. The stone industries of the early settlements throughout South Asia show considerable variation from site to site and from one region to another. They also vary from one cultural level to another at sites with prolonged occupation such as Amri and particularly Mehrgarh. At the latter there were local supplies of bitumen which survives in the excavation and, being used in hafting, allows us to see how stone artefacts form component parts of different tools. In all cases the lithic blade industries of the early settlement are closely related to those of the regional Mesolithic sites with which they share sources of stone and basic technology. The regional, cultural and chronological variations are in the types of artefacts made from blades and flakes, and in their relative proportions. All assemblages at this stage are varied and clearly intended to serve many purposes.

In the *Birth of Indian Civilization* (1968), we remarked on the geographical and environmental similarities of the western edges of the Iranian plateau and its junction with the Tigris–Euphrates plains on the one hand, and that of the eastern edges, with the hills of Baluchistan and the Indus plains, on the other. In this context we commented on the apparently unexplained disparity in the dates of similar events in the two areas. This statement calls for some new comment. Not only do the eastern and western fringes of the Iranian plateau share many common environmental features, but so too does the northern fringe, particularly to the east of the Caspian Sea, in the Elburz and Kopet Dagh mountains, and the plains that lie to the north as far as the valley of the Oxus. These three border regions of the Iranian plateau thus appear as interrelated parts of a larger whole – geographically, and even culturally. We may thus expect to find broadly parallel, though already distinct, cultural developments taking place in each, creating a vast area which may be loosely defined as a cultural interaction sphere, with contacts maintained by land routes in the interior of the plateau. As we shall see, new discoveries in Pakistan make the earlier disparities of dates appear to be more apparent than real, and suggest that they probably arose because of the limited extent of research in Baluchistan, and the Indus valley in particular.

Earliest settlements in Baluchistan

Baluchistan and the eastern parts of Afghanistan make up the Indo-Iranian border region. We have elected to deal first with this area as it is one of great potential interest for the archaeologist, although there has been less research here than in any other part of the subcontinent, and it is thus still relatively little known. The few excavations have mainly been on a small scale, with some done in difficult circumstances.

The climate is one of extremes, the summer temperatures being very high, and the winters often very cold, with snow lying for up to two months in the higher valleys. Given these climatic conditions, the choice of habitations for communities of the Neolithic period must have depended primarily upon their suitability for varying pastoral and agricultural requirements. As the rainfall is generally less than 10 inches per annum, mainly falling in the winter months, water for men and animals was obviously a prime necessity in site location. Because of the scarcity of water, settlements were never large, unless they coincided with a good permanent spring or source of water. This scarcity also set strict limits upon the production of crops. Consequently a pastoral element in the economy has predominated and has certainly been well represented up until the present day. There are signs that in Baluchistan, in prehistoric times, attempts were made to retain rain water in surface drainage tanks, behind earth or stone embankments. Another feature of importance in site location was the proximity of land suitable for cultivation. Today wheat is still the main crop, though a substantial part of the population still consists of pastoral nomads. Fairservis has pointed out that even now there is a reliance on water and soil resources very similar to that of antiquity, and this appears to lead to a continuity of settlement where there is a dependence on the same resources. Whether this continuity is unbroken, or whether the correspondence between the prehistoric and modern patterns of settlement is determined simply by geography remains to be seen; unfortunately, much less is known about the settlements of Baluchistan in later prehistoric or early historic times, as archaeologists have concentrated mainly upon the earliest period of settlement there.

There is comparatively little recent excavation to report from Baluchistan, and thus little to add to what was available ten years ago. In this arid mountainous region, in the isolated valleys, often at heights of four to five thousand feet above sea-level, there are many traces of early settlement. In the north these are particularly common in the Quetta valley, and to the east in the valleys of the Loralai and Zhob rivers.

Kili Ghul Muhammad is a small mound approximately 90 metres long and 55 metres wide, lying about two miles from the modern city of Quetta. Here in 1950 Fairservis carried out a small exploratory excavation, only 3.5 m square, reaching virgin soil at a depth of 11.14 m. Hence in the lower levels the area excavated was very small indeed. Period I, the lowest of the four cultural phases revealed at the site, produced radiocarbon samples from a hearth in its uppermost levels. These have given dates of 4400 and 4100 B.C. Below, there is a further deposit of nearly 4 m in thickness, doubtless representing a considerable time duration. These earliest data indicate that the inhabitants had domestic sheep, goats and oxen, and were probably initially nomadic. However, by the end of the period they had constructed houses of mud-brick or hard packed clay. Their material equipment included blades of chert, jasper or chalcedony, and a (broken) rubbing or grinding stone, but no metal objects. Awls or points of bone were also found, but no pottery was discovered, and hence the excavator treats the period as pre-ceramic, although on so small a sample this is perhaps to overstate the case. There followed two further periods, II and III, the earlier yielding crude handmade and basket-marked pottery. These levels contained further house walls of mud-brick, and a material culture otherwise little different from that of the preceding period. The predominant pottery had a red or yellow–red surface with a yellowish body, and a coarser ware with a sandy body also occurred. In period III the first copper was found along with distinctive pottery, both wheel-thrown and handmade, decorated with black or red painted designs including simple geometric motifs (see Fig. 5.17).

There are several sites in north and central Baluchistan which may on comparative grounds be associated with Kili Ghul Muhammad II and III. In the Loralai valley the mound of Rana Ghundai was excavated by Brigadier Ross in the late 1930s and an extensive sequence revealed. The lowest occupation (period I) was some 4 m in thickness, and consisted of a series of living surfaces and hearths in which no trace of any structures was discovered, although these may have been of mud-brick and hence undetected. Ross suggested that this level represented a sort of nomadic occupation. Throughout this period plain handmade pottery occurred along with bone points and a stone-blade industry. Animal bones included those of sheep, goat, ass and Indian cattle (*Bos indicus*). The four equine teeth recorded by Ross in this period have been shown by Zeuner to more likely be those of a hemione or semi-ass, and by themselves they certainly do not provide evidence of the domestication, or even the presence of the horse. Fairservis revisited the site in 1950 and confirmed

Ross's observations of the sequence. He discovered in period 1 sherds of painted pottery distinctly reminiscent of those of Kili Ghul Muhammad II. He also studied the trial excavations of the neighbouring site of Sur Jangal made in 1927 by Sir Aurel Stein, and concluded that the earliest period of occupation there was contemporary with at least the later part of Rana Ghundai 1.

In central Baluchistan, in the Surab valley, the excavations of Miss de Cardi revealed a similar picture of the earliest settlements at Anjira and Siah-damb. In the first phase (Anjira 1), immediately upon the natural gravel, there was no sign of structures. A chert-blade industry, including a small number of backed blades and lunates, occurred along with bone awls, spatulae, and a small bead. The pottery was of a fine buff ware, wheel-thrown and often with burnished red slip; it included both plain and decorated sherds, the latter painted with motifs comparable with those of Kili Ghul Muhammad II. Anjira 1 was followed by a further shallow deposit of about a metre associated with house walls of river boulders. This use at Anjira of stone instead of mud-brick, as is more usual elsewhere in Baluchistan, is noteworthy. The pottery may again be compared with that of Kili Ghul Muhammad II–III, and included a substantial number of cream-surfaced, handmade and basket-marked sherds. Although there are as yet no radiocarbon datings to relate the evidence of Rana Ghundai or Anjira to that of Quetta, there is a sufficient cultural uniformity, and even relationship of specific details of ceramic ornamentation, to make cross-dating over the relatively short distances possible.

Further evidence of the character of the earliest settlements in this region comes from south-east Afghanistan, where at Mundigak, on a now dry tributary of the Arghandab river, J.-M. Casal excavated a most important sequence. The initial occupation (periods 1, 1 and 1, 2) did not reveal any structures. Thus here too, the first settlers seem to have been semi-nomadic. There then followed, in period 1, 4, a level containing tiny oblong cells with walls of pressed earth. In the following layer (1, 5) larger houses appear, which have several square or oblong rooms, built of the new medium of sun-dried bricks, and these, as the excavator remarks, set the style of construction which is followed in all the subsequent periods at the site. Domestic hearths are found from the beginning, and ovens, presumably for baking bread, are situated at first outside the houses, and later, possibly in the courtyards. Wells are found between the houses. A terracotta figurine of a humped bull occurred in period 1, 3, a fact which emphasizes the very early occurrence of terracotta figurines in Baluchistan.

From the pre-structural phase onwards pottery is present, including painted ware (Fig. 5.2), apparently for the most part wheel-thrown. Some characteristic painted designs are similar to those of Kili Ghul Muhammad II and Anjira 1. Bone awls, alabaster vases, stone blades and beads in (?) steatite, lapis lazuli and frit, all make their first appearance during this period. So too do objects of copper, including a needle and a small bent blade, reminding us that copper is known from the earliest settlements in Baluchistan and on the fringes of the Indus system.

From period II has come evidence of club wheat (*Triticum compactum*), whilst also from this site has come jujube or ber (*Zizyphus jujuba*). Cattle, sheep and goat appear to have been the main domesticated species. Radiocarbon dates indicate that period I at Mundigak extended between *c.* 4000 and 3500 B.C.

There has been as yet no systematic investigation of any settlements of this period in southern Baluchistan or the Makran coastal region. That they exist is to be expected, but so far there has been less scientific excavation in this area. There are reports of mounds in which there appear to be a pre-ceramic Neolithic period, but we must await further work.

This limited evidence available suggests that in the western borderlands the earliest settlements grew out of what were originally pastoral nomadic camp-sites, and that there may have been a considerable period during which the change to permanent settlements and settled agriculture took place. However, the first permanent agricultural settlements indicate a highly organized, if still relatively simple society, demanding a substantial degree of social discipline and conformity.

The painting of pottery appears almost from the beginning of ceramics in Baluchistan. The most common elements are linear or simple geometric designs, but occasionally animals are represented as early as Mundigak III (Fig. 6.2). We will follow the further development of this Baluchistan province of pottery painting in the next chapter.

This earliest period in Baluchistan may be inferred to have come to an end by the first half of the fourth millennium B.C. In broadest terms the developments seem to match those reported for Turkmenistan by Masson and his colleagues at Djeitun, and from northern Iran, notably from Sialk I–III.

Earliest settlements of the Indus system

It is in the Indus valley, or more accurately (as Mughal has pointed out), in what

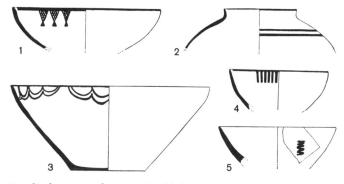

5.2 Mundigak I: painted pottery (1:6) (*after* Casal)

we may call the greater Indus system, that the most striking advances of the past decade have been made. In the *Birth of Indian Civilization* (1968) we pointed for the first time to the 'repeated evidence of continuity from pre-Harappan to Harappan times, suggesting that a large if not a major element in the Harappan civilization must derive from the pre-Harappan culture of the Indus valley itself' (p. 123). In itself this is significant enough, and several writers elaborated on the theme. However, the continuing advance of research means that now not only are there more sites of this 'pre-Harappan', or early Indus period, but that a whole new stratum of yet earlier settlements has been discovered. These hold out the expectation that, when dating is available, events in the greater Indus system will be found to parallel, perhaps even antedate those of the upland valleys of the borderlands to its west. Further, they reinforce our belief that the indigenous developments of this region are of central significance for the subsequent development of Indian civilization in its widest sense.

We shall here review the still very limited evidence for the earliest settlements, which may be called for convenience 'Neolithic', and in the following chapters go on to discuss the much more plentiful evidence for the second major period, that of incipient urbanism, or as we shall call it the Early Indus period. Because the earlier sites are so widely scattered and because the evidence is incompletely published and suggests considerable variations of age, we shall treat the period more as a series of vignettes than as representing any sort of coherent 'culture'. With the later period we are faced by the suggestions of a cultural convergence and simultaneous development or maintenance of regional characters, and we have to consider their significance in the light of the succeeding Indus period.

The Indus plains offer a very different environment from the upland villages of Baluchistan. The picture that we see today, even despite modern flood control measures, of a highly unstable river, constantly changing its course within a wide flood plain, and laying down quantities of silt in the course of its annual inundation over large areas of the plain, was probably the same in many respects at the time of the earliest settlements on the edge of the plain. The rate of accumulation of silt throughout the period (approximately 180 cm per millennium for the plain as a whole, or 250 cm near the river's banks) has been such that not only must many features of the valley have become submerged, along with any early sites associated with them, but the plain itself must have expanded in area, increasing the extent of highly fertile alluvial soil. The main channel of the Indus flows through a wide alluvial flood plain which, with the recession of the annual inundation of June to September, is of great fertility. Wheat and barley sown at that time ripen by the following spring, without either ploughing or manuring of the ground. The banks of the river and of its subsidiary channels are not cultivated and must then, as now, have supported a dense gallery forest. These forests were until recent times rich in game, and must have provided attractive hunting grounds. So too must the plains beyond the active flood plain, for they would have produced a rich and varied grassland vegetation and have provided grazing for wild no less than for domestic animals. Once the agricultural potentials of the new alluvium were realized, and means were discovered of overcoming the problems of protecting settlements on the flood plain from inundation, an entirely new type of life became possible. On present showing this development took place in several stages, reaching its culmination around the opening of the third millennium B.C.

The first and most important site for consideration is at Mehrgarh, at the head of the Kacchi plain, near the point where the Bolan river emerges from the hills, via the Bolan pass. The site is about 150 km as the crow flies from the Quetta valley, and its geographical position is essentially one of transition between the upland valleys of the eastern Iranian plateau and the beginning of the plains of the Indus system. The transitional nature of its position is fully demonstrated in the cultural remains found there. The site was discovered by the French Archaeological Mission, and their excavations, of which so far there have been several seasons, are proving of great importance. In the initial seasons, work was concentrated on a low mound rising above the plain, but subsequently it was realized that, below the surface of the plain and extending over an area of several hundred acres lay the scattered remains of settlements far older than those of the visible mound. In all (according to the preliminary report of the fourth season (1977–8)), there are seven periods of which four are represented in the upper mound and the remaining three on or below the surface of the plain. In this chapter we are concerned only with those which may be regarded as Neolithic, that is to say of periods I–III. The earliest part of the settlement, which was probably originally the camp of a group of nomadic pastoralists (as at other sites) is so far represented only at the northern end of the site, on the high bank of the Bolan river. The exposed section of this bank reveals that there is an 11 m deposit of occupation, of which so far only the uppermost level has been excavated on any scale. However, from the lower levels excavation has revealed a continuing series of mud-brick structures and occupation debris. The excavation also shows that in the final stage, which is convincingly dated by a run of five radiocarbon samples to 5100 B.C., there are mud-brick structures, which form an extensive settlement. The houses in this settlement use a distinctive mud-brick, for they are of a hitherto unknown type, with rounded ends and finger impressions on their upper faces. This settlement includes structures, perhaps granaries, with six-roomed and sometimes nine-roomed units (Fig. 5.3).

Associated with this period and near the houses are two groups of graves in which the bodies are lying on their sides, in a contracted position. This evidence is amongst the earliest which survives for institutionalized burial. The graves appear to have been dug beside a brick platform or wall (surprisingly reminiscent of much later Iranian burials). Grave goods include beads, one of which was of copper. This is the earliest occurrence of this metal at the site, and it certainly remains rare until period III (early fourth millennium). Baskets with bitumen coating have also come from these graves. These baskets probably had the function of pottery in this pre-ceramic period. So far we know relatively little of the material culture of period 1. Virtually no pottery at all is found in the final stages of period 1, and this leads us to believe that the whole of its duration must be pre-ceramic. We may therefore use this evidence to postulate a long pre-ceramic Neolithic occupation period at Mehrgarh. Bone points and awls are common. Stone blades are the principal tools, and some are found with traces of their bitumen mounts still clinging to them. There are also some trapezes, lunates and triangles. A single ground stone axe was discovered in a burial, and several more were obtained from the surface. These ground stone axes are the earliest to come from a stratified context in the Indian subcontinent, and they indicate that this type of tool goes back to the very earliest Neolithic. The techniques of pecking and grinding stone may be regarded as Neolithic innovations. By these means, tougher and less brittle rocks could be used for cutting and chopping than was previously possible; a ground stone axe once made would outlast many flaked tools. The same techniques were also used in making hammer stones, ring stones, querns and grinding stones.

Perhaps the most unexpected discovery in the final stage of period 1 is of turquoise beads found in the burials. This suggests that already at this early date these semi-precious stones were being imported from some distant source, perhaps in Turkmenia. Also pointing to such a link are the hump backed trapezes which very nearly match those found in the Djeitun culture, situated, suggestively, not far from the turquoise mines exploited at that time. The

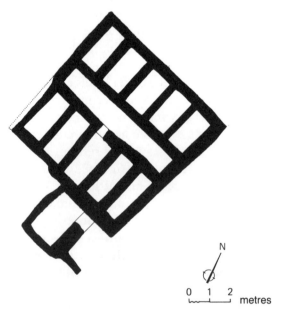

0 1 2 metres

5.3 Mehrgarh: compartmented building of mud-brick (MR 4) (*after* Jarrige)

strategically important position of Mehrgarh at the mouth of the Bolan pass, and thus at one of the major entrances to the Indus plains, no doubt increased its importance in the international trade network. However, the evidence quoted above for long-distance trade must indicate that trade in luxury goods, often over long distances, had already been established for thousands of years before the beginnings of Indus urbanism. This theory is further supported by finds from Rahman Dheri and Lewan (see p. 152).

Period II at Mehrgarh appears to be a direct continuation of the preceding period. In the lower levels of the small area so far excavated there are a few potsherds of coarse handmade pottery, while in the later part of the period (IIB) pottery (both handmade and wheel-thrown) is far more plentiful and painted decorations make their appearance. Amongst this pottery the first examples of basket-marked sherds occur, and these, and the painted decorations suggest striking parallels with the earliest levels of Mundigak I and with Kili Ghul Muhammad I. The stone industry continues, and one set of ten sickle blades was found hafted diagonally in a bitumen matrix to form a saw-like cutting edge (Fig. 5.4). There is further evidence of long-distance trade in this period, in the form of fragments of conch shells from the Arabian Sea, some 500 km away, and further objects of turquoise. Also a small perforated pendant of lead is recorded, perhaps too an object of trade rather than of local production. Whichever is the case, it is the earliest known occurrence of the metal before the Harappan period. Even more important as an indication of trade is the discovery of several beads of lapis lazuli – originally from Badakshan. Finally, we may note the appearance of a small unbaked clay figurine of a male torso. To what extent these earliest terracottas can be regarded as cult objects, it is impossible to say. Two further flexed burials were found in this period, without grave goods, in contrast to those of period I, but with a covering of red ochre on the body. This practice is already attested in Middle Palaeolithic burials in Central Asia, and is still to be found among untouchable groups in South India! Again the connection with Central Asia may be significant.

5.4 Mehrgarh: stone sickle blades set in bitumen (MR 4) (*after* Jarrige)

Period III is found in excavations slightly to the south-west of those of period II. Great quantities of pottery occur, permitting this period to be assigned to the first half of the fourth millennium (until radiocarbon dates are available). The painted motifs of the pottery – particularly in the later stages of the phase – resemble those of Kili Ghul Muhammad II and III, Mundigak and Togau A ware. Beads of lapis lazuli, turquoise and other semi-precious stones, as well as fragments of conch shell and the first objects of copper – beyond the single copper bead from period I – were found on the surface in this area. This suggests a continuity of the remarkable long-distance trading patterns of the preceding period, along with the developing metal technology, and the changing role of pottery in everyday life.

With the first appearance of pottery in the Indus valley and Baluchistan, it is perhaps worthwhile to remember that once the craft was discovered, pottery soon becomes so common that it becomes difficult to generalize about its production. Archaeologists, in India no less than in other parts of the world, have often been imprecise in the terms they employ in describing pottery, and no single system of description has so far been accepted. The attention given to pottery by archaeologists often quite ignores its relatively humble role in the life or economy of a society, and springs more from its usefulness as a common artefact which can provide cross-dating evidence from one site to another. The craft aspects of pottery have often been comparatively neglected.

Once potters started using painted decoration, it tended to grow more varied with the passing of time, and developed from monochrome to bichrome and even polychrome. There is throughout a tendency to abstract geometric or linear designs, although some animal motifs, such as those of the Togau ware, occur. There is not as yet direct evidence of the form of wheel employed, but from the pottery itself it may be inferred that it was some kind of footwheel, probably mounted in a pit. The skill exercised in control of firing likewise suggests that already at an early date a kiln with a separate fire-chamber had been introduced. Altogether the early Chalcolithic pottery of Baluchistan shows affinities with that of Iran and Mesopotamia. The craft traditions once established proved remarkably virile and, although fashions of painting and design changed, they persisted at least until the times of turmoil in the second millennium B.C., if not longer.

From the still-continuing excavations at Mehrgarh has come the earliest evidence yet available for settled agriculture in the subcontinent. We must stress that these excavations are still in progess, and that the scientific and interdisciplinary study of the materials has scarcely started. What we say must therefore be treated with reserve, as it may well be different from the final reports. It appears that during period I, i.e. pre-5000 B.C., there is already evidence for the cultivation of wheat and barley, and also of the date (*phoenix dactylifera*). The animal remains include both *Bos* sp. and water buffalo (these make up the majority), as well as wild sheep and goat, along with many other wild species.

During the course of this period there is a marked increase in cattle bones and a corresponding decrease in the proportion of sheep, goat and deer. Thus there appears to be some indication that the period witnessed a growing reliance upon domesticated species, and perhaps the first domestication of *Bos indicus* and *bubalus*, and the cultivation of cereals – all in an essentially stone-using, pre-ceramic society. The succeeding period (II) provided much evidence of cereal production: granaries and stone sickles set in bitumen reinforce the discovery of many samples of wheat. Also from this period comes the first evidence of the cultivation of cotton (*Gossypium*), some two thousand years earlier than its hitherto attested discovery in the Indus plains. This evidence, along with that of the variety of wheat (*Triticum aestivum*) emphasizes the local rather than the imported nature of the first agriculture of the region.

In the third period, the variety of seeds discovered in the settlement increases, suggesting a diversification of agriculture. Similar evidence comes from Mundigak. All this very early evidence provides the agriculture of the Indus civilization with a substantial background of several millennia, and takes us well back towards the earliest evidence from West Asia.

Another settlement of considerable antiquity, though not as ancient as Mehrgarh, is Gumla, north-west of Dera Ismail Khan. The location of this site is in some ways similar to Mehrgarh. Gumla lies on the right bank of the Indus, and on the alluvial plains of the tributary Gomal river. It is a small mound, and was excavated (in 1971) by Peshawar University. A sequence of six periods was discovered, of which only the first concerns us here. It is claimed in the report that the earliest stratum contained no structural remains and no pottery, but only hearths, community ovens, animal bones and stone tools (microliths). However, some doubt seems to exist in this respect. Elsewhere in the report (p. 130), it is stated that pottery of the subsequent period falls into two classes, of which one, consisting of coarse handmade sherds, was only found at the bottom of the deposit (i.e. on the surface of period I), while the other, of better made pottery, including painted wares, occurred in pits dug in the second period. We are inclined to think that the coarse pottery should be assigned to the first period. We are confirmed in our view of relative lateness when we compare the blade and microlith industry with that of Mehrgarh. None the less, as Gumla seems to be the first of the whole series of sites which appear in the neighbourhood of Dera Ismail Khan in the subsequent period, its importance is obvious.

There seems to be every possibility that similar early sites may be found on other tributary rivers or streams along the right bank of the Indus, either near their emergence from the hills or on the open plains. There are indications of such sites, for instance at Lewan in the Bannu basin to the north, excavated in 1977 by the Cambridge University Archaeological Mission, in company with members of Peshawar University (see below, pp. 151–3).

A third early settlement is at Sarai Khola, some 3 kms south-west of the early historic city of Taxila. This site is located on the Potwar plateau, to the east of the Indus, on the high alluvial plateau which marks the northern border of the Indus plains in this area. It was excavated in 1968–71 by the Pakistan Archaeological Department, and is well reported in *Pakistan Archaeology* nos. 7 and 8. Of the four periods only the first concerns us here. This may be described as a Neolithic occupation on account of the material culture. No structural remains were associated with this period, which is represented by a single layer. Ground stone axes, a stone-blade industry, bone points and burnished pottery formed the material culture. Subsequent investigations yielded several C14 dates between 3160–2360 B.C. for this period. The remains here, as at Gumla and Mehrgarh, are sequence dated by preceding those of the Early Indus period. Only a very small part of the blade industry came from period 1, the majority of the finds arising from the second period. The same is true of the ground stone axes, which are of a simple kind, generally with median ground edges and rounded butts. The pottery is coarse red–brown and frequently burnished (Fig. 5.5). There is a limited range of types, all handmade or built on a

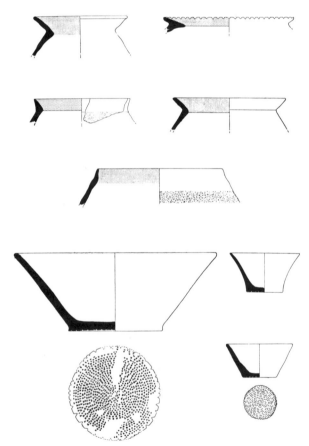

5.5 Sarai Khola, 1: handmade and burnished wares (note mat-impressed bases) (1:6) (*after* Halim)

simple turntable. Coiled mat impressions occur on the bases of some pots, as they do in the early pottery at Gumla, Lewan and Mehrgarh. Some of the pottery shows the addition of a coarse, gritty sand to the outer surface while the clay was still soft. Painted pottery is notably absent. There is no evidence of any metal in this period, although in the succeeding period it becomes relatively common. This excavation provides evidence of a period which, although in many respects differentiated from its successor, none the less has many continuing traits, suggesting that there was no complete abandonment of the settlement, nor change in population. A quantity of plant remains have recently been collected and their publication is awaited.

Our fourth early settlement of the Indus system is at Jalilpur in the south-western Punjab, some 65 km south-west of Harappa, standing near the left bank of the Ravi river, and therefore fully on the alluvial plain. It was excavated by the Pakistan Archaeological Department in 1971 and subsequently, but so far only preliminary reports have been published. Here too the early period may be called Neolithic, in that no copper or bronze has been reported, and the stone-blade industry and the bone points recall period 1 at Sarai Khola. There is some evidence for the use of mud-brick, although clear structures have not so far been reported. The presence of terracotta net sinkers suggests that fishing formed an element of the economy, and preliminary reports indicate that animal remains included bones of sheep, goat, cattle and gazelle. The pottery of the period is handmade of bright red clay, with a soft crumbling surface, perhaps the result of waterlogging and recalling the so-called 'O C P' of later times. A most distinctive feature is the roughening of the surface by the application, before firing, of a thick coating or slurry made up of clay mixed with fragments of crushed pottery, providing an equivalent to the granular sand roughening of pottery from Sarai Khola 1, in series 1A. This excavation is therefore of great interest and further reports are awaited.

Earliest settlements in the northern valleys

Sites which may be referred to as Neolithic occur in the valleys of the Himalayas, north of the Indus plain. The best known site is at Burzahom, in the Vale of Kashmir. Burzahom is situated on a terrace of Karewa clay above the marshy flood plain of the river Jhelum, about six miles north-east of Srinagar. A trial excavation was made some thirty years ago by the Yale–Cambridge expedition, but serious work was only taken up after 1959 by the Archaeological Survey of India. The earliest occupation (1), which radiocarbon dates indicate to be before c. 2920 B.C., took the form of a series of pits dug into the soft clay. The largest were presumably pit-dwellings, and post-holes around the perimeter probably indicate conical roofs (Fig. 5.6). In cross-section, these pits are narrow at the top, though they widen out towards the base. Floors and walls were occasionally mud-plastered. In the deeper pits steps were cut for part of the depth, though ladders must also have been used. The largest of these pits measured 3.96 m in depth and had a diameter at base of 4.57 m while the mouth was only 2.74 m. There were ashes both in the pits and at ground level in stone hearths near the entrances. Storage pits in the same area yielded animal bones. Obviously such 'earth houses' were intended to give protection from the cold, and it is improbable that the custom of making them would survive any excursion on to the plains of the Punjab or beyond. Indeed, at present, they form a type of habitation whose nearest parallel is at Sarai Khola in the Potwar region.

The ceramic material from Burzahom, which also represents a distinctly non-Indus, non-Baluchistan tradition, is a predominantly grey, buff or black burnished ware: heavy in section, coarse and ill-fired (Fig. 5.7). The mat-impressions on the bases and the irregular forms indicate that it is handmade, and there can be no doubt that it was fired in an open or bonfire kiln. The range of forms includes simple rimless bowls and bottle shapes with flared rims. Apart from the burnish, the only decoration is crude, incised and fingertip decoration. Other material remains included a wide range of bone points, awls, needles and harpoons (Fig. 5.8); stone axes, frequently pecked and ground, of both oval and oblong section; ring stones; and a distinctive pierced rectangular chopper or knife of a kind hitherto unknown in India (Fig. 5.9). Grindstones are reported to have been found in almost every house. The absence of a stone-blade industry is

5.6 Burzahom: Neolithic pit-dwelling (courtesy Archaeological Survey of India)

significant. There is as yet no clear evidence of the subsistence of these people, though it appears that hunting played an important part.

In period II the stone and bone industries of period I continue, but there are traces of houses of mud or mud-brick, sometimes with mud-plaster. The date of this phase is not yet clearly established, but a long run of radiocarbon dates suggests that it continued at least until *c.* 1700 B.C. A single copper arrowhead is reported from the end of this period. Also to the period belonged a number of burials, chiefly of crouched skeletons in oval pits, without grave goods, and situated among the houses. In some cases red ochre had been put over the body, and one skull had been trepanned during life. Dogs were also sometimes buried with their owners. This peculiar feature is without parallel in the subcontinent, and included the purposeful burial of other animals, such as wolves or ibex. This evidence from the graves is the only information which survives concerning religious beliefs at Burzahom, with the exception of a stray painted pot showing a typical Early Indus buffalo deity.

Another important site in Kashmir is at Gufkral, where three stages of early occupation were discovered. The earliest involved pit dwellings, as at Burzahom, some plastered with red ochre, and stone and bone tools, but no pottery. The animal remains in the first phase are of wild species, and are progressively replaced by domesticated sheep, goats and cattle; wheat, barley and lentils occur from the beginning. C14 dates indicate a span of *c.* 2400–1600 B.C.

Evidence of contemporary developments in the Swat valley is emerging. In

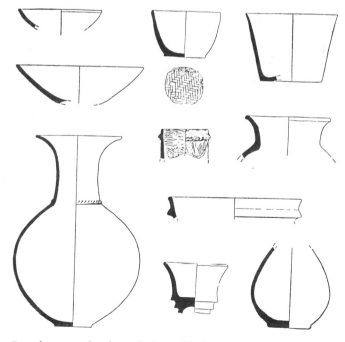

5.7 Burzahom, I and II: burnished grey-black pottery (1:8)

the Ghaligai cave the lowest levels produced coarse handmade pottery and no metal. Three radiocarbon dates give *c*. 2970–2920 B.C. In the succeeding stratum painted pottery of distinctly Early Indus character appears, only to disappear again in period III, when the northern Neolithic character continues. Further important evidence is coming from the current excavations of the Italian Mission at Loebanr, where dwelling-pits and wattle and daub structures are reported

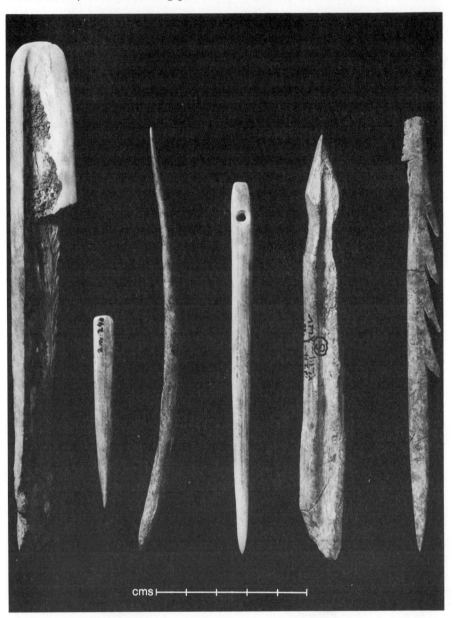

5.8 Burzahom: bone and antler tools (*courtesy* Archaeological Survey of India)

in period III. From the excavations at Loebanr III have come two varieties of barley and a little wheat, along with rice, lentils (*Lens culinaris*), and the field pea (*Pisum arvense*). Another exciting find is a grape seed (*Vitis vinifera*).

Radiocarbon dates from Loebanr, Aligrama and other sites suggest that this

5.9 Burzahom: ground and pecked stone tools: 1, 4, 6 and 7 axes; 2 rectangular harvesting knife; 3 hammer stone; 5 ring stone (*courtesy* Archaeological Survey of India)

cultural tradition continued into the opening centuries of the second millennium B.C. The material culture included stone celts, polished bone points and jade beads. The coarse and burnished grey and brown wares of the early Swat sites recall in general terms those of Burzahom and Sarai Khola I, and lead us to believe that all belong to a single complex. Although not yet securely dated we may expect this interesting site to belong culturally, if not chronologically, to the broad period of the early occupation at Burzahom.

In discussing the origins and affinities of these northern Neolithic sites certain things at once strike the eye as foreign to the Indian tradition. Among them are the forms of the bone tools, the rectangular perforated stone knives, jade beads, the pit-dwellings, and the placing of domestic dogs in graves with their masters. Each one of these features is found in Neolithic cultures of north China, the perforated knife in particular being a characteristic trait. Also dog burials are reported in the Ang-Ang-Hsi culture of Manchuria. The dog was apparently almost a cult animal in the Shilka cave culture of the upper Amur; and dogs were until recently sacrificed and buried with their owners among such peoples as the Gilyaks, Ulchis and Goldis of this region. The presence of jade beads at Loebanr is strongly suggestive of trade contacts with the areas north of the mountains. A bone industry, including harpoons, is also a frequent occurrence of north Chinese Neolithic sites. The Burzahom ceramic industry is not obviously comparable with any Chinese Neolithic pottery. In short, the Burzahom 'Neolithic' appears as a local adaptation to the special environment of the mountains, its people having rich sources of food from hunting and from agriculture. The presence of rice in Swat is particularly interesting. So too is the evidence of trade and other more profound contacts with the Chinese world. Another point which demands consideration is that although this culture must have co-existed with the Early and Mature Harappan developments in the Indus valley and Punjab, there is almost no indication that the two enjoyed any contact whatsoever. The question of relations with the other Indian Neolithic groups is more problematic, and we leave it on one side for the present.

Earliest Settlements east of the Indus system

We must now consider the situation in South Asia east of the Indus system and the Thar desert. In earlier chapters this part of the subcontinent has been shown to consist of a number of geographically distinct regions which, while presenting a range of different environments, taken as a whole have certain overriding features that contrast with the north-western third of the subcontinent. The western borderlands, Indus plains and Thar desert are all part of a major arid region where agriculture at all periods is almost entirely dependent upon water carried by rivers and streams whose principal catchment is outside the region. Moving east or south of the Indus system we enter more hospitable zones of higher monsoonal rainfall which lend themselves to more varied, less specialized forms of exploitation by man, anciently and at the present time.

In order to understand the nature of cultural developments in Eastern and Southern India we must go back to the situation described in the last chapter, recalling that during the early Holocene these regions supported a wide range of different Mesolithic cultures. They may be thought of as a continuous network or fabric, extending, with fairly large gaps or threadbare patches corresponding to the most intensely arid parts of the desert, from the relatively advanced centres of incipient urbanism in the western borderlands and Indus plain, described in previous sections, outwards to the east and south-east. The pattern of the fabric changes continually, but there is no break in the weave. The cultures forming this continuum had a number of material traits in common with the more urban cultures to the west yet were all based primarily upon different combinations of hunting, gathering and fishing. Notable among these items are microlithic industries, based upon the production of parallel-sided blades, and other stone artefacts such as hammer stones, mace heads, etc., such as are found in the occupation deposit at Adamgarh and elsewhere.

Some early communities forming part of the continuum east of the desert appear to have adopted the practice of keeping domestic animals, and it is probable that certain of them had also begun to practise small scale agriculture during this period, although we have little positive proof of this at present. This situation underlines the impossibility of drawing a line between so called Mesolithic and Neolithic cultures. Therefore we propose to use the term Neolithic only when we have some positive evidence of permanent settlement, or significant economic development beyond hunting, gathering and fishing. Using these criteria, we can see emerging among the Mesolithic communities of the east and south the first manifestations of local and regional cultures of the kind that came into prominence in succeeding phases, contemporary with and following the mature phase of the Indus civilization. The evidence to date is slight and may be briefly summarized, but it is of such a nature as to leave little doubt that further, more substantial evidence will be forthcoming in the course of time.

Evidence of early plant cultivation east of the Indus, of a somewhat equivocal nature, was published by Gurdip Singh in 1971. He suggested that the result of palynological studies in eastern Rajasthan indicated that around 7000 B.C. there was a marked increase in grains of cereal type. In the light of the discoveries at Mehrgarh, such a development now seems quite plausible. Even more important when they are more fully published seem likely to be the results of the excavations by G. R. Sharma and his colleagues from Allahabad University at sites south of Allahabad. At Koldihwa and the neighbouring Mahagara an interesting Neolithic occupation has been found stratified beneath Chalcolithic deposits. There are several strata of circular huts, marked by post-holes, with stone blades, ground stone axes (Fig. 5.11) and bone tools, along with a very crude, handmade pottery, frequently marked with cord or basket impressions (Figs. 5.10, 5.12). The animal remains are said to include bones of sheep, goat, bovids and wild species. Particularly interesting is the discovery of a small cattle pen, marked by post-holes around the perimeter and by cattle hoof impressions within (as in the case of the ash-mounds of Karnataka). The possibly early age of this culture is suggested by radiocarbon dates obtained from samples of charred rice from the upper levels of Koldihwa giving 5440 and 4530 B.C. (uncalibrated). One of the most striking features of these sites is that the Neolithic pottery frequently contains husks of rice. This would seem possibly to be the oldest evidence of rice in any part of the world. However, the early dating is not clearly established: subsequent radiocarbon dates from both Koldihwa and Mahagara suggest that the culture may more plausibly be dated to c. 1500–1600 B.C.; and the succeeding Chalcolithic phase certainly would support this dating.

In Bihar, on the alluvial plains of the Ganges, a group of early settlements have come to light in recent years. One of them, Chirand, has been excavated and preliminary reports published. This shows it to be a small village with huts of bamboo and mud-plaster. There is a 3.5 m deposit for the early period, and a radiocarbon date of c. 2000 B.C. for its upper limit. The material culture includes a rich bone and antler industry, ground stone axes and a stone-blade industry. Pottery was mainly handmade and includes grey and red burnished ware. A mat impression on a base is recorded, as well as post-firing ochre paint. Rice husks

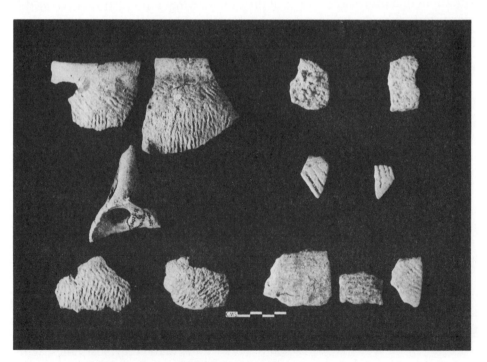

5.10 Koldihwa, district Allahabad: cord-impressed pottery (*courtesy* G. R. Sharma)

and fish bones are indications of diet. As the radiocarbon dates for the end of the period indicate that it was contemporary with the Late Harappan, we may expect that the beginnings of the culture were probably contemporary with Early Indus settlements to the west. The blade industry is closely comparable to Mesolithic industries from western Central India. An industry of this kind in the alluvial plain indicates, as it does at Sarai-Nahar-Rai in Uttar Pradesh, trade with adjacent regions, probably to the south, and the ground stone axes carry the same implications. Bihar appears to be the western focus for the development of an East Indian Neolithic based partly upon rice, and as such is of the greatest interest.

Collections of stone axes made in many parts of Central India probably belong to this period, and like microliths and other stone artefacts may in the future be a means of relating sites in what appear to be two complementary geographical regions. Typological studies of these collections, many of which were made a century or more ago without much reference to context or location, show them to fall into two major groups. One has affinities with axe types found in Eastern India and further east but not in the south or west, and the other with the southern Neolithic group of axes, and those from sites extending as far west as

5.11 Mahagara, district Allahabad: stone axes (*courtesy* G. R. Sharma)

the western borderlands of the subcontinent. The first group includes small axes of triangular and rounded outline, and shouldered or tanged axes of both angular and rounded types closely similar to axes from Assam and other eastern regions. The second group consists of rather heavier axes of lenticular section and more or less triangular outline, with curved median ground cutting edges. Some assemblages consist almost exclusively of axes of one group or the other, and others are mixed, while others again include what appears to be factory debris and therefore were probably collected at factory sites. The chronological and cultural relationships of the two major groups are far from clear, but the distribution of the eastern group corresponds in a general sense with other eastern traits noted in eastern Central India, Bengal and increasingly in Assam and the eastern frontier regions.

The existence of Neolithic settlements in Eastern India in the hills and valleys of Assam has long been postulated on the basis of widely spread surface collections of ground stone axes, often of distinctive forms, with their main comparisons with those of South-east Asia and southern China (Fig. 5.13). So far there is very little cultural evidence to throw light on the makers of these axes, and little or not dating evidence. Excavations at Sarutaru, near Gauhati, revealed shouldered celts and round-butted axes associated with crude cord- or basket-

5.12 Mahagara: cord-impressed pottery (*courtesy* G. R. Sharma)

marked potsherds. Another site of the East Indian Neolithic is that of Daojali-Hading. Here crude handmade pottery with external cord-marked or striated beaten-impressed decoration was produced. Such pottery has perhaps some connection with the early Central Indian potting tradition noticed above. It strongly recalls the Neolithic wares of south China, and seems thus to belong to an eastern culture zone.

Earliest settlements in Peninsular India

In South India we have the most decisive evidence of new patterns of subsistence contemporary with the early Indus cultures of the north-west.

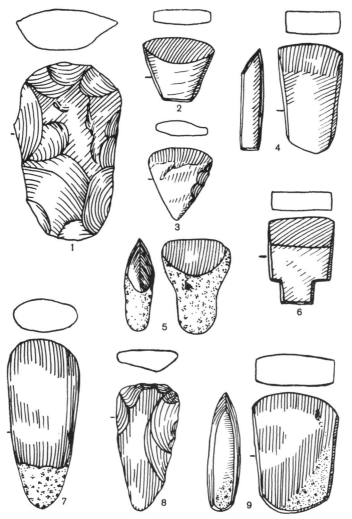

5.13 Stone axes from Assam: 1 North-east Frontier Agency; 2, 3 and 6 Cachar hills; 4 and 8 Garo hills; 5, 7 and 9 Naga Hills (1:3) (*courtesy* T. C. Sharma)

In that part of the Deccan plateau where this new pattern first developed, the predominant physical features are residual granite hills rising from a rolling 'sea' of black cotton soil. The hills were favoured for settlement, and wherever they contained suitable caves or rock shelters, these were used for habitation, and often enlarged by the construction of a levelled stone terrace in front. Small plateaux on the summits of hills or level areas on hillsides were likewise exploited and artificially levelled or extended. In some cases there seem to have been single large terraces, while in others there were many small ones, rising one behind the other up the slope of a hill (Fig. 5.14). At this early period, sites are only rarely found on the banks of rivers away from hills. There is as yet no evidence for structures associated with the earliest settlements in this area.

The further development of the southern Neolithic is discussed in more detail in chapter 10 (p. 286ff.). However, it is appropriate to note here that the early

5.14 Modern fields on terraces yielding evidence of Neolithic occupation, Kallur, Karnataka

radiocarbon dates (from *c.* 3000 B.C.) obtained from certain excavated sites in the southern Deccan correspond with the Early Indus phase, and are thus the earliest settlements known from the south. The sites concerned are the so-called ash-mound type of Neolithic settlement, which Bruce Foote correctly deduced in the last century to be the sites of Neolithic cattle pens. There are some indications that correspondingly early settlements may come to light in other parts of India, between the southern Neolithic sites and those of Central India, but so far we only have secure evidence for these ash-mound sites. Ash-mounds have been excavated in Karnataka (from whence comes all our information), at Utnur, Kupgal, Kodekal and Pallavoy, and were undoubtedly places where cattle (*Bos indicus*) were herded. These pens were surrounded by two heavy stockades of palm trunks. The inner of the two provided the area in which the cattle were penned, while the outer provided a space within which the herdsmen lived. Some of these pens are attached to permanent settlements, but others, probably the oldest known sites in the region, are in the forest, remote from any settlement, and thus, probably, only temporarily occupied.

It has been suggested that the ash-mounds were in origin places where wild cattle were captured and tamed. Indeed, they seem comparable to both the 'keddahs' used today to capture and tame wild elephants, and the large traps used by hunting peoples in various parts of the world to secure large animals. There is no doubt that the ash-mounds continued to be used over a long period as places for herding cattle and protecting them from wild animals and raiders. Communities that breed cattle in forest areas of Central and Peninsular India today pen them in much the same way. Given this, it seems most likely that the first settlers were probably heavily dependent on cattle husbandry, and at least partly nomadic. This clearly implies that plant agriculture did not form a major part of their economy, and there is certainly no evidence presently available to support a different view.

So far there is only limited evidence available for the form of the structures at these sites. Most of what we know in this area is derived from the excavations at Utnur (Fig. 5.15). Here the stockade was burnt and then rebuilt several times,

5.15 Utnur: hoof impressions from floor of cattle pen in ash-mound

the burning being associated with the conflagration of great accumulations of cow dung. Whether this was done by accident or design is still not clear, but it has been suggested that it may have been connected with seasonal festivals marking such events as the beginning or end of the annual migrations to the forest grazing grounds. Among modern pastoralists in Peninsular India bonfires are still lit at festivals at such times. Cattle are also driven through fires as prophylaxis against disease. Whatever the reason for this burning, it gave rise to the Deccan ash-mounds – those features which mystified archaeologists for so long.

The occupation material includes small quantities of ground stone axes (Fig. 5.16), stone blades and coarse pottery similar to some found at other, later and

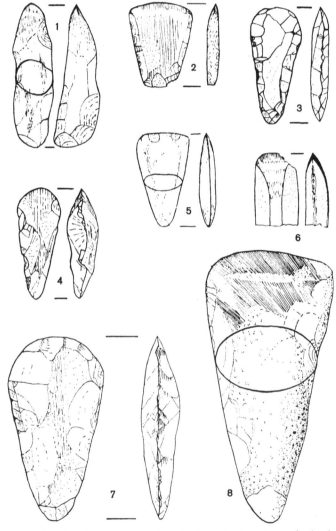

5.16 Ground and pecked stone axes from Bellary district, Karnataka (1:3)

more substantial Neolithic settlements on the terraced slopes of the granite hills of the same region, such as at the site of Piklihal (from c. 2100 B.C., and thus contemporary with the Mature Indus and later periods). At Kodekal and Utnur, however, this pottery represents the first stage in the formation of a distinctive potting tradition. Initially it combines several separate wares. First was a burnished grey or buff ware, generally plain, but including a decorated group usually with simple bands of red ochre apparently applied after firing. This pottery is handmade, probably built on some kind of turntable, and very rarely bearing mat-impressions upon the base. The second element is also hand-built, having a red, black or brown dressing applied before burnishing and firing. Some of the vessels of this ware are painted before firing with black or purple paint. Throughout the whole industry the evidence suggests that pottery was handmade upon a turntable, and that it was fired in an open, bonfire kiln.

Looked at as a group, this forms a major ceramic tradition, apparently unconnected with that of the Indus or Baluchistan, though linked up in some way with the northern Punjab and the northern valleys, and perhaps too having affinities in South-east Asia. This region we may regard as a Peninsula ceramics province as opposed to the Indus–borderlands province. In the earliest period, the group would probably be represented by the pottery from Sarai Khola I, Burzahom I, Ghaligai I, perhaps also Chirand I and the burnished wares of the southern Neolithic.

There are as yet no clear indications of when the first related cultures spread throughout other parts of the southern peninsula or across to Sri Lanka. Such signs as there are at present suggest that these were later developments, perhaps in the form of a secondary spread from the nuclear region in the low rainfall areas of Karnataka, and there is scarcely evidence at all from Sri Lanka.

Conclusion

The evidence we have been reviewing leads us to form certain broad conclusions. The earliest settlements in the Indian subcontinent to date come from the west of the Indus system, on the borders of the Iranian plateau. Here at Mehrgarh there is a pre-ceramic Neolithic, which we may expect to have lasted for a long period, perhaps for as long as two or three millennia (c. 8000–5000 B.C.). At the close of this period there was already a developed mud-brick architecture, wheat and barley were cultivated, and cattle, sheep and goat were domesticated. This was followed by a period of ceramic Neolithic, when comparable settlements are found at several points, notably at Mundigak, Kili Ghul Muhammad, and in Kalat (Anjira and Siah Damb). One of the most striking things about both these early periods is that trade links with the Arabian Sea coast and with Central Asia seem already to have been established. Until positive evidence is available to disprove it, we must assume that during all this time there were no settled agricultural communities elsewhere in the subcontinent,

Time scale B.C.	Baluchistan				Amri	Indus system						Stage
	Kalat (Anjira)	Quetta valley	Mundigak (after Jarrige 1979)	Mehrgarh		Mohenjo-daro	Kot Diji	Harappa	Kalibangan	Lothal (Surkotada)	Rahman Dheri	
2000			V	Sibri cemetery	d	Late		CEM. H	?	II (Ic)	III Late	IV Mature Indus
2500	V	III	IV 3 2 1	VII	c b III a b II a	Inter-mediate Early	II Mature Indus	II	II Mature Indus	(Ib) I (Ia)		III Early Indus
			6 5 4	VI		→ ?	I Early Indus	I →	I Early Indus		II	
3000	IV	II	3 2 III 1	V	d c b			?			I Early	II Chalcolithic
3500	III	DS I	II	IV								Ic Final Neolithic
		IV	6 5	III	I a							
4000	II	III	4 3 2 II 1	b								Ib Ceramic Neolithic
4500	I	II		II a								
5000		KGM I		c b I a → ?								Ia Non-ceramic Neolithic
6000												

5.17 Sequence chart 1: Baluchistan and the Indus system (c. 6000–2000 B.C.)

and that those regions were peopled by Mesolithic communities living by hunting and collecting, and perhaps by pastoralism. The third stage at Mehrgarh shows greater use of pottery and, at the end of the period, the first introduction of copper tools. It seems probable that this period lasted until *c.* 3500 B.C. During this period we may guess that settlements were beginning to appear in other parts of the Indus system, notably in the north and in the valleys beyond, at Sarai Khola, in Kashmir, and in Swat, and maybe also more widely on the Indus plains themselves, although here the settlements have almost certainly been submerged under the steadily rising alluvium. We may also guess, in the absence of absolute dates, that the ancestors of the Neolithic communities of Eastern, Central and Peninsular India also emerged at approximately this time. Thus the foundations of the subsequent period of incipient urbanism in the Indus valley may be seen to have been well and truly laid in the Neolithic period, and to have roots far deeper than hitherto believed. At the same time it is interesting to note that certain traits of the 'Neolithic' period of the Indus borderlands appear to be shared by the apparently later 'Neolithic' adaptations east of the Indus system. This suggests that the transition from 'Mesolithic' to 'Neolithic' in all these areas may be considerably older than present evidence indicates.

PART II
INDUS URBANISM

CHAPTER 6

THE EARLY INDUS PERIOD

In the previous chapter we have outlined the evidence for the varied ways in which settled 'Neolithic' cultures developed in different parts of South Asia. We must again recall that the prior, or at least broadly contemporaneous, existence of groups who lived by hunting and collecting, and by various sorts of pastoral nomadism, is often suggested in the archaeological record in all areas. Their structures were probably not unlike the tents of the modern nomads of the North West Frontier, or the temporary huts of light wooden frames, matting and thatch still constructed in many parts of the subcontinent to this day. Evidence of huts of this character was obtained recently in the excavations at Lewan, near Bannu, a fourth millennium site. At this site the similarity between the excavated huts and local modern examples was remarkable.

During the second half of the fourth and early part of the third millennium B.C., a new development begins to become apparent in the greater Indus system, which we can now see to be a formative stage underlying the Mature Indus civilization of the middle and late third millennium. This development seems to have involved the whole Indus system, and to a lesser extent the Indo-Iranian borderlands to its west, but largely left untouched the subcontinent east of the Indus system. Therefore we shall now concentrate upon the developments of those regions which may be seen to contribute directly or indirectly to the emergence of the Indus civilization.

The borderlands in the fourth to third millennia

The early patterns of settlement established in the valleys of Baluchistan continued with little major change for more than two millennia. The principal change so far recorded is in the development of highly individual styles of painted pottery – from the archaeological point of view the main recorded surviving feature of the sites. It was this feature which led some earlier writers to describe distinct 'cultures' on the basis of pottery painting style alone: in the north the Zhob and Quetta, and in the south the Nal and Kulli styles were particularly cited. Recently Shaffer has drawn attention to the inadequacy of previous 'models' for understanding Baluchistan during this period, and has pointed to the related roles of pastoralism and agriculture in articulating both local and long-distance trade, thereby producing some of the distinctive elements of the archaeological record as it is known to us. Undoubtedly one

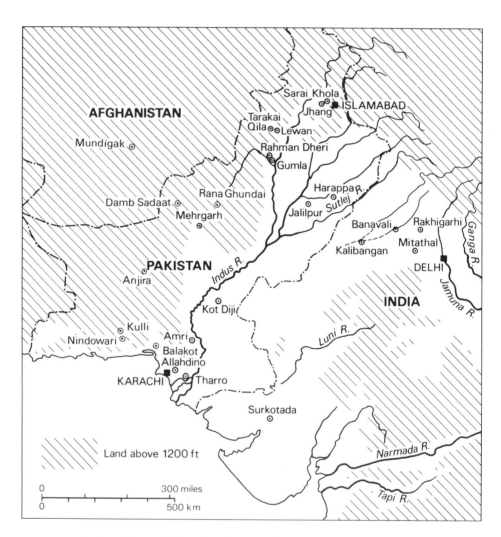

6.1 Map of sites of the Early Indus period

important element must be the relations established between the upland valleys and the flood plains of the neighbouring Indus system. Another must have been the arteries through which long-distance trade flowed, particularly those originating in the main centres of wealth wherever they may have been. It is probably this trade which provided stimuli for the development of an incipient urbanism in one part of the region, in southern Afghanistan and Seistan, leading to the growth of sites such as Shahr-i Sokhta or Mundigak into towns or even 'caravan cities'. One result of this interaction must have been that the many parallels between the material culture of this region and that of Central Asia, witnessed at sites of the Namazga I and II period continued to be a prominent feature. The links between Central Asia, the Indo-Iranian borderlands and the Indus valley appear to have been particularly strong and enduring, and must lead us to enquire whether they may not have involved more than mere trade. In the light of later history, and of the continuing movements of peoples down into South Asia from the north, one may legitimately expect movements of peoples to have been a major, if nowadays unfashionable, factor. We must also recall that – on the evidence of Mehrgarh – the beginnings of such contacts were already at this time at least fifteen centuries old.

Because Mundigak appears to represent a point on one such trade route we shall first consider what developments took place there. In period II the houses, now larger than before, are well constructed and the settlement is notably more compact than in the earlier period. In one house a well with a brick head was discovered. Many of the rooms had hearths constructed in the centre. The pottery of this period, by contrast to that of the first, was mainly handmade, and undecorated, whatever this may signify. On the other hand, the second period produced the first crude stone disc seal (Fig. 6.8, No. 1), and the first of a series of bifacially worked stone leaf-shaped arrowheads. Mundigak III, in which there are six phases of construction, represents a time of great activity, the structures forming a logical development of those of the preceding period. A cemetery was discovered at the foot of the mound outside the main living area, in which there were contracted burials generally without grave goods in its earlier phase. In its later phase there were more frequently communal ossuaries. The bones in these ossuaries had evidently been exposed, or otherwise excarnated, before deposition. In some cases single pots were added as grave goods. The pottery shows an increasing proportion of wheel-made vessels and an exciting range of painted decoration (Figs. 6.2 and 6.3). In particular, black geometric designs on a red surface and polychrome designs appear – both having many parallels at other sites in Baluchistan. The stone-blade industry continues and there is a considerable increase in the use of both copper and bronze. In period III.6 a bronze shaft-hole axe and a shaft-hole adze were found (Fig. 9.3, nos. 3 and 4). Terracotta figurines are numerous and include the humped bull and crudely formed human females. There are numbers of flat stone seals, both square and circular (Fig. 6.8).

Mundigak IV saw the transformation of the settlement into a town with massive defensive walls and square bastions of sun-dried bricks. The main mound was capped with an extensive building identified as a palace, and another smaller mound with a large 'temple' complex. The brick walls of the palace had a colonnade of pilasters (Fig. 6.7). The city was destroyed and twice rebuilt during the period. An increasing quantity of pottery was decorated with a red slip and black paint, and there was a growing use of naturalistic decoration showing birds, ibex, bulls and *pīpal* trees (Figs. 6.4 and 6.5). Female figurines of the 'Zhob mother goddess' type are found, and these have their closest parallels in Mehrgarh VII, Damb Sadaat III and Rana Ghundai IIIC. This suggests that Mundigak IV corresponds with these periods in its earlier phase, while in its later phase it is contemporary with the Mature Harappan period. Further support for this may be found in the male head with hair bound in a fillet, made of white limestone, assigned to Mundigak IV.3 (Fig. 6.6). This piece has a certain relationship to the celebrated priest-king of Mohenjo-daro even if the relationship is not a direct one.

6.2 Mundigak, III: painted pottery (1:6) (*after* Casal)

The developments we have just witnessed at Mundigak appear to be closely paralleled in the Quetta valley. At the opening of this period, i.e. around the beginning of the third millennium, the settlement at Kili Ghul Muhammad came to an end, but the sequence is taken up by a new site some ten miles south, at Damb Sadaat, also excavated by Fairservis. Here too there is a noticeable

6.3 Mundigak, III.6: painted pottery (*after* Casal)

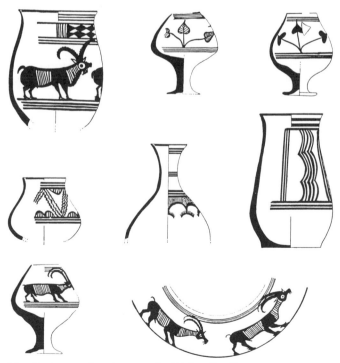

6.4 Mundigak, IV: painted pottery (1:6) (*after* Casal)

advance in the scale of the houses, but mud-brick is still favoured, and hearths and bread ovens were found. There were three phases of occupation of which the earliest (I) produced two radiocarbon dates of 3180 and 3150 B.C., and the second (II) three dates of 3150, 2920 and 2630 B.C. In the third phase a more ambitious structure with brick walls of monumental proportions was constructed. The material culture of the three phases is homogeneous; distinctive figurines of terracotta, both human female and animal forms, were found in periods II and III. Among the animal figurines the humped bull with painted decoration was noteworthy. Two button seals of clay occurred in periods II and III (Fig. 6.9), and copper objects in the earlier period included a dagger blade. Bone tools and a stone-blade industry, mainly of chert, continued, as did the alabaster bowls. The presence of numbers of grinding slabs and stone balls, perhaps used as corn-crushers, suggests the preparation of cereals. Once again varieties of painted pottery proliferate, and Quetta ware with its black-on-buff bichrome decoration shows numerous parallels with Mundigak III. The beginnings of this style are found in Damb Sadaat I, and its elaboration continues through periods II and III. Polychrome decoration (named 'Kechi Beg Polychrome' after the type-site) occurs in Damb Sadaat I and II; and a painted grey ware (named 'Faiz Muhammad grey') is another feature. A characteristic of the plain pottery is a surface roughening, as in the Quetta 'Wet' ware, while another variety of this ware has circular stamping on the shoulder of the vessel. The similarities of form, fabric and design point to a general relationship between Damb Sadaat I–III and Mundigak II–III.

In the north-east lobe of Baluchistan, in the Loralai and Zhob valleys, further convincing concordances may be found. Here as yet there are no radiocarbon dates. At Rana Ghundai in the Loralai valley the second major period (II) coincides with an important change and the introduction of a new, finely made painted pottery with friezes of humped bulls in black, upon a buff-to-red surface. These vessels are frequently in the form of bowls or cups, often with a ring base or a hollow pedestal. Period III follows, and is divided by its excavator into three

6.5 Mundigak, IV: painted pottery (*after* Casal)

sub-periods. The division was traced by him in a stylistic evolution of the painted pottery. In IIIA appears a bichrome painted style with red-on-red tones, occurring also nearby at Sur Jangal in period III. In the upper levels of this period there appear a number of wares with parallels in Quetta, including the 'Wet' ware, and a polychrome akin to Kechi Beg ware. The third period ended with a conflagration and was replaced by a very different potting tradition. A larger excavation is required to provide a more certain chronology for the Loralai valley.

From the Zhob valley in the extreme north of Baluchistan further evidence comes from the site of Periano Ghundai, excavated by Sir Aurel Stein in 1924

6.6 Mundigak, IV: sculptured head in limestone (height 9.3 cm) (*after* Casal)

and revisited in 1950 by Fairservis. The earliest phase here seems to coincide with Rana Ghundai IIC. The finds include leaf-shaped bifacial arrowheads, stone blades and female figurines of the sort commonly known as 'Zhob Goddesses'. A distinctive type of surface-roughened ('Wet') ware again suggests its date. Another special feature of Periano Ghundai was the large terracotta figurines of humped bulls. The assemblage from this site is discussed in greater detail by Fairservis.

In central Baluchistan, de Cardi's work at Kalat provides a valuable extension of our knowledge of this period, or at least of its earlier half (Fig. 5.17). Anjira III seems to coincide with Damb Sadaat I–II, and Anjira IV with the flowering of Damb Sadaat II–III. Here the principal painted pottery was that named after the typesite of Togau – fine red ware with painted designs including friezes of animals, usually caprids. De Cardi has traced the stylistic evolution of this motif

6.7 Mundigak, IV: palace building (*after* Casal)

in the succeeding levels of the excavation. Other characteristic painted wares are bichrome and polychrome, the former with cream or red slip, and decoration in red or black. These same varieties are found again in Anjira IV. Also common in this last period are the black-coated Anjira ware, and a surface-roughened ware having obvious affinities with the Quetta 'Wet' wares.

The situation in south Baluchistan for this period still lacks clarity. Several important excavations have been conducted or published in south Iran since 1968, and these provide valuable comparative data, and an indication of the sort of evidence which may be found. The most important of these are at Tal-i Iblis, Bampur and Tepe Yahya. Within the borderlands there are two new contributions: the unfinished excavations at Nindowari, some 15 km south of Kulli, where a Kulli culture settlement has been found stratified below occupation of

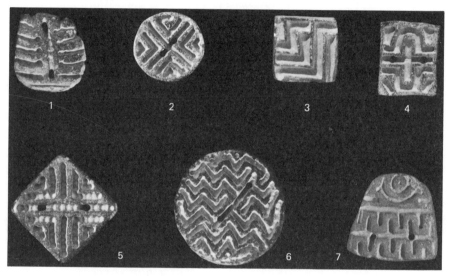

6.8 Mundigak: stone button seals: 1, period II.2; 2–4, period III; 5–7, period IV (*after* Casal)

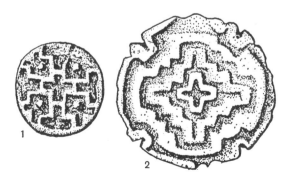

6.9 Damb Sadaat: clay seals: 1, period II; 2, period III (2:3) (*after* Fairservis)

the Harappan period; and the excavations at Balakot, about 80 km south-east of Las Bela, where Dales discovered a deep occupation deposit in a similar context. The importance of the former site is that it has begun to reveal for the first time a clear picture of the so-called Kulli culture, with massive monumental structural remains, and all the signs of incipient urbanism. It is greatly to be regretted that it has not proved possible to continue this work. Balakot is equally important and in some ways quite unexpected. The mound lies a short distance from the modern seashore, and doubtless anciently was still nearer. There are some 12 m of occupation for the early period. From the start a dominant element of the pottery is painted in characteristic polychrome Nal style. In the upper levels of the period this is more or less completely replaced by pottery whose affinities are with the Early Harappan period of the Indus valley, particularly with Amri IC and D. Four radiocarbon dates from this period give calibrated dates of between 4000 and 2900 B.C. There is thus a suggestion that even before the ensuing Harappan occupation at the site its relations shifted from the interior of Baluchistan towards the Indus valley. Nevertheless, Dales has remarked that there is an impression of continuity running through the whole period, while there is equally a clearly marked break before the reconstruction of the settlement in Mature Harappan times. There is therefore a striking contrast between the evidence found at Nindowari and at Balakot. Continuing work by the Danish expedition in the Persian Gulf, notably at Bahrain, indicates significant trade contacts between the Kulli sites and that region, although only slight evidence for such trade, curiously, seems to have been discovered at Balakot.

In the previous chapter we mentioned the emergence of a Baluchistan 'province' of ceramic decoration. We can now take this discussion further in relation to the evidence outlined above. The first decorative designs, as at Mundigak I, soon blossom into more complex patterns, including quite elaborate geometric motifs, as in the Quetta ware or the pottery of Mundigak III (Fig. 6.4). Already friezes of cattle and other animals occur in north or central Baluchistan showing a measure of stylistic evolution, as in the Rana Ghundai 'bull' pottery or the Togau ware. Stylized plant motifs, particularly the *pīpal* leaf, occur as well as less obvious plant and bird motifs. The art of pottery painting seems to have reached its peak in these regions in the late fourth and early third millennia, with the graceful fish or animals of the polychrome Nal ware, the naturalistic friezes of animals or *pīpal* leaves of Mundigak IV, the 'Animals in landscape' motifs of Kulli ware, recalling the 'Scarlet' ware of Diyala and Susa in southwest Persia, and many more. The whole of this development shows strong Iranian parallels, and many of the patterns and motifs can – in a general, rather than a precise way – be paralleled in Iran. Indeed, in broadest terms, the Baluchi style of pottery appears as a regional development. It is also interesting to wonder whether any of the designs were shared in the decoration of textiles. It is often striking to find in modern carpets motifs recalling those used anciently in Baluchistan.

The Early Indus period

Around the middle of the fourth millennium B.C. a development which is of profound importance seems to have begun throughout virtually the whole Indus system. One is aware of a spread of settlements, doubtless resulting from a growth of population caused by, and centred upon, the vast possibilities of agricultural productivity which were opened up by exploiting the flood plains of the Indus system. This first settlement of the Indus plains, when viewed from the Indian subcontinent, marks an event of great cultural significance.

Also characteristic of these new settlements is a convergence of traits of material culture suggestive of the sort of cultural unification which will appear in the succeeding Indus civilization. It is scarcely yet possible to say how far this process was accompanied by the maintenance of separate regional traditions, though this is to be expected. We shall make our survey broadly on a regional basis, trying to consider a representative site in each region, and in the conclusion attempt some sort of general synthesis of the evidence.

The first region for consideration includes Lower Sind and the edges of the Indus delta.

The southern group of sites is that associated with the type-site of Amri. The settlements still rise for the most part well above the flood plain of the Indus, and are found in tributary valleys, as is the site of Othmanjo Buthi; or on piedmont ground, situated between the western hills and the plain. Amri is notable both because it was here that Majumdar, by his excavations of 1929, first demonstrated the existence of a pre-Harappan phase laying beneath the Harappan culture, and because some thirty years later, the excavations of the French team directed by J.-M. Casal provided a much clearer picture of the stages of this change. The ancient settlement lies within a mile of the river Indus, on the right bank, near the edge of the alluvial plain (Fig. 6.10).

The Early Indus occupation of Amri is divided into two periods, the first being further sub-divided into four phases. In the earliest of these (IA) no structures were discovered, but it yielded a number of ditches, buried storage jars and other pottery. Most of the pottery was handmade, a few sherds having bichrome and many others monochrome decoration, including motifs recalling the Togau c ware and thus probably contemporary with Anjira III–IV (Fig. 6.11). Fragments of copper and bronze, a chert-blade industry and a number of stone balls (perhaps slings or bolas stones) completed the assemblage. The second sub-period followed without any break, and contained two phases of mud-brick buildings, with bricks of irregular sizes and, in some instances, footings of stone. The pottery constitutes a definite development from that of the earlier phase and includes a wide range of painted motifs. However, the chert blades and bone tools continue. The third phase (IC) represents the high point of the Amri culture and contains no less than four structural phases. Houses are built of both mud-brick and stone, and a curious feature is the presence of multiple cellular compartments about a metre square which seem to have served as grain stores or as platforms, probably to raise buildings above ground level. The pottery now includes a majority of wheel-thrown vessels, and shows a wide variety of painted motifs, mainly geometric, in both plain and polychrome styles, with brown or black, and ochre or orange-upon-pink (Fig. 6.12). The range of forms is a direct development from the earlier phases. The other categories of the material culture, bone points, stone blades, etc., continue. The final phase of the first period is represented by only one building level and a continuation of the essential features of the culture. From this period comes a beautiful painted sherd with a humped Indian bull, while another painted vessel has a row of quadrupeds, two of which appear to be caprids and one a carnivore, perhaps a cheetah or a dog.

In discussing the external affinities of the Amri culture we must regret the paucity of radiocarbon datings and base our estimates upon cross-dating to other excavated sites (Fig. 5.17). The earliest phases (IA–B) provide links with Anjira III, Kili Ghul Muhammad III and IV, and Mundigak III: while phase ID gives comparisons with the upper levels of Mundigak III and Anjira III and IV. Two plausible radiocarbon dates for periods IB and C respectively give dates around 3540 B.C. and 3240 B.C. The presence of a few sherds of Harappan pottery in phase ID and the further correspondences with Kot Diji (to be discussed below) are significant. Period II at Amri follows without any cultural break, but after a

6.10 Amri: view of Indus from the top of the mound

general levelling and reconstruction of the site. It is divided into two phases, A and B, and is characterized by an increasing presence of sherds of Harappan type alongside the Amrian. It may thus be regarded as transitional between the purely Amrian culture of I and the Mature Harappan of III. From period II the cross-datings of pottery are with Mundigak IV.I and Damb Sadaat II, and more especially with Kot Diji and sites of the Indus valley proper. There is a suggestion that the site was burnt at the end of the period.

A number of sites have been identified as belonging to an equivalent Early Indus, Amrian phase. In the south, on a promontory which in those days was probably on the coast, although now far inland behind deltaic formations, is the fortified settlement of Tharro (Tharri Gujo). Another fortified site is at Kohtras Buthi, south-west of Amri. To the north lie other small sites such as Pandi Wahi

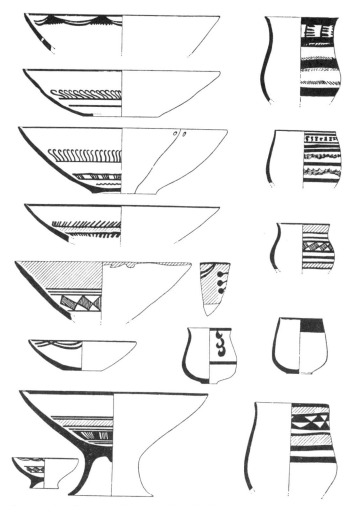

6.11 Amri: painted pottery from period IA (1:6) (*after* Casal)

and Ghazi Shah. West of Tharro, Allahdino has been recently excavated by Fairservis and his colleagues. The main settlement is of the Harappan period, and relatively little can be said of the earlier occupation.

About 160 km north-east of Amri, on the left bank of the Indus, today some twenty miles from the river, but still near one of its ancient flood channels and thus close to the agriculturally productive land, lies Kot Diji. The ancient site is located on the solid ground below a small rocky outcrop, which forms part of the limestone hills of the Rohri range (Fig. 6.13). The site was excavated between

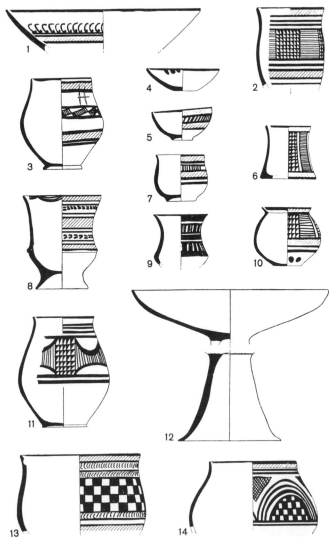

6.12 Amri: painted pottery: 1–10 and 12, period 1B; 11, 13 and 14, period 1C (1:6) (*after* Casal)

1955 and 1957 by the Pakistan Archaeological Department, and the published results are of great interest, although they leave many questions unanswered. The first settlement was constructed upon bed rock, while immediately above were discovered house floors, contained within a massive defensive wall of which the lower courses were of limestone rubble and the upper of mud-brick. The wall was strengthened by bastions and preserved in places to a height of 4–5 m. Whether the inhabitants were defending themselves against the fury of the flood-waters (there seems to be some evidence to suggest this) or human or animal intrusion – or indeed all of these – is unclear. Within this great wall there were some 5 metres of occupation deposit, the lower portion being excavated only in a restricted area. Throughout the upper 3 m, house walls of stone and mud-brick occur, and it is probable that further excavation below this level would reveal similar structures. The material culture included a chert-blade industry with some serrated blades, and other blades bearing 'sickle gloss'. A small number of leaf-shaped arrowheads suggest parallels with Periano Ghundai I and Mundigak II–V. Stone querns, pestles, balls (corn-crushers, sling or bolas stones?), and at least one fine terracotta bull were found. It is not clear whether there were any objects of copper, but a fragment of a bronze bangle is reported. The pottery was of a distinctive character with a restrained use of painted decoration (Fig. 6.14). It was mainly wheel-thrown, and much of it was decorated with plain bands of dark or brownish paint. An interesting motif appears to have developed from bands of loops and wavy lines into the well known fish-scale pattern which later appears on Harappan pottery. As in Amri II, in the later levels of Kot Diji I many characteristic Harappan forms occur. The excavators report a clear typological evolution of the principal forms throughout the period. Of the painted pottery one may note the common bichrome with

6.13 Kot Diji: view of excavations (*courtesy* Department of Archaeology, Government of Pakistan)

a cream slip and red-, sepia- or black-painted decoration; parallels for this ware are found in Mundigak III.5 and IV. A small number of vessels had distinctive painted motifs. The roughening of the outward surface of some vessels is reminiscent of Anjira III–IV and Damb Sadaat II–III.

The early occupation of Kot Diji closes with evidence of two massive conflagrations and is replaced with a mixed but predominantly Harappan culture. The date of this event, carrying with it as it does the suggestion of violent overthrow and conquest, is suggested by the radiocarbon evidence. The Early Indus occupation yielded three samples; one from near the beginning of the settlement gave a date of 2880 B.C.; and two others from nearer the top, 3180 and 2700 B.C., respectively. A fourth date of 2520 B.C. corresponded with the second great conflagration. The comparison of the pottery of Amri and Kot Diji should provide an all-important check on their relative ages. There is little doubt that Amri IA–C is earlier than the beginning of Kot Diji. Parallels between Amri ID and IIA and B, unfortunately not well represented in the excavations, and Kot Diji, are more numerous. However, even here there is considerable individuality in the two assemblages. The suggestion is clearly that in Early Indus times there were fairly marked divergences in potting tradition between these two sites.

About 50 km west of Kot Diji, on the right bank of the Indus, lies Mohenjo-daro, now some three miles from the river, but squarely on the flood plain. The continuing deposition of alluvial silt with each year's floods has raised the whole land surface in this area more than 10 m since Harappan times, and as the water table has risen correspondingly, archaeologists have so far been unable to plumb the lower levels of this vast site. It is tempting to speculate that here, too, beneath the Harappan occupation there may lie an Early Indus culture corresponding to that of Kot Diji. Support for this may be found in such pre-Harappan features as surface-roughened ware reported in the lowest levels reached by Mackay. Further support is probably to be found in the results of the borings conducted in the HR area by Dales and Raikes. Here occupation deposits were encountered to a depth of 39 feet below the modern level of the plain. In the same way at Chanhu-daro Mackay reported further occupation levels below the water table and speculated that these too might well contain a pre-Harappan, or Amrian culture.

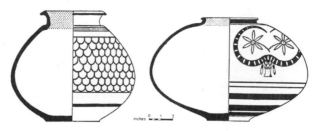

6.14 Kot Diji, 1: Early Indus pottery (*after* F. A. Khan)

The current excavations at Mehrgarh, to which we referred in the previous chapter, have also yielded a clear sequence for this period. We have discussed Mehrgarh periods I–III in the previous chapter. The settlement seems to have become consolidated in the southern part of the site around the middle of the third millennium, and the four final periods (IV–VII) are stratified one above the other. Until now, comparatively little has been known of these periods. Their chronology has been established mainly on the basis of the comparisons of pottery with other sites. Thus period IV shows affinities with Damb Sadaat I and the ealiest stages of Amri I, with fine wheel-thrown pottery with monochrome, bichrome and polychrome decoration (Fig. 6.15). Of peculiar interest, because of what is to follow, is the discovery of female figurines in terracotta, reminiscent

6.15 Mehrgarh, period IV: polychrome goblet (*courtesy* Jarrige)

of examples from Namazga III and Kara Depe in Central Asia, and also of early Rahman Dheri. This level also produced the first stamp seals in terracotta, and a single bone seal. Much domestic debris is reported, including thousands of cereal husks, so we may expect more information to be forthcoming as the study of this material proceeds. A number of ring stones, and further examples of stone blades set in bitumen in wooden handles to form sickles are also recorded, as well as a copper chisel. The succeeding period v is still comparatively little known. It produced a painted grey pottery reminiscent of the Zari ware of Kalat; a developing series of female figurines, also with parallels to the north in the sites of the Derajat plain (see below); and further examples of stamp seals. The third phase, period vi, shows parallels with Mundigak III, Shahr-i Sohkta I, Damb Sadaat II and Amri IIA. It is relatively much better documented than the previous period, and among the architectural remains a huge mud-brick plat-form was discovered. A large quantity of pottery, much of typical 'Quetta' style was discovered, including the so-called 'Faiz Muhammad' grey ware, with various decorative designs including some examples of the use of *pīpal* leaf and fish motifs. The so-called 'Quetta Wet ware' becomes very common. There is still a stone-blade industry but it appears to have become relatively less com-mon, stone leaf-shaped arrowheads occur, and many beads are found including lapis lazuli. Special features of this period are terracotta compartmented seals, and large numbers of figurines, both male and female, with elaborate hair styles (Fig. 6.16a). These recall an example found by Fairservis in Damb Sadaat II.

The final period on the southern mound at Mehrgarh is relatively well known as a larger area has been excavated. There are mud-brick houses and indications of buildings used for specialized craft activities. The pottery of this period shows a development of the relationships of the previous period, that is to say de-veloped 'Quetta' characteristics of Damb Sadaat III, relations with Mundigak IV and Shahr-i Sokhta II, and, most significantly, elements of early Kot Diji and Amri IIB are in evidence. Thus we see alongside the continuing and parallel development with that of the Quetta valley a new tendency towards a 'Kot Dijian' character. This evidently coincides with the development of a new, interprovincial style throughout a large part of the Indus system. The produc-tion of terracotta figurines, both male and female, continued on a large scale (Fig. 6.16, b–c). Hundreds of these were found, still with elaborate hair styles, but now much closer to the well known 'Zhob' figurines of Quetta and north Baluchistan. A small percentage of figurines from this level show an unexpected naturalism, a feature also seen in some specimens from Mundigak IV. Seals of terracotta continue. Among the plant remains recovered and already identified are wheat and barley and large numbers of grape pips. The stone-blade industry, including several new artefact types, among them leaf-shaped arrowheads, and bead drills persisted to the end.

The extended Mehrgarh sequence continues in the neighbouring mound of Naushahro, excavated during the late eighties, where period IA represents the

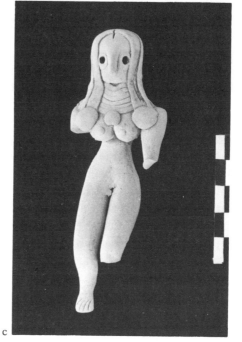

6.16 Mehrgarh: terracotta figurines: a, period VI; b–c, period VII (*courtesy* Jarrige)

final stage of the pre-urban Early Indus culture, followed by IB, a stage which is truly transitional between the Early and Mature Harappan. This in turn leads to two further phases of the Mature. The last of these takes us up to the end of the mature urban phase and provides links to the post-urban cemeteries referred to below (p. 233).

Mehrgarh thus forms a wonderfully documented sequence through from earliest times to the end of the Mature Indus stage. Among the developing styles of its material objects the terracottas stand out. The oldest human figurines (in unbaked clay) go back to periods I and II (sixth and fifth millennia), while the first baked clay animals occur in period III. But it is particularly in periods IV–VII that a remarkable evolutionary series begins, starting with the stick-headed figures of IV, and developing through the elaborate coiffure of period VI to the 'late' Zhob types of period VII. The sequence continues with the highly distinctive male terracottas of Naushahro IB, and the typical Mature Harappan types of the succeeding phase. This series provides an interesting opportunity for cross–dating to the terracottas of less well dated sites elsewhere in Baluchistan, and to the much less complete series from sites in the Dera Jat.

Further evidence of the Early Indus period comes from a number of sites in the area known as the Dera Jat, that is, the western plains of the Indus, particularly in Dera Ismail Khan and Bannu districts. In the former we have already mentioned the excavation at Gumla. Far more important, when it is published, will be the current work at nearby Rahman Dheri. This is a large mound, which on the aerial photograph shows an extraordinary regularity of plan. It appears to be a well laid out oblong, surrounded by a massive wall and divided into two by a street running north-west to south-east. At right angles to this road, houses, divided by regularly laid out, straight narrow lanes, are visible. The current Peshawar University excavations have revealed three phases of occupation, corresponding approximately to Gumla II–III. The excavations indicate that the surrounding mud-brick town wall and probably also the basic layout of the streets go back to the very beginning of the occupation, which we may expect to date to the first half of the fourth millennium (Fig. 6.17). So far, four radiocarbon dates are available, and these confirm the evidence of cross-dates based on the painted pottery and terracottas. Two samples show that the early period dates between 3340 and 3160 B.C., while two others confirm that the Early Indus period at Rahman Dheri dates from around 2600–2480 B.C. The settlement is approximately 550 by 400 m, providing an area of 22 hectares, and suggesting a population of around 12,000 persons. As such it probably antedates any of the town plans known from elsewhere in the Indus valley.

The early period shows a regionally distinctive painted pottery tradition, closely reminiscent of Gumla II. In the two succeeding periods this is gradually modified and supplemented by an increasing element of pottery identical to that of Kot Diji. That the early period may be expected roughly to equate in time with Mehrgarh IV is indicated by a number of factors. A remarkable square bone seal, engraved with scorpions on either side of a female figure with drawn-up legs on one side, and two goats on the other, dates from this period (Fig. 6.18). Beads include lapis lazuli and turquoise. Grains of wheat and barley are reported, as well as bones of cattle, sheep and goat. The stone-blade industry appears to have been a major source of tools for the population, but copper and bronze tools also occur. Again there are many terracotta figurines. Those of the early period have curious stick-like heads. in marked contrast to their well-modelled breasts and torsos, and are paralleled at Gumla and in Mehrgarh iv. In the two succeeding periods these develop in a distinctive way, forming a major stylistic difference from those of the Quetta–Mehrgarh region.

Very large numbers of graffiti occur on the pottery of all periods at Rahman Dheri. The excavators have questioned whether these may not be the forerunners of the Harappan script. This excavation, when it is published, should provide very valuable evidence for the Early Indus period in the Dera Jat.

Exploration in the Bannu basin, one hundred miles to the north, has revealed a group of sites which appear to parallel those of the southern Dera Jat. One site, Lewan Dar Dariz, was excavated in 1977–8, and shown to be a huge factory site manufacturing great numbers of specialized stone tools, including perforated

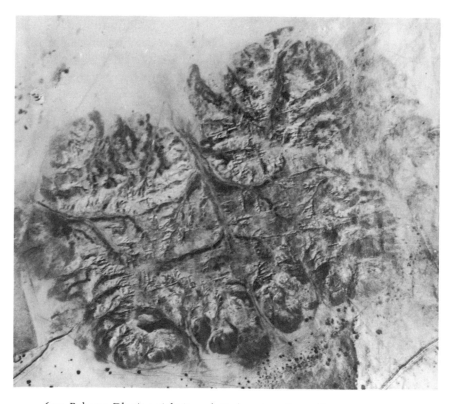

6.17 Rahman Dheri: aerial view of site (*courtesy* Durrani)

ring stones, ground stone axes, hammers and querns from locally available materials (Figs. 6.19–20). Here also were found the typical grinding grooves on portable stones used in the production of ground stone axes. There was also a prolific stone-blade industry. The painted pottery shared many elements with that of Rahman Dheri, including fish and *pīpal* leaf motifs. However, in its later stages it resembled more closely the Kot Dijian style. Terracotta figurines largely parallel those of Rahman Dheri (Fig. 6.21). It seems probable that the largest of the Bannu sites so far reported, Tarakai Qila, is similar to, though somewhat smaller than, Rahman Dheri (10 hectares only, compared with 22 hectares). However, both of these sites, with their major mud-brick defensive walls, are indicative of an incipient urbanism developing in this area in the centuries preceding the beginning of the Mature Indus phase.

At both Rahman Dheri and Lewan there is evidence, in the form of turquoise and lapis lazuli beads, of continuing trade links with Central Asia. Links are also suggested by the appearance of a type of female terracotta figurine, which has striking parallels with some known from Namazga Tepe in Turkmenia. As yet, no intensive studies of economic interaction of the kind recently carried out at Tepe Yahya or Shahr-i Sokhta have been made in Pakistan, and this is something which will clearly produce important results. For example, at Lewan, near Bannu, there is evidence of the careful exploration and importation of suitable rocks and stones for a number of specialized crafts – making ground stone axes, ring stones, as well as microliths, and beads. The raw materials are mainly locally available, although some, such as lapis lazuli, were not. It is evident that the special products of this site, including such heavy items as querns, must have been exported for sale to communities on the Indus plains which were far removed from sources of raw material.

6.18 Rahman Dheri, early period: bone seal (8:5) (*courtesy* Durrani)

6.19 Lewan: stone axes

6.20 Lewan: ring stones

With the publication of Tarakai Qila, the information concerning Early Indus agriculture will be substantially augmented. The period produced massive samples of seeds and grains, among which so far identified are several varieties of wheat and barley, lentils (*Lens culinaris*) and a field pea (*Pisum arvense*). Here too, cattle, water buffalo, sheep and goat are reported. Many examples of microliths or stone blades with silica gloss add support for grain harvesting (Fig. 6.22).

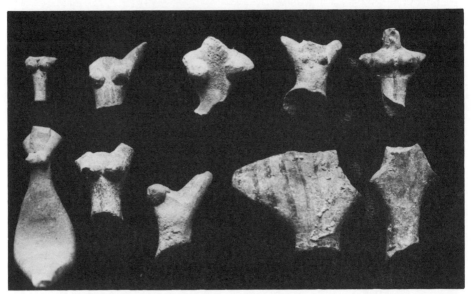

6.21 Lewan: terracotta figurines

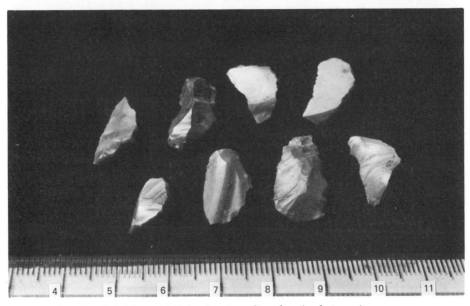

6.22 Tarakai Qila: microliths showing silica gloss (scale in cm)

We have already referred to the early settlement at Sarai Khola, some 240 km north-east of Bannu, in the northernmost parts of the Punjab. Here again the second period witnessed a development which is parallel, if not identical, to those we have been discussing. In the earliest part of the period pit dwellings were observed in the sections, thereafter presumably replaced by mud brick structures. Kot Diji style pottery becomes predominant indicating the influence of the pervasive early Indus style. C14 dates indicate a span of *c.* 2600–2200 B.C. for this period (Figs. 6.23–24). The stone industry continues, with microliths, celts, chisels, etc. The number in most of these categories, however, is small, even if greater than in period I. There are, for example, eleven ground stone axes in period II. The main change is the appearance of metal objects

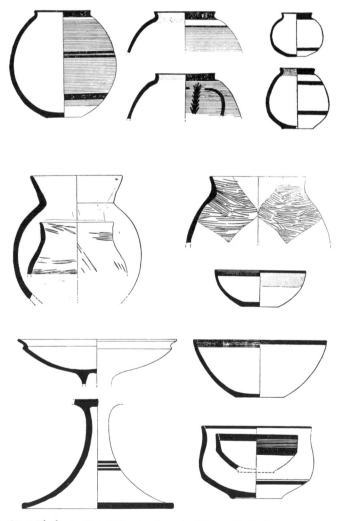

6.23 Sarai Khola, II: 'Kot Dijian' pottery (1:6) (*after* Halim)

(including tools), absent in period I. They all appear to be of copper, and include bangles, rings, pins, rods, etc. Beads include one of lapis lazuli, and disc beads of steatite paste make their first appearance. Terracotta figurines include seated females of distinctly similar appearance to those of the Dera Jat sites, as well as animals. Several other sites of this period are reported from this area.

Related developments seem to have extended very widely. Pottery was discovered by Wheeler during his excavations at Harappa in 1946, in stratified positions under the Mature Indus defences, in the earliest structural level and among the mud-bricks of the rampart. He drew the inference that this pottery represented a 'non-Harappan' or pre-Harappan culture phase, but in the light of Kot Diji and Kalibangan it can be seen that, in all probability, he had stumbled on part of the brick rampart of an Early Indus settlement at Harappa itself. It therefore seems legitimate to add Harappa to the list of sites, and to expect further excavation at the great citadel mound to reveal a brick-walled settlement analogous to those of Kalibangan and Kot Diji.

In the southern Punjab, at Jalilpur, there seems to be evidence for a similar development during the Early Indus period. There is no break in the sequence, but rather a gradual evolution, witnessed by the increase in characteristically Kot Dijian pottery, and by the appearance of the first metal objects. Recent exploration has been carried out by Rafique Mughal of the Pakistan Archaeological Department in the Cholistan, the desert belt south of Bahawalpur, marked by the dried-up beds of the Ghaggar–Hakra river courses. A similar sequence to that farther west appears to be represented widely at sites in the area, many well preserved by the desert and by the absence of later human activities.

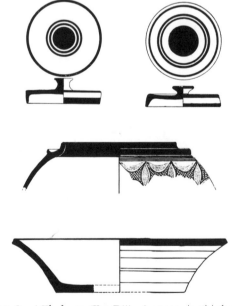

6.24 Sarai Khola, II: 'Kot Dijian' pottery (1:6) (*after* Halim)

Following this river course north-eastwards into the territory of modern India, further important developments may be assigned to the same period. At Kalibangan, on the bank of the now dry Ghaggar river, about 200 km south-east of Harappa, and 480 km east-north-east of Kot Diji, nine seasons of excavations were undertaken with impressive results by the Archaeological Survey of India from 1959 onwards. Unfortunately, only short summaries have as yet been published in *Indian Archaeology* and elsewhere. The Early Indus settlement which was situated beneath the Harappan citadel mound, as at Kot Diji and Harappa, consisted of five building phases (Fig. 6.25). Again, as at Kot Diji, the data so far published give us little information regarding house plans. However, throughout these five periods at Kalibangan, both dried brick and stone were used, domestically and for town walls. At this same site there appears already to have been a standardization of brick sizes, and although the ratio (3:2:1) differs from that of the Mature Harappan period, it clearly suggests the way in which the Early Indus anticipates what is to follow (Fig. 6.26). The settlement at Kalibangan was surrounded by a massive rampart, also of mud-brick. Just as at Kot Diji the exact reason for this – defence against floods, humans or animals – cannot now be determined. This tradition however, once established, continues

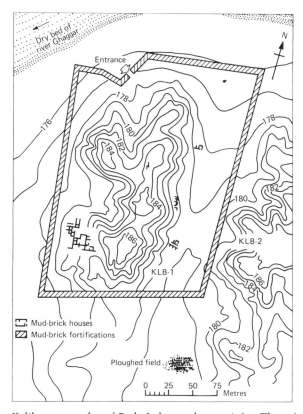

6.25 Kalibangan, I: plan of Early Indus settlement (*after* Thapar)

into the Harappan period. Pot-like hearths were found in the rooms, and one house contained a series of ovens, both above and below ground. A feature of the material culture was a stone-blade industry, with some serrated blades. Shell bangles, steatite disc beads and beads of various other materials were found. Copper and bronze were rare, but copper objects included a bangle and several flat axes.

The pottery of this early period at Kalibangan is varied and of great interest (Figs. 6.27 and 6.29). The range of forms and painted motifs differs quantitatively from those of either Amri or Kot Diji, although a proportion shares an important element, particularly with the latter. As at these sites some features anticipate the Harappan ware, including the presence of such forms as the offering stand. The predominant pottery (Fabric A) is red or pink with black, or bichrome black and white painting. Among the painted motifs may be noted a distinctive arcading, a 'moustache-like' bifold scroll also found at Kot Diji, as well as occasional plants, fish and cattle. A number of features anticipate the Harappan Wares, such as the internal incised decoration upon bowls, and offering stands. One group of pots of Fabric B shows a surface roughening technique somewhat similar to the Quetta 'Wet' ware, but sometimes overpainted with animal or other motifs. Another group (Fabric D) has elaborate incised or combed decora-

6.26 Kalibangan: Early Indus settlement (*courtesy* Archaeological Survey of India)

tion on the inside of open bowls or basins, a technique seen occasionally in Amri II (Fig. 6.28). On the whole the pottery of Fabric A is distinct, while that of Fabrics B, C, D and E is closer to that of the Early Indus pottery of Kot Diji, both in point of manufacture and of painted decoration – mainly in the form of plain bands of red and black. One of the most remarkable finds of this period was a ploughed field surface with furrows in two directions. The significance of this is discussed in a later chapter (Fig. 6.30, and see p. 192). An extensive series of radiocarbon samples has been obtained from Kalibagan, those from the 'pre-Harappan' or Early Indus period ranging from 2920 to 2550 B.C. A cluster of six, between 2550 and 2440 B.C., gives dates for the beginning of the Mature Harappan period provocatively close to that obtained at Kot Diji.

In his tour of exploration of 1950–1, Ghosh discovered many sites in the

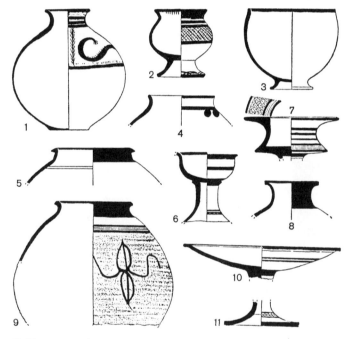

6.27 Kalibangan: Early Indus pottery: 1–4 fabric A; 9 fabric B; 5, 7, 8, 10 and 11 fabric C; 6 fabric E (1:8)

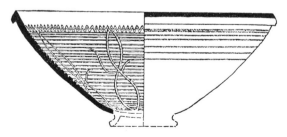

6.28 Kalibangan: Early Indus bowl, fabric D (1:8)

valley of the Ghaggar (Sarasvati) river and its tributary, the Chautang (Drishad-vati) just as Mughal was to do later, further west. They produced a pottery which was apparently identical to the pre-Harappan pottery of Kalibangan. This complex he named the Sothi culture, but so far little has been published concerning it, and it remains a somewhat shadowy entity. However, recent exploration by

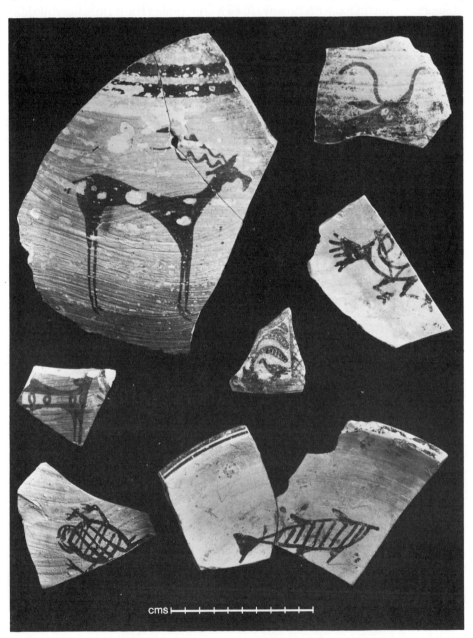

6.29 Kalibangan: Early Indus painted pottery (*courtesy* Archaeological Survey of India)

Mrs K. F. Dalal has revealed further sites and clearly established the existence of an Early Indus complex extending right up to the frontier and closely paralleling that reported by Mughal in Pakistan Cholistan.

Yet further east, in the plains of the Indo-Gangetic divide, we enter a rather different region, in which an Early Indus culture phase can be recognized, even if in a rather different form. The main sites in this region are Banawali, in the dried-up Sarasvati valley, excavated in 1974 by Bist, of the Haryana State Archaeological Department; and Siswal and Rakhigarhi, to the south in the Drishadvati valley, discovered and excavated by Suraj Bhan of Kurukshetra University. These sites show close affinities to period 1 of Kalibangan.

We have already introduced the concept of varying stylistic provinces in relation to ceramic decoration. We can now take this idea one step further, for in the regional variants of the Indus system we encounter a further province, which is characterized by several elements. On the western borders there is considerable Baluchi influence, while on the eastern there is the development of a style which for the moment we may refer to as 'Eastern Indus'. During the Early Indus period the painted wares from sites in the Dera Jat, such as Gumla and Rahman Dheri, show individual character which differentiates them from contemporary Baluchistan. Alongside polychrome patterns there are occasional

6.30 Kalibangan: field surface with furrow marks of Early Indus period (*courtesy* Archaeological Survey of India)

figural representations, and symbolic subjects, including examples of bull's and buffalo's horns with accompanying *pīpal* leaves, and remarkable fish motifs. Slightly later, these sites share the more austere painting of the central Indus sites, as represented by Tarakai Qila in Bannu, and by Kot Diji and early Harappa. In all these, plain bands of black or red occur with occasional wavy lines, either singly or in groups. Thus it appears as though there is a development still related to Baluchistan, but increasingly removed from it. On the eastern periphery, Kalibangan shows a somewhat similar combination of the austere style with other elements. The buffalo-horned head or 'deity' is common to all three areas, as are flower-petal motifs, fish, cattle and repeated arches or arcades, often with dissecting, wavy or diagonal lines. There are also clear anticipations of elements of the following Mature Harappan style, including the distinctive 'fish scale' motif.

Conclusion

With so many of the major sites that we have just reviewed still largely unpublished, and with so many of the excavations themselves only partly published, it is still impossible to make an analysis, or fully to comprehend the meaning of this Early Indus period. We can, however, at least go some way in this direction. Throughout the whole Indus plain regular agricultural settlements, based on wheat and barley, and domestic cattle, sheep and goats, began to appear during this period. These settlements had regularly constructed houses, often with surviving traces of town walls, and some of considerable size. While they still relied on stone for some purposes – for blades and bead-borers for instance – they also used copper, and probably bronze. Copper objects are reported regularly from the excavated sites of the Early Indus period, though they are not plentiful. There is as yet no clear evidence of when the use of tin, or some other alloy for the production of bronze, first occurred. In many areas these Early Indus settlements can be traced back to an earlier, sometimes Neolithic stage, and in those crafts where local fashions had already appeared, such as pot making, these antecedent traces often remain visible. Indeed, the pottery of the entire Indus system from the late fourth and early third millennia B.C. may be said to belong to a single craft province, closely related to that of Baluchistan. Although direct archaeological evidence is still wanting, a technological examination of many of its products permits us to infer that it was predominantly made on the footwheel. Archaeological evidence confirms that kilns were made with separate fire and kiln chambers. Only on the eastern and northern borders, for example at Kalibangan or in Swat, do we encounter evidence of contact with a separate eastern province, with markedly different craft traditions.

Despite this, however, it is clear that during the Early Indus period a striking new development begins to exert itself. The strongly local, regional character of, for example, Balakot or Mehrgarh or early Rahman Dheri begins to be replaced by a new style of relatively less artistic painted decoration. This style we may call Kot Dijian, since this site was the first where it was clearly identified, though we do not as yet know where it first developed, nor why and how it did so. But with its appearance we begin to find throughout the whole extent of the Indus system, from Balakot in the south-west to Sarai Khola in the north or Kalibangan in the north-east, a tendency towards a more unified style. This tendency, whatever it means, is likely to be a reflection of greater communication and trade between the communities spread out across the Indus plains, and to indicate a resulting process of cultural convergence. This same tendency reaches its apogee in the subsequent Mature Indus period. Because this Early Indus period corresponds with the Early Dynastic of Mesopotamia and the most affluent period of such Iranian sites as Shahr-i Sokhta, we may expect, and indeed evidence is forthcoming to confirm these expectations, that there would have been an unprecedented increase in trade with these regions.

The process of cultural convergence and the increase in homogeneity that we have mentioned above is also evident in the realm of ideology and religious beliefs. The terracotta mother goddesses of the early period continue at most sites, although in some cases they become increasingly rare as the Mature Indus period approaches. However, a more dramatic example of this convergence is seen in the appearance upon pottery of painted designs representing a horned head, which, as the horns are those of the buffalo, we may name the Buffalo deity. Representations have been found at Kot Diji, Burzahom, Gumla, Rahman Dheri, Sarai Khola and Lewan. That it anticipates the horned deity of the Mature Indus period seems beyond doubt. An incomplete example from Sarai Khola has a plant growing between the horns; at Kalibangan a similar plant appears beside a horn on another incomplete sherd, and again on a triangular terracotta cake from the Mature Indus period, between the horns of an anthropomorphic figure (Fig. 6.31). At Kot Diji the whole head is clearly visible, with two six-petalled flowers rising between the horns. Similar flowers occur on pots at Kalibangan. At Lewan, the incomplete head has three *pīpal* leaves rising between the horns. *Pīpal* leaves appear as motifs quite frequently on pottery at this period. The Lewan pot, however, has another horned deity on the opposite side, and this one is more or less complete (Fig. 6.32). Here the horns are those of the *Bos indicus*, and we may call it, by extension, the Bull deity. This has a group of six *pīpal* leaves rising between the horns. It seems reasonable to infer that there were already certain associations of buffaloes and cattle with a horned deity or deities, and that they anticipate the horned deity of the Mature Indus religion. It is also clearly possible to see that these ideas continued to exert their influence on Indian folk religion down to modern times, and that the Early Indus period is in every way part of the continuing growth of Indian civilization.

From all these things we conclude that, whatever the changes which occurred between the Early and Mature Indus stages and however they are to be accounted for, the Early stage must be seen as the formative period, the stage of

6.31 Kalibangan, Mature Indus period: terracotta cake incised with horned deity (*courtesy* Archaeological Survey of India)

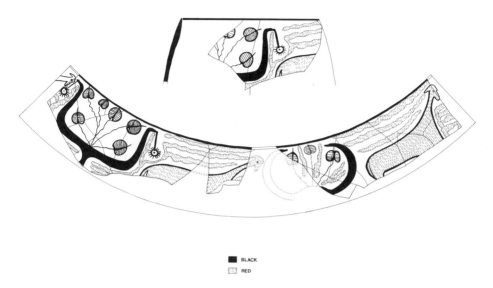

BLACK
RED

6.32 Lewan: polychrome painted pot showing heads of buffalo and *Bos indicus* with *pīpal* leaf decoration)

incipient urbanism. The current excavations at Naushahro are providing striking new evidence of the actual transition to the Indus civilization. Their further publication is eagerly awaited. The essential basis for the mature urbanism must be seen as the gradual build-up of population, and its spread through the Indus plains (a process now seen to be as old as the first settlement at Mehrgarh); the growth of technology and agricultural know-how; and the establishment of a socio-economic interaction sphere over an enormous area. These things are all to be deduced to have reached their fulfilment during the Early Indus stage.

CHAPTER 7

THE MATURE INDUS CIVILIZATION – 1

It has been remarked that books on the prehistory of India and Pakistan are often Indus valley centred. If this be true, it is understandable, for until recently the Indus civilization occupied the centre of our knowledge. The past decades have changed this, and we venture – at the risk of erring in the other direction – to try to put the civilization in a better perspective. Its importance is still, however, unique, both because it represents a great and astonishing cultural achievement and because it may be seen as the formative mould for many aspects of classical and even modern Indian civilization. The preceding pages have shown how the stage is set in the Indus valley and Punjab and how there is a direct cultural continuity between the Early and Mature Indus periods. It is in the light of this that we may now proceed.

We remarked in the previous chapter that at the beginning of the Early Indus period there was a marked spread and increase in population. This probably resulted from the successful control and exploitation of the tremendously productive agricultural potentialities of the Indus plain. The basic geographical determinants of the region remained constant, and therefore in almost every case the earlier sites remained in occupation. However, this increased pressure of population meant that not only did settlements expand, but that many new ones were founded. Our present dating evidence – either sequential or absolute – does not, however, permit any certain conclusion to be made concerning the rate at which the Harappan culture expanded, nor of where the new culture traits first evolved, other than within the Indus valley itself. There is indeed, some evidence, both at Mohenjo-daro and Harappa, of a general cultural evolution, but the earlier excavations of Vats and Marshall are not helpful on this point. What is, however, clear is that the Harappan cities in magnificence and size represented the culmination of a steady development. After the Harappan period the society of the Indus system as a whole, however much depressed during unsettled periods of its development, was never to return to the uncomplicated simplicity of earlier times.

We must admit that we are still very much in the dark as to what were the causes of the many changes which took place between the style of the Early or incipient urban phase, which we discussed in the previous chapter, and the Mature Indus style. The search for some area outside the Indus system from which to derive the latter ready made to supersede the Early Indus style appears to be a chimera. At base the one must have evolved out of the other in the Indus valley itself, implying a continuity of population and technical skills, and probably recognizable more by the introduction of such important innovations as writing and all the implicit concomitants of political, administrative and social organization. This process of evolution is everywhere apparent in the basic aspects of the culture, the pattern of settlements, crops and agricultural life, and in the basic crafts involved. It is sometimes less obvious in the 'super-structural' aspects of life, although even here it is present in many important features. If it be objected that the changes in style from Early to Mature Indus rule out the possibility of such continuous evolution, we would reply that the Mature style was the special product of the cities which lay at the core of the whole society, and that the changes were an intrinsic part of the actual emergence of the cities themselves.

We have already mentioned the environment of the Indus valley and the opportunities it offered once the annual inundation had been understood. There is no convincing evidence of any drastic change in climate during the past four or five millennia in this region. Thus, while it is reasonable to expect a slightly higher rainfall throughout the area before the natural vegetation cover was reduced by man's steady intensification of agriculture and grazing, no major shift in climate need be postulated. A vital necessity of settlement in the Indus plain itself would have been flood defence, and here it seems that burnt-brick must have played an important role. For, in these areas where stone was not readily available (and this includes the majority of Harappan sites) mud-brick would have been rapidly destroyed by rain or flood water. Thus the discovery and utilization of burnt-brick was one factor. It has sometimes been suggested that the Indus valley could not have produced sufficient timber for this oper-ation unless the climate were damper than today. However, Lambrick, writing with many years of administrative experience of Sind, has shown that timber growing along the riverine tracts today is sufficient for all the burnt-bricks made in the province, and anciently cannot have been less abundant.

Extent and distribution of sites

The area enclosed by a line joining the outermost sites at which the material culture of this civilization has been discovered is little less than half a million square miles, considerably larger than modern Pakistan (Fig. 7.1). Within this area over seventy sites are known, of which the great majority lie on the plains of the Indus and its tributaries, or on the now dry course of the Hakra or Ghaggar river which once flowed to the south of the Sutlej and then southwards to the east of the Indus, with the Thar desert on its left bank. Outside the Indus system to the west a few sites occur on the Makran coast, the farthest being Sutkagen Dor near the modern frontier of Pakistan and Iran. These were probably ports or trading posts situated in an otherwise separate culture region, for the uplands of Baluchistan appear to have been outside the Harappan zone. To the east of the

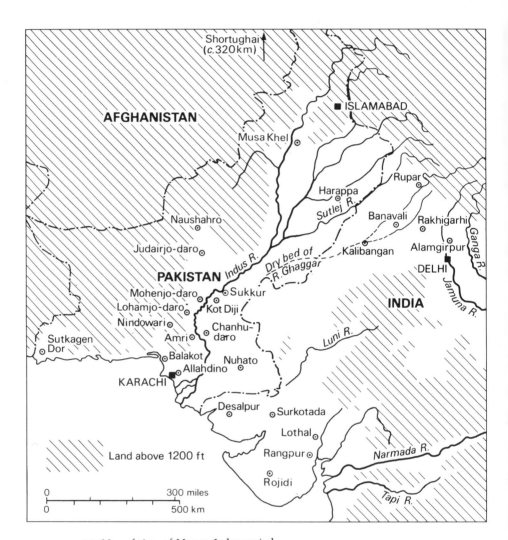

7.1 Map of sites of Mature Indus period

Indus further sites occur on or near the coast beyond the marshes of Cutch (Kacch), the most impressive being the trading post at Lothal, on the gulf of Cambay. Among recent discoveries the most remarkable is the Harappan site at Shortughai on the south plain of the Oxus in north-eastern Afghanistan. This appears to be an isolated colony, doubtless exploiting the trade in lapis lazuli from the neighbouring mines of Badakshan, and perhaps other materials such as copper. The large quantity of excavation data now available, in contrast to the preceding period, enables us to study the evolution of patterns of settlement – and leading on from that, the study of interregional relationships. This enables us to put all these excavation data into perspective. It is worth stressing once more that in the past, as today, in addition to the normal range of sites of different size and importance by which any cultural phase is always represented throughout the Indian subcontinent, distinct cultural groups at very different levels must be envisaged as living in more or less close proximity to one another. The inhibitions and the stimuli provided by the interrelationship of these groups are factors which the archaeologist can never afford to lose sight of, and to which we must return again and again.

Of all the excavated Harappan sites two stand out, both on account of their size and of the diversity of the finds that excavations have revealed. These have generally been hailed as cities, the twin capitals of this extensive state. It is perhaps hardly necessary to mention that this glib sentence conceals the cold archaeological truth that to date there is no positive evidence that the cities were 'capitals', either of separate 'states' or of a unified 'empire'. For any society lacking written records, or whose script is still undeciphered, evidence of such matters as political conditions is clearly hard to come by, and is at best inferential. Generations of archaeologists have felt that some such interpretation better fits the Harappan evidence than any other, but necessarily it remains hypothetical. The reader must therefore draw his own conclusions from the available data: the apparent conformity of weights and measures, the common script, the uniformity – almost common currency – of the seals, the evidence of extensive trade in almost every class of commodity throughout the whole Harappan culture zone, the common elements of art and religion. Even if the political and economic unity is admitted, there remain the profound and tantalizing problems of how it came about and how it was maintained. These have yet to be tackled satisfactorily.

The southern city is Mohenjo-daro, on the right bank of the Indus. Here the Indian Archaeological Survey under Marshall, and later Mackay, excavated between 1922 and 1931; after the partition of India and Pakistan in 1947 further work was done by Wheeler, and more recently by Dales. In all these excavations the bottom of the Harappan occupation has never been reached, let alone the level of the first settlement, because, as we have already seen, the alluvial deposition of the centuries has raised the level of the plain by more than thirty feet, and the water table has risen correspondingly. The second and northern city is Harappa on the left bank of a now dry course of the Ravi in the Punjab. The vast mounds at Harappa were first reported by Masson in 1826, and visited by Cunningham in 1853 and 1873. Their rediscovery some sixty years later led to the Archaeological Survey's excavations between 1920 and 1934, directed by Vats. A short but important further excavation was made in 1946 by Wheeler; the natural soil was reached and evidence of a pre-Harappan culture phase revealed. In the earlier excavations of both these sites a mass of information was obtained relating to their planning and architecture, and much material relating to arts and crafts and to the way of life of the people was recovered. However, the excavations prior to 1947 did not achieve a satisfactory picture of the development of the cities, and in the absence of radiocarbon dating no absolute chronology was obtained.

A second series of sites have in some cases features which recall the basic layout of the cities, and although smaller, they may reasonably be regarded as provincial centres of government. Among them several have been excavated. Most recent of these is Kalibangan, where extensive excavations of the Harappan township took place in the 1960s. From the viewpoint of technical excellence this work does credit to the Indian Archaeological Survey: we greatly regret however that its publication has been so delayed. Kalibangan shares with Harappa and Mohenjo-daro the layout of citadel and lower town, and it has produced a series of radiocarbon datings. At Kot Diji the excavators also treat the site during the Mature Indus phase as comprising a citadel and outer town of Harappan style. It was excavated in 1955 and 1957. Other large sites which may also be included in this category are Sandhanawala in Bahawalpur and Judeirjo-daro in Sind, north of Jacobabad, but these have not as yet been excavated, nor has the great mound at Dabarkot in the Loralai valley of north Baluchistan, apart from trial trenches made by Sir Aurel Stein. Farther south in Sind are Amri and Chanhu-daro, the former on the right and the latter on the left plains of the Indus. The French excavations revealed much interesting information at Amri and have shown not only the pre-Harappan development, but also three distinct phases of Harappan occupation, as well as an immediately post-Harappan period. Chanhu-daro was excavated in 1935–6 by Mackay and produced a great deal of interesting material relating to the two latter periods.

Among other excavated sites we may mention Sutkagen Dor on the Makran coast, where Stein dug some trial trenches. More recently Dales has shown the existence of a great fortification around this Harappan outpost. Another important excavation of the post-war period has been that at Lothal, where the Indian Archaeological Survey's team under the direction of S. R. Rao revealed a great artificial platform with streets and houses of regular plan, and a series of building phases which have been dated by a number of radiocarbon samples. Besides the township was discovered a remarkable brick basin, probably used to provide a fresh water supply. Two other smaller sites excavated in recent years are Rojaidi in Saurashtra, and Desalpur in Cutch. Both provide evidence of an initial occupation in the Harappan period, and of continuing occupation during post-Harappan times. More important is the excavation at Surkotada, also in Cutch, where three stages of Harappan occupation are in evidence. In southern Sind and Baluchistan two small Harappan sites have recently been excavated at Allahdino by Fairservis, and at Balakot near Las Bela, by Dales. Several sites have been reported or excavated in the eastern borderlands of the Indus system. Among these are Mitathal, excavated in 1968 by Suraj Bhan, Banawali excavated by Bisht, and Rakhigarhi, a large twin mound on the old Drishadvati river bed. Finally mention may be made of two outlying sites at Rupar in the Punjab, and at Alamgirpur in Uttar Pradesh outside the Indus system, and indeed east of Delhi. At several of these sites excavations have shown the presence of Mature Harappan and Late Harappan settlements. The extension of the civilization eastwards towards the Ganges–Jamuna Doab raises various interesting possibilities, which call for further elucidation.

As a result of more than fifty years of excavations, there is a great body of evidence relating to the life of the civilization which gave rise to them. Our overwhelming impression is of a sophisticated and highly complex society whose hallmark is, nevertheless, cultural uniformity – both throughout the several centuries during which the Harappan civilization flourished, and over the vast area it occupied. This permits us to infer from the larger and better known sites the common features of architecture and planning of the smaller and less well known. Unfortunately, little attention has hitherto been paid to this last category, and much remains to be learnt of the village communities which may be expected to have formed the basis of the Harappan system, as indeed they always have in India. Similarly, far too little is yet known about the nomadic or semi-nomadic communities who must have then as now lived on the periphery of the plains, breeding cattle and other livestock, and no doubt providing transport for trade and communication. At the present moment we have no idea how much of the population was centred upon the cities, and how much was dispersed through the villages.

Town planning and settlement types

This uniformity, probably reflecting the imposition of a superimposed pattern, is nowhere clearer than in town planning (Fig. 7.2). The basic layout of the larger settlements, whether cities or towns, shows a regular orientation. At Harappa, Mohenjo-daro and Kalibangan, this consists of two distinct elements: on the west a 'citadel' mound built on a high podium of mud-brick, with a long axis running north–south, and to the east – apparently broadly centred upon the citadel, and dominated by it – a 'lower' city, consisting of what must have been in the main residential areas (Fig. 7.3). Probably the latter was originally more or less square. The citadel certainly, and probably also the lower town, was surrounded by a massive brick wall. At Kalibangan traces have been discovered of

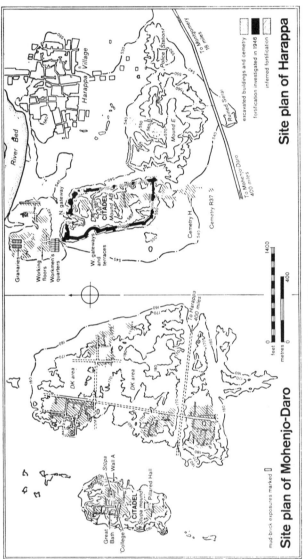

7.2 Outline plans of Mohenjo-daro and Harappa

the remains of massive brick walls around both the citadel and the lower town. The citadel in particular had square towers and bastions. An entrance was set into the main line of the north wall, and there was another from the south. The principal streets at best were laid out with controlled skill (although at Mohenjo-daro they are not in precise alignment) and the widest streets appear to have run across the lower city from north to south. At Kalibangan the roads on the east–west axis only partly run across the whole town, some being staggered from block to block; and the same feature, at least in part, is repeated at Mohenjo-daro. There appears also to have been a general co-ordination of measurements of the streets, the largest being twice the width of the smaller, and three or four times that of the side lanes. The imposition of this new layout on the older, Early Indus settlement at Kalibangan, with its haphazard disposition, dramatically emphasizes the suddenness and completeness of the change. The general population probably lived in the blocks in the lower town, while on or beside the citadel mound were buildings of a civic, religious or administrative status, including perhaps granaries.

The layout of the settlement at Lothal – a site of intermediate size – was in some respects different, perhaps because of the different role that it played as a Harappan trading station. The site was nearly rectangular, with the longer axis running from north to south (Fig. 7.4). It was surrounded by a massive brick wall, probably as flood protection, as the site is situated on low-lying ground near a tributary of the Sabarmati river. Along the east side of the settlement was a brick basin, 219 by 37 metres in length, with extant brick walls of 4.5 metres in height (Fig. 7.5). It is claimed by its excavator to have been a dockyard, connected by channels to the neighbouring estuary. A spill-way and locking device were apparently installed to control the inflow of tidal water and permit the automatic desilting of the channels. On its edge the excavator discovered several heavy pierced stones, similar to the modern anchor stones employed by traditional seafaring communities of West India. This interpretation, however, has been challenged, and indeed the published levels of the basin and its entrance relative to the modern sea level seem to argue against it. Leshnik has cogently suggested that it was a tank for the reception of sweet water, channelled from higher ground inland to an area where the local water supplies were anciently, as still today, saline. We regard either interpretation as still unproven, but favour the latter. Beside the basin was a massive brick platform which ran along the entire eastern side of the town. The south-eastern quadrant abuts this area, and takes the form of a platform of brick and earth filling, rising to a height of about 4 metres, and perhaps serving a similar function to the citadels of the cities, either as simple flood defence, or to provide added security for the food and materials stored there, or even perhaps to provide added prestige for the ruling group. An important part of the raised platform contained further brick platforms intersected by ventilating channels, representing perhaps the foundations of warehouses or granaries comparable to those of the other sites. The overall

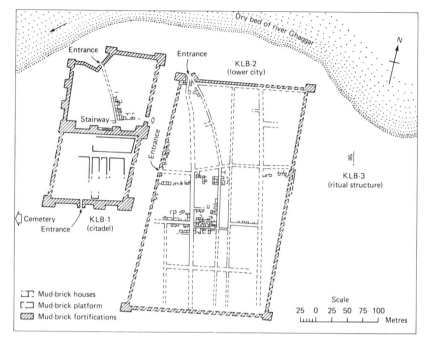

7.3 Site plan of Kalibangan, II (*after* Thapar)

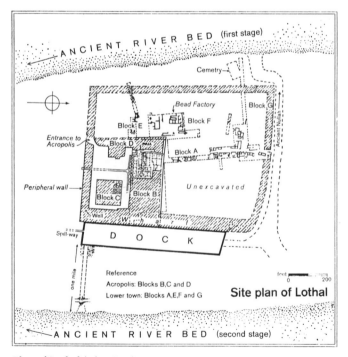

7.4 Plan of Lothal (*after* Rao)

dimensions of this block were 48.5 by 42.5 metres. Evidently there were other buildings on the platform, for a row of twelve bathrooms and drains was discovered there. The remaining three-quarters of the town seems to have been the principal living area, divided by streets of 4 to 6 metres in width and narrower lanes of 2 to 3 metres. The main street ran from north to south. In this area numerous traces of specialists' workshops were found, including copper and goldsmiths' shops, a bead factory, etc.

Another recently excavated Harappan site is at Surkotada in Cutch, where a small settlement was discovered (Fig. 7.6). This settlement was surrounded by a stone rubble fortification with square bastions at the corner and in the centre of the longer sides. The area enclosed comprised two oblongs each of roughly sixty metres. The western square represented the original settlement and when this had risen to some height it was augmented by the 'lower' half.

Throughout the Harappan structural crafts there appears to be a uniformity similar to that noted in town planning. There is a standardization of brick sizes, both of burnt- and mud-bricks, and this too is in basic contrast to that of the Early Harappan period. The skill of the bricklayers is particularly clear in the great public buildings of the citadel complexes – for example, in the great bath at Mohenjo-daro, and in the granaries at both Mohenjo-daro and Harappa. On the other hand, one cannot but be struck by the regularity of the plain, undecorated brick-work of the acres of uniform houses of the lower town at Mohenjo-daro.

7.5 Lothal: brick basin, sometimes referred to as a 'dockyard' (*courtesy* Archaeological Survey of India)

This is a notable feature at many other Harappan sites – particularly in the 'lower' cities.

The most usual material throughout was brick, both burnt and sun-dried. The latter was used at Mohenjo-daro mainly for fillings, but at Harappa it sometimes alternated with burnt-brick course by course, and at Kalibangan it seems to have been if anything more common, burnt-brick being almost exclusively reserved for wells, drains and bathrooms. The predominant brick size was 28 by 14 by 7 cm, that is a ratio of 4:2:1. The bricks were mainly made in an open mould, but for special purposes, such as bathrooms, sawn bricks were invariably used, and wells were constructed with wedge-shaped moulded bricks. The flooring of houses was either beaten earth, or sun-dried or burnt-brick. In some bathrooms a sort of plaster of brick dust and lime was reported. Worked stone was rarely employed structurally, and the true arch was not used, but the corbelled arch in brick is frequent. Certain pieces of worked stone suggest segments of pillars, but it is not clear whether these were ever employed structurally. Hammer-dressed limestone slabs, however, are occasionally found covering brick drains. Probably such blocks were quarried with the assistance of copper chisels and stone hammers, which had been specifically designed for this work. Transport of such blocks would have required exacting teamwork. Timber was used for the universal flat roofs, and in some cases the sockets indicate square-cut beams with spans of as much as 4 m. In certain rare instances timber also seems to have formed a semi-structural frame or lacing for brickwork.

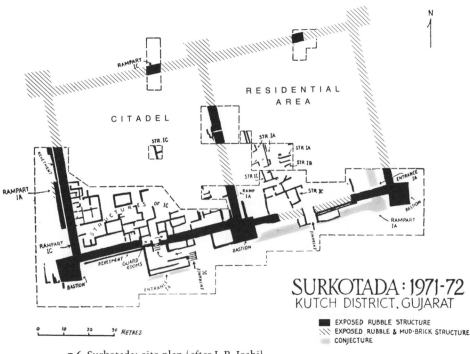

7.6 Surkotada: site plan (after J. P. Joshi)

Considerable variation is seen in the size of dwellings, which range from single-roomed tenements to houses with courtyards and upward of a dozen rooms of varying sizes, to great houses with several dozen rooms and several courtyards. Nearly all the larger houses had private wells. A recent study by Sarcina shows that the great majority of the houses at Mohenjo-daro conform to one of five basic modules, depending mainly on the position of the courtyard (Fig. 7.7). Several of these basic types can be found widely among village houses in Pakistan and West India to this day. In many cases brick stairways led up to what must have been upper storeys or flat roofs. Hearths are commonly found in the rooms. Almost every house had a bathroom, and in some cases there is evidence of bathrooms on the first floor. The bathroom is indicated by a fine sawn brick pavement, often with surrounding curb, and by its connection by a drainage channel to chutes built in the thickness of the wall, giving access to the main street drains. A number of pottery drainpipes was also found. Mackay has shown that many of the smaller examples of these fine brick pavements in fact

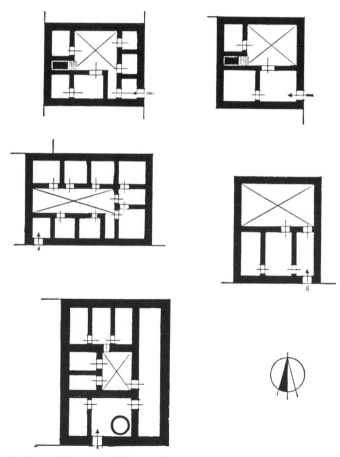

7.7 Mohenjo-daro: typical house plans (*after* Sarcina)

represented privies, and that the chutes for these are vertical as against the sloping chutes of the baths.

The entrances to the houses were from the narrow lanes which were set at right-angles to the main streets (Figs. 7.8–9). A distinctive feature of the construction was thus that the roadward side of a block presented a plain blank facade broken only where drainage chutes discharged. The houses seem often to have been built with an oblong perimeter wall, and adjacent houses were separated by a narrow space of 'no man's land'. If the general batter of the brickwork in the walls be allowed for, this interstice would grow wider with the height of the walls.

One other feature of the lower city deserves comment. Many of the lanes and streets had brick drains, covered over by bricks or sometimes stone slabs, into which the house drains flowed, while others led directly into large soak pits or jars. The street drains were equipped with manholes, and sometimes flowed into soakage pits, but nothing is known of their final discharge on the edge of the city. Altogether the extent of the drainage system and the quality of the domestic bathing structures and drains are remarkable, and together they give the city a character of its own, particularly in its implication of some sort of highly effective municipal authority. It may be noted in passing that privies and drains of identical kind may be found in many modern towns of North India and Pakistan, and were also built in cities of the early centuries of the Christian era.

7.8 Mohenjo-daro: plan of part of lower city (HR area)

There are some barrack-like groups of single-roomed tenements at Mohenjo-daro which forcibly recall the rows of tenements beside the granary at Harappa. These must belong to a much poorer class than the houses with a courtyard and many rooms. The lower town must also have contained a wide range of shops and craft workshops: among these potters' kilns, dyers' vats, metal-workers', shell-ornament-makers' and bead-makers' shops have been recognized, and it is

7.9 Kalibangan: view of street (*courtesy* Archaeological Survey of India)

probable that had the earlier excavators approached their task more thought-fully much more information would have been obtained about the way in which these specialists' shops were distributed through the settlement. Another class of building to be expected in the lower city is the temple. Wheeler has argued convincingly that one building in the HR area of Mohenjo-daro which com-prised a monumental entrance and double stairway, leading to a raised platform on which was found one of the rare stone sculptures – of a seated figure – may be identified as a temple. Several other buildings of unusually massive character, or unusual plan, have also been tentatively identified in this way. A major project is currently under way to study the architecture and utilization of the excavated structures of Mohenjo-daro. This work is being conducted by a German team, and may be expected to add greatly to our knowledge of these aspects.

We may well wonder what would have been the population of these cities. Lambrick has made a convincing case for a figure of 35,000 at Mohenjo-daro, based upon comparison with the population of a city of comparable area in Sind in 1841. An independent estimate by Fairservis suggests a slightly higher figure (41,000). As Harappa appears to have been of roughly equivalent size, its popu-lation may well have been more or less the same, but Fairservis has suggested a figure of 23,500 for the lower city at Harappa, excluding the citadel.

Turning to the buildings of the citadel mounds, or their vicinity, we encoun-ter a series of major structures of a very different character (Fig. 7.10). Their special nature is emphasized by the great podia of brick or mud-brick and earth filling upon which they stood. The floods which at Mohenjo-daro devastated the lower city several times probably provide the *raison d'être* for the citadel mounds. The great brick embankment, some 13 m in height, which ran round the platform at Mohenjo-daro must also have served the same purpose, and is no doubt the counterpart of the massive defensive wall which surrounded the Harappan citadel.

Perhaps the most remarkable feature of the citadel mound at Mohenjo-daro is the Great Bath (Fig. 7.11). This finely built brick structure measures 12 m by 7 m, and is nearly 3 m deep from the surrounding pavement. It is approached at either end by flights of steps, originally finished with timber treads set in bitumen. The floor of the bath was constructed of sawn bricks set on edge in gypsum mortar, with a layer of bitumen sealer sandwiched between the inner and outer brick skins. Water was evidently supplied by a large well in an adjacent room, and an outlet from one corner of the bath led to a high corbelled drain disgorging on the west side of the mound. Surrounding the bath were porticos and sets of rooms, while a stairway led to an upper storey. The signi-ficance of this extraordinary structure can only be guessed. It has been generally agreed that it must be linked with some sort of ritual bathing such as played so important a part in later Indian life. If so, it must mean that this part of the citadel was connected with civic–religious life.

Immediately to the west of the bath excavation has revealed an equally remarkable group of twenty-seven blocks of brickwork criss-crossed by narrow ventilation channels. Wheeler interpreted this structure as the podium of a great granary (akin to that of Harappa, although of somewhat different design), and believed that below the granary were the brick loading-bays from which corn was raised into the citadel for storage. This interpretation is not proven, and further investigation is called for. What does seem certain, however, is that the brick platforms were part of a building of civic importance. Around the bath on the north and east were other large blocks of buildings which may be inferred to

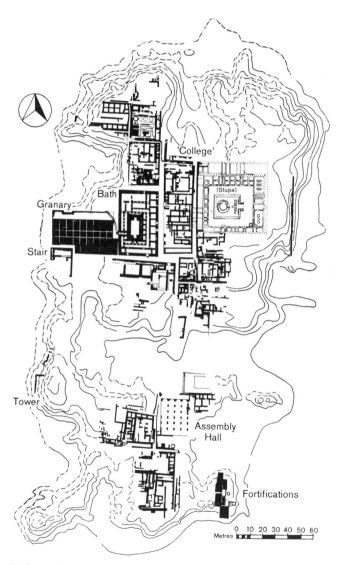

7.10 Mohenjo-daro: plan of citadel

be associated with the group of administrators (perhaps priests) who controlled not only the city but the great empire which it dominated. Further excavation on the south of the citadel mound may corroborate this view. Here an oblong assembly hall was unearthed having four rows of five brick plinths upon which no doubt wooden columns were erected. The floor between these plinths was of finely sawn brick-work, recalling that of the bath. In the complex of rooms immediately to the west a seated male statue in stone was discovered, and nearby a number of large worked stone rings, possibly pieces of architectural masonry but more probably part of a ritual stone column. These finds recall those associated with the reputed temple in the lower city, and probably indicate the presence of a temple in this part of the citadel.

The citadel mound at Harappa is comparatively much less well known, both because it has been less excavated, and because it is more disturbed by subsequent occupation and depredation. However, immediately to the north, between it and the old river bank, lies an area of ground of comparable interest to the citadel at Mohenjo-daro. Here was another series of brick platforms which constituted the basis for two rows of six granaries, each 16 m by 6 m, lying within a few yards of the river's edge (Fig. 7.12). The combined floor space of the twelve units must have been something over 800 square metres, approximately the same area as that of Mohenjo-daro. To the south of the granaries was an area of working floors consisting of rows of circular brick platforms, evidently for

7.11 Mohenjo-daro: the Great Bath

threshing grain: wheat and barley chaff were found in the crevices of the floors. Immediately below the walls of the citadel were two rows of single-roomed barracks, recalling the smallest dwellings in the lower city at Mohenjo-daro and artisans' or slaves' quarters in such sites as Tel-el-Amarna in Egypt.

The smaller citadel mound at Kalibangan has not yet been fully excavated, but it shows a number of corresponding features. In the southern part are brick platforms, while the northern, separated by a wall with a narrow entrance reached on either side by steps, contained ordinary houses. Both parts were approximately square and measured 120 metres along each side. The brick platforms are separated from each other by narrow brick-paved passages. Their surfaces had been damaged, but on one there was a row of seven of the distinctive 'fire altars', found also in the houses of the lower town, as well as a brick-lined pit containing animal bones and antlers, a well head and a drain (Fig. 7.13). There seems to be little doubt that this complex marked a ritual centre where animal sacrifice, ritual bathing and perhaps also the cult of sacred fire took place. The main entrance to the southern part was from the south via a broad flight of steps, while the northern residential section was entered by a doorway in the north-west corner. In the light of this extraordinarily interesting discovery, we may wonder whether the brick platforms beside the Great Bath at Mohenjo-daro may not have had some similar ritual function rather than have served as the bases for granaries.

Trade

In the Harappan culture the elaborate social structure and the standard of living must have been maintained by a highly developed system of communication and trade. How far trade supplied basic essentials such as food, and how far it was simply a means of obtaining luxury goods is a question of importance. However, there can be no question that with the inception of the full urbanism of the Mature Indus period the volume of trade and interaction, both within the Harappan economic circle and without it, must have increased in scale and variety to a quite unprecedented extent.

In some cases common products were distributed throughout the state. From the limestone hills at Rohri and Sukkur (Sakhar) came nodules of fine flint and finished flint blades which were worked at vast factory sites nearby. Thence they were imported, no doubt by river wherever possible, to form a uniform item of equipment at Harappa, Mohenjo-daro, Lothal, Rangpur, Kot Diji and Kalibangan (Fig. 8.3). At Rangpur they are present only in period IIA and are replaced by tools made of local stones in the subsequent period. In the same way Balakot, near Las Bela on the coast of Baluchistan, and Chanhu-daro were centres for shell-working and bangle-making; Lothal and Chanhu-daro were centres for the manufacture of beads of carnelian, etc.

It may be confidently assumed that many other specialist products, such as

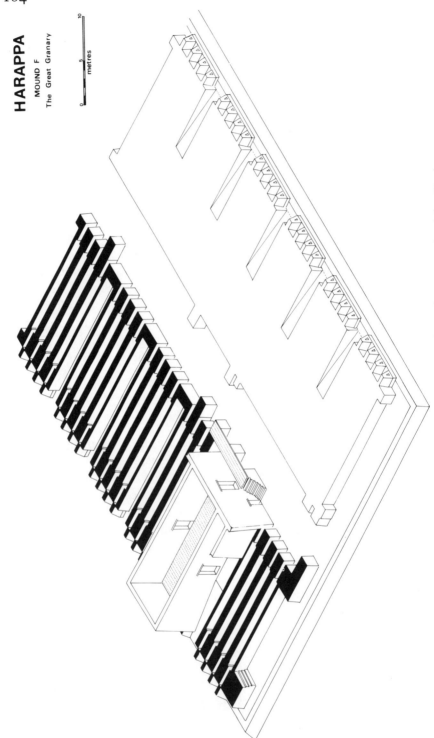

HARAPPA
MOUND F
The Great Granary

0   5   10
metres

7.12 Harappa, the granary: isometric projection showing conjectural partial reconstruction (*after* Vats)

weights, seals, copper artefacts, etc., were equally much the work of craft groups in the cities, and were disseminated in similar fashion throughout the Harappan state. A glance at the finds from Mohenjo-daro will suffice to recognize the presence of specialized groups of craftsmen – potters, copper- and bronze-workers, stone-workers, builders, brick-makers, seal-cutters, bead-makers, faience-workers, etc. Other groups are implicit – scribes, priests, adminis-trators, sweepers, farmers, caravan-leaders and, of course, traders.

Trade in the Indus valley implies, as in Mesopotamia, a regulation of ex-change and of weights and measures. Sir John Marshall remarks upon the extraordinary profusion of stone weights at Mohenjo-daro, and the system of weights has been analysed in some detail by Hemmy. The weights proceed in a series, first doubling, from 1, 2, 4, 8 to 64, then going to 160; then in decimal multiplies of sixteen, 320, 640, 1600, 3200, 6400, 8000 (i.e. 1600 × 5) and 128,000 (i.e. 16,000 × 8). The measures of length were based upon a foot of 37.6 cm and a cubit of from 51.8 to 53.6 cm. The use of writing must also have been essential. There can be little doubt that the Harappan seals were (at least as one of their functions) necessary elements in the mechanism of trade. The seals carry two principal kinds of information: first there is an animal, often before an object which is, perhaps, either a manger or a standard, and second is an

7.13 Kalibangan: row of 'fire altars' on brick platform in citadel area (*courtesy* Archaeological Survey of India)

inscription varying from one or two to a dozen or more ideograms (Figs. 8.15–17). The script has unfortunately still to be deciphered, but it has been proven that it was written from right to left. Many of the seals appear to carry numerals as a part of their information. An interesting context is established for their use in applying clay sealings to bales of merchandise from impressions of cords or matting which are not infrequently found on the backs of such sealings. Further proof of this use is derived from the discovery of several such sealings lying among ashes in the ventilation shafts of the brick platform of what is considered to have been a granary or warehouse at Lothal. How the exchange was regulated is not yet apparent, but it is easy to picture Lothal as being an outlying trading post of the Harappan state. To reach it implies either a journey by sea down the Indus and around the coast of Saurashtra, or by land. The goods must have included such objects for internal consumption as the stone blades, and perhaps even seals, and also beads and other items for trade or exchange with the barbarian people who lay outside the empire. Again they must have carried back to Mohenjo-daro and the urban centres objects of trade or raw materials derived from the coastal provinces or from neighbouring territories. Although there is plentiful evidence that the Indus merchants or caravan-leaders carried their trade far beyond the frontiers of the empire, and established contacts with other peoples, either still in a state of barbarism or belonging to contemporary civilizations, yet they also had another function – that of linking together the city and the countryside. This function has long been an important factor in Indian life and culture.

Of the less civilized groups with whom the traders were in contact we can form some impression by a study of the raw materials imported into Mohenjo-daro. Gold was almost certainly an import, and the presence of clusters of Neolithic settlements contemporary with the Harappan civilization around the goldfields of north Karnataka suggests an important source. Silver was imported, probably from Afghanistan or Iran. The sources of copper may have been several: predominantly the ore came from the vicinity of Khetri in Rajasthan; other sources were perhaps South India towards the east, and Baluchistan and Arabia to the west. Lead may have been derived from either East or South India. Lapis lazuli, though rare, can only have come from the region of Badakshan in north-east Afghanistan; turquoise from Central Asia or Iran; fuchsite from north Karnataka; alabaster could have come from a number of sources both east and west (but the large-scale manufacture of alabaster vessels in contemporary Shahr-i Sokhta suggests the probable source); amethyst probably came from Maharashtra; agates, chalcedonies and carnelians from Saurashtra and West India; jade from Central Asia.

A dramatic indication of the extent of such Harappan trading activity, even beyond its own frontiers, has come with the discovery of a small settlement or colony in north-east Afghanistan, at Shortughai. This site is situated not far from the lapis lazuli mines of Badakshan, and the large quantities of lapis discovered at the site clearly show that it was one reason for the establishment of this Harappan trading outpost, beyond the high passes of the Hindu Kush.

Of trade with other civilized states, notably with the cities of Mesopotamia, there are two kinds of evidence, archaeological and literary. Of the former we may list objects imported from the Indus and exported in return. The most convincing sign of the presence of Indus merchants is the discovery of some two dozen seals, either actually Harappan, or copying Harappan, or of intermediate 'Persian Gulf' types, from Susa and the cities of Mesopotamia (see below, pp. 217–20). Of actual imports, the certain origin is often not easy to determine, but carnelian and etched carnelian beads, shell and bone inlays, including some of the distinctly Indian 'kidney-shape', leave little room for doubt. From the Indus the reciprocal evidence is even less sure: only three cylinder seals of Mesopotamian type from Mohenjo-daro, all probably of Indian workmanship, and a small number of metal objects suggesting Mesopotamian origin. It is probable therefore that the trade included many objects of less durable kind, cotton, spices, timber, etc. A more definite indication of foreign trade comes from Lothal where a circular button seal of a distinctive kind was discovered (Fig. 7.14). This belongs to a class of 'Persian Gulf' seals known otherwise from excavations at the port of Bahrain, and also found occasionally in the cities of Mesopotamia, notably at Ur. The Persian Gulf sites such as Bahrain and Failaka near Kuwait were beyond doubt entrepôts for sea trade between Mesopotamia and outlying regions, and these seals therefore provide very convincing evidence of some sort of trade activities. Also from Lothal come bun-shaped copper ingots, which may be compared with ingots found on the Persian Gulf islands and at Susa.

The literary evidence from Mesopotamia helps to fill in the gaps in the archaeological record. It shows that in the time of Sargon of Agade and during

7.14 Lothal: seal of 'Persian Gulf' type (*after* Rao)

the succeeding centuries, merchants particularly from Ur carried on trade with various foreign countries. Among those mentioned most frequently are Tilmun, Magan and Meluhha. The first is now fairly confidently identified with Bahrain and must have served largely as an entrepôt. The second, reputed as a source of copper, has been sometimes identified with Oman or some other part of South Arabia, although the similarity of its name to the modern Makran coast certainly tempts one to locate it in Baluchistan; and the third is now generally identified with India, the region of the Indus river, Mohenjo-daro or Saurashtra. Comparison of the name with the Sanskrit word *mleccha*, barbarian, is suggestive. We learn of Tilmun merchants residing in Ur, of a Meluhha village (apparently a village in which families of merchants from Meluhha lived in Mesopotamia), and once at least of an official interpreter of the Meluhhan language in the period of the empire of Akkad. We hear also of boats of Meluhha. Among the imports from Meluhha are various kinds of timber, including a black wood identified as ebony, copper of a quality different from that of Oman, gold, a red stone identified as carnelian, of which were made monkey- and kidney-shaped beads, and ivory, of which were made multi-coloured birds and combs. Pearls are often mentioned, but their Meluhhan source is not specified. It can be argued that these imports could have originated in Africa, and that the absence of cotton, although this seems to have been known as an import at Ur, is significant. However, we feel that probability favours India as the source of all these items.

The discussion of trade focuses attention upon methods of transport. Several representations of ships are found on seals or as graffiti at Harappa, Mohenjo-daro (Figs. 7.15–16), etc., and a terracotta model of a ship, with a stick-impressed

7.15 Mohenjo-daro: representation of ship on a stone seal (length 4.3 cm) (*after* Mackay)

socket for the mast and eyeholes for fixing rigging, comes from Lothal. We have
seen above that the great brick tank, interpreted by Rao as a dock at Lothal,
cannot yet be certainly identified. The evidence of sea trade and contact during
the Harappan period is largely circumstantial, or derived from inferences from
the Mesopotamian texts, as detailed above.

Of the inland travel on the plains there is plentiful evidence from terracotta
models of bullock-carts, to all intents and purposes identical with those of
modern times (Fig. 7.17). Further, cart-tracks were found on the roads of the
cities which indicated that the wheelspan of the Indus carts was also little
different from that of their modern descendants. From Harappa and Chanhu-
daro come copper or bronze models of carts with seated drivers, and also nearly
identical models of little carts of the modern 'ikka' or 'ekka' type, still common
in the Punjab. These have a framed canopy over the body in which the passenger
sits. For longer journeys and through rougher and more wooded country there
can be little doubt that the chief means of transport would have been by
caravans of pack-oxen. Such caravans continued to be the principal means of
carriage in large parts of the subcontinent until the advent of the railways and
motor traffic. The more recent historical and anthropological evidence is of
particular interest because we learn that the caravan trade was largely conducted by the same communities as the breeders of cattle and the organizers of
the cattle trade. Moreover, Saurashtra and the north Karnataka region are often

7.16 Mohenjo-daro: representation of ship on terracotta amulet (length 4.5 cm) (*after*
Dales)

interlinked among the surviving caravan communities, and this leads one to speculate that already cattle may have been one of the links between the southern Neolithic and the Indus valley. Traditional methods of transport and their organization, as they have been observed and recorded during the past century and a half, leave little doubt of their extreme antiquity. One may question whether other aspects of the trade which was carried on both within India, and by Arab dhows or country boats around the coast, and westwards to the Hadramaut, may not also have followed equally ancient patterns which time has done little to disturb.

Agriculture

In the Mature Harappan period there is a considerable volume of information available concerning animal husbandry and agriculture. It appears to have been extraordinarily like that of recent centuries in the Indus valley. The range of domesticated animals, or of wild animals used for food, is quite large. In addition to sheep and goats there is, as we have seen, repeated evidence of the predomi-nant role of Indian humped cattle. One strain of these is depicted on the Harappan seals (along with a humpless bull of a *Bos primigenius* variety), and is beyond doubt the ancestor of a strain still bred in parts of Western India and Sind

7.17 Mohenjo-daro: terracotta cart

(Fig. 8.15). Zeuner has suggested that the zebu may be descended from *Bos namadicus*, a wild cattle which occurs throughout the Indian Pleistocene, and in this case it is probable that the centre of its domestication may have been in South Asia, just as *Bos primigenius* was probably first domesticated in Western Asia or Europe. Another species whose bones are of frequent occurrence at more than one site is the Indian boar, *Sus cristatus*, which must have been either domesticated or regularly hunted. The buffalo (*Bubalus bubalis*) is another such species, but its bones are less common. Yet more rare are bones of both elephant and camel, but as the former is a fairly common motif upon seals, where it appears to be caparisoned, it may be assumed that the Indian elephant was already domesticated. Camel bones are reported at Kalibangan. Among the birds, bones of the domestic fowl are noteworthy. There is also a wide range of wild animals which were undoubtedly hunted for food: these include the Sambar deer (*Rusa unicolor*), the spotted deer and the hog deer, and several varieties of tortoise. From Amri comes a single instance of the Indian rhinoceros, of interest because it too is depicted on the seals, and remained a native of the Lower Indus valley at least until the fourteenth century A.D. It is perhaps worthy of note that the only plausible evidence of the horse comes from a superficial level of Mohenjo-daro. A terracotta figurine from Lothal is scarcely unequivocal. It is not possible to rule out Zeuner's cautious appraisal of the supposed equine teeth from Rana Ghundai as those of hemiones, and indeed with the present state of evidence it would be unwise to conclude that there is any proof of the regular use of the horse in pre-Harappan or Harappan times.

Wheat is frequently recorded, apparently of two varieties – the club wheat (*Triticum compactum*) and the Indian dwarf wheat (*Triticum sphaerococcum*). Barley (*Hordeum vulgare*), probably of a small-seeded six-rowed variety, is also found both at Harappa and Mohenjo-daro. Both wheat and barley are found at Kalibangan, and indeed these two crops must have been the most important at all Harappan sites. Other crops include dates, and varieties of leguminous plants, such as field peas. Sessamum and mustard were grown – presumably for oil. Unfortunately, no excavation has yet revealed evidence of that typically Indian crop the sugar-cane, though its presence is to be expected. At Lothal and Rangpur (period IIA) rice husks and spikelets were found embedded in clay and pottery. Another find of great interest was a fragment of woven cotton cloth at Mohenjo-daro. The plant belonged to one of the coarser Indian varieties closely related to *Gossypium arboreum*, and the fibre had reputedly been dyed with madder, indigenous in India. The prehistory of a textile industry is necessarily elusive, as so much of the evidence disappears unless climatic conditions favour its survival, but we have already noticed the presence of cotton at Mehrgarh some two thousand years before the finds at Mohenjo-daro. That woven textiles were already common in the Indus civilization, and that the craft for which India has remained famous was already in a mature stage of development, must be inferred from these finds, and from occasional impressions of textiles upon earthenware, pottery and faience from the Harappan sites. A whole class of small faience vessels were evidently formed upon a cloth bag filled with sand or some other suitable substance, leaving the textile impression upon the interior of the pot. The employment of fabric for this and for other equally humble tasks, as in baling goods (evidenced by the cloth impressions upon sealings) surely testifies to its common availability. Whether both cotton and flax were spun, as they were in post-Harappan times in the Narbada valley, is not yet clear.

Lambrick, from his intimate personal knowledge of Sind, has been able to suggest the way in which the various crops would have been grown, and how they exploited the flooding of the Indus. The principal food grains (wheat and barley), would have been grown as spring (*rabi*) crops: that is to say, sown at the end of the inundation upon land which had been submerged by spill from the river or one of its natural flood channels, and reaped in March or April. In modern practice such land is neither ploughed nor manured, nor does it require additional water. Lambrick remarks that 'the whole operation involves an absolute minimum of skill, labour and aid of implements'. It was the first development of this which made possible the development of Indus urbanism. Cotton and sessamum would be sown as autumnal (*kharif*) crops: they would be sown at the beginning of the inundation and harvested at its close, in the autumn. For this fields surrounded by earth embankments would be required, most probably along the banks of natural flood channels. Although this method is more precarious than the former, both exploit the natural fertility of the alluvium, and the annual inundation. Both systems are still in use, and they provide a very convincing explanation of the means by which the Harappans filled their vast granaries; and yet neither of them have left any surviving traces for the archaeologist.

There is as yet comparatively little evidence for the actual tools employed for agriculture. It must be assumed from the finds at Mehrgarh of hafted stone lunates set in bitumen, and the occurrence of sickle gloss on stone tools at many other sites, that stone was hafted in this way to make composite sickles. It seems likely that this already ancient practice was followed also during the Mature Indus period. There is some very interesting evidence from Kalibangan where a field surface was uncovered, which had been covered by builder's debris at the opening of the Mature Indus period (Fig. 6.30). This surface still retained the marks of furrows laid out in two directions at right-angles to each other. The marks suggest that a wooden plough or 'ard' was employed. Incidentally, the pattern of the crossed furrows, closely spaced in one direction and more widely spaced in the other, is still used by the population of the area for planting two crops simultaneously, in one direction horse gram or sessamum, in the other mustard, etc. This finding therefore provides a dramatic suggestion that an agricultural practice was already in use during Early Indus times which has survived locally till today.

CHAPTER 8

THE MATURE INDUS CIVILIZATION – 2

Technology

The products of the Mature Harappan craftsmen exhibit a degree of uniformity similar to that found in town planning and structure plans. Indeed, it is so marked that it is possible to typify each craft with a single set of examples drawn from one site alone. It is not yet established whether this feature was achieved by the centralization of production, linked with efficiency of distribution, or whether by other factors, but in either case it calls for special attention. From the outset of the Mature Indus period, there is a greater quantity of evidence for copper and bronze technology than previously; clearly there was easy access to plentiful supplies of copper. Analysis indicates that the principal source of copper ore was in the Khetri–Ganeshwar area of Rajasthan (see below p. 253). A standard range of tools of copper and bronze is recorded at site after site (Fig. 8.1). Many among them set the pattern for later Indian types for centuries to come, and the majority exhibit what Piggott called 'competent dullness' – a simplicity of design and manufacture linked with adequate but not great functional efficiency.

Nearly all the basic tool-types – flat axes, chisels, knives, spearheads and arrowheads, small saws, etc – could have been made by simple casting, and/or chiselling and hammering. Daggers, knives or dirks with mid-ribs and flat tangs begin to appear in the upper levels of Mohenjo-daro. Although they may show foreign influence, we concur with Childe's remark that they are 'technically very Indian'. Bronze appears to have been present from the lowest levels at Mohenjo-daro, but it is noticeably more common in the upper levels. Four main varieties of metal were present: crude copper lumps, in the state in which they left the smelting furnace, with a considerable quantity of sulphur; refined copper containing trace elements of arsenic and antimony, doubtless deriving from the original ore; an alloy of copper and arsenic having from 2 to 5 per cent of the latter substance, probably present as a natural constituent of the ore; and bronze, having a tin alloy content often as high as 11 to 13 per cent. The copper–arsenic would have been harder than the pure copper.

The splendid copper and bronze vessels which are among the outstanding examples of the Harappan metal-workers' craft were either raised or sunken by hammering over a form (Fig. 8.2). In the Late Harappan period an additional technique, that of lapping or joining two parts to make a composite jar, appears.

There is little doubt that such special objects as the cast bronze figures of people or animals, or the little model carts (of which nearly identical examples come from sites as far apart as Harappa and Chanhu-daro) were the products of specialists' workshops in one or other of the cities. These products of the casting of copper and bronze illustrate that the process was well understood throughout the Harappan period. Copper bun-shaped ingots are among the finds. Apart from using simple casting moulds, well ventilated complex moulds were also employed with great skill, particularly in making bronze figurines of humans and animals (Fig. 8.11). Kilns of brick have been discovered at a number of places and some of them were probably associated with copper-working, as for example in block 1 of the DK area of Mohenjo-daro.

No doubt gold, because of its attractive native appearance, was one of the first metals to be sought after by man. Panning or washing of gold-dust were probably the principal means employed anciently to obtain gold. There is as yet insufficient evidence in the Indian subcontinent to indicate the character and use of gold in pre-Harappan times. With the Indus civilization there is more evidence. Objects of gold are reasonably common, though by no means prolific. Gold occurs in the form of beads (some of minute size), pendants, amulets, brooches, needles, and other small personal ornaments, including small hollow conical

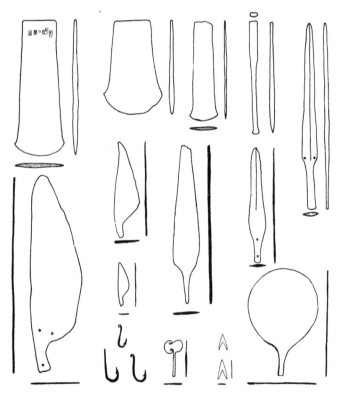

8.1 Mohenjo-daro: copper and bronze tools (1:10)

caps with interior soldered loops, doubtless for use as forehead ornaments, and identical with modern examples. Much of the Indus gold is of light colour, indicating a high silver content, or rather that it is unrefined electrum. This suggests that it originated from the quartz reefs of Karnataka, rather than from panning, and the possibility is certainly not discouraged by the numbers of Neolithic settlements which are reported from that region, particularly clustering around the Hatti gold bands.

Silver makes its earliest appearance in India–Pakistan to date in the Indus civilization. That it was relatively more common than gold is indicated by the number of large vessels made of silver, and by the frequency of other finds. Beads and smaller ornaments apart, the forms of the utensils almost always repeat those made in copper. Among examples of finer workmanship is a silver buckle from Harappa, with soldered scroll pattern of gold wire and gold-capped beads, and a boss of silver inlaid with conch-shell. Of the manifold possible sources of

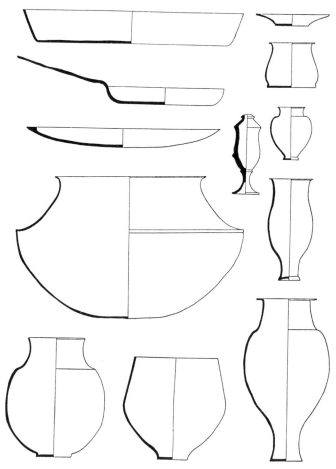

8.2 Mohenjo-daro: copper and bronze vessels (1:4)

this metal available to the Indus merchants, it is difficult to determine which were exploited. Objects of silver are almost unknown in later prehistoric or protohistoric contexts in the subcontinent. A rare, indeed unique, occurrence is in the copper hoard from Gungeria (see p. 257) where about a hundred thin silver plates in the form of (?) bulls' heads were discovered. Their age is still a matter for speculation. The Indus cities also provide testimony that lead – often found naturally in association with silver – was imported in ingot form, and occasionally used for manufacturing objects such as vases or plumb-bobs.

In spite of the common use of metals, stone was not abandoned, and chert blades were prepared at the settlements from cores which in turn had been exported from great factories such as that at Sukkur (Figs. 8.3–4). At Sukkur blades of the type found in Mohenjo-daro and other settlements were also made in large quantities at extensive working areas using the same sources of material as Palaeolithic craftsmen had done earlier. The Harappan craftsmen cleared the earlier materials and flint nodules that had suffered long exposure to the elements, and piled them up in long ridges, or threw them down the sides of convenient hills. They then used the freshly exposed nodules of flint for blade production. The craftsmen appear to have sat cross-legged at chosen spots in the cleared area, and the actual places where they sat could still be recognized when we visited the site in 1976 – some four thousand years later! Small kidney-shaped areas were completely cleared of flints down to the residual soil, and concentrations of waste materials, cores and blades could be seen beside them. Studies of the stone industries from settlements of the Mature Indus period show a distinct and probably rapid development and convergence from the more varied, individual assemblages recorded at Early Indus and all earlier settle-

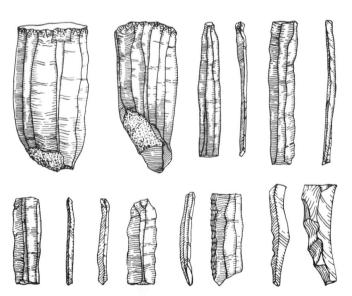

8.3 Mohenjo-daro: stone-blade industry (1:2)

ments. The range of artefacts made from blades (in which the local and regional distinctions were seen), drops away almost entirely. What is left is an industry consisting of long, regular blades made from carefully prepared cores of very high quality material obtained from outstandingly good sources of supply. The blade industry of this period is highly professional, and this craft shows an effortless competence, without apparently any desire to produce novel or special results. This is a clear example of the kind of craft specialization that took place at the beginning of the Mature Indus urban period.

On the other hand, the products of the potters must have been mainly local, and the uniformity of forms and painted decoration which they display (Figs. 8.5, 8.6, 8.7) cannot be accounted for by trade. How it was achieved is not easy to determine; mere uniformity of potter's wheels or equipment cannot alone supply the answer, even though it may have played a substantial role.

Mature Harappan pottery represents a blend of the ceramic traditions of Baluchistan on the one hand, and those of India east of the Indus (as exemplified in Fabric A at Kalibangan) on the other. Although this Mature period pottery shares the wheel, kiln and firing patterns with Baluchistan, it developed its own somewhat stolid character, less sensitive or exciting than the finest Baluchi pottery, but competent and self-assured. Throughout the whole range of forms, flat bases are dominant, and many show the string-cutting marks of their removal from the wheel.

8.4 Rohri hills: Harappan factory site near Sukkur, area cleared where craftsman sat

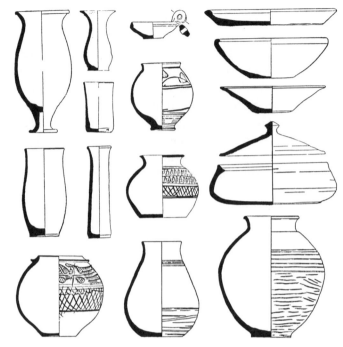

8.5 Harappa: plain and painted pottery (1:8)

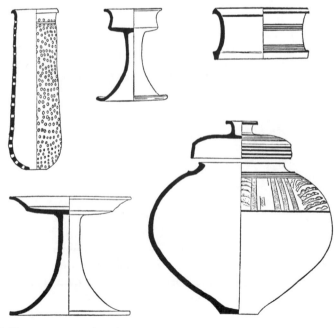

8.6 Harappa: pottery (1:10)

The foot-wheel is still in use in Sind and parts of the Punjab, Saurashtra, and the North West Frontier Province, in contrast to the Indian spun-wheel found east of the Indus, and may be taken with some degree of certainty to be a legacy of this period. The modern foot-wheel closely resembles those which are found right across Iran and into Mesopotamia, both today and probably in ancient times. The wheel is set in a pit, and an axle connects it to a smaller, lighter turntable on which the pot is thrown. The potter sits on the side of the pit and regulates the speed and duration of the movement of the wheel with his foot.

The majority of the pottery is plain, but a substantial part is treated with a red slip and black-painted decoration. Polychrome pottery is rare. Abstract geometric motifs are comparatively unusual, the nearest approach being in 'scale', leaf or petal designs. Natural motifs such as birds, fish, animals, plants, trees and *pīpal* leaves, however, are not infrequent (Fig. 8.7). Varieties of the 'animal in landscape' style are by no means rare. As with the uniform repertoire of forms of the Harappan potter, so the painting often has a utilitarian quality and a kind of heavy insensibility. On the other hand, some pieces show a remarkable delicacy of line and artistic feeling, as for example the pots from Lothal, which we illustrate here. This quality may indicate the existence of regional variations.

Comparatively few examples of ivory carving have been found. They include combs, probably the cousins of those imported to Ur, carved cylinders, perhaps for use as seals, small sticks and pins. A unique piece of a much-damaged plaque carved with a human figure in low relief is notable. Another craft was that of working and inlaying shell. The shell most commonly used was probably obtainable locally from the coast, being the *Fasciolaria trapezium* variety. This was used for several kinds of beads, bracelets and decorative inlays. The conch-shell, more commonly used in later millennia, is much less frequently encountered. The making of objects of faience was probably another area in which Harappan craftsmen were competent. Extensive craft centres for the manufacture of shell objects are known from Chanhu-daro and Balakot. The latter excavations have revealed a splendid body of data from which the whole craft can be reconstructed.

The lapidary's craft was widely practised, and its products included the range of steatite seals – whose artistic aspect is discussed elsewhere in this chapter – beads and various ornaments, and numerous weights. Beads were manufactured from a wide variety of semi-precious stones brought to the Indus valley from many different regions. As we saw above, turquoise and lapis lazuli were imported into Mehrgarh from Central Asia, even during the pre-ceramic Neolithic. The large number of beads discovered in sites of the Early Indus period, and the evidence for local factories, shows that it continued without a break. The craft of the Indus civilization marks a logical development. In Chanhu-daro and Lothal bead-makers' shops were discovered, with their equipment, which included stone borers and drills, anvils, grinding stones and furnaces, and large numbers of beads in all stages of completion. The beads and the

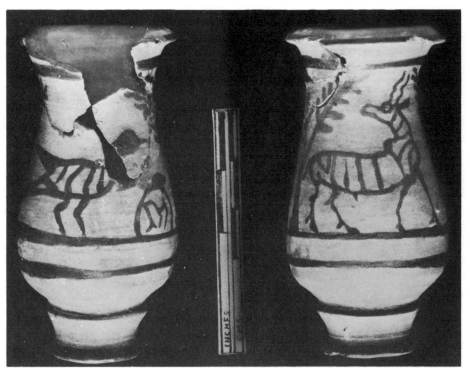

a

b

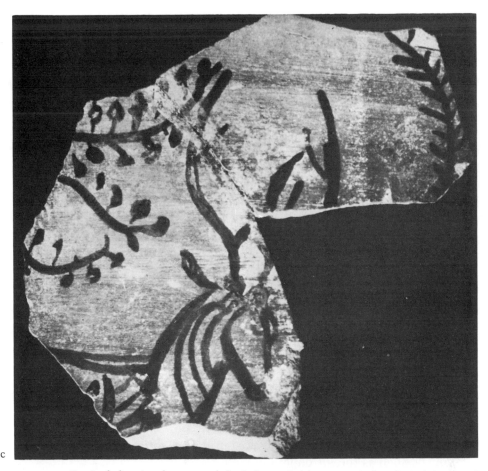

c

8.7 Lothal: painted pottery of the Indus period (*courtesy* Archaeological Survey of India)

weights were made by flaking techniques similar to those used in the preparation of blade cores, and then ground, polished and drilled, with extraordinary skill and accuracy. The seals were intaglios, made of steatite and first cut to shape with a saw. The boss was then shaped with a knife and bored from either end. The carving of the animal motif was done with a burin, probably of copper, and at some stage the seal was baked to whiten and harden its surface (Fig. 8.15). An alkali was probably applied to the surface before firing to assist in the whitening and to glaze it. Their importance was doubtless linked in some way with their role in trading activities, but for the modern observer of even greater interest are the short inscriptions in the unread Harappan script, and the subjects of the intaglio, many of which represent scenes of a cultural or religious nature.

Steatite was used for a wide variety of other objects: beads, bracelets, buttons, vessels, etc., but its use for making faience is of particular interest. In this material, numbers of beads, amulets, sealings and even animal models have been found. Several techniques are indicated, using a body paste of either powdered steatite or perhaps sand, and a glaze of some related substance. Minute disc-cylinder beads of this material were apparently extruded in plastic form, fired and then snapped off. Pieces of glazed earthenware and even faience pots, some with coloured decoration, are recorded, and again testify to a remarkable level of technical achievement.

Another semi-precious stone utilized for bead-making was carnelian. Long barrel beads of this material rank among the technical achievements of the Harappans. A related technique is the decoration or etching of carnelian beads. Carnelian was mined in the form of agate nodules which were subsequently toasted in a furnace to produce the distinctive red–brown colour. To decorate them further the beads were painted with an alkali paste and again toasted to produce a white pattern where this was applied, or decorated with black lines obtained from metallic oxides. It seems probable that India was anciently a source of carnelian beads, and therefore that etched beads may well have been among the items of export to Mesopotamia. On the other hand disc beads, apparently of steatite, and faience barrel beads occur already in Mundigak I. The technique of making beads of semi-precious stones must long have remained a special feature of Indian craftsmanship (Fig. 8.22). Archaeology is able to supply a mass of evidence from sites from the earliest Neolithic and Chalcolithic settlements in many regions to testify to its longevity. Another, most comprehensive body of evidence comes from a bead-worker's shop at Ujjain, dating from about 200 B.C., which was excavated by N. R. Banerjee. The same basic techniques continued to be used until recent times, and are still used by lapidaries in many parts of India and Pakistan, only slightly modified by modern technology, such as the introduction of electric drills.

Summing up, we may say that the technical level achieved over so great an area as is demonstrated in the Harappan civilization, is probably unique in the ancient world, and that Harappan technology deserves Childe's acclaim as 'technically the peer of the rest' (that is, of Egypt and Babylonia). However, its limitations should not be overlooked. The majority of the products are unimaginative and unadventurous, in some ways reminiscent of the products of the Roman provinces, but also suggesting either that the people of Mohenjo-daro and Harappa had their eyes on things beyond this world, or more probably that they gave their attention to less permanent crafts such as textiles. Indeed, we may not be altogether wrong if we detect in this aspect of their way of life the roots of the cultural style which distinguishes the Indian cities of the historic period.

Arts

The boundary between the field of craft and technology, and that of art is never very distinct, and constantly overlaps. Where works of art survive, they add greatly to our comprehension of prehistoric cultures, for they provide an insight into the minds of the artists. Not only do they often reflect the spirit and atmosphere of a culture, but in some cases they also give an indication of social values and religious beliefs in a way in which other material remains cannot possibly do. This is certainly true in the Mature Harappan period. Owing to either the destructive climatic conditions, or the sensibilities of the artists, we have been left a somewhat biased view of the achievements of the Harappans in this sphere of human activity. Only a very few sculptures survive; of those in stone about a dozen pieces only come from Mohenjo-daro and two or three from Harappa. Most are mutilated or fragmentary. The stone employed was usually soft – either steatite, limestone or alabaster. The function, wherever indications are available, seems always to have been as cult icons. The size is never great, and in each case well under life-size. The outstanding pieces are the bearded head and shoulders from the D K area at Mohenjo-daro (Fig. 8.8), and two small

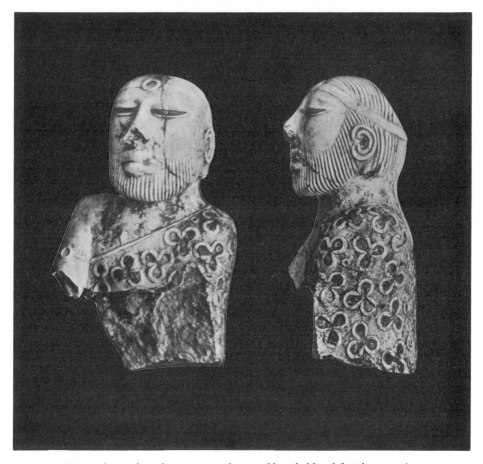

8.8 Mohenjo-daro: limestone sculpture of bearded head (height 19 cm)

figures from Harappa (Fig. 8.10 a and b). The Mohenjo-daro fragment is one of a series of male figures, either seated or kneeling, with hair tied in a bun or hanging in a long plaited lock. In some the hair is tied in a fillet. It is with this series that two fragmentary terracotta pieces from Chhalgarhi and Mundigak iv may be compared. The latter, which is more complete, is evidently a kneeling figure, and in both cases the head is tilted backwards and the eyes are half-closed. Another outlier of the same group is a stone head discovered by Stein at Dabarkot among Harappan remains. A further piece which suggests more remote Harappan affinities is the limestone male head from Mundigak iv.3. In some of these cases there are indications that an inlay was used for decoration and for the eyes. At best the modelling of these pieces is convincing, but the inferior examples are distorted and improbable. Stone carvings of animals are even more rare than those of human beings, but from Mohenjo-daro come two reclining animals, evidently either bulls or rams, in each case carved from a block of limestone of which a solid part remains as the base. One has an elephant's trunk recalling the composite beasts of the seals (Fig. 8.9). The head in both instances is missing. The modelling of the larger of the two, which incidentally was finished by polishing, is surprisingly sensitive, and bears somewhat the same relation to the human figures as many of the terracotta animals do to their human counterparts.

The two examples of stone sculpture from Harappa have sometimes been held to belong to a much later period, but there are several cogent arguments to

8.9 Mohenjo-daro: composite animal, bull with elephant's trunk and ram's horns

favour their Harappan date. First of all no comparable sculptures are known from North India of the Early Historic period, and secondly both have drilled sockets to take dowel pins to attach head or limbs, a technique not found in later sculptures. The first figure is a tiny nude male torso of red sandstone, less than 10 cm in height, with a pendulous belly. As Sir John Marshall pointed out, its chief quality lies in the 'refined and wonderfully truthful modelling of the fleshy parts' (Fig. 8.10a). Indeed it is far finer than any other Harappan stone sculptures. The two tubular drill holes on the front of the shoulders may have been intended to take an inlay. The second figure is no larger, made of a grey stone. It is a nude dancing figure, also male, with twisting shoulders and one raised leg. A dowel pin was used to attach the now missing head (Fig. 8.10b). It is quite unwarranted to suggest an association of this figure with the much later icon of Śiva as Natarája, Lord of the Dance, and yet it is as convincing and tempting an ascription today as when Marshall proposed it nearly half a century ago.

Even less plentiful than the remains of stone sculpture are those of cast bronze, which come mainly from Mohenjo-daro. The most significant specimen is a little figure of a dancing girl about 11.5 cm in height (Fig. 8.11). The head is inclined back, giving the eyes a characteristically dropping quality, the right arm rests on the hip, and the left, which is heavily bangled, hangs down. She is

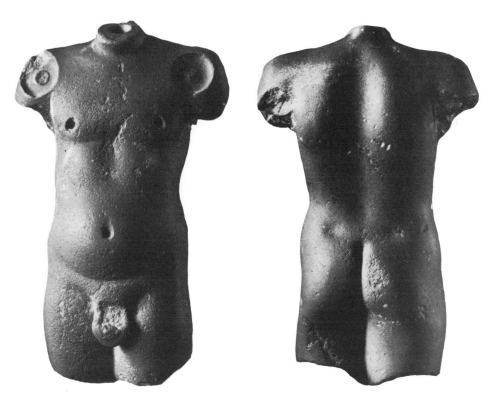

8.10(a) Harappa: red sandstone figure (height 9.3 cm)

8.10(b) Harappa: stone figure of dancer (height 10 cm)

naked, except for a necklace, and her hair is plaited in an elaborate manner. A second figure of comparable size also comes from Mohenjo-daro, as do one or two cast-bronze feet from figures of about the same size. Among animals of bronze one may mention a fine buffalo and a ram. Finally, even if only toys, the little models of bullock-carts and 'ikkas' from Chanhu-daro and Harappa are interesting examples of the skill in casting. Incidentally, the two ikkas, though discovered over 650 km apart, are virtually identical in all details. Although so few, these specimens testify to a remarkable degree of skill in bronze-working and suggest that this area was well developed in the Harappan cities.

From this sparsity in the fields of stone and metal sculpture, we now turn to the much better represented area of terracotta figurines. A great number of these survive, as they seem to have been universally popular, either as toys or cult objects, or more probably as both (Figs. 8.12, 8.13, 8.14). Technically they show little to distinguish them from those of Baluchistan – hand-modelling and applied detail being general. A few pieces are certainly made in single moulds. However, the style of both the human and animal figures is marked by its own character and individuality. The main corpus includes a range of birds and animals, including monkeys, dogs, sheep and cattle. Both humped and humpless bulls are found, the pride of place seemingly going to great humpless bulls, clearly of the *primigenius* stock, well modelled and with sticked details of eyes, head and neck (Fig. 8.13, No. 2). These probably had some cult significance. Both male and female human figurines are found, the latter being if anything more common. Some of these female figurines are heavily ornamented and have exaggerated features, and are generally seen as representations of the Great Mother, the descendants no doubt of those of Mehrgarh and other earlier sites, while others have elaborate head-dresses and appliqué dress or ornament on their bodies. Seated women and mother and child groups are often among the most vividly modelled. Of special interest is a group of heads with either horns or horn-like appendages. These appear on both male and female torsos, and may be associated with the horned figures on seals and elsewhere so that with some certainty we may regard them as deities. The male heads sometimes have small goatee beards. One other group of figurines deserves notice; these are models of

8.11 Mohenjo-daro: bronze figure of dancing girl (height 10.2 cm)

carts made of terracotta and almost certainly used as toys (Fig. 7.17). The various types of carts are recognizably the ancestors of actual vehicles surviving in the modern countryside of India and Pakistan, and once again bear remarkable testimony to the extraordinary continuity of the culture during the past four millennia. With these Harappan terracottas we notice for the first time a general

8.12 Mohenjo-daro: terracotta birds and animals

tendency which is repeated many times in later Indian art: the plastic qualities of the animals are as a rule more noteworthy than those of the human beings, and show considerable skill on the part of the artists in representing natural observation.

We have already mentioned the seals of the Indus civilization in terms of their role in economic life, and discussed their techniques of manufacture. They form further an impressive part of the surviving examples of Harappan art (Figs. 8.15–17). The number so far discovered in excavation must be around 2000. Of these the great majority have an animal engraved on them, and a short inscription. The animal most frequently encountered is a humpless bull, shown in profile with its horns superimposed on each other and pointing forward (Fig. 8.17). From this feature it has generally been called a unicorn. In front of the beast stands a short decorated post, variously interpreted as a standard, manger or even an incense-burner. The animal interests us for two reasons: first because it would appear to be a relation of *Bos primigenius* rather than of *Bos indicus;*

8.13 Mohenjo-daro: terracotta figurines; 1 toy bull with moving head; 2 bull of *primigenius* type

and more immediately because the schema that is used to depict its head and
horns is one which was a commonplace in Mesopotamia from Uruk times at
least to the Achaemenid period. What is at present not clear is whether this was
merely the loan of an art-form, or whether it is an actual representation. It may
be that the Indus unicorn was a mythical rather than real beast. The less
common representations of Indian humped cattle in terracotta must indicate
that these were the main breed in the region. Here the portrayal of hump, horns,
head and dewlap is Indian, and it is drawn according to a different schema,
which is also occasionally found in the Middle East, generally being seen there
as evidence of contact with India. The *Bos indicus* is never accorded the honour
of a 'standard', suggesting that sacred status was given only to the humpless
breed.

Other animals on the seals are sometimes accorded a trough or manger, or are
represented by themselves, among them the elephant, the bison, the rhinoceros
and the tiger. Of special interest is a considerable group of seals with 'cult'
motifs, evidently containing material of a religious character. The craftsmanship of these seals is generally excellent and shows at once considerable skill in

8.14 Mohenjo-daro: terracotta figurines

8.15 Mohenjo-daro: seals with animal motifs

8.16 Mohenjo-daro: seals with mythological or religious content: 1 mythological scene, showing worship of horned deity in *pīpal* tree; 2 seated deity frequently identified as prototype of Śiva; 3 symbolic *pīpal* tree with unicorn heads; 4 starfish form with unicorn head; 5 horned tiger covered by female horned spirit; 6 composite animal, bull–elephant–tiger

8.17 Mohenjo-daro: 'unicorn' seals

the depiction of animals, though it is combined with a tendency to run into accepted schemata or clichés. This is particularly marked with the hundreds of 'unicorn' bulls, which repeat with only minor changes the same motifs again and again. The cult scenes show a refreshing originality, but many of them are so small that they give little scope for artistic expression.

Having considered the artistic manifestations of the Harappan period, we may feel somewhat disappointed at the limitations of the materials it provides us. (Indeed, the same may be said for the whole of the Indian prehistoric art.) In quantity India cannot compare with the repertoire of either Egypt or Iraq. We find neither the variety of expression, nor the range of exploitation of media which both these countries witnessed. Stone sculpture is very rare and often comparatively undeveloped, however excellent unique pieces may be; terra-cotta sculpture was not exploited as it was in Mesopotamia. Even metal-work, in spite of the excellence of the unique pieces, did not develop at all widely.

The total absence of any surviving painting on house walls too is disappointing, when we consider the varied uses it finds in many parts of modern India. Thus the evidence is paradoxical and perplexing. We are left wondering whether less durable forms of artistic expression have completely vanished, and whether such crafts as textile design – for which India has been justly renowned during the historical period – can have filled this role as in more recent centuries.

Language and script

The language of the Harappans is at present still unknown, and must remain so until the Harappan script is read. Broadly, there would appear to be two main contestants as to the nature of the language: that it belonged – however improbably – to the Indo-European or even Indo-Aryan family; or that it belonged to the Dravidian family. In spite of the careful analysis of the corpus of Harappan inscriptions – now in the region of 2500 – by Hunter, Langdon and others, the task of decipherment remains problematic and the shortness of the inscriptions, nearly all on seals or amulet tablets, renders it difficult. Perhaps because it offers such a challenge the associated problems have attracted a whole series of scholars to attempt their solution. Since no two attempts have so far been in agreement, as their number increases only one thing becomes more certain: that the probability of any one being correct is correspondingly reduced. With the wisdom of hindsight many of the earlier attempts appear to be abortive, and using similar criteria, many of the more recent attempts show little advance on the earlier. Some scholars have recently pointed to the need for a constructive methodology, but others still proceed on idiosyncratic lines. Several of the major attempts to read the inscriptions have been made by groups of scholars, using a variety of techniques, including computers.

Parpola and his Scandinavian colleagues have produced an impressive concordance of the known inscriptions, and proceeded with a hypothesis that the language was Dravidian and that the script relied upon homophones; a group of Soviet scholars have also concluded that the language is closer to Dravidian than to any other known language; and an Indian scholar, Mahadevan, has also published an impressive computer concordance. There appear to be some areas of agreement between all these attempts, both in accepting the Dravidian hypothesis and in reconstructing from the inscriptions elements of an astronomical system. A rather different approach is to be found in a recent attempt to read the contents of the inscriptions in terms of analogies between Harappan and Sumerian signs or groups of signs. This does not lead us to the language of the inscriptions, but it may lead us to the meaning of some of them. Its author, Kinnier-Wilson, has developed Ross's analysis of the numeral system which is an element in many of the inscriptions, and proposes to read information which would be appropriate for the commercial use of the seals. S. R. Rao has also produced a quite different attempt to read the script as containing a pre-Indo-Aryan language of the Indo-European family, and as clearly ancestral not only to the later Indian Brahmi script, but also to the early Semitic alphabet. This attempt has so far not been supported by other workers.

Religion

In spite of the mystery of its undeciphered inscriptions, there is still a considerable body of information concerning the religion of the Mature Indus civilization. As we have seen, a number of buildings both on the citadel and in the lower town at Mohenjo-daro have been tentatively identified as temples. It is from these that a part of the small repertoire of stone sculptures, almost certainly all cult icons, derive. But our information goes far beyond this. Forty years ago Sir John Marshall, in his brilliant chapter upon the religion of the Indus civilization, was able to propose certain basic elements. He concluded that the great numbers of female terracotta figurines were popular representations of the Great Mother Goddess; and he rightly drew parallels between this evidence and the ubiquitous cult of goddesses, and particularly that of Pārvatī, the spouse of Śiva, both throughout modern India and in Indian literature. He further postulated the presence of a great male God, whom he identified with the later Śiva, who shared many of his attributes. We are of the opinion that the stone cult icons, and therefore probably also the temples, were dedicated to this same deity. One of the most significant representations is to be found on a series of seals. These show him seated in a Yogic posture, upon a low throne flanked by wild goats, and wearing a great buffalo-horned head-dress; he is ithyphallic, he has perhaps three faces, and he is surrounded by jungle creatures (Fig. 8.16) – a veritable Lord of the Beasts. In several instances he has a sprouting plant emerging between his horns (Fig. 6.32). Every one of these features can be found in the descriptions of the Śiva of later times. Moreover, stones identical in form to the *lingam*, the phallic emblem of Śiva, were found in the cities (Fig. 8.18).

Another group of human figures on seals and amulets, whether male or female, have horns on the head and long tails; they sometimes also have the hind legs and hoofs of cattle. From the seals, seal impressions, amulets and copper tablets (Fig. 8.19), we may derive a series of items which must belong to the religious iconography of the Harappans. On one seal, rearing cobras accompany the Yogi figure. A recurrent theme is of a tree-spirit, of indeterminate sex, shown in a *pīpal* or other tree, with a tiger or other animal standing before it (Fig. 8.16). This motif is occasionally combined with a pair of worshippers bearing rooted plants or saplings. Another theme shows a row of seven figures, also of

8.18 Mohenjo-daro: stone (?) *lingam* and two decorated bases

uncertain sex, with long hair plaits, standing before a *pīpal* tree, with a horned figure standing in it. The seven have been variously identified with the seven Rishis (or seers), and with the seven Mothers of later times. Some scenes are strongly suggestive of Mesopotamian mythology: for example, a man grappling with a pair of tigers recalls the Gilgamesh motif, and the horned god, with the legs and tail of a bull, recalls the Bull-man Enkidu of the same epic. From Chanhu-daro comes another remarkable seal, which shows a bull bison, with erect penis, standing over and fecundating a supine human figure, from whose head emerges a sprouting plant. Both wild and domestic animals are depicted. Many of these are naturalistic representations, and the extent of their religious significance is not clear, although the bull and cow may be expected to have had a special role comparable with that of later times. We need have no doubt in assigning such a role to the composite animals, such as the creature with the forepart of a human and the hindquarters of a tiger – perhaps the ancestor of the Tiger Mother (Huligammā) of modern South India – or the composite bull–elephant, the ram–bull–elephant, and so on. The last has been compared by Mode and Kosambi with a similar beast from Jemdet-Nasr. It also demands comparison with compound creatures, such as the Lion–elephant (*Gajasimha*) of folk-tales and medieval iconography. Even abstract symbols and motifs seem to anticipate those of later Indian religion. Among these are the maze-like closed patterns which recall the auspicious rice-flour designs made by house-wives upon thresholds or in courtyards; the *svastika* in several variant forms; and the *pīpal* leaf or *pīpal* tree.

8.19 Mohenjo-daro: copper tablets (1:2)

If the evidence of the earlier excavations is not very helpful with regard to the layout or function of actual temples, the more recent excavations of the Archaeological Survey of India at Kalibangan are far more informative. At this site, as we saw above, there was in the southern square of the citadel mound a series of brick platforms, raised to a considerable height and crowned with 'fire altars', a well and bathing places, and brick-lined pits containing ashes or animal bones (Fig. 7.13). This complex must represent a civic ritual centre where animal sacrifice, ritual ablution and some sort of fire ritual featured. The excavators have noted that in the houses of the lower town, apart from the normal domestic hearths and ovens, one room was set aside for a similar fire altar, a feature which is strikingly suggestive of the 'fire room' (agni-śālā) of late Vedic and later Indian tradition. This, therefore, one may interpret as representing a domestic fire ritual or worship. There was, however, a third context in which these fire altars were found at Kalibangan, in a small brick-walled courtyard outside the lower town towards the east. Here several fire altars were discovered along with pits containing ashes, but no other structures. This may be interpreted as a further ritual centre, belonging to the lower town and perhaps of lower hierarchical importance than those of the citadel.

To sum up, there is every reason to see in the iconography of the Mature Indus civilization many features which have developed from elements first seen in the Early Indus stage, or even earlier. Equally, it is possible to find many features which seem to have their counterparts perhaps in Vedic mythology and also in later Indian religion. But at the present stage of research it is hazardous to carry such identifications far, and further systematic study is needed. Another very problematic set of data are those from Kalibangan, where there is evidence from the beginning of the Mature Harappan period of distinctive ritual hearths. Fire-worship being considered a distinctly Indo-Aryan trait, do these carry with them an indication of an Indo-Aryan presence even from so early a date? This

8.20 Lothal: burial and double burial (*courtesy* Archaeological Survey of India)

too is a crucial question which requires very careful consideration and further excavation so that it may be objectively evaluated.

Burial customs

The earlier excavations at Mohenjo-daro and Harappa revealed surprisingly little clear evidence of Harappan burial customs, particularly as it is not certain whether any burials were found inside the cities. Marshall rightly believed that the main cemeteries of Mohenjo-daro lay outside the inhabited areas and that they would be deeply buried by the rising level of the plain. However, in the final seasons at Harappa Vats discovered the Late-Harappan Cemetery H (to be discussed below), and between 1937 and 1941 a second Harappan burial ground, known as Cemetery R37. Both these were further investigated by Wheeler in 1946. Since 1940 three other Harappan cemeteries have been reported, although none is yet published; at Derawar in Bahawalpur, discovered by Stein; at Lothal; and at Kalibangan. The two latter have been excavated. It appears that the predominant burial rite was extended inhumation, the body lying on its back with the head generally to the north. Quantities of pottery were placed in the graves, and in some cases the body was buried with ornaments. A number of graves took the form of brick chambers or cists, one at Kalibangan being of unusual size (4 × 2 metres), and from Harappa is reported a coffin burial with traces of a reed shroud. At Kalibangan two other types of burial were encountered: smaller circular pits containing large urns, accompanied by other pottery, but, perplexingly, no skeletal remains, at any rate in the examples so far excavated; and more orthodox burial pits with what are evidently collected bones. From the Lothal cemetery comes evidence of another burial type with several examples of pairs of skeletons, one male and one female in each case, interred in a single grave (Fig. 8.20). It has been suggested that these may indicate a practice akin to *sati*.

Chronology

We shall now turn to a more detailed discussion of Harappan chronology and internal development, and the circumstances of the downfall of the civilization. The first estimate of the duration of the occupation at Mohenjo-daro was made by Sir John Marshall in 1931. His estimate, based upon general concordances with Mesopotamia, was from 3250 to 2750 B.C. In the following year C. J. Gadd published a paper listing a number of Indus, or Indus-like, seals discovered in Mesopotamian sites, particularly Ur, and discussing their ages. Here, apart from two examples which were listed as pre-Sargonid, the majority of finds of seals belonged to the Sargonid and Isin-Larsa periods, and might therefore be expected to indicate active trade contacts between 2350 and 1770 B.C. A few seals were also found in Kassite contexts indicating a yet later date. Since then Piggott

(1950) and Wheeler (1946, 1960, etc.) have reviewed the evidence, including cross-dates to the as yet imprecisely dated sites of Iran (Hissar, Giyan, etc.), and other categories of objects apparently imported into Mesopotamia, such as etched carnelian beads, stone house-urns, etc. There has been general agreement upon an overall span of 2500–1500 B.C., with principal trade contacts with Mesopotamia between 2300 and 2000 B.C. In the past twenty years little additional evidence has come to light to change this view, so far as archaeological cross-datings are concerned. However, in 1955 Allbright concluded that the end of the civilization must have been around 1750 B.C., in order to coincide with Mesopotamian evidence. The advent of radiocarbon dating has provided a welcome new source of information on what must otherwise have remained a very vague position, and may well necessitate a revision of the earlier views. By 1956 Fairservis had seen in the (as yet uncalibrated) radiocarbon dates of his excavations in the Quetta valley a need to bring down the dating of the Harappan culture to between 2000 and 1500 B.C. In 1964 D. P. Agrawal, of the radiocarbon laboratory attached to the Tata Institute of Fundamental Research in Bombay, was able to plot some two dozen dates, including those for Kot Diji, Kalibangan and Lothal, and to draw the conclusion that the total span of the culture should be between 2300 and 1750 B.C. (based on uncalibrated dates). This evidence still appears to be most plausible.

In view of the proximity of Kot Diji to Mohenjo-daro, it seems improbable that any great time lag would be experienced in the culture sequence of the two. Thus the radiocarbon dates relating to the general destruction by fire which heralds the intermediate period following the end of the Early Indus stage at Kot Diji, and any dates relating to the subsequent developments, would be of tremendous interest. Unfortunately, the published report on Kot Diji leaves some vital gaps. The detailed description of the layer numbers of two of the four samples is not clearly stated, but we gather that only one date, 2520 B.C. relates to the final destruction at the end of the Kot Dijian occupation. With this we may compare the series from Kalibangan, where a cluster of dates between 2500 and 2490 B.C. indicates the beginning of the Mature Harappan period, and two dates around 2110–2040 B.C. indicate its conclusion. At Lothal another Mature Harappan series gives dates between 2490 and 2120 B.C., and a single date from a late level at Mohenjo-daro gives 2110 years. A series of dates derived from samples collected by Dales during the excavations of 1964–5 gives a span for the occupation in the HR area at Mohenjo-daro of between 2590 and 2160 B.C.

During the past decade important new data have been derived from the excavations of J. P. Joshi at Surkotada. Here, there are three sub-periods of the (?) Mature Harappan, and there are ten radiocarbon dates. In view of the careful excavation, considerable reliance may be put on them (Fig. 8.21). Period 1A dates from 2480 to 2300 B.C.; 1B from 2290 to 2140 B.C.; and 1C from 2130 to 2020 B.C. There is a clear degree of conformity between these and those from other sites mentioned above. They indicate that the Mature Harappan period began *c.* 2550 B.C., and lasted for about five centuries until *c.* 2050. Thus, the use of the MASCA calibration for radiocarbon dates removes one part of the difficulty formerly felt in relating the Indus chronology to that of Mesopotamia. It must be admitted that there is still plenty of room for uncertainty, particularly regarding the late dates and the final stages of the Mature Indus civilization, which is still imprecisely known.

There is another category of dating evidence which may be invoked, in the textual references from Mesopotamia to objects imported from Meluhha (probably the Indus valley or Western India), or the entrepôts of Tilmun (probably in the Persian Gulf, perhaps Bahrain) and Magan (perhaps in southern Arabia or on the Makran coast). There is good reason to suppose that many of these objects originated in India, and therefore the dates of this literature are likely to be significant, being indicative at least of the period of maximum trade activity on the part of the Harappans, if not of the duration of the civilization. The first reference is in the time of Sargon of Agade (*c.* 2350 B.C.), but the volume of literature only grows during the third dynasty of Ur (2130–2030 B.C.) and the subsequent Larsa dynasty (2030–1770 B.C.). Thereafter it declines markedly. This therefore suggests that the maximum trade contacts coincide with the second half of the Mature Indus period as indicated by the radiocarbon samples.

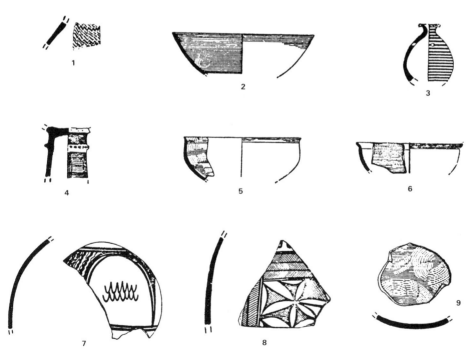

8.21 Surkotada: 1, 3 reserved slip ware, period IA; 4, 7 and 8 varieties of painted ware of 'non-Harappan' type, period IA; 2, 5, 6 and 9 white-painted black-and-red ware, period IC (*after* J. P. Joshi)

There are, however, indications that the beginning of the trade goes back well before 2500 B.C., and thus would have coincided with the Early Indus period, rather than the Mature. The discovery of a 'Persian Gulf' seal at Lothal highlights the interest attached to finds at Failaka, Bahrain and other sites on the southern shores of the Persian Gulf. In recent years the Danish expedition working in this area has discovered a large number of these distinctive seals, some almost identical to imported specimens found at Ur and other sites in Mesopotamia. Buchanan has reported the impression of one such seal on a dated cuneiform tablet of the tenth year of King Gungunum of Larsa, that is about 1923 B.C., according to the middle chronology. Of all the findspots of these seals and of objects supposedly imported into Mesopotamia from the Indus region, Frankfort's excavations at Tell Asmar in the Diyala valley supply perhaps the most convincing evidence of the age. But even so there seems to be some latitude in the interpretation of the evidence. According to Buchanan the earliest seals and imports are not earlier than the late Agade period, and he concludes that 'the Mesopotamian evidence therefore does not require a date for the Mature Indus civilization much, if at all, before the twenty-third century B.C.' On the other hand, it would seem dangerous to use the absence of textual references, or even of certain categories of evidence of direct trade contacts, as an argument for a later chronology for the Indus civilization, since in archaeology such arguments from silence are as often as not proved by later discoveries to be incorrect.

At almost every site of the Harappan period there is at least some evidence of internal development. Unfortunately, much of the earlier work at Mohenjo-daro and Harappa was of such a kind that its analysis is now scarcely possible, while the more recent work there and at Kalibangan or Lothal is still incompletely published. It is thus not easy to make a close comparison of the development at each site, although one is led to feel that parallels might be found, if only more evidence were available. At all those sites where excavation has revealed an Early Harappan phase below the Mature Harappan (Amri, Kot Diji, Kalibangan), there is a clear indication of cultural continuity. Even at Kot Diji, where a massive burnt layer intervenes, the evolution of decorative motifs on pottery continues. Further, at the same three sites, there is a transitional level in which both Early and Mature styles of pottery are found together. Of this level there is no evidence at Chanhu-daro or Mohenjo-daro, as the height of the subsoil water prevented excavation below a certain point, but at Mohenjo-daro Mackay's deep digging in Block 7 of the DK area revealed an early period, related by him to the 'Early' eighth stratum of Marshall on the citadel mound, where some pottery of non-Harappan type, such as incised comb decoration, recalling the pre-Harappan Fabric D at Kalibangan, was found. This may indicate that the earliest period reached in the excavations at Mohenjo-daro goes back to the transitional phase of the other sites.

At Harappa, Mohenjo-daro and Chanhu-daro the early period ends with the massive construction of brick platforms of the citadel areas, and above are found the remains of the high period of the civilization. At Mohenjo-daro this included three principal structural levels of Marshall's intermediate period and was succeeded by a great and disastrous flood, and by three levels of the late period; at Harappa there were six structural levels of which the uppermost produced some pottery of Cemetery H type. At Kot Diji there are also apparently six or seven building phases within the Harappan period, while at Kalibangan nine are reported. At almost every site there succeeds a 'late' period during which planning and construction decline, brickbats from former houses are re-used, new motifs appear on pottery, etc. This is generally seen as a decline, though whether associated with natural calamities or with political factors is still a matter of debate in each case. At a number of sites it is apparent that the typical Harappan material culture flourished alongside local regional styles. Thus at Surkotada the three sub-periods are marked by the presence of three distinctive styles of painted pottery alongside the typical Harappan wares. In the earliest period IA there is a red slipped polychrome ware (in some ways reminiscent of the Early Indus fabric of Kalibangan), a cream slipped painted ware, and a curious reserved slip ware, said to have been found also in the earliest levels of Lothal and recalling the reserved slip ware of Mesopotamia. In the second period, IB, a coarse red ware with painted designs in black, with decidedly local Saurashtran features becomes common; and in the third, IC, there is a white-painted black and red ware reminiscent of that of Ahar and sites in Rajasthan. There appears to be similar evidence from other sites remote from the heartlands of the Indus culture. Thus in the south at Allahdino there appears to be a local element, so too at Gumla in the Dera Jat; and also in the sites of the east Punjab and Haryana, where at Mitathal a local style continues alongside the Harappan.

Conclusion

It is when we seek to interpret all this evidence and to reconstruct something of the life and culture-history of the men and women who were responsible for leaving it that the need for a framework or model becomes apparent.

In the light of what we have already said, we may now conclude that the Indus civilization in its maturity was the result of the concurrence of three major factors. The first and perhaps the most important in terms of its actual character was its direct development from the cultures and existing population of the Early Indus period in the Indus plains and on their margins. These included many incipient urban communities, and centres of local trade and craft specialization, already involved in long-distance trade. They also included a wide spectrum of semi-urban and non-urban communities engaged in a whole variety of activities with widely differing life-styles. This pattern and the interrelationships it involved was already very ancient. The second factor was the environment offered by the Indus system, whose principal character is that of a great river flowing through a desert, and all that this implies. One is inevitably reminded of Egypt and Mesopotamia, but it is important to remember also that the Indus and its major tributaries have laid down a much larger area of alluvial plains than either, extending through other contiguous auxiliary plains into adjacent regions, and providing the means of interlocking with a variety of other regions, notably the western mountain borderlands and the Thar desert. A further aspect of the environment that must be borne in mind is that it was subject to continuous and often rapid change and development. This was principally due to the continuing deposition of rich alluvium throughout the plains to such an extent that it not only raised the level but must have correspondingly made significant increases in their area during the Early and Mature Indus phases and thereafter. The effect of man upon this environment could only be to hasten these processes. Thus the environment offered by the plains would have varied somewhat with time and have provided the optimum conditions for intensive agriculture at certain stages and places. The third, and perhaps least important factor, must have been the stimulus offered by contacts with other societies outside the Indus system, and particularly by those of Central Asia and Mesopotamia. It cannot be mere chance that the Early and Mature Indus stages coincide with the Early Dynastic and Sargonid periods in Sumeria.

There are many indications that by the Mature Indus period urban society had

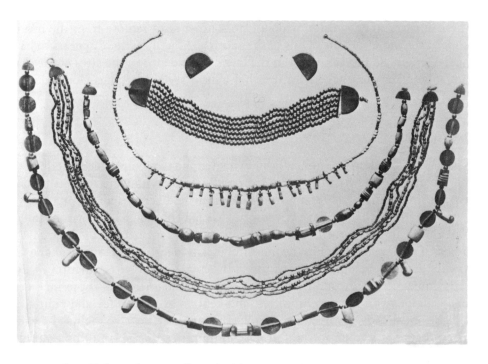

8.22 Mohenjo-daro: jewellery of gold, steatite and semi-precious stone

evolved considerable social stratification and division. The varied and often highly specialized crafts alone indicate this, and some scholars have seen in the variations of house sizes and the localization of blocks and barrack-like dwellings further evidence of class divisions, perhaps even amounting to slavery. Whether we should speak of class divisions, or rather of something akin to the later caste system, is also worthy of consideration. In addition to craft specialists and artisans there must have been an agricultural population, whether living wholly in villages or also in part living in the 'cities'. There must also have been a ruling group who have generally been supposed to have combined the roles of administrators and priests. Further, there is growing evidence of the extent and variety of trade. First, there are the 'granaries' or warehouses at Harappa, Mohenjo-daro and Lothal, implying great concentrations of wealth. Next, there is the evidence of unprecedented trade in goods produced within the Indus culture region, such as stone, metal, shell, etc. Thirdly, there is the evidence of very widespread trade with distant parts, both in the form of exports to Mesopotamia and of the trading 'colony' at Shortughai, in northern Afghanistan, and in the form of other exotic imports. As we have seen, this aspect was already extremely old, and contacts with Central Asia for such purposes already went back several thousand years, to the pre-ceramic Neolithic of the western borderlands. In the new context of the Indus civilization it was evidently more sophisticated and more highly organized than ever before. This is shown by the presence of regulated weights and measures, and of a script which was evidently used for trading purposes, as were the elaborate and well-made seals.

The widely diffused use of a uniform script, and the extent of the trade itself indicate that there must have been an all-embracing and well organized network of communications, both between the cities of the Indus world and beyond to other major centres. This implies the use of pack-animals and the organization of caravans, and the presence of further specialized groups to carry out this function. Recent evidence suggests that such communities may have been clearly divided, in terms of their way of life and domicile, from those who inhabited the major settlements of the plains, perhaps as pastoral nomads or semi-nomads, not unlike the modern Powindahs who combine with their nomadic and pastoral way of life a major role in the trade of Afghanistan and the Indus region. The cultural uniformity of the settlements over such a wide area leaves no doubt that the relationship between the city-centred communities of agriculturalists and craftsmen, and those who provided the means of transport and communication, must have been a stable one. This in turn indicates a strong and firmly based system which held them together and maintained their relations. Precisely what this system was and whence it drew its authority is not yet clear, but of its existence there can be no doubt, nor that it represented a special achievement in the world of the third millennium B.C.

Finally, we must remark that the indications of the superimposition of a uniform language and script (which seems to be the inescapable inference we may draw from the distribution of the seals and inscriptions), and of a uniform mythology and iconography, over so vast an area, are still and must remain sources of real wonder. They remind us of the similar indications of the rule of Asoka Maurya in the third century B.C., or of the Mughal empire at its height, although neither survived for so long as did their first model. But they are above all the indications of the first great promulgation of an interprovincial 'Indian' style, and as such they carry profound implications for the future of Indian thought and culture.

However the system came into being, it must have been built upon remarkably sound foundations, since the 'Indus Empire' appears to have lasted for around five centuries as a major cultural entity, including a number of major cities and regions, at a time when in other parts of the world the largest effective unit was little more than the city state. We may envisage throughout the period a continuing growth of population no doubt linked to an outward expansion of the Indus life-style, and resulting in a variety of encounters with other cultures. In the central regions the Mature Indus culture appears to have completely taken over all aspects of urban life; though in some peripheral centres local Early Indus cultures continued to exist alongside, or in combination with, that of the centre. In each region the situation appears to have been somewhat different, and at present we do not know exactly what was involved – military conquest, colonization, or economic and ideological takeover.

Just as the creation and maintenance of the system was the outcome of the successful combination of several factors, so too its breakdown could have been caused by the weakening of any one of these or the upsetting of their harmonious balance and interaction. It has been suggested that there was a slight increase in rainfall in the region around 3000 B.C., and thereafter a decrease in the early centuries of the second millennium. Although this in itself is unlikely to have had much effect upon the agriculture of the plains, it may well have affected peripheral regions and especially those where animals were bred and through which trade caravans had to pass. It has been suggested too that there was a 'wearing out' of the land due to over-cultivation. But this too seems unlikely, as the population pressure can never have been very great, and in later times the land retained great fertility. Another theory that has been advanced for the end of Mohenjo-daro is that it was engulfed in a great flood affecting a wide area of the plains over a long period. While the specific theory advanced by Raikes has been questioned by Lambrick and others, the occasional flooding of Mohenjo-daro has been long known and cannot be entirely discounted as a cause of local destruction. The whole region lies in a major earthquake zone, and there is no means of estimating the effect of a period of major tectonic disturbance on the whole Indus system. This may well have been associated with changes in the course of the river such as those Lambrick has suggested as a major cause of the desiccation of agricultural lands supplying Mohenjo-daro, and its subsequent deprivations. Any or all of these natural factors would have weakened the structure of the system, and laid it open to internal dissension or to attack from without. Another possibility which cannot be ignored is of epidemic diseases following in the wake of floods, etc. The fertile and productive regions of the Indus valley have throughout history been subject to marauding raids and conquests from the less fertile western hills. Childe (1934) and Wheeler (1946) have both suggested that the end of the Indus cities may have been precipitated by the major incursions of Indo-Aryan speaking people. Whether this view is still tenable must depend upon more accurate dating than is presently available, for the final stages of the Indus civilization and the succeeding centuries. But we shall reserve consideration of this question to a later chapter.

What in conclusion we would like to stress is our view that the Indus civilization arose as a social, economic and cultural phenomenon, produced by the build-up of population on the fertile Indus and Punjab plains. The resultant urban society was a delicate balance of internal relations between cities, towns and villages, and of external relations with neighbouring peasant societies and more distant urban societies. The end of the Indus urban phase probably arose from some major upsetting of this balance. Such an upset could have been produced by any one or more of the causes we have discussed, operating either alone or in combination. Whatever they may have been, what is beyond doubt, and what from our point of view is of primary concern, is that at a certain point the urban phenomenon came to an end.

PART III

THE LEGACY OF THE INDUS CIVILIZATION

CHAPTER 9

THE AFTERMATH OF THE INDUS
CIVILIZATION IN THE INDUS AND
GANGES SYSTEMS

In Chapter 5 we saw that the earliest settlements at present identified in any part of South Asia are on the borders of Baluchistan and the Indus valley, and we commented in conclusion that a new pattern developed after *c.* 5000 B.C., which in time spread throughout the whole Indus system, paving the way for the incipient urbanism of the Early Indus period and the full urbanization of the Mature Indus period. We remarked that these developments took place over an area of great extent in the north-western part of the subcontinent, but that in India east of the Indus system there was at that time no comparable urban development. In contrast, we saw that there are still only a few known traces of developments of separate and probably different adaptations to the differing environments offered in these areas, and that on current showing these developments took place at a somewhat later date, perhaps during the third millennium, more or less contemporarily with the Indus civilization, though apparently largely in isolation from it. With the breakdown of the highly developed socio-economic system of the Indus civilization a major change took place, in that city life seems to have disappeared for several centuries before emerging afresh in the Ganges valley. At the same time a pattern of more or less uniform peasant agricultural settlements appears both inside the Indus region and beyond it. During the second millennium there is plentiful evidence of already developed regional cultures, frequently referred to as 'Chalcolithic' or 'Neolithic–Chalcolithic', in almost every part of the subcontinent. In the next two chapters we propose to review this material, necessarily in a somewhat summary fashion, treating the archaeological evidence as such. In the chapter which follows we shall retrace our steps over the same period, while considering how far archaeology can throw light upon the related question of the movement of Indo-Aryan speaking peoples into India during the second millennium. We shall divide the present chapter into three major sections; first, treating areas peripheral to the Indus civilization on the west and north; secondly, developments within the Indus culture region itself; and lastly, North India east of the Indus system. In the following chapter we shall consider developments in the peninsula.

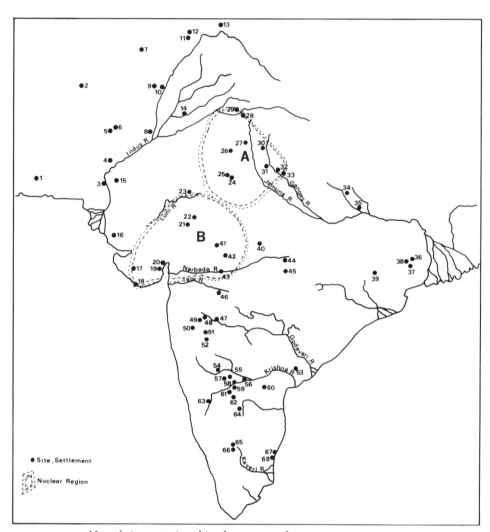

9.1 Map of sites mentioned in chapters 9 and 10

Key
1. Shahi-tump 2. Mundigak 3. Amri 4. Jhukar 5. Naushahro 6. Pirak 7. Shalozan 8. Fort Munro
9. Gumla 10. Rahman Dheri 11. Ghaligai 12. Loebanr 13. Gilgit 14. Harappa 15. Chanhu-daro
16. Desalpur 17. Rojadi 18. Somnath (Prabhas Patan) 19. Rangpur 20. Lothal 21. Ahar 22. Gilund
23. Khurdi 24. Jodhpura 25. Ganeshwar 26. Mitathal 27. Bhagawanpura 28. Bara 29. Rupar
30. Alamgirpur 31. Lal Qila 32. Jakhera 33. Atranjikhera 34. Sohgaura 35. Chirand 36. Mahisadal
37. Pandu Rajar Dhibi 38. Bharatpur 39. Barudih 40. Eran 41. Nagda 42. Kayatha 43. Navatoli
44. Tripuri 45. Gungeria 46. Prakash 47. Nevasa 48. Daimabad 49. Jorwe 50. Chandoli
51. Inamgaon 52. Sonegaon 53. Kesarapalli 54. Kodekal 55. Maski 56. Utnur 57. Piklihal 58. Kallur
59. Tekkalakota 60. Patpad 61. Sanganakallu 62. Kupgal 63. Hallur 64. Pallavoy 65. T. Narsipur
66. Hemmige 67. Gaurimedu 68. Mangalam

The Indus system

Baluchistan

The archaeological evidence for developments to the west of the Indus system after the end of the third millennium is still so fragmentary that it is not really possible to interpret it with any assurance. In north Baluchistan, Piggott has drawn attention to the thick layers of burning which indicate violent destruction of whole settlements at about this time at Rana Ghundai, Dabarkot, etc. In south Baluchistan the cemetery at Shahi-tump, dug into an abandoned Kulli settlement, shows copper stamp-seals, a copper shaft-hole axe (Fig. 9.3, no. 2) and painted grey pottery, including footed goblets and bowls. The seals may be compared with Iranian examples from Anau III and Hissar III; the shaft-hole axes, unknown until this time in the Indian subcontinent, are of Iranian type and compare with those from Maikop and Tsarskaya in South Russia. A mid-second millennium date seems acceptable. At Mundigak in period v the picture is rather different. On the main mound a considerable reconstruction of a massive brick structure is found over the ruins of the palace of period IV. The massive structure is perhaps in some way connected with the brick granaries of the Harappans and may well indicate a need for fortified storage of grain. Copper stamp-seals, of patterns sometimes reminiscent of those of Shahi-tump, make their first appearance during period IV, and continue into v. Copper pins with spiral loops, also reminiscent of Shahi-tump and Chanhu-daro, appear in IV (although related types are reported already in II, and shaft-hole axes and adzes are already present in III.6). None of these finds, however, is datable in itself. What the evidence seems to indicate is that there was a substantial change in the settlements. Many older ones were abandoned and new ones have not been discovered, suggesting that there may have been a shift towards nomadic life. There is also a change in the style of the pottery. The fine tradition of painted pottery with a great variety of naturalistic and abstract designs, in monochrome, bichrome and polychrome, seems to have come abruptly to an end. The pottery of Mundigak v includes a much greater proportion of plain ware whose forms

cm

9.2 Fort Munro, Dera Ghazi Khan district: bronze dirk

indicate a corresponding shift in techniques of manufacture, much of it being handmade and some burnished. The use of paint continues, but the repertoire of

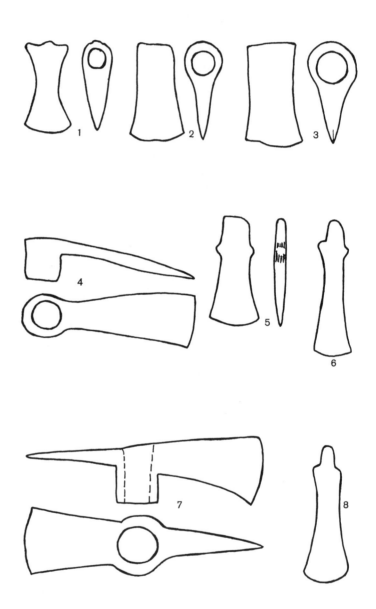

9.3   Copper and bronze objects from the Indus system (1:4 approx.): shaft-hole axes: 1 Chanhu-daro (Jhukar culture); 2 Shahi-tump cemetery; 3 Mundigak III.6; shaft-hole adze; 4 Mundigak III.6; trunnion axes; 5 Shalozan; 6, 8 Gilgit Karakoram; shaft-hole axe-adze; 7 Mohenjo-daro

designs is greatly curtailed (just as at Chanhu-daro in Jhukar times). At Rana Ghundai in periods IV and V quantities of coarse handmade pottery with appliqué bands and fingertip or nail decoration occur.

Rather different evidence comes from the fringes of the Indus plains, from sites in the Dera Jat and from Pirak, near Sibi. These areas strictly belong to the Indus culture zone, but in both cases they are marginal. In the Dera Jat the many sites of the Early Indus period seem to have been abandoned and there is so far little evidence of a Mature Indus presence, except in the small mound at Hisam Dheri, near Rahman Dheri, where a small Harappan 'industrial' site seems to have been located, and at Gumla where period IV shows an admixture of typical Harappan pottery alongside local pottery of continuing Early Indus tradition. At the end of this period the site was abandoned or destroyed, and thereafter was used as a graveyard by a later population. The date of these graves is not established, but terracotta figurines of horses and horse bones were found in them. As yet no other sites of the second millennium have been noted in this area.

At Naushahro, near Mehrgarh, the final phase of period II contains, alongside late Mature Harappan objects, distinctive plain pottery similar to that of the cemeteries of southern Soviet Central Asia (for example, Sapalli Tepe). A cemetery south of Mehrgarh and another at Sibri contain equally distinctive pottery and bronze objects, including a shaft-hole axe-adze. These sites also show remarkable affinities to the cemeteries of north Afghanistan and Soviet Central Asia, and probably date to c. 2000 B.C. (Fig. 9.4). At Pirak, the French excavations have produced clear evidence of an initial Harappan occupation followed, after a period of desertion of unknown duration, by an occupation which extended from the beginning of the second quarter of the second millennium B.C. into the early part of the first millennium B.C. The excavator records three phases of unbroken occupation. In the first period, structures of unburnt brick associated with a large platform were found with pottery which combined its coarse clay and hand manufacture with a painting tradition clearly related to that of earlier periods in this area. A major part of the pottery, however, was a coarse ware decorated with appliqué bands and fingertip impressions. Both terracotta and unburnt clay figurines of horses and camels occurred, along with numerous bones of both species. Terracotta button seals of circular, square or curved forms were common. Objects of copper or bronze occurred; and a stone-blade industry is recorded which included many serrated edges, evidently employed for working bone or ivory. The second period showed a rather similar assemblage (Fig. 9.6), with large numbers of clay and terracotta figurines, including not only Bactrian camels and horses (Fig. 9.7, No. 4), but human figures, including riders. Along with numerous tools of copper and bronze came the first pieces of iron. The third period produced a greater quantity of iron and a continuation of all the elements of the earlier periods (Fig. 9.7, No. 3). Radiocarbon dates indicate for period III a span of c. 1000–800 B.C., and an earlier date, c. 1370–1340 B.C., perhaps represents the second phase. Along with three varieties of wheat and two of barley, rice (*Oryza sativa*) and sorghum are found at Pirak. This is the first recorded appearance in this region of the latter two cereals, and is indicative of the distinctly regional character of agriculture in the second millennium B.C. The evidence from Pirak is, till now, the best from any part of the whole Indus system during this period.

The impression provided by these sites is supported by stray finds of metal objects. From Fort Munro in the foothills west of Dera Ghazi Khan comes a bronze dirk with a fan-shaped decoration on the pommel of its hilt (Fig. 9.2).

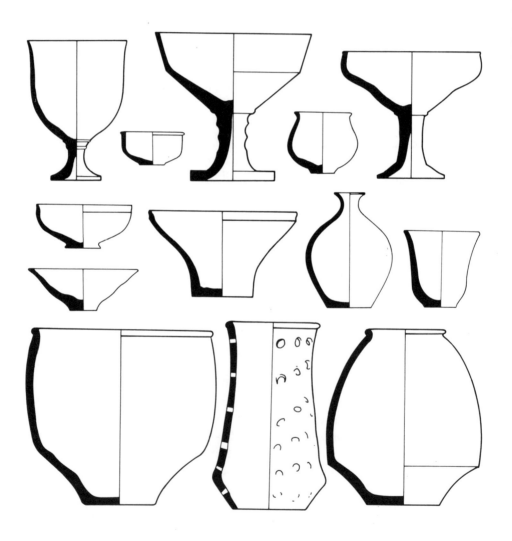

9.4 Plain pottery from Mehrgarh, south cemetery (*after* Jarrige)

This piece is very close to dirks from Luristan and Sialk VI and should date to *c.* 1150 B.C. At Moghul Ghundai, in the Zhob valley, Sir Aurel Stein excavated cairn graves which Piggott assigns to the period of Cemetery B at Sialk (*c.* 1000–800 B.C.). These graves produced an array of bronze objects typical of the latter site, including a tripod jar, horse bells and a bangle. In some of the graves iron arrowheads were found, but these are in no way out of keeping with the probable date. At Shalozan, high up in the Kurram valley, a characteristic trunnion axe of copper was discovered, belonging to type III of Maxwell-Hyslop's classification, and comparing with examples from Hasanlu and other Iranian sites, where they belong to the second millennium and indicate contacts between Anatolian and Iranian smiths (Fig. 9.3, No. 5). This evidence from Late Harappan or post-Harappan contexts in the western part of the subcontinent suggests the movement of peoples, as well as of trade from the direction of Iran, during the second millennium B.C. Apart from the new designs and the probably greater efficiency of some of these weapons, we have regrettably few data on their composition, ore source and the smelting technique that was used in the extraction of the metal from the ore, or how they were manufactured. Some indication may be found in the evidence recovered from Ahar, to the east, where there is clear evidence of copper working (see p. 262).

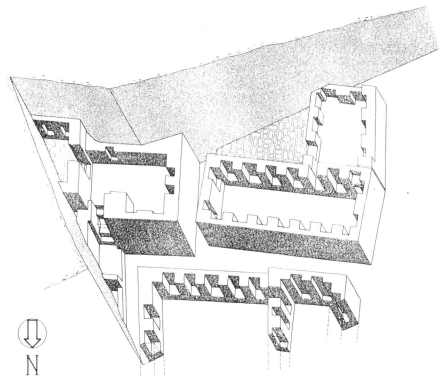

N

9.5 Pirak, period IIB: isometric projection of brick house showing characteristic wall niches (*after* Jarrige)

The Northern valleys

We now turn to the northern valleys of the Indus system where, as we saw in a previous chapter, a local Neolithic culture had long been established. There is surprisingly little evidence of any trade contacts or cultural influence from the Indus plains reaching this area during the Mature Harappan period, although in the Ghaligai cave a brief Early Indus influence seems to have been in evidence.

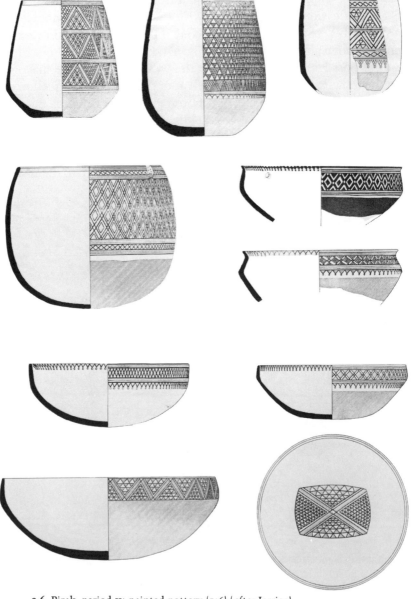

9.6 Pirak, period II: painted pottery (1:6) (*after* Jarrige)

At a certain date, as yet not definitely established, an interesting development takes place, not only in Swat but in many neighbouring valleys – Dir, Chitral and the Indus itself. This is the appearance of a large number of cemeteries having a distinctive range of grave goods and evidently remaining in use over many centuries. These are the cemeteries of the so-called 'Gandhara grave culture'. They first became known from the work of the Italian mission in Pakistan, and their work has now been augmented by excavations of the Peshawar University Department of Archaeology. Considerable material about the graves has been published, but there is still a need for synthesis as the different accounts appear to be mutually inconsistent on some matters. In these circumstances we must accept that any attempt to classify the graves or their contents must be tentative. The principal sites so far published are Katelai 1, Loebanr 1 and Timargarha, all in Swat.

The broad chronology of the graves, both in terms of cross-dating parallels with sites outside India and Pakistan, and in terms of the dozen or more radiocarbon dates so far published, appears to cover a wide spread. Katelai 1 produced five samples dated between 1500 and 200 B.C.; from Timargarha two samples give dates of 1710 and 1020 B.C.; while from Barama two samples were dated to 800 and 430 B.C.

The graves consist for the most part of an oblong pit sometimes with dry stone walling and generally with stone slabs to form a roof (Fig. 9.8). The pit is often

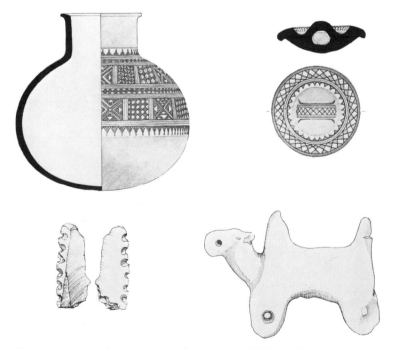

9.7 Pirak: 1–2 painted pottery, period II; 3 notched blade of stone, period IIIA; 4 terracotta Bactrian camel, period IIIB (1:6) (*after* Jarrige)

dug in the floor of an upper larger pit, which was filled with soil and charcoal after the burial and often surrounded by a rough stone circle. Children's remains were sometimes placed inside a smaller cist with stone slabs for walls. The great majority contain inhumations with one or two skeletons. The body was laid on its side with legs drawn up and arms raised and bent. A minority of the graves contained cremated ashes, sometimes gathered in a pottery cist or 'box-urn' with flat lid, or large urn with a 'face' decoration consisting of appliqué and cut-out features (Fig. 9.11). Some burials were of collected bones. The grave goods included large quantities of distinctive plain pottery, either buff-red or grey, and of a distinctive range of forms (Fig. 9.9). These included tall 'champagne goblets', pedestal cups, beakers with flared mouths, bottles with tall narrow necks, occasional jugs with raised lips, spouted pots – some with small handles – and one curious triple pot on three stems rising from a base. There are also sometimes terracotta figurines of distinctive type, generally flat tablets with rough human form, appliqué breasts and highly stylized heads, some with incised necklaces and eyes (Fig. 9.10). Metal objects include those of copper or bronze, most commonly pins with decorated tops, and much more rarely objects of iron. Of special interest was the discovery of two horse burials in separate graves, presumably alongside their masters; and a bronze model of a horse, all three from Katelai. Another important find was an iron cheek-piece of a snaffle bit from Timargarha. The obvious comparisons for all these classes of objects

9.8 Loebanr, Swat: burial of 'Gandhara grave' series (*after* Antonini and Stacul)

9.9 Pottery from Gandhara grave sites in Swat, red and grey burnished ware: top row, period v (*c.* 1400–800 B.C.); middle row period vi (*c.* 800–400 B.C.); bottom row, period vii (*c.* 4th century B.C.) (*courtesy* Stacul)

and for the graves themselves are not to be found in India or Pakistan, but in Iran and the Caucasus. Many parallels can be found for the pottery, in Tepe Hissar III, Hasanlu IV, Shah Tepe, Marlik, Sialk Cemeteries A and B, and the cemeteries of Lenkoran and Talish. The copper or bronze pins may also find their nearest parallels in these sites. Stacul has shown that the graves may be divided into four groups of which only the last, associated with the thin-sided grey and red ware, produced iron tools. Thus there seems good reason to think that a fair proportion of the graves pre-date the arrival of iron in this area. We shall further discuss the interpretation of this evidence in a later chapter.

As in the western region, here too there have been some unassociated finds of metal objects. In 1958 Professor Jettmar photographed the residue of a large hoard of bronze objects discovered shortly before at a spot far up the Indus valley, high in the Gilgit Karakoram. This included several good specimens of trunnion axes of a similar type, along with shaft-hole axes with narrow necks (Fig. 9.3, Nos. 6 and 8). This hoard also suggests Iranian contacts during the second half of the millennium. It may be argued – however improbably – that the stray items of copper and bronze found in these western border regions indicate trade contacts rather than movements of peoples.

A somewhat perplexing surface find is a golden stag from the Hazara district of the Punjab, now in the Peshawar museum. This piece has a distinctly

9.10 Female terracotta figurines from the Gandhara graves: Nos. 1, 5, period v; Nos. 2–4, period vii (*courtesy* Stacul)

Caucasian appearance and may be compared with many examples, made in various metals from such sites in the south-west Caspian area as Talish, Samthavro and Lenkoran, and from Marlik, where they date from *c.* 1450–1200 B.C. The age of this piece is open to debate. M. Bussagli has assigned it to the Animal style of the Scytho-Sarmatian period, and dates it accordingly to the last centuries B.C. (*La Civiltà dell'Oriente*, 4, pp. 137–8, and Pl. 191). We can only comment that it is far removed from other Indian objects which exhibit the influence of the Animal style at that period (for example, some of the pierced ring stones of Mauryan date), and appears to us to be considerably earlier. It is difficult to believe that at so late a date it would exhibit no trace whatsoever of contemporary Indian influence: a date in the 7th or 8th century B.C. would seem acceptable.

Sind

Although there is no evidence that Mohenjo-daro continued to exist as a settlement, let alone as a city during this period, there are other sites which convey a different picture. The excavations at Chanhu-daro, Jhukar and Amri all seem to point in the same direction, namely that occupation continued after the end of the Mature Indus period without any major break. As yet the only published report which throws light on this period is for Chanhu-daro, but the Pakistan Archaeological Department's excavations at Jhukar (which, following Piggott,

9.11 Gandhara graves, face-urns, Swat, period v (*courtesy* Stacul)

has given its name to this 'culture', or what we now may better call 'phase') are likely when published to provide strong support. At Jhukar there appears to be a gradual change with a steady reduction in the characteristic Harappan elements and their replacement by the new Jhukar style which, while it is no doubt of Harappan derivation, reflects a distinct 'shift' of craft techniques. At Chanhu-daro also there appears to be no break between the final stage of Harappan house building and the subsequent 'squatter' occupation, with the re-use of earlier bricks and the breakdown of the older planned layout. The distinctive Jhukar pottery, a buff ware with red or cream slip often in bands, and bold painting in black, suggests a degree of continuity with local Harappan and even Western Indian traditions, and leads us to infer that the population remained substantially unchanged.

The picture in this way is generally comparable to that of Saurashtra, although the two regions show important differences. By contrast with the Harappan pottery, a fair proportion of the Jhukar ware gives evidence that it was finished by beating, after removal from the wheel. This later became a typical Indian potting technique. All these things may suggest that the population remained basically unchanged, but that there was a withdrawal for whatever reasons of certain distinctive elements of life, such as the Harappan seals and the use of writing. However, this is not the whole picture: there are a number of objects of metal which suggest either an increase of foreign trade (in our view unlikely at the moment when the urban system had broken down) or (more probably) the presence of foreign immigrants in the population. The same may be implied by the sudden appearance of circular or square stamp-seals of stone or faience. These things have been generally seen as indications of an influx of immigrants into the Indus valley from the west. The analogues of the distinctive objects suggest the direction of the movement, since their sources are generally in Iran, the Caucasus or Central Asia. A shaft-hole axe (fig. 9.3, No. 1) and copper pins with looped or decorated heads recall Shahi-tump and more significantly Hissar iiib. Circular, or occasionally square, stamp-seals of stone or faience again recall Hittite parallels from Asia Minor, and also Shahi-tump. Another foreign object is a small cast bronze cosmetic jar (or mace head) comparable to examples from Luristan, the Oxus valley and Hissar iii.

At Mohenjo-daro direct evidence of a Jhukar occupation is wanting, although Dales has noticed Jhukar elements in the late Mature period. The absence is probably due to natural causes, such as erosion; but on the other hand the groups of hastily buried or unburied corpses left in the streets of its final occupation, and the buried hoards of jewellery and copper objects, have been interpreted by some as testimony to the proximity of foreign invaders. More precise evidence of such a presence in the upper levels at Mohenjo-daro is found in the copper shaft-hole axe–adze, whose Iranian or Central Asian parallels date from c. 2000 to 1500 B.C. (Fig. 9.3, No. 7); while two dirks and two daggers with thickened mid-rib and rivet holes, are also of this time (Fig. 8.1, Nos. 5 and 9). We shall see below that thickened mid-ribs of bronze and copper appear to have spread into the peninsula of India between 1500 and 1300 B.C. In southern Sind and neighbouring Baluchistan the Harappan settlements at Balakot and Allahdino seem to have been abandoned, but comparable evidence for the subsequent period is not yet forthcoming.

Cutch and Saurashtra

The south-eastern province of the Indus civilization embraced Cutch and Saurashtra. We have already seen that at both Lothal and Surkotada there is evidence of the co-existence of local styles of material culture alongside the Harappan. The implication seems fairly clear: that the Harappans for a time established control over these areas which they exploited, probably because of their locally available raw materials or products – cotton, rice, etc. The picture of the period following the end of the Indus rule is in many respects comparable to that of Sind, except that there is not as yet the same suggestion of foreign immigrants (as evidenced by their seals, etc.).

At Lothal, throughout the Harappan occupation, a sprinkling of local pottery is found, including a distinctive black-and-red ware and a cream-slipped ware. The Mature Harappan character of this site seems to have ended around 2160 B.C., and the succeeding period II is characterized by new pottery forms and styles of painting, including animals of striking naturalism. In some publications periods I and II at Lothal are referred to as A and B respectively. This 'sub-Harappan' phase produced two radiocarbon dates of 2160 and 2140 B.C., and it must, we feel, indicate the partial withdrawal of colonial rule and the emergence of an independent provincial culture. Apart from Lothal, there are three principal excavations where the subsequent development can be followed; these are Rangpur, Somnath (Prabhas Patan) and Rojadi. Between them these sites give a complete sequence from the Mature Harappan period down to the arrival of iron. We shall summarize here the main phases of this development, as recognized at present:

1. Mature Harappan. During this period settlements show a combination of Harappan and local pottery. Constructional techniques – the use of mud- and burnt-brick for houses and drains – indicate Harappan influence. Rangpur IIA is our main source of information for this period (Fig. 9.12); Rojadi IA is also probably contemporary, as too may be Desalpur IA, in Cutch. It will be interesting as research advances to see whether it is possible to differentiate Harappan settlements such as Lothal from other sites, and whether the local cultural elements predominate at some sites more than others. One would like to know, for example, whether Harappan seals or sealings are found at the smaller sites. From what is already published it appears that, if not seals, at least inscribed potsherds are known at Rangpur and Rojadi.

2. Post-Harappan. This phase is represented by Lothal II, Rojadi IB, Rangpur IIB, and by the earliest settlement at Somnath (Prabhas Patan) I. At both Lothal and Rangpur, Harappan features are less common, following the withdrawal of Harappan trade and

influence. The pottery and other items of material culture continue without any marked break, but elaborate town planning and drainage, so characteristic of Harappan culture, disappear. Huts were probably built of wooden frames which supported some non-durable material such as thatch or matting. This period should commence around 2100 B.C., and at Rangpur the occupation is of about 4 metres in depth. A radiocarbon date from Rojadi gives 2090 B.C.

3. The third period is described by its excavators as coinciding at Rangpur IIC with something of a 'revival' (whatever that may mean). Certainly mud-brick was once again in common use, although floors were still of rammed earth, and post-holes, perhaps for the timbers to support the roofs, are found. No complete house plans are as yet available. This period may be equated with Rojadi IC and Somnath II. Again there is no real break with the preceding period. Some further distinctive Harappan forms of pottery, such as the footed goblets, disappear, and new painted motifs are found, including examples of antelopes and bulls (Fig. 9.13). A bright red burnished pottery known as the Lustrous Red ware makes its appearance. The terracotta cakes disappear.

4. The final development of the series corresponds with Rangpur III, Somnath III and Rojadi II. The Lustrous Red ware becomes a dominant pottery trait, as do the painted antelope and bull motifs, and a wide range of geometric designs painted on small carinated bowls. Another new trait is the black-and-red pottery, often with white-painted designs (Figs. 9.13, Nos. 8, 9, etc.).

The chronology of these periods is not yet clear. A series of radiocarbon dates from Prabhas Patan indicates that the early occupation there may be far older than hitherto suspected (the earliest date goes back to 2950 B.C., after calibra-

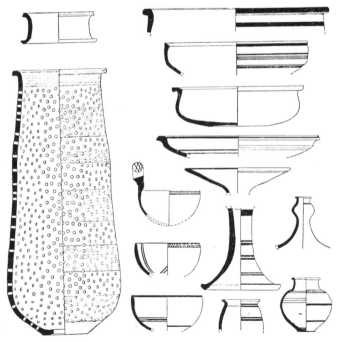

9.12 Rangpur, IIA: red ware pottery (1:6)

tion). Period II is dated by samples to *c.* 1900, while other dates (not as yet published in relation to their stratigraphic positions) suggest that the occupation continued without break to around 1400 B.C.

The stone-blade industry of the Harappan period, made of almost certainly imported materials, gives way in all the subsequent phases to a blade industry of locally available jasper and agate, but copper tools are found throughout. A study of the large quantity of plant remains obtained from Rangpur showed the cultivation of rice already in period IIA, and some millet, possibly *bājrā* or bulrush millet (*Pennisetum typhoideum*) in period III. The trees identified are mainly acacias, tamarisk and albizzia, indicating a dry forest and therefore a climate little different from that of today. Considering this evidence, and noting the apparent continuity of the settlements from the Harappan period forward, we may well ask at what stage Indo-Iranian languages were first introduced. Already before the Christian era Somnath was associated with Shri Krishna, the hero of the Mahābhārata story, who became identified with an incarnation of Vishnu. Another feature of the sequence is the way in which it apparently parallels that of Sind, where also a Late or Post-Harappan (Jhukar) culture phase succeeded almost immediately after the Harappan.

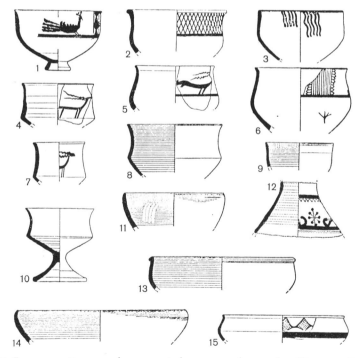

9.13 Rangpur pottery: 1 red ware, period IIB; 2, 3 and 5–7 red and Lustrous Red wares, period IIC; 4, 10, 12 and 15 red and Lustrous Red wares, period III; 8, 13 and 14 black-and-red ware, period III; 9 and 11 white-painted black-and-red ware, period III (1:6)

Punjab

The period coinciding with the end of the Harappan civilization in the north of
the region, in the Punjab, is of a rather different character from that of Sind, and
may well prove of fundamental importance to our understanding of later Indian
civilization. All over the citadel mound at Harappa, and in the topmost stratum
of the area F immediately to the north, Vats discovered a decadent period of
structures of re-used brick and pottery, including a significant quantity similar
to that discovered in Cemetery H. Even in the second stratum of the citadel
mound instances of pottery of this sort were noted. As this pottery is clearly
identified only in the cemetery, we propose to refer to it as belonging to the
Cemetery H culture. Wheeler showed conclusively by his excavation in 1946
that the cemetery bore a stratigraphic relationship to an earlier cemetery (R37) of
the Harappan period. Between the two there intervened a great mass of debris,
mainly of Harappan pottery, including some late-Harappan forms such as footed
goblets. Above and into this debris burials of Cemetery H were dug at two levels.

In the lower of the two strata (II) there were predominantly extended inhumations with grave goods. The pottery from some graves (which we may suppose,
following Vats, to have been the earliest) is reported to resemble that 'of the
mounds', that is to say, of the main Harappan occupation. In other cases the
pottery introduces both new forms and new painted patterns (Fig. 9.14). In the
upper stratum (I) we find the new, and probably intrusive rite of burying collected, disarticulated bones with other goods in large urns, but without other
accompanying grave goods. The painted urns tell us all that is so far known of
the beliefs of their makers (Fig. 9.15). On their shoulders these urns bear
registers bounded by straight or wavy lines. Common motifs are peacocks, with
long streaming feathers on their heads. In one case their bodies are hollow and
contain small horizontal human forms. A second motif is of bulls or cows, some
with curious plant-like forms springing from their horns, reminiscent of the
Harappan Bull deity, one with a *pīpal* leaf appearing from the hump. Another
shows two beasts facing each other, held by a man with long wavy hair, while a
hound stands menacingly behind one of them; in yet another a little man of
similar form stands on the back of a creature which shares the features of a
centaur with the Harappan bull–man. Other painted designs are mainly natural:
stars, leaves, trees, etc. Vats suggested that the tiny human forms within the
peacock are the souls of the dead; that the broad registers represent the river
across which they must be carried, and that the peacocks, bulls and so forth are
other aids to their crossing. In support of this he quoted possibly related extracts
from the Rigveda. Perhaps the most convincing detail is the hound, which he
compares with the hound of Yama, the god of death. We are inclined to interpret
the peacocks along similar lines, seeing in them the 'One bird' of the Rigveda,
variously identified with Agni (Fire), Sūrya (Sun) and Soma. Whether we are
already in the age of the Vedas, or whether these are part of a common heritage to

be soon absorbed by the migrating Aryans, is immaterial. However, it is clear that in the pottery of Cemetery H, the religious content of its decorations, no less than the pottery itself, suggests on the one hand a continuum with Mature Harappan elements, and on the other the presence of new features which we may be tempted to associate with the arrival of Indo-Aryans.

We are given almost no information by the excavators about the other aspects of the related material culture: thus at present all we have to go by is the pottery. Our view is that the differences between it and the earlier Harappan pottery have been exaggerated, while the many technical similarities and even the forms have not been given sufficient attention. A substantial range of forms – the urns themselves, the carinated vessels, the graceful footed vases – are no doubt foreign to the Mature Harappan style; the painted decoration with its distinctive stars and ring-and-dot patterns, is also foreign. On the other hand, it shows overwhelming craft continuity with that of the preceding period. In the same way the painting, with its continuing use of black upon a red ground, may

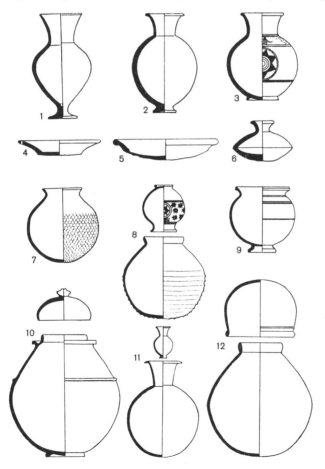

9.14 Harappa: Cemetery H red ware: 1–6 (1:8); 7–12 (1:16)

be said to form a logical development, rather than a break. The star and rosette motifs which are characteristic of the Cemetery H pottery are to be found also in both Early and Mature Harappan levels, as are the peacock and the humped bull. It cannot be denied, however, that the often bare vessels with single friezes of decoration, and the extraordinary painted covers with their bird or *pīpal* leaf themes have no counterparts in the Harappan itself, and seem to reflect contemporary styles found in western Iran (for example in Tepe Giyan II or Djamshidi II).

The evidence, therefore, seems to indicate an integration of existing potter communities with newcomers whoever they were. This conclusion was also

9.15 Harappa, Cemetery H: painted decoration from pottery

reached by Vats, who supported it by a careful consideration of relative stratigraphy. He stated that the Cemetery H culture was the final stage of the Harappan, and continuous with it; but that it must indicate the presence of foreign
conquerors or immigrants. In our view this is a fact of considerable importance,
suggesting the sort of cultural synthesis which may be represented by the
Cemetery H culture itself. The date of this event is clearly of great interest, but it
is not easy to estimate with precision in the absence of radiocarbon dating. It
may be expected to open at about the time when the Mature Harappan period
ends (i.e. after 2000 B.C.). The comparative material already suggested for the
urns from stratum I at sites in the far west of Iran, such as Tepe Giyan II/III and
Djamshidi II (c. 1550–1400 B.C.) and Susa D give some approximation for dating
the Cemetery H culture. At these comparative sites stars and birds occur in
registers in a manner strikingly recalling those of Cemetery H. Certain of the
evolved Harappan forms, particularly the offering stands, may be compared
with those from Rangpur IIB and C (see above). Altogether we feel that this
period may extend over some three centuries or more in the Punjab, and is
probably to be placed between 2000 and c. 1500 B.C. We shall continue below the
discussion of the eastward extension of this and related cultures.

India east of the Indus system

When we move eastwards beyond the frontiers of the Indus system we encounter two regions which are of great importance for our understanding of the
succeeding periods. These may be regarded during Harappan times as contact
zones with India east of the Indus; and during post-Harappan times as nuclear
areas in which cultural developments over a wide area are foreshadowed. The
two regions, moreover, occupy geographically significant positions, in that they
represent the logical termini of routes which have been diverted by the position
of the Great Indian desert. The northern route follows up the rivers of the Punjab
until it reaches the sub-montane tract, and then turns south-eastwards across
the Indo-Gangetic divide towards the Doab of the Ganges and Jamuna rivers.
The southern route leaves Lower Sind and crosses between the desert and the
marshes of Cutch, re-emerging in southern Rajasthan and the fertile Malwa
plateau. The two Nuclear Regions are further important to our understanding
because they form the entrances to two broad corridors through which movements, trade and contacts have flowed, following largely natural, geographical
lines. We shall organize what we have to discuss in this and in the following
chapters bearing in mind these two great corridors. The first, which we may call
the northern corridor, coincides closely with what in later Indian literature is
referred to as the *Uttarapatha*, or northern road, leading up from the Ganges
valley towards the north-west, and thence through the mountains to Central
Asia. The second, southern corridor, may also be likened, though less exactly,
to the ancient *Daksināpatha*, the southern road, which in later times was

conceived of as leading from the Ganges valley into the south. The northern corridor passes from the Nuclear Region through the Doab into the middle Ganges valley and thence into Bengal and the deltaic Ganges regions. The southern corridor leaves the Southern Nuclear Region and passes through Maharashtra and Karnataka into all parts of the southern peninsula.

In these Nuclear Regions and the corridors we enter another world in terms of the patterns of settlement and housing. The use of mud-brick or pressed earth, and the construction of compact houses in regular spatial relationship to each other, disappears, at least for the early periods, to be replaced by more loosely clustered, single-roomed huts of less solid construction. These are frequently built with a wooden frame infilled with a wattle of split bamboo or other substance, and a daub of mud-plaster and cow dung. Two main types are found: circular huts, with – it may be inferred – pitched roofs covered by thatch; and oblong huts – also probably with pitched roofs. Huts of both types are still to be seen in almost every state of India from the far south, to Rajasthan in the west, and Bengal in the east.

In view of the apparent longevity of the contrast between the housing patterns within the Indus system and to its east, one may enquire when the pattern of more extensive, many-roomed houses of brick or more solid materials first spread eastwards. This is still not altogether clear, but the evidence from the northern and southern nuclear areas is suggestive. It appears as though some sites of the Harappan and immediately post-Harappan periods retained the building patterns of the former. Brick houses are referred to in connection with Bara, Sanghol, Rupar IB and Mitathal IIB. Very interesting evidence from Bhagawanpura in Haryana, suggests a slightly different picture. At this site in the subsequent period, with the first appearance of the Painted Grey ware pottery, the structures 'revert' to round, or partly rounded huts with thatched roofs; but still later as the Painted Grey ware becomes more common, extensive houses, with as many as thirteen rooms, and walls of earth or mud-brick reappear. From farther east, in the Doab, evidence from the excavations at Jakhera indicates that there the settlers of the black-and-red ware and Painted Grey ware periods continued to occupy circular huts of wattle and daub.

The Northern Nuclear Region

The Northern Nuclear Region comprises a considerable area (Fig. 9.1, A). In the west it includes much of the modern states of east Punjab, Haryana and parts of northern Rajasthan, and in its eastern half the Doab of the Ganges and Jamuna rivers. Indeed the former area consisted at one time of the Doab of the now dry Sarasvati and Drishadvati rivers, and the latter with the ancient kingdoms of Matsya, Kuru, Surasena and Panchala, and the whole of the area may therefore be compared with the ancient Āryāvartta, the 'home of the Aryans' of Indian tradition, also known as Brahmāvarta.

Dealing first with the western half of this region, we find a curiously compli-cated situation. The earliest settlements yet known there belong to the Early Indus period. These appear to have been augmented during the Mature Indus period by a number of colonies, while exisiting settlements show indications of culture contact with the Harappans. A number of sites belonging to the post-Harappan period have been excavated, and these suggest that there may well be several regional variants of pottery style. A good example is Mitathal, excavated by Suraj Bhan. Here period I is the final stage of Early Indus and is culturally closely parallel to Kalibangan I (Fig. 9.16); period IIA shows the blending of this local style with Mature Harappan elements, indicative of some sort of Harappan presence; period IIB shows a further direct development which its excavator names Late Harappan and which shows clear Cemetery H affinities (Figs. 9.17–18). It appears probable that all the variants belong to a broader cultural unity, indicated in the pottery by the presence of a redware, sometimes with painted decoration and with a number of notably 'Harappan' forms surviving. This pottery has been called locally by various names: 'Bara ware', 'Late Siswal ware', Ochre Coloured Pottery, etc. We would prefer to all these local variants under the one style, 'redware of Harappan tradition'. The distinctive redware of Cemetery H is closely related to that found at Bara and other sites near Rupar, north-west of Chandigarh, and at Sanghol in Ludhiana district. It has also been reported at a number of sites to the east as far as the Jamuna and southwards into Rajasthan, where it is probably represented by the early period at Jodhpura. The relations of this pottery are still not clearly established. Surprisingly

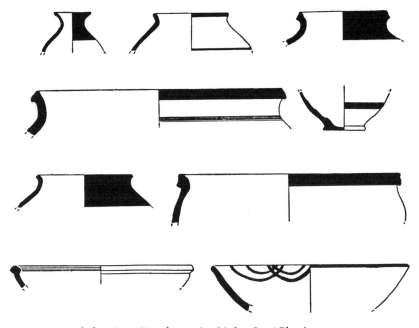

9.16 Mitathal, I: Late Siswal ware (1:6) (*after* Suraj Bhan)

reminiscences of the painted decorations of Tepe Giyan IV are found at Bara and Mitathal IIB. These incline us to expect that the phase belongs to the first half of the second millennium. As this region is of such importance, and as this period probably coincides with the foundation of the early settlements of Indo-Aryan speaking tribes in the area, it calls for special attention, and further research of all kinds.

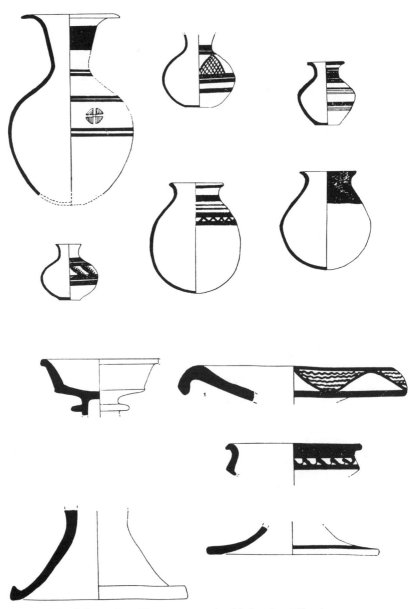

9.17 Mitathal, IIB: Late Harappan ware (1:6) (*after* Suraj Bhan)

The southern part of the Nuclear Region abuts on the northern extremes of its southern counterpart. This junction is an area of crucial importance: not only does it abound in remains of early settlements, but in the Khetri region there are copious deposits of copper. R. C. Agrawal has shown that there are many ancient copper working localities, often associated with red pottery of OCP affinity, and also many copper objects. In excavations at Ganeshwar, in Sikar District of Rajasthan, over 400 copper arrowheads, 50 fish-hooks, 58 copper flat axes and dozens of smaller objects are reported. No radiocarbon dates are as yet available, but at the neighbouring site of Jodhpura, a sequence of Iron Age levels succeeds a comparable OCP period. Here one radiocarbon date for the latter suggests that it may be as old as 2800–2700 B.C. The forms of the copper objects resemble Mature Harappan types, but there is so far absolutely no other indication of Harappan influence in this area. Clearly the further determination of the chronology and character of these sites is called for. Spectrometric analysis suggests that these areas were the source for the copper found in sites of this period from Haryana, Rajasthan, Gujarat, Madhya Pradesh and even the Deccan. Some of these artefacts show a very pure copper; while others show an alloy of 3–12% of tin. Metallographic analysis reveals that the axes were cast in moulds, and that their edges bevelled by hot and cold forging. Some were cast in unventilated moulds, but others give evidence of well ventilated ones. Examples of the latter are from Prabhas Patan and Navdatoli.

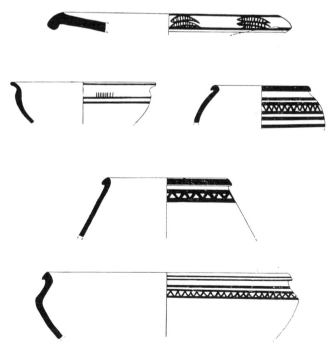

9.18 Mitathal, IIB: Late Harappan ware (1:6) (*after* Suraj Bhan)

The Ganges Doab and the Ganges valley

As we have already seen on the eastern borders of the Harappan culture region in the north, Mature Indus cultural influences appear to have penetrated almost as a colonial process among settlements whose culture continues at least for a time to reflect more nearly that of the Early Indus stage. As we move eastwards out of the Punjab into Haryana and the Doab we progressively leave behind the Harappan zone and encounter other related indigenous cultures. Since virtually no fully Harappan sites occur east of the Jamuna – the single possible exception being Alamgirpur, which in most respects appears to be closer to the Late Harappan of Rupar and Bara – we may for convenience treat the line of the Jamuna as the frontier between the western and eastern halves of the nuclear area. To the east is the area known as the Doab. This territory, and the lands to its east and south, has long been famous for being the home of what came to be known as the 'Copper hoard culture'. Ever since 1822 hoards of copper implements have come to light from time to time in the Ganges–Jamuna Doab, the hills of the Chota Nagpur and Orissa, and at odd places in Central India and the Deccan. In 1951 B. B. Lal listed thirty-seven such hoards. We may consider them as divided, culturally, into two main groups, those of the Doab and those of the more easterly province, the former comprising about half of the total (Fig. 9.19). Until two decades ago there was no indication of the cultural context of the copper hoards, but since that date their associations have become clearer. At Bisauli and at Rajpur Parsu exploration and trial excavation in the vicinity of the findspots of hoards revealed a thick, red, rolled and waterlogged pottery, nicknamed 'Ochre-washed' or Ochre Coloured Pottery (sometimes abbreviated to OCP) from its distinctive quality. A third hoard site at Bahadarabad in Saharanpur district yielded similar evidence. Excavation at Hastinapura revealed the OCP below the Early Iron Age (Painted Grey ware) levels, but in so small a quantity as to give no indication of complete forms. Further exploration has revealed a number of sites, some producing Late Harappan elements, such as stone blades, and even a copper bracelet, in association with this pottery. All the sites at which the elusive Ochre Coloured ware has so far been recorded are on the alluvial plains of the Ganges river system, and frequently finds have been reported as having been subjected to flooding, or redeposition. This may explain the worn and waterlogged condition of so much of the pottery and its disintegrated surface. Trial excavations at Ambakheri and Bargaon revealed quantities of pottery including many Late Harappan forms. It seems probable that when this material is published it will show two or more phases, corresponding to those of the east Punjab. Thus we may expect to find two parallel and interleaving series: one deriving ultimately from an Early Indus source, comparable to the Siswal tradition in the Punjab; and the other deriving from sites where there was a direct Harappan presence, degenerating in later times into the so-called 'Late Harappan' character (as is witnessed at Bara or Alamgirpur). Explorations during the past decade have revealed a very large number of sites in the Doab both to the east and west. There have been a number of excavations, notably at Atranjikhera in Etah district, at Lal Qila in Bulandshahr district, Saipai in Etawah district, and at Ahicchatra in Bareli district. At many of these sites the pottery sequence is similar: in the earliest period of occupation there is the red 'Ochre Coloured Pottery' which is the name hitherto used for the red wares of this series. This is generally followed by a short second period in which black-and-red burnished ware is discovered. The earliest evidence of iron comes from this period. In some sites there appears to have been no black-and-red ware

9.19 Map of finds of copper and bronze objects

phase, but a gradual appearance of Painted Grey ware which too is associated with the earliest appearance of iron at several sites. The absolute dating of the early period is still somewhat unclear. At present it depends upon a small series of thermoluminescence dates from Atranjikhera, Lal Qila, Nasirpur and Jhinjhina. These record a spread of 2650–1180 B.C., three dates being between 2650 and 2030, and five between 1730 and 1180. However slight the evidence it provides general confirmation for our hypothesis. A feature of some sites on the Ganges–Jamuna alluvium is that they appear to have been flood-washed during the early period, suggesting that the second millennium may have witnessed considerable tectonic uplift, leading to widespread shifts of river courses and flooding. As none of the excavations has as yet been published in more than summary form, further information about the economy and subsistence of these settlements must await fuller publication.

The associational evidence now seems quite clear. The copper hoards belong to the period of the 'OCP' or red ware of Harappan tradition, and may be expected to date from the last half of the third and the whole of the second millennia. Much of it thus coincides with a 'Late Harappan' time scale. We may expect that further research and publication will help to establish the chronology more precisely.

The chronological and cultural horizons being thus defined, we may now consider the typology of the objects found in the hoards (Fig. 9.20). The metal of specimens so far analysed suggests that it is of impure copper throughout, with traces of tin, lead and arsenic in many instances. Agrawal has suggested that the source of the copper is likely to have been from the Rakha mines of Bihar, in contrast to the Harappan source, which as we noted above was most probably the Khetri region of Rajasthan. The tools are made by a limited range of techniques, further distinguishing them from the much wider range of Harappan metal technology.

The common flat axes sometimes with slightly splayed blades require no discussion: as we have already noted, they are common in the Indus civilization and at several post-Harappan Chalcolithic sites. A second type of flat axe has a semi-circular cutting edge and a pronounced shoulder (Fig. 9.20, No. 4). A third type has the cutting edge extended to form two wings, as in the modern *Parasū*. The most elaborate type is that often referred to as an anthropomorphic figure (Fig. 9.20, No. 1). These curious pieces have sharpening on the rear of the 'arms' while the inner sides of the 'legs' are left blunt. They bear some resemblance to 'anthropomorphic' sacrificial axes of iron or steel used by the Santals and other tribal people of Chota Nagpur, but their actual function was more probably as some kind of ritual figures. Next there are heavy spearheads or swords having a solid tang, often with a single barb, presumably for hafting, and a blade with a mid-rib, ranging in length to over 71 cm (Fig. 9.20, Nos. 6 and 10). There is no doubt that the examples with antennae hilts were swords or dirks (Figure 9.20, No. 2). Another distinctive type is the barbed harpoon, with triangular tip and with three pairs of barbs below. In some instances these are hafted with a tang and single barb, in others with a pierced lug and tang (Fig. 9.20, Nos. 7 and 8). These again have a stout mid-rib and were undoubtedly cast in a mould.

The second distributional group of copper implements is still less easy to fix culturally. The objects are found south and east of the first, in the hills and forests south of the Ganges in Bihar and Bengal. The groups include flat axes, long bar celts, often 18 inches in length, and shouldered axes. An outlier of this group is from Gungeria, in the Balaghat district of Madhya Pradesh south of Jabalpur, where along with over 400 copper objects about 100 thin silver plates in the form of a bull's head with down-turned horns were discovered. This

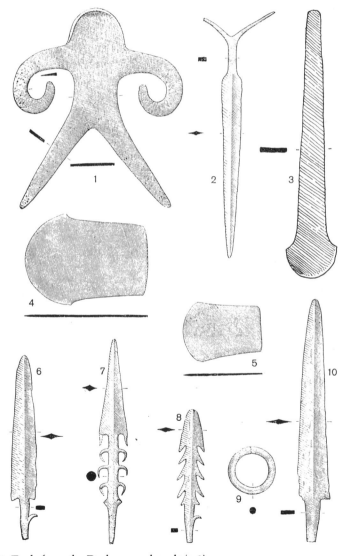

9.20 Tools from the Doab copper hoards (1:8)

occurrence of silver in a prehistoric context from east of the Indus is unique. This hoard is reported to have weighed in all 829 lbs (376 kg), quite dwarfing the copper weight of the Daimabad hoard! Its age is still a matter of speculation. Indeed, throughout all the hoards of the Doab, of Chota Nagpur, and between, one is struck by the excessive weight of the individual items, surely making them functionally unwieldy. They may well have had a mostly non-utilitarian use. The majority of the tools are of plain copper, although occasionally specimens of bronze have been reported. One may expect such a prodigal use of the metal to indicate a cheap and plentiful source, and D. P. Agrawal may well be correct in associating it with the mines in the Singhbhum and Dalbhum area of Chota Nagpur.

The copper hoards of these two groups, those of Doab, and of the eastern area or Chota Nagpur, thus appear to form a separate cultural entity. They are for the most part clearly distinct from the stray hoards from Pakistan, Western India or the Deccan, including the Mehsana and the Kallur hoards. They seem to reflect a mainly copper-using craft tradition, and the evidence of alloying is still rather unclear. That it is an indigenous tradition, not expressly linked with any external influences may be concluded, although the picture is somewhat uncertain. Certain types, such as the antennae dirks, have exact parallels in northwest Afghanistan, and less exact comparisons with specimens from Iran and the Caucasus. These elements may indicate trade or other indirect culture contacts with those areas.

In contrast to the distribution of hoards, the easternmost extension of the distinctive Doab 'Copper hoard culture' is roughly the confluence of the Ganges and Jamuna at Allahabad. Beyond this the middle Ganges valley is still relatively little known at this period. The early settlements in this area are widely scattered and few in number. The indications are that they are relatively late in date, and poor in material culture. The earliest known is at Chirand in north Bihar, to which we have already alluded in an earlier chapter. Here the first period appears to be a true Neolithic, in that there is so far no evidence of metals. The proximity of such a culture to the copper rich culture of the Doab or Chota Nagpur, gives food for thought. The succeeding period, II, is described as Chalcolithic, but to date very little has been published about it. It appears to be substantially a continuation of the preceding period I. Pottery included black-and-red ware along with black and red wares. Copper objects were discovered. The period is dated by a run of radiocarbon dates, between 1500 and 800 B.C. The further dates from Sohgaura in the Gorakhpur district are between 1500 and 1400 B.C. This period is also in evidence in the latest levels of Sonpur in Gaya district. Evidence of huts of wattle and daub, along with objects of copper, is reported. There is also some evidence of rice, as well as wheat (*Triticum p. sphaerococcum*) and a species of barley, though, unfortunately, it is insecurely dated.

At Pandu Rajar Dhibi in the Burdwan district of West Bengal, the excavation

Time scale B.C.	Northern valleys & Kashmir					Potwar			Pirak
	Ghaligai	Aligram	Loebanr	Gandhara graves	Burzahom	Sarai Khola	Hathial (Taxila)	Bhir mound (Taxila)	Pirak
250	VII	VI						IV	
500	VI	V		← III	← ?			III / II	III
750	V	IV			III	III ?		I	II
1000	IV	III	III	II			? ← II → ?		I
1250	III	II		I	II				
1500		I							? ← I ?? → ?
1750	II						? ← I → ?		
2000					I ——————→ ?	II b			
2250	I → ?					II a			
2500						I →			
2750									
3000	?								

9.21 Comparative sequences of the northern valleys and Pirak (c. 3000–250 B.C.)

9.22 Comparative sequences in the Northern Nuclear Region and Ganges valley (c. 2250–250 B.C.)

of a mound produced a culture sequence with two pre-iron periods, characterized by a crude stone-blade industry, ground stone axes, and a number of copper
objects, including fish-hooks. Wheat and barley are recorded – as is rice. The
pottery included painted red ware and black-and-red wares. Channel-spouted
bowls are also common. Taking this assemblage as a whole, we would expect it
to belong to something equivalent to the Jorwe phase (see onward, p. 273) at the
earliest, but more probably slightly later than that phase in the west. A single
radiocarbon sample gives a date of 1110 B.C., and seems plausible. At Mahisadal
in the adjacent Birbhum district, another recent excavation has yielded confirmation of this sequence. Period 1 was Chalcolithic, with simple huts of plastered reed. The finds included a typical blade industry and a flat copper celt;
pottery included black-and-red ware, sometimes white-painted, and red ware,
some with black-painted decoration. The forms of pottery recall those of Pandu
Rajar Dhibi, channel spouts being prominent. A quantity of charred rice was
discovered, confirming again the evidence from Pandu Rajar Dhibi. This period
is dated by three radiocarbon samples to between 1380 and 855 B.C. The succeeding period 11 saw a combination of the new somewhat coarser pottery and
the arrival of iron, and a single radiocarbon sample suggests that this event took
place before 690 B.C. Other sites yielding somewhat similar evidence are Barudih in Singhbhum district where a profusion of ground stone axes and an iron
sickle were found in deposits radiocarbon dated to *c.* 1100–700 B.C.; and at
Bharatpur in Burdwan district, radiocarbon dated to *c.* 1350–1000 B.C.

CHAPTER 10

THE AFTERMATH OF THE INDUS CIVILIZATION IN PENINSULAR INDIA

The Southern Nuclear Region

Southern Rajasthan

Leaving the Indus valley and skirting the southern fringes of the Thar desert, we enter, in a very real sense, another major culture zone. Almost at once we are in a region in which direct contacts with the Indus system become much rarer and in which from the earliest settlements known there is a new and different cultural style. We have in fact entered our Southern Nuclear Region (Fig. 9.1, B).

About three hundred km north-east of the Kathiawar peninsula, in the hilly country east of the Aravalli range, a somewhat different culture has been brought to light in recent years, called the Banas culture after the river of that name. Certain features suggest that it may have played a significant role in the formation of later Indian civilization. In this area no Harappan sites are yet known, and it is therefore a matter of great interest to speculate on the origins of the Banas culture and its relation with the Harappans.

The early occupation at Ahar, near modern Udaipur, is divided into three phases, IA, B and C. Radiocarbon dates indicate that IA extended from 2580 to 2170; IB produced one date of c. 2080; and IC continued down to 1500 B.C. or later (Fig. 10.30). These dates thus indicate that the site was occupied during the lifetime of the Indus civilization, as well as after it. One of the special features is the complete absence of any stone tools, either axes or blades; copper axes and objects of copper were correspondingly numerous. At Ahar heaps of semi-fused glass-like copper slag, along with copper tools, were discovered in a context dated to c. 1800 B.C. Clearly Ahar was a copper-smelting centre, and there are indeed extensive copper deposits in the nearby Aravalli hills, sometimes associated with old shafts and slag heaps, of as yet undetermined age.

Much of the pottery is also rather different from that of the Saurashtran sites, though one of the dominant wares throughout is black-and-red ware with white-painted decoration (Fig. 10.1). Another important ware present in the earliest phases only is a cream-slipped pottery with black-painted decoration. Red-slipped ware is present from the beginning, and in the third phase (IC) Lustrous Red ware makes its appearance. Grey ware, with incised or appliqué decoration, was found, and some of these vessels had surface roughening on the lower part of the exterior, recalling examples from both Baluchistan and South India. A noteworthy form, the dish-on-stand, was present throughout. The large numbers of rubbing stones and saddle querns may be taken as indicating some sort of grain production, and deer were evidently hunted. Terracotta figurines (a comparative rarity from Rajasthani sites, and indeed also to the south in Maharashtra) included humped cattle, and these were evidently an important element in the economy, to judge by the large number of bones discovered. Less common,

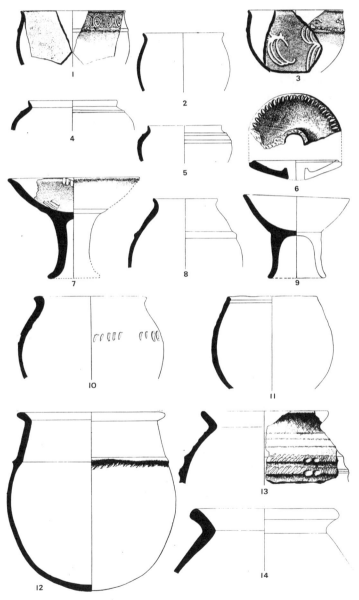

10.1 Ahar: pottery: 1, 3 and 7 white-painted black-and-red ware period IA; 2, 4, 5, 8, 11 And 14, red ware, period IA; 10 and 13 grey ware, period IA; 6 and 9 grey ware, period IB; 12 scarlet slipped ware, period IC (1:5) (*after* Sankalia *et al.*)

but also identified in period 1 were domestic fowl, domestic ass, buffalo, sheep, goat and pig. Among cultivated grains rice was common, and sorghum was present in the final stage of period 1. There is also a possibility that *bājrā* or the bulrush millet (*Pennisetum typhoideum*) was cultivated here. Along with the similar evidence from Rangpur this is the earliest known occurrence of this crop. The picture presented suggests a continuation of the earlier crop-patterns like those of the Harappan province, but augmented by millet.

Houses at Ahar were ablong and often of not inconsiderable size; one completely excavated example measured 10 by 5 metres. The walls were of stone and mud, or mud-brick, and perhaps also of wattle and daub. Apparently the roofs were flat, made of bamboo and matting, and covered with earth or thatch. No indication is recorded of any development or change during the occupation.

Among the numerous other sites identified as belonging to this period, Gilund has been excavated. It is about 80 km north-east of Ahar. The site was obviously a large settlement, and interesting structural remains were revealed from the earliest occupation, including a system of mud-brick walls which seemed to have formed part of a great platform, a feature recalling Harappan planning. The pottery appears to have been much as at Ahar, with painted black-and-red ware appearing throughout. In the upper levels only, painted cream-slipped ware was found. Terracotta figurines of humped cattle were again present, but in contrast to Ahar a stone-blade industry was recorded. More precise correlation will be possible when the publication of this interesting excavation is completed. It appears that this culture can be compared with those adjoining it to the south and east. The reason for the absence of any trace of Harappan influence is again problematic. The button seals and other things found associated with the Jhukar period are also absent, as are traces of western imports comparable to those found in the Gandharan grave culture. There are, however, some traces of western imports towards the end of the period. A copper hoard from Khurdi (properly Kurada) in the Nagaur district of Rajasthan including a fine bowl with a long protruding channel spout, of a form with numerous analogues in both pottery and metal at Giyan 1, Sialk (Necropolis B), etc. Also from the hoard came another simple bowl of copper recalling examples from Sialk, and several flat double choppers of copper (Fig. 10.2). We may expect this hoard to date to *c.* 1300 B.C. Another small hoard from the Mehsana district contained four dirks of copper and bronze. One at least has a distinctly 'Iranian' bifurcated hilt, although the others are clearly local.

We have mentioned the evidence of metal-working at Ahar, and of the ore sources in the nearby Aravalli hills. This must be taken in relation to the evidence from the north-east, in the Ganeshwar area, referred to in the previous chapter. It seems certain that these two areas, and therefore the two Nuclear Regions, must have had contacts with each other at all times, and may well have formed a major cultural grouping which in one way or another checked the eastern spread of the Mature Indus civilization into Rajasthan.

Malwa

Directly to the east of the Banas valley and the Aravalli hills lies the fertile
Malwa plateau. Drained by the river Chambal and sloping gently toward the
north, the region is bounded on the south by the valley of the Narbada river. Two
sites of importance have been excavated in this area – Kayatha, some fifteen
miles east of Ujjain, and Navdatoli on the banks of the Narbada, near Mahesh-
war. Kayatha has been the subject of two excavations, one by its discoverer, V. S.
Wakankar, and the other by the Deccan College. The settlement revealed a
Chalcolithic occupation of considerable interest. There are three periods. The
first is dated by radiocarbon to between *c.* 2400 and 2120 B.C., and produced a
distinctive range of pottery including Kayatha ware, painted in violet over a
broad band of deep brown slip; a buff-painted ware and a combed ware. We have

10.2 Hoard of copper objects from Khurdi, Nagaur district, Rajasthan (*courtesy*
Jodhpur Museum)

not ourselves seen this pottery, but the impression is that like the pottery from Ahar it is throughout either handmade or made on some sort of turntable. The excavators tell us that up to 85% is handmade. A more specific examination of the decorative tradition of Malwa and Maharashtra ceramics is made later in this chapter, see p. 284. As at Ahar, copper objects appear to have been common, and finds included flat axes and copper rings, both recalling Ahar examples. There was also a typical blade industry of chalcedony and similar stones. The second period is dated to between 2100 and 1800 B.C., and it shows, alongside a continuation of most of the main features of the previous period (such as use of copper and stone blades), a marked change in the style of pottery. Whether this change reflects political or other developments, or even actual folk movements, as the excavators have suggested, or merely a change in fashion, has still to be demonstrated. The pottery shows, ware by ware, a direct resemblance to the pottery of Ahar, with white-painted black-and-red ware, fine burnished red and grey wares, and red-slipped ware and coarse grey ware. Houses appear to have been of wattle and daub. A prominent feature of the material culture is provided by a series of terracotta figurines, mainly of bulls (Fig. 10.3). These include many examples of stylized horned heads standing on flattened bases. These are evidently intended to be boucrania, and along with other evidence suggest that, as elsewhere in the subcontinent, the cult of the bull was also present here. This unfortunately is presently the only evidence available for religious beliefs in this area. The third period, which is dated to c. 1800–1500 B.C., shows a gradual evolution to a style of pottery virtually identical with that of Navdatoli, and known therefrom as Malwa. The other elements of material culture continue much as in the preceding period, though of note is the recorded occurrence of wheat at Kayatha. Unfortunately, it comes from an insecurely dated context.

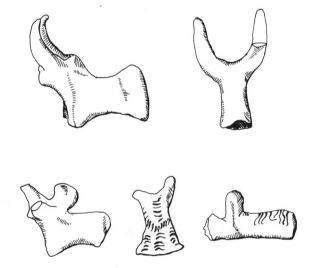

10.3 Kayatha: terracotta bulls (1:2) (after Ansari)

However, this evidence, along with the much more comprehensive material from Navdatoli, suggests that wheat would have been cultivated at most sites in the Malwa region.

The excavations at Navdatoli provide eight radiocarbon dates. They suggest that the Chalcolithic settlement, which the excavators divide into four phases, may be dated between *c.* 2020 and 1660 B.C. The earliest settlement at Navdatoli is period I. A stone-blade industry existed and copper tools were made. The stone blades are particularly numerous and often very finely made. As in Karnataka, there is a regular minority of retouched blades, giving backed or geometric forms. The inhabitants kept cattle, sheep, goat and pig, and hunted deer. The excavations have provided excellent botanical evidence. Finds from period I include wheat grains of the *Triticum compactum* and *Triticum vulgare* types. Their pottery, which again provides the chief distinguishing feature in the culture, included painted black-and-red ware, a distinctive red-slipped pottery with black-painted decoration (known as Malwa ware), and a creamy-white slipped ware with black-painted decoration, also closely related to the Malwa ware in point of manufacture (Figs. 10.4–5). A grey ware recalling that of Maharashtra and Karnataka was present throughout. Among distinctive pottery forms are many handmade bowls. The painted decoration is rather fussily applied, and gives the impression that its authors had a good deal of time on their hands!

In the second phase at Navdatoli (II), which in parts of the site followed a minor burning, evidence of rice cultivation is encountered. The chief change in the pottery is the absence of the black-and-red painted ware, while a series of small goblets on solid pedestals is distinctive. The third phase followed a more extensive burning and seems to have coincided with the arrival of new traits and perhaps also new elements of population from the west. Among these new traits is a fine red pottery, frequently wheel-thrown, with black-painted decoration (Fig. 10.6). This has been named Jorwe ware. Characteristically it is unburnished, but some of its forms seem related to those of the Lustrous Red ware of Kathiawar. Along with the Jorwe ware came a new vogue for spouted vessels, and distinctive forms which recall those from the second phase of the Neolithic of the Karnataka region. Copper fish-hooks from the surface collection probably belong to this phase. Rice is again found in period III, but there are several pulses, including the lentil (*Lens culinaris*), black gram (*Phaseolus mungo*), green gram (*Phaseolus radiatus*) and grass pea. It is interesting that linseed appears, as well as two fruits, the Indian jujube or ber, as at Mundigak, and the myrobalan (*Phyllanthus emblica*). This picture again is remarkable for the sense of continuity which it affords; almost all the crops are still grown in the region.

The final stage of the Chalcolithic at Navdatoli (period IV) saw the addition of channel-spouted bowls and of further pottery recalling the Lustrous Red ware.

The huts throughout the Chalcolithic period at Navdatoli – unlike Ahar – were both round and oblong, but all seem to have employed a wooden frame and

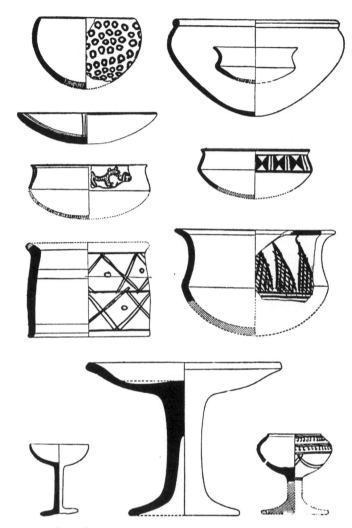

10.4 Navdatoli, Malwa: pottery (1:6)

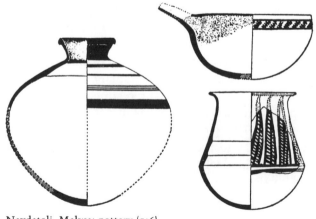

10.5 Navdatoli, Malwa: pottery (1:6)

wattle and daub walls. The floors were made of clay and cow dung, and sometimes given a lime-plastered surface. The oblong houses were the larger, and one measured 12 by 6 m, while the round huts did not exceed 2.75 m in diameter, clearly indicative of their subordinate status. The smallest of these round huts must have been used for no more than the storage of grains or other materials. There is no evidence of roof tiles, and the probability is that roofs were thatched. Every house had its own hearth, of a pattern identical to those of Ahar, with three compartments, side by side, made of clay and lime plaster; the store-rooms within the houses contained lines of jars, the larger standing on raised earth stands.

The eastward extension of Chalcolithic cultures of Malwa type is soon told. Geographically and culturally, the regions of Central India are to this day somewhat complex, presenting a picture of islands of settled agricultural life amid an ocean of hills and forests. No doubt in ancient times the forest was far more prevalent than it is today, but fundamentally the pattern is ancient. At Eran, some 300 km north-east of Navdatoli, on a tributary of the Betwa river, and at Tripuri, near Jabalpur, on the Narbada river itself, excavations have revealed Chalcolithic settlements below those of a later period; in both cases the material culture suggest that of Malwa. A series of radiocarbon dates from Eran has recently been published, but they do not seem to bear a uniform relationship to their reported stratified provenances. The indication they provide is that the Chalcolithic culture at this site extended from *c.* 1700 to 1170 B.C., and probably gave way to the Iron Age around that date. However, the published evidence from both these sites is too slight to present a very definite

 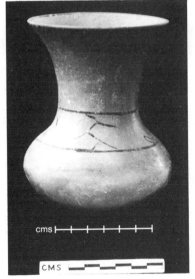

10.6 Navdatoli: high necked vessel and water pot of Jorwe ware (*courtesy* Deccan College, Pune)

picture. There is a suggestion at Eran that the final phase of the Chalcolithic (IIA) may be associated with black-and-red ware.

The area included in the Banas and Malwa cultures forms a Southern Nuclear Region, shut off from direct influence from the Indus valley by the desert, but open to such influence via Saurashtra. It cannot yet be said why no – or at most very slight – traces of Mature Harappan contacts have been found in the region but, as we have seen, it is now clear that a distinctive and characteristic style of culture developed in it from around the time when the Mature Indus civilization arose in Sind. From this nuclear area a great corridor runs towards the south through the low rainfall areas of the Deccan plateau, and there can be no doubt that this corridor has throughout formed a major means of culture contact

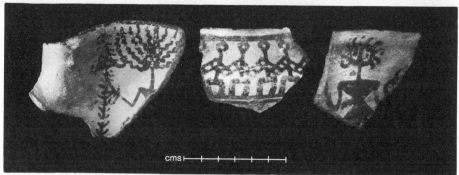

10.7 Navdatoli: painted Malwa ware and white slipped ware from period 1 (*courtesy* Deccan College, Pune)

between the north and south. From it subsidiary corridors run eastwards, rather like the veins of a leaf, into the forests of Central India in the north, across the Deccan plateau to the Andhra coast in the centre, and towards the Tamil plain in the south. The evidence of culture contacts and the spread of influence suggests that this corridor was already recognizable in the period under discussion, and we shall therefore do well to bear it in mind as articulating the series of regional cultures which we shall now describe.

Maharashtra

South of the hills which border the lower course of the Narbada valley lies the northern part of the great plateau of the Deccan. In terms of the Chalcolithic period this is one of the most extensively excavated parts of India, thanks in large measure to the activities of Sankalia and his colleagues of Deccan College, Poona. Thus during the past two decades excavations have been undertaken at Jorwe, Prakash, Bahal, Nevasa, Daimabad, Chandoli, Sonegaon and Inamgaon. Two of the sites, Prakash and Bahal, lie in the valley of the westward-flowing Tapi (Tapti) river; the remainder are all on the plateau itself, in the country drained by the headwaters of the eastward-flowing Godavari and Krishna river systems which abut to the south upon Karnataka or the central Deccan. A special problem is presented because, apparently, out of eight sites only Daimabad, which is unfortunately incompletely published, yields cultural remains of an antiquity comparable to the earlier stages in Saurashtra and Malwa to the north, or Karnataka to the south. Thus we must treat the evidence for this earlier period with some caution.

1. The first period is represented at present only at Daimabad (1). Here the occupation was found to produce ground stone axes, a perforated ring-stone and a stone-blade industry. The pottery was mainly coarse grey or black, frequently burnished, and sometimes decorated with unburned ochre paint. A second ware was again unburnished, but with a buff surface sometimes painted in black or brown. Fingertip decoration and appliqué bands occur, and it is claimed that at least one painted spout was recovered from this period. Comparatively speaking, this assemblage may be compared with the second or Upper Neolithic phase of the Karnataka sites to the south, though its more immediate affinities are with Navdatoli and Malwa. Several extended burials were discovered between the houses. This type of burial rite, with adults laid on their backs in pits, in extended posture, frequently with grave goods, is typical of the Deccan sites, in the Chalcolithic period. The grave goods included stone axes, blades and pottery.

    In the mid-1970s the chance discovery of a remarkable hoard of copper objects at Daimabad (see p. 278) focused fresh attention on this site, and since that date further excavations have been undertaken there, but so far little has been published and the results appear to be inconclusive. However, the first period has now been divided into three, linking the earliest levels with the so-called Sawalda ware of the Tapi valley, hitherto not clearly established in a stratigraphic context. This deposit was apparently no more than 20 cms in depth. Above it is a second shallow deposit said to have produced a red ware, described as of Harappan affinity, and a sherd reported as having three letters in the Indus script. The exact nature of this purported Harappan connection clearly needs to be explored. The deposit is little deeper than the preceding one. Finally, in the uppermost part of the first period occurs a new buff and cream pottery with associated white-painted grey ware, reminiscent of the white-painted black-and-grey of Prakash, described below. Coarse grey ware is reported throughout all three phases of this period.

2. The second period is reported at several sites, notably Inamgaon, Daimabad II (from whence has come a rare gold pendant of spiral form) and Prakash IA. At Daimabad copper is markedly more plentiful than in the first period. Among the copper objects was a knife blade (Fig. 10.9, No. 11), reminiscent of Harappan types. The common grey ware continues, but a fine reddish-brown ware with painting is now common. Spouts and a channel spout are found, once again comparable to the Malwa ware. The painted decoration includes a remarkable series of small animals, mainly bulls, and a (?)

cms

10.8 Daimabad, Ahmadnagar district: painted pot, Malwa ware (*courtesy* Archaeological Survey of India)

peacock. One unusually fine example (Fig. 10.8) may be assigned to this period. However, the first instances of this distinctive style are already present in period I, and it continues into period III. It is also closely related to the adjacent Malwa style. The excavator of Prakash divides period I into earlier and later parts. The earlier, sub-period IA, produced painted red ware akin to Malwa ware, a distinctive black-and-grey ware with white-painted decoration (apparently related to the painted black-and-red ware tradition), and a coarse grey burnished ware, occasionally with unburnt ochre decoration. No radiocarbon dates are available from this site, but the pottery suggests that this sub-period is contemporary with Navdatoli II and III and may therefore be assigned to c. 2000–1600 B.C.

Although we can say that the settlements of Maharashtra, as represented by the excavations of Nevasa, Daimabad, Chandoli, etc., appear to have been very similar to those of Malwa, it is now possible, from the important site of Inamgaon, to give very detailed evidence concerning the life-style of these Chalcolithic peoples of Maharashtra. Here the archaeologists of the Deccan College have over the past decade made great advances, particularly in attempting to recover the total cultural information, period by period. The earliest period, which corresponds with our second phase, is dated by a series of radiocarbon samples to between 1800 and 1500 B.C. (calibrated) and called by the excavators the Malwa period, for obvious reasons. Huts were either rectangular, with a light wooden frame and wattle and daub filling for the walls, or circular, occupying shallow pits with the post-holes of the roof around the perimeter of the pit. The layout of the huts has been established (Fig. 10.16). In one rectangular hut, a circular platform in one corner was probably the base for a storage bin; in another corner a cooking hearth with a central clay 'pillar', probably for supporting the cooking pot was recorded, and elsewhere a series of hollowed bases for standing pots are detailed. In a third corner was a large painted storage jar set in the floor, and near the entrance a saddle quern. The floor was of earth.

Bones of domestic animals were found, as well as those of wild ones. The botanical evidence from Inamgaon is typical of that for the whole of Maharashtra, in that it appears as a southern extension of the Malwa complex, in this respect. At Inamgaon wheat and barley are found, augmented by sorghum, field peas, lentils and horse gram (*Dolichos biflorus*). Interestingly, there are some suggestions that some form of limited irrigation was employed here.

3. The third phase may be named after the type-site, Jorwe. It represents a great expansion of settlement and hence of population, and it may be dated with some confidence, from runs of radiocarbon datings at Nevasa, Chandoli, Sonegaon and Inamgaon, to between c. 1500 and 1050 B.C. There is a great deal of cultural information regarding the way of life of the Jorwe communities. The houses, like those of Malwa, were rectangular, of wattle and daub on a wooden frame, and the floors were often mud-plastered, or finished with mixed sand and gravel (Fig. 10.10). The stone-blade industry dominated the material equipment, but copper played an important part, flat axes of rectangular form being found at Jorwe and Chandoli, and copper chisels at the latter site (Fig. 10.9, No. 3). A copper spearhead with faint midrib and antennae hilt was found at Chandoli, as was a copper fish-hook. The people used a variety of stone tools. A small stone-axe factory was discovered at Nevasa, and stone axes are reported from Chandoli. Once again, as at Navdatoli and the Karnataka sites, the stone-blade industry demands our admiration (Fig. 10.11). The predominant raw materials are chalcedony and other semi-precious stones; and because of their gem-like quality and the technical excellence of their manufacture, the finished tools are often things of great beauty. Used and unused blades, without retouch, predominate, but backed blades, various geometric forms, and serrated blades, are regular occurrences.

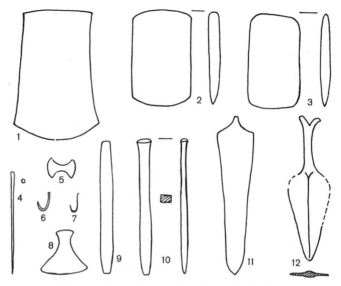

10.9 Copper and bronze objects from Peninsular India (1:4): 1, Navdatoli; 2, Tekkala-kota; 3, 6 and 12, Chandoli; 4 and 9, Nevasa; 5, 7 and 8, Hallur; 10, Piklihal; 11, Daimabad

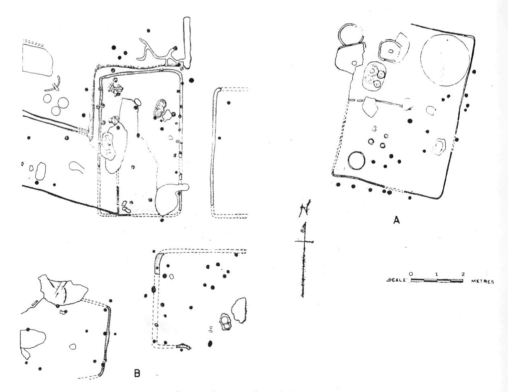

10.10 Inamgaon, period II: Early Jorwe huts (*after* Sankalia)

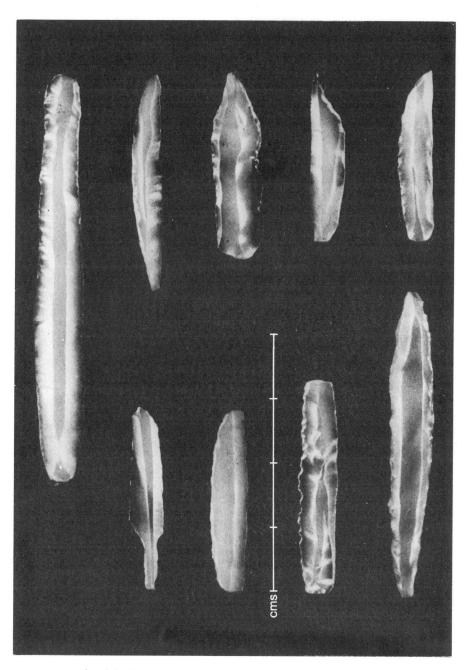

10.11 Chandoli: blade industry of Jorwe period (*courtesy* Deccan College, Pune)

The domestic animals included cattle, sheep, goat and buffalo. Apart from domestic species, bones of deer, nilgai and pig were discovered, and remains of barley, wheat, horse gram, lentil and several other pulses, thus being very similar to what is known from the previous period. A scratched representation of a bullock cart from Inamgaon indicates that these vehicles were in use (Fig. 10.17). Another discovery of peculiar interest is of beads strung upon a thread of silk with a cotton nep from a Chalcolithic burial at Nevasa; a second such string from a similar context at Chandoli had a thread of flax. These finds, taken with the presence of linseed at Navdatoli, show that during the second millennium B.C. cotton was already being spun in Maharashtra, which in later centuries has always been famous for this commodity, and that at this time, at any rate, flax was also used.

The pottery included a continuing coarse grey ware, and the painted red Jorwe ware with its characteristic long-spouted vessels and shallow carinated food bowls (Figs. 10.12–13). There is a tendency for the painted decoration to become more slapdash, often giving the impression of wheel application, while burnishing becomes correspondingly rarer. At Prakash, sub-period IB is differentiated from IA by the appearance

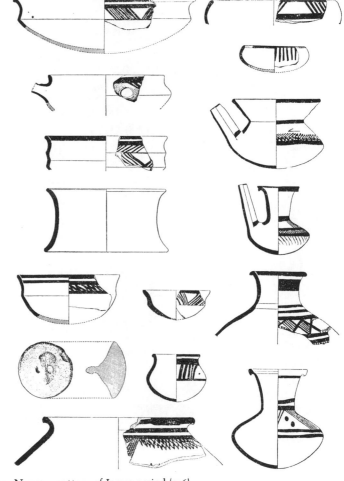

10.12 Nevasa: pottery of Jorwe period (1:6)

of new pottery wares. The Malwa ware continues, being now augmented by a small proportion of Jorwe ware. Also noteworthy is the presence of a small quantity of Lustrous Red ware, suggesting some sort of contact with Rangpur IIC and III. At Inamgaon a potter's kiln was discovered. At several of the sites there is evidence of some of the burial customs; skeletal remains of infants or children were found buried in double urns of grey ware beneath the house floors, together with other grave goods (Fig. 10.15). During the course of the second millennium B.C. a new custom, with multiple urns, forming a sort of sarcophagus for the collected bones, and other grave goods, makes its appearance. Another important find was of terracotta figurines, both male and female: from Nevasa have come two terracotta mother goddesses of crude form, with oblong tabular bodies and crudely modelled heads. These are the first indications of a type which becomes fairly widespread in the Iron Age. At Inamgaon was discovered a female figurine with a bull, both lying on top of a small terracotta box

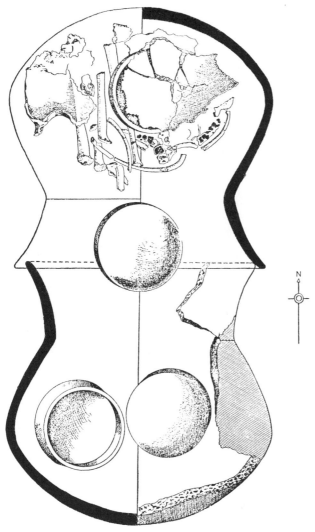

10.13 Nevasa: pot burial of Jorwe period (1:6)

in which was a second female figure (Fig. 10.18). The first figure was apparently joined to the bull by a stick. This is inferred from the small impressions on the back of the bull and front of the body of the woman. These terracottas give us one of our few insights into religious beliefs at this time in Maharashtra.

From this phase in the recent excavations at Daimabad the discovery of grains of sorghum and millet is reported. Sorghum had earlier been reported at Inamgaon. Its appearance at this time would appear to lend weight to the early date of the discovery of sorghum at Ahar.

We are inclined to assign the hoard of fine, non-utilitarian copper objects found at

10.14(a) Daimabad hoard, copper rhinoceros (*courtesy* Prince of Wales Museum, Bombay)

Daimabad to this period. It is reported to have been discovered by chance, when local agriculturalists were digging out the roots of a tree on the top of the mound. Below this point there was a deposit of 1.2 m belonging to the third or 'Jorwe' period. The hoard consists of four massive pieces – an elephant, rhinoceros, buffalo, and a chariot drawn by two bullocks with a rider standing on it (Figs. 10.14–15). Three pieces have copper axles and wheels. The four are all solid cast, and are reported to weigh over 60 kg. The heaviest is the elephant, which stands on a cast copper platform with four brackets beneath, pierced to take axles. The overall height is 25 cm and the platform is 27 cm long. Although the modelling is rather heavy, the piece already has something

10.14(b) Daimabad hoard, copper elephant (*courtesy* Prince of Wales Museum, Bombay)

of the special character attached to the elephant in later Indian sculpture. The rhinoceros is slightly smaller. It too stands on a cast platform, and in this case the brackets contain two solid copper axles with cast wheels attached. The treatment of the figure inevitably recalls that of the seals of the Indus civilization, which provides almost the only comparative examples. The same is true of the buffalo which is of roughly the same size, also with wheels and axle in position. This too must recall the figures of buffaloes in both terracotta and cast copper or bronze from Mohenjo-daro. The fourth object is the most elaborate: it consists of a two-wheeled chariot with a standing rider. It is attached by a long pole to two yoked oxen, which stand on two cast

10.14(c) Daimabad hoard, copper buffalo (*courtesy* Prince of Wales Museum, Bombay)

copper strips, but neither has brackets for wheels. The chariot is a light affair with two uprights supporting a cross-bar behind which the driver stands. This piece has no analogues in the Indus civilization, and remains unique.

These objects appear to belong to the same technological group as the Kallur hoard. Spectrometric analysis of their metal content as published by Agrawal suggests that they are in all cases copper unalloyed by tin or other elements. The copper compares closely with that of other objects found in the excavations, although it differs from the copper so far analysed from the Indus civilization or from other Chalcolithic sites of West and Central India, or Maharashtra. Agrawal has concluded that the metal composition and great weight of the objects argues against their antiquity, but we cannot agree. We remarked above on the weight of copper in several of the Gangetic hoards. The Gungeria hoard weighed over 400 kg, and this, with the similiarity of the metal to the other objects found in the excavations at Daimabad, suggest to us that they all originated from a common copper source at a time when such weights of copper were neither debarred by economic nor technological considerations. The important thing is that the four pieces reveal considerable skill in casting and controlling copper in such volume. The publication of all this important material is awaited.

4. At Inamgaon there is evidence of a final period which the excavators name Late Jorwe and which is dated to between 1100 and 800 B.C. by calibrated radiocarbon. This is important, as it has not been clearly identified at other sites. The huts of this period are without exception round, varying in diameter between 2.5 and 4.5 m. They are closely clustered, more so than in the previous periods, and in some cases appear to have had a small verandah (Fig. 10.19). Several dozen such huts have been uncovered.

10.15 Daimabad hoard, copper chariot (*courtesy* Prince of Wales Museum, Bombay)

10.16 Inamgaon: excavated house of Malwa period (1) (*courtesy* Deccan College, Pune)

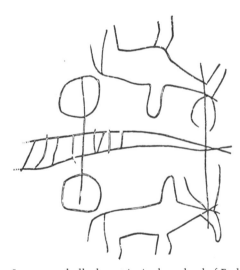

10.17 Inamgaon: bullock cart incised on sherd of Early Jorwe period (*after* Sankalia)

In this period at Inamgaon there is a suggestion that there was a deterioration in climate, leading to a greater reliance upon varieties of wild grains and also animal husbandry. This interesting thesis (advanced by Dhavalikar) deserves to be subjected to further investigation. The pottery includes two elements, one deriving from the Jorwe ware, though in a debased form, and the other black-and-red burnished ware. Although we should expect to discover the first iron during this period this has so far not been the case. However, the presence of quantities of black-and-red ware, which elsewhere is so often found in association with early iron, gives us reason to think that its absence may be due to the economic depression of the population at this time, or some other cause, not yet fully understood. This impression is strengthened by the appearance of new burial sites. A large urn of unburned clay with four hollow legs was found to contain a contracted human skeleton, together with a spouted Jorwe jar and carinated bowl of terracotta. This mode resembles burials found in Iron Age graves in other parts of Southern India (Fig. 10.20).

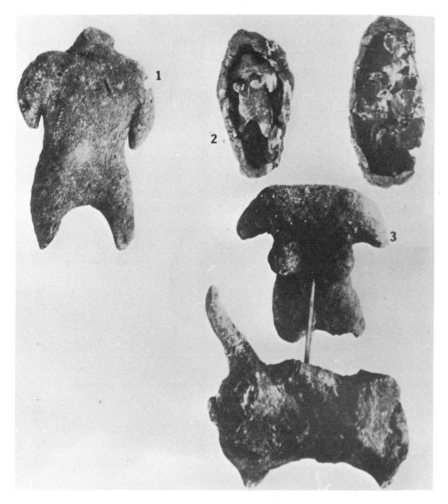

10.18 Inamgaon, Early Jorwe period: terracotta cult figurines (*courtesy* Deccan College, Pune)

In Malwa and Maharashtra throughout these four periods, the settlements reflect the geography of the trap regions; they are invariably sited on the edges of rivers or streams, and usually on a high and solid part of the bank.

In Malwa and Maharastra one may identify a distinctive province in terms of ceramics decoration. East of the Indus one enters a large and rather ill-defined area in which painting, as a rule, is much more restricted in use than it is to the west. The earliest occurrences date from the late third millennium, or early second. The most interesting regional group is that from Malwa and Maharashtra which shows a wide variety of animal and human motifs, in addition to simple linear designs and geometric patterns (Fig. 10.7). Some of the Malwa patterns are drawn with a fussy, uncertain line. The style is quite distinct from anything in the Indus region, and forms a separate stylistic province. Such geometric patterns as are employed are frequently unsurely drawn, and limited to an elementary range, including cross-hatched panels or bands of square, triangular or lozenge shapes, wavy lines and loops. Far more prominent is the range of naturalistic motifs. Cattle and antelope are not uncommon, the horns often swept back in wavy lines, recalling those of Cemetery H at Harappa; sometimes registers of indeterminate animals, perhaps panthers or other felines, are found; and birds include the peacock. Humans feature mainly as lines of dancing figures with interlocked arms, strikingly reminiscent of rock paintings from both Central India and Karnataka, but there are also single figures, some with long wavy hair standing on end and some grasping long staffs. A few special motifs, including stars or rosettes, quite elaborate cross patterns, horn patterns and curious tufted spirals all deserve comment.

The pottery of the succeeding Jorwe phase has two styles: one a continuation of that of Malwa, and the other a new style whose keynote seems to have been speed and deftness of application. The fussiness disappears and the linear patterns are simplified (Figs. 10.12–13). The geometric patterns continue, but the

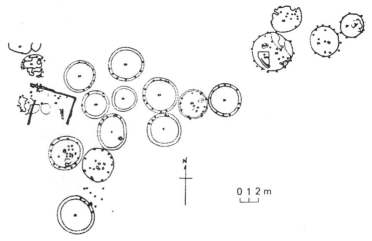

10.19 Inamgaon, period III: Jorwe houses (*after* Sankalia)

number of animal and human motifs diminishes. Among animals, there are several which almost certainly represent horses. Continuous spirals and tufted spirals occur regularly. The restricted range of motifs recalls developments which were taking place elsewhere at the time, including the Indus province, particularly in the Jhukar style from Chanhu-daro.

10.20 Inamgaon: Late Jorwe burial urn (*courtesy* Deccan College, Pune)

During the second millennium there seems to be a general tendency throughout this broad province for painted decoration to be reduced to simpler forms.
This is exemplified in the Prabhas ware of Saurashtra, where a long series of
bowls shows registers filled with short strokes, in various simple geometric
patterns. Others make use of longer obliquely crossing strokes. A related, and
somewhat similar style occurs on the white painted black-and-red ware of
Ahar, where short strokes are found alongside spirals and roughly drawn concentric circles and arcs. A third, again probably related style of painting, is that
associated with the Painted Grey ware of the Punjab and Uttar Pradesh. Many
of the same motifs occur on this pottery with its different fabric and rather
different range of forms. The so-called russet-coated wares of southern India
(see p. 330) probably represent a fourth related style of painting. Why these different wares, widely separated in space and time, should bear so interesting a
resemblance to one another in terms of painted style is an interesting question.

South India

In chapter 5 we saw that there is evidence that a 'Neolithic' culture had already
developed in parts of South India, initially in Karnataka, by c. 3000 B.C. This
early phase is known to us so far only from sites of the ash-mound type, that is to
say cattle pens, used either for the capturing of wild cattle and/or herding of
domestic cattle thereafter (see p. 123). This first period may be called Neolithic,
period 1. Radiocarbon dates suggest that it comes to an end around 2000 B.C.
Thereafter a further set of dates derives from settlements of more permanent
character frequently located on the slopes and tops of granite hills. This second
period is fixed by radiocarbon dating to between c. 2100 and c. 1700 B.C. It is
followed by a third period during which developments recalling those of the
Jorwe phase of Maharashtra are witnessed. This phase continues down to
c. 1000 B.C. We shall briefly discuss the evidence for each of these three periods,
because they show a marked degree of continuity, without any major breaks in
the material culture.

The presence of very large numbers of ground stone axes in Karnataka in the
valley of the river Krishna and its tributaries, was first established by Bruce
Foote. Largely on account of the foundation provided by his researches, it has
now become the best documented of the Neolithic groups of Peninsular India.
Since 1947, when Wheeler excavated at Brahmagiri, there have been excavations at several settlements, such as Sanganakallu (1948, 1964–5), Piklihal
(1951), Maski (1954), Tekkalakota (1963–4), and Hallur (1965). In addition
'ash-mounds' at Utnur (1957), Kupgal (1965), Kodekal (1965–6) and Pallavoy
(1967) have been excavated. The southern extension of the culture is represented by T. Narsipur at the confluence of the Kaveri and Kapila rivers, and
the neighbouring site of Hemmige near Mysore. It is possible, on the basis of

comparisons, to provide some sort of tentative sequence for the periods which precede the introduction of iron at these sites:

1. The earliest settlements (briefly touched on in chapter 5) were made by a people who possessed a ground stone-axe industry and a somewhat rudimentary stone-flake or blade tradition. It is evident that they had domesticated cattle, sheep and goats. Their pottery was predominantly handmade grey or buff-brown, but a less common ware had a black or red burnished slip, often with purple-painted decoration. A feature of the grey ware was the use of bands of red ochre applied after firing. Other noteworthy features of this early pottery are the applied ring feet and hollow pedestals, recalling those of pre-Harappan Amri or Kalibangan. They utilized forest cattle stations, probably for seasonal grazing. From the earliest levels numbers of rubbing stones and querns are found, suggesting some sort of grain cultivation or collection. This phase is represented by the occupation at Utnur, Kodekal and Pallavoy. In the – so far – complete absence of metal it may be regarded as a truly Neolithic phase.

2. During the second period some important developments took place. The first settlements were made on the tops of granite hills, or on levelled terraces on the hillside, or on saddles or plateaux between such hills (Fig. 5.14). Mud floors are in evidence, as are circular hutments of wattle and daub on a wooden frame. A small number of objects of copper or bronze belong to this period. However, the stone-axe industry is everywhere common, without any clear evidence of typological development. There is a great increase in the number and regularity of stone blades prepared from small blade cores of various siliceous stones.

    There is evidence in this period for the presence of gold from such sites at Tekkalakota I. Although this is a rare example, gold was probably in use at a good number of other sites, given that this region is well known for its gold mines.

    There are some changes in the pottery and some new elements appear, suggesting contact with regions to the north (Fig. 10.24). Among these are perforated and spouted vessels. The practice of roughening the outer surface in a manner distantly reminiscent of that employed in the Indus and Baluchistan in Early Indus levels, also makes its first appearance. There is nevertheless a basic continuity discernible between these two periods.

    Period II is in evidence at Piklihal (Upper Neolithic), Brahmagiri, Sanganakallu, Tekkalakota I and Hallur IIA. The occupation of Hallur I and T. Narsipur appears to date from the beginning of this phase, and represents a southern, slightly later, extension of period I. The first metal objects, of both bronze and copper, appear with increasing frequency towards the end of this period. Although few, if any, good radiocarbon dates are available, we may expect this period to begin around 2100 B.C.

3. A third period is in evidence, particularly at Tekkalakota II, Hallur, and perhaps Paiyampalli. It is also present at Piklihal (intrusion period), Sanganakallu 1.2 and Brahmagiri (although not discernible in the excavated sections). It coincides with an increase in the number of tools of copper and bronze, although the axe and blade industries in stone continue right up to the early Iron Age. A copper fish-hook was discovered at Hallur. The predominant tool types – other than the fish-hook – were chisels, flat axes, etc. (Fig. 10.9, Nos. 2, 10) and are all reminiscent of those of the Southern Nuclear Region, Malwa and Maharashtra. This repertoire was augmented by certain new and exotic types, such as the copper or bronze antennae swords of Kallur (Fig. 10.21) and the antennae dagger or spearhead of Chandoli.

    In pottery a new and harder surfaced grey and buff ware becomes common, together with a wheel-thrown unburnished ware with purple paint, akin to the Jorwe ware of Maharashtra (see p. 276). The presence of a bone of *Equus cabalus* in the beginning of this phase at Hallur is suggestive, particularly if it is considered in conjunction with an extensive group of rock paintings showing horses and riders, and with such exotic metal objects as the Kallur swords. Few radiocarbon dates have as yet been published for this period, but comparing it with the Jorwe phase in Maharashtra, with which it shares its new traits, it may be expected to have extended from *c.* 1500 to 1050 B.C.

These three periods show every indication of remarkable continuity, and settlements once established do not appear to have shifted. As with Maharashtra we now know quite a lot about the way of life of the people of this region, and we may consider the evidence from all three periods in synthetic form. At some sites dry stone walls, rising to a height of only a couple of courses, are found marking the circular outline of huts. Excavations at Tekkalakota, Sanganakallu,

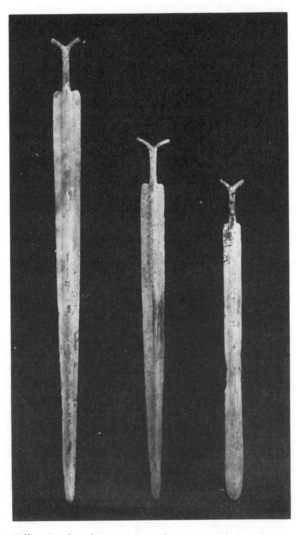

10.21 Kallur, Raichur district: copper/bronze swords from hoard

and Hallur have all produced evidence of circular huts (Fig. 10.22). The floors were coated with mud, or perhaps cow-dung plaster. Hearths, sometimes associated with tripods of small upright slabs of granite, were found either within the house or nearby, and so too were grinding stones, some with mullers still in position. Large pots, buried up to the neck, probably served as storage jars. In the later 'Chalcolithic' phase which covers the transition from the Neolithic to the Iron Age, walls of more massive boulders were built. In many parts of southern India circular huts are still in use among the poorest strata of society, and their construction, furniture and utilization can scarcely have changed since Neolithic times. At Tekkalakota, Nagaraja Rao reported several such huts in the modern village at the foot of the hill on which the Neolithic inhabitants first constructed their dwellings some 4000 years earlier (Fig. 10.23). In the authors' excavations at Piklihal, fragments of the clay moulding of door frames were discovered in the excavations which were identical with those of huts in the modern village of Mudgal. Even though settlements as a whole covered a large area, these scattered groups of huts on hill terraces cannot, we believe, have housed a very large population, and certainly numbers cannot be estimated with reference to modern settlements in the same region in the way that they may be in Sind or Baluchistan.

At these sites stone axes occur in large numbers in all three phases, and fine stone blades in the two later phases (Fig. 5.16). The most common tool is the stone axe with medial ground edge, with a generally triangular form and curved

10.22 Tekkalakota: circular hut floor, phase II (*courtesy* Nagaraja Rao)

blade, and an oval or lenticular median section. Full grinding is usually reserved for small, flattish axes, and pecking for larger tools made from suitable raw material. The commonest axe form is that often spoken of as a pointed-butt axe. There are several processes involved in the production of stone axes, and each finished item must have taken a considerable time to complete. Rocks such as dolerite, basalt and gneiss were first brought to the required shape by flaking. The blade, and sometimes the whole, or part of the body of the axe was then ground. The method for this grinding is quite clear from the deep grooves of several feet in length which are found in the rocks at several regular factory sites in Karnataka, where the grooves fit the width and curve of the typical axe blades of the area. After grinding, the axes were polished. Crystalline rocks such as granite or gneiss which would not flake regularly were hammered or pecked into shape, and then treated like the first group. The grinding process must have taken a long time. In Australia, in recent years, we know that the manufacture of a flaked and ground axe took an experienced man two to four days. Despite the regular use of copper in Maharashtra to the north, stone axes continued in use in the south until the end of this period. The blade industry commands our attention because it shares many features in common with those of the Mesolithic of Central India and the Deccan. The excavations reveal that somewhat less than three-quarters of the assemblages are blades, without retouch and frequently with both bulb of percussion and distal ends snapped off. Reworked, backed or truncated blades occur in small numbers (around four to five per cent

10.23 Tekkalakota: modern Boya hut in village

of the total), and lunates, points or borers, together occupy only about two per cent of the total. There can be little doubt that the predominant blades were hafted in gum to make composite knives or sickles, but evidence is lacking so far in this region. All told, the industry compares closely with that of the Chalcolithic sites in Maharashtra and Malwa.

As far as can be seen, the economy largely depended throughout on cattle raising, but horse gram (*Dolichos biflorus*) and finger-millet or *rāgi* (*Eleusine coracana*) are reported at Tekkalakota I and at Hallur in period II, while the

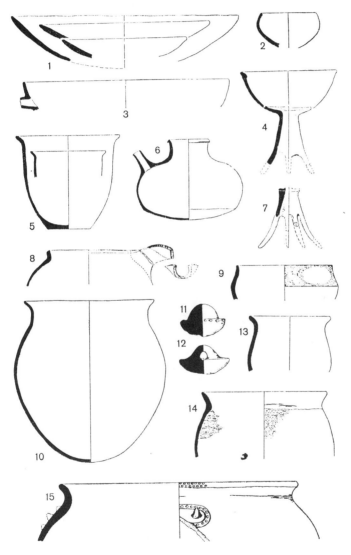

10.24 Piklihal and Brahmagiri, phases I and II: typical pottery; 1–3, 5–6, 10–15 grey or buff burnished ware; 4, 7 burnished red slip ware; 8 and 9 grey ware with unburnt ochre painted decoration (1:8, except 15 which is 1:12)

former is reported at Paiyampalli, along with green gram (*Phaseolus radiatus*). These two pulses are still grown throughout the region, and *rāgi* is to this day one of the most important millets grown by the poorest groups in many parts of Peninsular India. This millet, along with the bulrush millet or *bājrā* (*Pennisetum typhoideum*), is of particular interest as wild varieties are unknown in India, and they are thought to have been first cultivated in Africa. How they first came to India is presently a matter of surmise. Wood of the date palm is reported from Tekkalakota and was probably also used at Utnur.

We noticed above that the terracing of hills was an important feature of the settlements of the Neolithic period, and it is probable that it was increasingly employed for making tiny fields for growing crops (Fig. 5.14). Such terraces, behind a stone retaining wall, would incidentally help to conserve both soil and moisture after the Monsoon. Terracing would further provide a logical first step towards the earth or stone embankments which, from the Iron Age at least, served as surface drainage tanks throughout the areas of impervious granite rocks. Field-terraces are still widely constructed by the villagers throughout this region, and even by such tribal groups as the Badaga of the Nilgiris.

We have some evidence respecting the animal husbandry of the southern Neolithic settlements. Bones of humped cattle are most numerous at all sites, from the earliest period onwards. This corroborates the evidence (listed above) of the importance of stock raising. Next among domestic species come goat and sheep, though these are far less common. As mentioned, rock paintings and also terracotta figurines depict humped cattle, the earliest almost always having long curling horns (Figs. 10.25 and 10.26). It is evident that the cattle were used

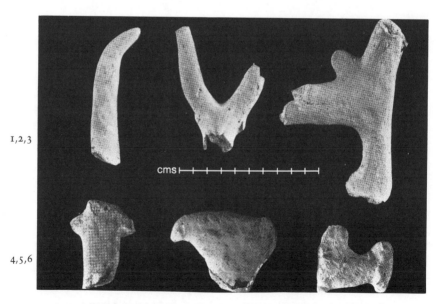

1,2,3

cms ⊢+++++++⊣

4,5,6

10.25 Piklihal: terracotta figures: 1–3, 6 bulls; 4 human male; 5 fowl

for food, and split and cut bones commonly occur. The buffalo is far less common, and indeed it seems uncertain whether it was domesticated or hunted in this region. Bones and terracotta figurines of fowls are reported. Among other animals there are references to deer, tortoise, and a unique bone of an Indian elephant, and as noted above from the final phase of the Chalcolithic at Hallur comes a bone of a horse (*Equus cabalus*).

In the areas in which the southern Neolithic flourished – Karnataka and Andhra – there are granite rocks which provide suitably protected surfaces for rock art. This can be seen at such sites as Kupgal, Maski, Piklihal, etc. Most of this can be attributed – on account of its content – to the Neolithic people who settled on these hills, but it is quite possible that a few can be attributed to the hunting people who preceded them. Others again are certainly later. The

10.26 Maski: rock bruisings of cattle, dancing figures and bullock cart

pictures are made by crayoning rather than painting, in a similar range of colours to those seen in Central India (see p. 82). The most frequent subjects depicted are cattle: long-horned humped bulls, unmistakably *Bos indicus*. They are shown singly and in groups, some with their horns decorated as though for a festival. Other animals, such as deer and tigers, are occasionally illustrated, and it is these which suggest links with the hunting peoples. There are also elephants, some with riders; and human figures, again like pin-men. Some of the men carry axes or spears, and occasionally they ride horses. The presence of horses in the region in the second half of the second millennium is further supported by horse bones found at Hallur (see p. 287). The elephants, the horses and the armed men almost certainly belong to the final phase of the Southern Neolithic, or even to the Iron Age, but the method of representation is the same as in earlier times, although lacking the grace of some of the finest early bulls.

Alongside the rock paintings there is a whole series of rock bruisings (Fig. 10.26). These are done by hammering or pecking the surface of the granite and so changing its colour and producing a pattern. These again show animals, chiefly bulls. The rock bruisings, however, unlike the paintings, continued to be made at certain sites until the present day, the principal subject throughout being cattle. The style changed steadily, until the most recent bulls closely resemble the emblem of the Congress Party. The bulls shown in the earliest rock bruisings, on the other hand, are similar in style to the early rock paintings, and both are parallel to the terracotta figurines of bulls which are found in the early phases of the Southern Neolithic. All these early representations emphasize the long horns, the hump and sometimes also the pronounced dewlap of *Bos indicus*. At Piklihal a group of headrests like those found in excavations of Neolithic levels at T. Narsipur and Hemmige are found bruised on the rocks.

There is some information on burial customs: extended inhumations, usually with some grave goods. In a male example, these grave goods consisted of two stone axes and five large blades; and in another, a female, a spouted pot and a deep (?) milking vessel are reported. Infants were buried in pottery urns, as in Maharashtra, to the north. Burials of all types appear to have been among the houses of the settlement, rather than in separate burial grounds. In the third phase multiple pot burials at Tekkalakota are reminiscent of those of Maharashtra during the Jorwe phase (Fig. 10.13). From a burial at T. Narsipur, and from other phase II contexts, some pottery headrests of a distinctive form (Figs. 10.27–28).

The terracotta art of the peninsula in Neolithic–Chalcolithic times is – like that of Maharashtra – less prominent than that of the Indus, but in the Southern Neolithic it is present from an early date: humped cattle, birds and human male figurines are recorded (Fig. 10.25).

Closely related to the sites of Karnataka and Tamilnadu are those of eastern Andhra Pradesh. In the Kurnool district a large group of sites, first identified by Bruce Foote, produces a distinctive painted red ware which we may name after the type-site Patpad ware. The culture which produced this pottery at Patpad (Pattupadu) and elsewhere flourished within a few scores of miles of the sites of the Karnataka region, and yet it shows a remarkable difference in the style of painting, and in other details. The channel-spouted bowl is here again a special feature. The age of this culture is as yet unclear. Another site of perhaps about the same age is reported to have been excavated in 1961 at Kesarapalli in the Krishna district, revealing a considerable deposit of late pre-iron material.

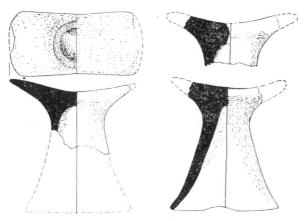

10.27 T. Narsipur: Pottery headrests (1:4)

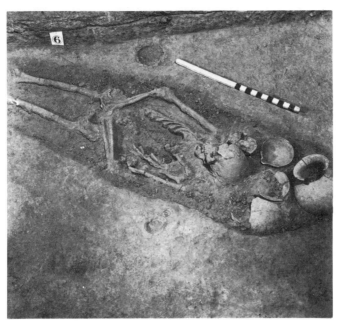

10.28 T. Narsipur: burial with pottery headrest beside skull (*courtesy* Director of Archaeology, Karnataka)

Neolithic axes have been found in surface collections, often in quantities, particularly towards the south-east, where they occur in large numbers in the Shevaroy and Javadi hills and thence eastwards towards the Tamil coastal plains, southwards to Madura and even in the extreme south of the peninsula. In this area, sites are reported producing a typical blade industry and pottery of forms and wares reminiscent of those of the Karnataka area. Several pots have mat-impressions on their bases. Further south, in Pondicherry, Casal discovered and excavated a number of urn burials at Gaurimedu and Mangalam. The predominant red pottery associated with them, the pot forms, and the absence of any metal objects other than copper or bronze, all indicate that these belong to a cultural phase anterior to the Iron Age. There is, of course, no inherent improbability that further, earlier stages of 'Chalcolithic' or 'Neolithic' settlement may be found in all these eastern areas, but in our view those so far reported are more likely to belong to a late Chalcolithic phase chronologically akin to the Jorwe phase of Maharashtra. There is as yet no evidence that this distribution extends into Sri Lanka, although stray ground stone axes have been reported there.

It is important to remember that in many parts of the south, just as in the hills of Central India, stone axes continued to be made and used even after the introduction of iron. Thus, while stray finds may be regarded as useful pointers, until actual settlements with all the other components of culture and economy are found and excavated, they have very little real meaning.

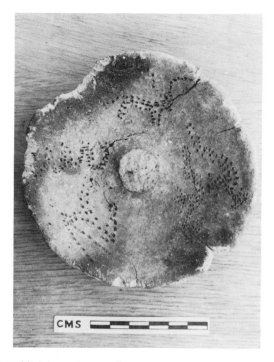

10.29 Tekkalakota: decorated pottery lid (*courtesy* Nagaraja Rao)

Time scale B.C.	Saurashtra			Southern Nuclear Region			Maharashtra			Karnataka			
	Lothal	Rojadi	Somnath (Prabhas Patan)	Ahar	Kayatha	Navda-toli	Daimabad	Inamgaon	Prakash	Kodekal	Utnur	Piklihal	Hallur
1000			III A	? ↑ I c Iron		? ↑ IV	? ↑ III	III	II A Iron →			III	III Iron
1500		II	II b / II a / I b / I a	I b	III	III	II	II	I b		? ↑ 4 / 3	I B	b / II a
2000	IV / III / II / I	c / b / I a	?	I a	II	II / I	I c / b / a	I	I a		2 / I	I A	I
2500					I					? ← I → ?	1		
3000													

10.30 Comparative sequences of sites in the southern zone (c. 3000–1000 B.C.)

CHAPTER 11

THE ARRIVAL OF INDO-ARYAN
SPEAKING PEOPLE AND THE SPREAD OF
THE INDO-ARYAN LANGUAGES

In previous chapters we have reviewed the evidence from the various regions for cultural developments during the second millennium B.C. We concentrated our discussion on the archaeological data, on the principle that this was the only surviving evidence which was firmly datable. We shall now break into the roughly chronological sequence and retrace our steps over the same ground, attempting to reconstruct an event of great significance for the subsequent course of Indian civilization, namely the arrival in the subcontinent of peoples speaking Indo-Iranian, or more particularly Indo-Aryan, languages. We have adopted this somewhat pedantic device because there has been much confusion over the relationship between archaeological and linguistic evidence, and there is no accepted methodology for interrelating them. Therefore we must first make our aims clear.

As archaeologists we are fundamentally concerned, at the level of interpretation, with reconstructing evidence of the total culture and life of the peoples of South Asia from period to period, and our aim may be classed as the reconstruction of cultural history. Where there are no written records, it is reasonable to accord the material findings of the archaeologist the prime place in providing such data, but once written records begin these assume a place of equal, if not greater importance. In India the earliest written records so far available (apart from the still unread inscriptions of the Indus civilization) are the inscriptions of Asoka (third century B.C.), but there exists a body of earlier literature of very considerable size and variety which was composed and passed on for many centuries in an oral form. This literature goes back to the oldest surviving text, the Samhitā, or 'compilation' of the hymns of the Rigveda. A reasonable estimate of the date of the compilation of the Rigveda is c. 1500–1300 B.C., and the composition of many of the individual hymns may be expected to have extended over several previous centuries. The Samhitās of the other Vedas, the Yajur, Sāma and Atharva, and the subsequent literature generally classified as Late Vedic, may be taken to belong to the subsequent seven centuries or so. Thus there are well over a thousand years for which there is textual evidence of a limited sort before the earliest surviving inscription. Viewed in this light we may refer to the second millennium as 'protohistoric'. Once the existence of this literary history has been established it becomes incumbent upon the would-be cultural historian to attempt to relate it to the archaeological evidence, if it all possible; since written sources, no matter how meagre, open up possibilities of understanding a culture in a way which can never be achieved without their aid. To gloss Sir Mortimer Wheeler's memorable dictum, 'The archaeologist may find the tub but altogether miss Diogenes' – but what a treasure if he could find even fragments of his diary!

There seems to be general agreement that the Indo-Iranian languages, one of the branches of the great Indo-European family of languages, were originally spoken in the steppes of Eurasia, and that over a period of time they spread, undoubtedly largely though the medium of movements of groups of speakers, into the regions where they are later traceable through written records or where they are still spoken. A similar state of affairs may be accepted for the other branches of the family, moving down from the steppes into Central and Western Europe and the Mediterranean region. Misunderstandings and distortions have arisen because of the inadequate conceptual framework and terminology which have often been associated with the discussion of these movements in archaeological writing. For instance, it is often treated as though the arrival of Indo-Aryan speaking people in any area involved the complete and simultaneous disappearance or displacement of the already existing population, their culture and languages. Yet, as we have seen above in almost every part of India and Pakistan, settled agricultural communities had already been established for many centuries, if not millennia, before this time, and there are all sorts of indications to show that much of that population, together with its languages and cultures, survived to maintain the already established character of each region, and to influence the development of the Indo-Aryan languages themselves. Another source of misconception is the tendency of archaeologists to identify single traits or groups of traits with people. Thus one reads of the first appearance of a certain type of pottery at a given site as evidence of the presence of the Indo-Aryans, that the Painted Grey ware was the pottery of the Indo-Aryans, etc. While this may be partly true for some traits in special circumstances, perhaps for example with the first arrival of horses in a region, or of a new and different burial pattern, such cultural traits can and almost universally are acquired by one group from another without necessarily having reference to ethnic origins or language, or other aspects of culture. We would like to insist that the arrival and spread of the Indo-Aryan languages must have been associated with the movement of Indo-Aryan speaking people, and that their relations with the populations they encountered must be conceived as a dynamic process of culture contact, producing a variety of cultural reponses. This process must have continued over many centuries. Its result was to produce a cultural synthesis which we may refer to as culturally Indo-Aryan, that is, a synthesis of Indus or Indian, and Aryan elements.

The discovery that there was a close relationship between Latin, Greek, Sanskrit, German and the Celtic languages, was made by Sir William Jones in

1786, and its systematic study and elaboration was the work of Bopp and other philologists during the first half of the nineteenth century. The initial work was linguistic, but it was soon followed by attempts to interpret and explain the relationship in cultural and anthropological terms. Interest was early centred upon identifying the original homeland of the speakers of the Indo-European languages, and various views were put forward. Since 1871 there has been general acceptance that this early homeland must have been somewhere on the steppes of Eurasia, from the frontiers of China in the east to those of Western Europe in the west, and we must conceive of already widely dispersed Indo-European speaking tribes inhabiting these regions, and gradually separating from one another. It is generally agreed that the steppes were also the homeland of the wild ancestors of the horse, and that this animal was exploited and then domesticated by the human population, who learned both to ride and to harness the horse for draught purposes. Gimbutas has recently suggested that archaeological traces of these people may be found in the Early, Middle and Late stages of what she has named the 'Kurgan culture' (after the characteristic Kurgan or barrow type of graves), which can be identified during the late fourth and third millennia as occupying the steppes to the west of the Urals. Their way of life was dominated by stock breeding, with horses outnumbering cattle. They practised metallurgy, having a characteristic range of copper and bronze tools and weapons. They or their neighbours seem to have invented the spoked wheel and the horse drawn chariot. Recent Soviet archaeological research supports the earlier view that the domestication of the horse may have taken place first in the South Russian steppes before the end of the fourth millennium, and spread thence eastwards into the Kazakh steppes around the end of the third millennium. These eastward moving tribes were probably the ancestral speakers of the Indo-Iranian languages, and may be identified with the archaeological timber-grave–Andronovo culture. In the east they must have come in contact with an earlier population. Thus we may expect the Indo-Iranian branch of the Indo-European family to have become separated from the other branches at the latest, during the third millennium, and, further, before the end of the millennium we may expect the Indo-Aryan and Iranian tribes to have become separated from each other. Both these developments may well have taken place considerably earlier.

The next development is still not clearly understood, but it would appear that somewhere around 2000 B.C., or perhaps a century or so earlier, or later, some of the tribes moved southwards into the lands long occupied by agricultural communities. The causes of this movement, as indeed of the similar movements of the Mongols and other Central Asian peoples in later times, are not altogether clear. Increasing desiccation of Central Asia has often been invoked, but the evidence for major climatic change at this time has not been substantiated, although there are indications of minor fluctuations of climate, both regional and general, which might well have contributed to more complex situations, historical or political, which set in motion shifts in the regular patterns of movements of nomadic people. Their advance was no doubt facilitated by their horses and chariots and perhaps too by their effective weapons. To the east of the Caspian it appears that the Indo-Aryans moved south into the Iranian plateau around 2000 B.C., and we find the first evidence of their languages at this time. The Kassite rulers of Babylon at the opening of the sixteenth century bore what were probably Indo-Aryan names, as did the Mitannian rulers of the succeeding centuries. A treaty of the Hittite king Subiluliuma and the Mitannian Mattiwaza of *c.* 1380 mentions the Aryan gods Mitra, Indra and Varuna, all familiar from the Rigveda itself, and among the Boğazköy tablets is a treatise on horse training by Kikkuli of Mitanni using chariot racing terms in virtually pure Sanskrit. As far as is known, during the first half of the second millennium the Iranian speaking tribes were still located further north, in the southern parts of Central Asia, in Sogdia and Bactria, while the Indo-Aryans fanned out across Iran, and also eastwards into India proper. It is believed that after some centuries the Iranians too advanced southwards into Iran, around the fourteenth century B.C., probably thereby displacing some of the earlier Indo-Aryans who in turn moved on to the east. Thus we would expect there to have been at least two main periods of Indo-Aryan migration into north-western India and Pakistan, the first or early period dating from around 2000 B.C., and the second some six centuries later.

We have now reached the point where we may consider the evidence from the Indian subcontinent in more detail, and we may begin by discussing the linguistic evidence. The Indo-Aryan languages of India have been divided into two major groups by Grierson and subsequent scholars. The first, which has been called 'non-Sanskritic' or 'pre-Vedic' (also known as Dardic), comprises a small cluster of languages spoken in the mountains of the north-west, in Gilgit, Chitral, Kafiristan and Laghman. It has been argued that these languages, which are not directly related to the Sanskritic languages, represent a separate and perhaps somewhat earlier movement of Indo-Aryans southwards from Central Asia directly into the mountains, in the Pamirs and eastern extremities of the Hindu Kush. The second group has been called 'Sanskritic' or 'Vedic', and its speakers are supposed to have moved southwards further west, through the passes of the Hindu Kush and Kopet Dagh ranges, into Iran and Afghanistan. It was this second group which spread out, some westwards towards Mesopotamia, and some turned eastwards entering the Indus plains, probably by a variety of routes. What is not clear, and perhaps can never become clear from the very limited evidence available, is whether any members of the first 'pre-Vedic' group also entered India and Pakistan by these western routes, or whether any of the earlier settlers who entered the north-western valleys ever moved on into the plains of India and Pakistan proper. A further interesting theory was advanced in the last century by Hoernle, arguing that certain differences within the modern Indo-Aryan languages of India proper might be explained by reference to two main waves of immigrants: an earlier (represented by an 'outer band' of languages – Bengali, Oriya, Marathi, Sindhi and Kashmiri); and a later represented by a central group of languages, comprising mainly Hindi, Rajasthani and Panjabi. This theory has not been universally accepted, but some scholars have believed that the languages of the outer band might represent elements surviving from an earlier, possibly even 'pre-Vedic', wave, while those of the central group might represent a later, 'Vedic' wave. Another, perhaps more plausible, theory would make the outer band languages an earlier wave of the Vedic group itself.

The linguistic models we have outlined are based upon the modern Indo-Aryan languages and their distributions, and they necessarily provide very slender evidence upon which to base theories relating to the first arrival of Indo-Aryan speaking peoples, nearly four millennia ago. It must also be recognized that the models offer very little, if any, hope of establishing absolute chronologies of any kind. We mentioned above the Mitannian and Hurrian evidence for the presence of Indo-Aryan speaking peoples, including experts in the management of chariots, on the western borders of Iran in the middle of the second millennium. No such positive evidence is yet known from India and it can only be expected to come from the discovery of texts or inscriptions. Furthermore, the chronological position of the Rigveda and other Vedic and late Vedic texts is necessarily extremely vague. All this makes our aim of relating linguistic and archaeological evidence problematic, and we must allow for several possible hypotheses, none of which at the present can be firmly established or rejected. Another difficulty which we now encounter is that while it may be reasonably simple to identify archaeological cultures with the movements of Indo-Iranian speaking people in the sparsely populated steppes, it is quite a different matter to make such identifications when these same peoples moved down into southern Central Asia, Iran or India, where there were already substantial populations of agriculturalists with long established settlements and craft and cultural traditions. If we are to recognize the arrival or presence of the Indo-Aryan barbarians, it is probable that it will be in the form of evidence of culture contacts between the two communities, rather than in the sudden or total extinction of one by the other. It seems likely that the Aryans would have brought with them not only their 'secret weapon' – the horse and chariot – but also other more effective bronze weapons, as well as their horse- and fire-cults, and perhaps such distinctive traits as their burials. However, they would largely have taken over the crafts and settlement sites of the existing populations, whom in general they came to dominate. We must also expect different types of culture contact in different situations: among the small population units of the Himalayan valleys there would have been many fewer specialized crafts for the immigrants to exploit; while in the comparatively more sophisticated, richer and more populous plains there must have been rather more.

We may now review the archaeological evidence marshalled in the previous chapters, asking whether it gives us any clues to this sort of culture contact. Three principal questions require attention: first, is there any evidence which would allow us to identify an early 'pre-Vedic' movement; secondly, can we distinguish between such a movement and a second, major series of 'Vedic' movements; and thirdly, what were the stages by which the Indo-Aryans spread through the land, and can we distinguish areas of primary settlement from those of secondary or even tertiary settlement?

The most obvious candidate for consideration as an early and therefore possibly 'pre-Vedic' group is from the valleys of the north-west, from very much the same areas as the modern speakers of Dardic languages. We saw how in Swat there is clear evidence that in period IV of Ghaligai cave, a new element entered the valley, associated with the Gandharan graves, and bringing a marked increase in the use of copper and bronze, horses and horse furniture, distinctive burial rites, and a cult of fire, inferred by the presence of some cremations, etc. The parallels for the material culture are in the Caucasus, north Iran and southern Central Asia, and they lead us to expect that somewhere during the first quarter of the second millennium these new traits were introduced into the area by people who we may believe spoke ancestral languages to the modern Dardic ones. They must have settled alongside the indigenous population, perhaps driving them back into the higher valleys, or more remote areas, and thereby establishing a recurring pattern of the driving back of one language by the more dominant speakers of another, which is still recognizable today. It is not yet clear, from the archaeological record, whether there was also a subsequent arrival of one or more further waves of immigrants in the valleys, and therefore of possible 'Vedic' groups following 'pre-Vedic'.

We may well wonder whether there was a corresponding 'pre-Vedic' movement into the plains of India and Pakistan proper, to match the somewhat doubtful linguistic evidence. There is some very problematic evidence which may point in this direction. For example, at Kalibangan, where the main Harappan occupation seems to have come to an end before 2000 B.C., there are reports of curious and distinctive fireplaces, recognizably different from domestic hearths, occurring along with pits of animal bones on top of the brick platforms of the 'citadel' mound, in an enclosed courtyard outside the main settlement, and in small rooms inside houses. Such 'ritual hearths' are reported from the beginning of the Harappan period itself. It has been suggested that they may have been fire altars, evidence of domestic, popular and civic fire-cults. Such evidence appears to us strongly suggestive of the fire-cults of the Indo-Iranians, which are described in detail in the late Vedic literature. It may then be an indication of culture contact between an early group of Indo-Aryans and the population of the still flourishing Indus civilization. With this possibility in mind one may wonder whether similar indications of contact may not be noticeable in other regions, during the early centuries of the second millennium. There is also the possibility that some of the foreign metal tools and weapons which we noticed from various parts of north and west Pakistan, and the destruction of settlements in Baluchistan, may not be unconnected with the same movement. But we must not forget how vague is the dating of most such objects, and that they may well relate to later movements. If, however, the contact of an Indo-Aryan group with the flourishing Indus settlement of Kalibangan could be substantiated, and the suggestion is put forward with every admission of its being as yet quite unproven, it would clearly have very important implications in terms of the formation of an Indo-Aryan cultural synthesis. Against this whole hypothesis must be set the fact that little if any other evidence so far published from Kalibangan shows any trace of the sort of data recorded in the Gandharan graves, etc. While in part this might reflect the different geographical context and relations with the earlier population, it seems unlikely that no traces of, for example, imported metal objects would occur in such a situation. Again, the virtual absence of bones of horses in Harappan contexts, and of representations of horses on Indus seals, seems to argue against the hypothesis.

At present there are no really unequivocal indications by which we may identify separate pre-Vedic and Vedic waves or movements. Rather there is a mass of generally imprecisely dated evidence indicating a whole series of movements or contacts, starting already before the end of the third millennium and continuing through much if not all of the second.

In Baluchistan, the picture is of a major change in the life-style of the population around the end of the third millennium, with the subsequent appearance of metal tools and weapons with Iranian or Caucasian affinities, a new pattern of burials in kurgans (barrows and cairns) or simply in cemeteries dug into earlier settlements, and evidence of the use of the horse and horse furniture, etc. The cemeteries with plain pottery closely analogous to that of Namazga VI and the cemeteries of southern Uzbekistan and Tajikistan at or near Mehrgarh are highly suggestive. In Sind, the Jhukar period suggests that after the breakdown of the Indus civilization many settlements continued to exist and to display a typically Indian culture pattern, while new exotic traits with eastern Iranian or Central Asian affinities, such as button seals, appear. This may indicate the presence of an extraneous element in the population, and in view of the linguistic hypotheses it is to be expected that the new elements were Indo-Aryan speakers.

In the Punjab there is different, but parallel, evidence. The culture represented by Cemetery H at Harappa appears to be a post-urban (or Late Harappan) phase, when suddenly certain new elements appear alongside many traits which continue from the preceding Mature Indus period. The iconography of the paintings on the Cemetery H pottery, to which we shall revert in a later chapter, was seen by Vats as indicating a 'Rigvedic' pattern of belief. We are inclined to agree. Thus Cemetery H and the related Bara culture may also represent a culture contact situation, with perhaps an Indo-Aryan military aristocracy dominating and interacting with a local population. It may well be that the distribution of diagnostic traits, the distinctive metal objects, axes and dirks, the metal pins, the faience and metal circular seals, etc., mark the approximate extent of the first waves of immigrants – that is to say, the areas of primary settlement – and that the general absence of these traits to the east of the Indus system, with one or two slight extensions in Gujarat and Rajasthan, serves to show areas in which mainly secondary expansion of Indo-Aryans took place. In the Northern Nuclear Region in east Punjab, Haryana and the Ganges–Jamuna Doab, we pass through a series of stages of increasingly attenuated western influence. This is not unexpected, as the area was a contact zone between Harappan and surviving pre-Harappan cultures already during the lifetime of the Indus civilization, and the same tendency may be expected to have persisted into the post-urban (or Late Harappan) period. To the south, in Saurashtra, Gujarat and Maharashtra, the picture may have been similar, although it is not easy to detect traces of the Indo-Aryan infiltration which must have been going on. Here too events in the Southern Nuclear Region may represent the first stage of Indo-Aryan secondary expansion. In our view the changes witnessed in the Jorwe phase, with the several curiously Iranian traits to which Sankalia has drawn attention, are certainly indications of the process, and it may well be that it began even earlier, during the Malwa phase. The spread of Indo-Aryans to the east and into the interior of the peninsula undoubtedly continued during the final centuries of the second millennium and into the first, but as these movements relate to the period in which the smelting and use of iron began to gain currency, we shall discuss them in the following chapter.

In looking for this sort of evidence for the expansion of Indo-Aryan speakers we must guard against over-simple explanations. We shall see that the Rigveda suggests that both inhumation and cremation were current in the society of that time and place. As burial rites tend to be among the most conservative of human institutions we must therefore expect to find similarly complex indications in the archaeological record. A few examples will bring out this point. We noticed the difficulty in interpreting the two strata of burials at Cemetery H, Harappa, where the lower contained simple inhumations and the upper secondary burials in large urns. The burial practices of the Gandharan graves are still far from clearly defined: certainly there were both inhumations, cremations and multiple secondary burials; but their relationship in time has not been, and perhaps can never be, definitely established. It is to be expected that as the Aryan rites of cremation became widespread evidence for inhumations would dwindle. Yet there are several early Iron Age cemeteries (at Gumla, Sarai Khola and Bhagawanpura IB, for example) where simple inhumations, with no or only very few grave goods occur. Finally, we have seen that there is evidence of horse burials and of the burial of items of horse furniture in the Gandharan graves, in the Baluchistan cairn graves, and in the Nagpur graves, and to a lesser extent elsewhere in the South Indian Iron Age graves. Yet, there is no clear evidence for the circumstances of such burials to be derived from the Rigveda or other sources.

We are now on the threshold of history, in a protohistoric period, when it is becoming possible to examine the evidence of texts, insofar as they can be reasonably dated, and to compare their evidence with that of archaeology. The chronology of the Vedic literature remains imprecise, and hence it must be used with considerable caution. Nevertheless, there seems to be at least a possibility of establishing the broad horizons. As we have seen, we may expect the first waves of Indo-Aryan movement into the subcontinent to have begun at the opening of the second millennium, or even before. Our view is that the earliest material contained in the Vedic Samhitās began to be composed from that time. This 'Early Vedic' period probably lasted down to c. 1500 B.C., and was followed by a second 'Mature Vedic' stage, during which the compilation of the hymns into the 'Samhitā' took place. This may have lasted for some two or three centuries, and probably coincided with the second and major influx of Indo-Aryans from Iran. Thereafter we enter the third or 'Late Vedic' stage, which continued from c. 1300 B.C., down to c. 600 B.C. During this time, several strata of later material were added to the Rigveda Samhitā, and the extensive schools of exegetic literature developed. If this chronology is accepted as a working hypothesis it should enable us to use materials from the Samhitās, and particularly the Rigveda, to augment the archaeological data for the first three quarters of the second millennium; and similarly to use the later Vedic literature for the last quarter of the second and for the opening centuries of the first millennium B.C.

The geographical horizons of the Rigveda are interesting. On the west they are bounded by the western tributaries of the Indus, the Gomati (modern Gomal), the Krumu (modern Kurram) and the Kubhā (modern Kabul) rivers. Other rivers are mentioned even to the north of the Kabul, notably Suvāstu, the modern Swat. This latter signifies 'fair dwellings' and may therefore indicate Aryan settlements in this beautiful valley. The centre of Rigvedic geography is the Punjab. The rivers most often referred to are the Indus itself, the Sarasvati and the Drishadvati and the five streams which collectively gave their name to the Punjab (Panjāb, five waters), the Sutudri (Sutlej), Vipās (Beas), Parushni (Ravi), Asikni (Chenab), and Vitastā (Jhelum). The eastern horizons are the Jamunā river and the Gangā (Ganges), which is mentioned only in one of the latest hymns. These must have been the confines within which the first generations of Indo-Aryans settled. It is the sacred heartland remembered later as Brahmāvarta or Brahmarṣideśa.

From the Vedas we learn that stock breeding was still a most important part of the Indo-Aryan economy, and that along with cattle and sheep the horse occupied an outstanding role. They cultivated barley and probably also wheat. Among their crafts the manufacture of wheeled carts and particularly of chariots was important. There has been much discussion as to whether the references to metal (*ayas*) included iron or only copper and bronze; but archaeological evidence would seem to show that for the Early and Mature Vedic stages iron was not in use. They were still organized as tribes, each having a king and a tribal assembly. The names of several tribes and of a number of rulers are recorded. The most important tribe were the Bhāratas who were to give their name to the whole territory (Bhāratvarsa). They fought a great battle with a confederacy of five other Aryan tribes, led by the Purus, and five other tribes who may have been non-Aryan, or at least less closely connected with the rest. The leader of the Bhāratas at that time was Sudās, and the 'Battle of the Ten Kings' (*Dasarājña*) became a subject of heroic record which has sometimes been supposed to have provided one of the sources for the later epic story of the Mahābhārata. It has been estimated that the battle of the ten kings took place during the Mature Vedic period, around the fourteenth century B.C. In another battle the Bhāratas fought three tribes whose names are surely non-Aryan.

The Vedic hymns are addressed to Indo-Aryan gods, such as Indra, the warrior charioteer whose thunderbolt destroyed their enemies and who boasts of his inebriation on the sacred *soma* drink; Agni, the fire god, who also shares something of this warlike character as the consumer of the enemy, as well as being the intermediary between gods and men; Varuna, the Asura or righteous king; Mitra, who has solar characteristics, and so on. Their cult revolved around the fire sacrifice. The Aryan funeral rites are already complex: cremation and burial were evidently both in practice.

From the Vedas it is evident that the Aryans were not the only inhabitants of the region, for which they themselves used the name *Sapta-Sindhava* or land of seven Indus rivers, and that their original stay was not entirely peaceful. We learn of a people called *Dāsas* or *Dasyu* (the word later means 'slave') who were dark-complexioned, snub-nosed, worshippers of the phallus (*śiśna deva*), etc. They were rich in cattle and lived in fortified strongholds, *pura*. We learn of another people, the *Panis*, who were also wealthy in cattle and treasures. In later literature this name is invariably associated with merchants and wealth. Although many of the hymns refer to battles between one Aryan tribe and another there is an underlying sense of solidarity in the fight against the Dāsas, and Indra is named *Purandara*, the 'breaker of cities'. Already in the Vedas the first encounters of Indra (the Aryan people personified) and the fortified settlements of the Dāsas were being forgotten and the former Dāsa rulers were regarded as demons. We hear of the destruction of many cities by fire, and of a battle on the banks of the Ravi at a place named Hariyūpīyā (which – although it is quite unprovable – many have been tempted to identify with Harappa). Professor Burrow has recently shown the unambiguous character of such references as 'Through fear of thee the dark-coloured inhabitants fled, not waiting for battle, abandoning their possessions, when, O Agni (fire), burning brightly for Puru (an Aryan tribe), and destroying the cities, thou didst shine' (VII.5.3). He has further recognized the importance in both the Rigveda and later Vedic texts of the word *arma, armaka,* meaning ruin. For instance, in the Rigveda we read 'Strike down, O Maghavan (Indra), the host of the sorceresses in the ruined city of Vailasthānaka, in the ruined city of Mahāvailastha (Great Vailastha)' (1.133.3). There were then, by the end of the Mature Vedic period, great ruin-mounds which the Aryans associated with the earlier inhabitants of the area. The same idea recurs in a later Vedic text, the *Taittiriya Brāhmana* (II.4, 6, 8), in the statement that 'The people to whom these ruined sites belonged, lacking posts, these many settlements, widely distributed, they, O Agni, having been expelled by thee, have migrated to another land.' Also in one of the later Vedic texts we read 'On the Sarasvati there are ruined sites called Naitandhava; Vyarna is one of these'; and, for the archaeologist perhaps even more suggestively, 'He should proceed along the right bank of the Drishadvati, having reached the ruined site near its source he should proceed towards the right,' etc.

Not all the culture contacts suggested by the Rigveda need have been of a violent kind. For example, the name of the father of Sudās was Divodāsa, and this may indicate that this tribal ruler was himself partly of Dāsa stock. More significantly, it is certain that the language of the Vedic period, after perhaps centuries of culture contacts, had already absorbed a major element, both phonetic and semantic, from an indigenous non-Indo-Aryan source, which appears to have been primarily Dravidian. Such a development seems certain to have resulted from intermarriage and other forms of intercourse between Aryans and non-Aryans. Further evidence of this same development may be seen in the way in which the contents of the hymns develop, so that those of the latest strata (admittedly datable to the late Vedic period) reveal a profound shift from the ideology of the earlier. Whether the new material reflects in any degree the still unknown ideology of the priestly class of the Indus civilization, or rather the positive results of what we called the Indo-Aryan cultural synthesis, has still to be established, but it is certainly not impossible.

CHAPTER 12

THE IRON AGE AND THE EMERGENCE OF CLASSICAL INDIAN CIVILIZATION

The earliest known occurrences of iron used as a human artefact are from West Asia, and are of meteoric iron. The discovery of the smelting of iron ore to produce a spongy bloom and of the forging of the bloom to make wrought iron tools probably first began in the third millennium, though from that period only very rare examples have been found, and these also in the same area of West Asia. During the second millennium smelting begins to occur more widely, but what may be called the 'Iron Age' probably nowhere began before c. 1300 B.C. From that time onwards iron becomes gradually more common, and we may trace several further stages in its exploitation in any area – first still comparatively rare, then vying with copper and bronze, and finally assuming a more or less general role as a utilitarian metal. Cuyler Young (1967) has suggested for Iran three periods of the Iron Age which probably correspond with these stages and which start respectively at c. 1300, 1000 and 750 B.C. This offers a rough chronological framework against which we may compare the evidence from India and Pakistan.

It must be remembered that several divergent views have been current until recently, one holding that India, for reasons not entirely clear, only developed iron smelting at a very late date. Thus Gordon (1950) could find no evidence for the use of iron in India before 250 B.C.; and Wheeler (1959) held that India received the necessary knowledge only c. 500 B.C. as a result of the incursions of the Achaemenids. Another school of thought suggested on the contrary that South India might have been the home of the world's first discovery of iron-working! Needless to say, such extreme views are quite unacceptable; between them the more acceptable view is that of Banerjee (1965) who held that iron working in India began as early as 1000 B.C. and became more common around 800 B.C. We shall try to record the current evidence for the development of the working and utilization of iron, without any preconceived hypotheses.

Until recent years tribal peoples in many parts of the subcontinent continued to smelt their own ores by methods which are not only relatively primitive, but which share much with the techniques observed, for example, among iron-smiths in many parts of Africa. For, once discovered, the techniques involved are relatively simple, and we may expect that the picture of the modern Agaria smiths of Central India recorded five decades ago by Verrier Elwin differs little from that which archaeology has recently reconstructed. The excavation of an

Early Historic smelting site at Dhatwa in southern Gujarat and the subsequent investigations by Hegde into the metallurgical technology have revealed many salient features of ancient Indian smelting and iron smithery. Locally available ore and fuel were employed; the ore was first roasted, then crushed; it was next mixed with charcoal and fed into small furnaces in which a draught was created with bellows. The resultant bloom was removed from the furnace and again heated for forging in an open hearth. The slag was removed by hammering, while the surface of the metal was simultaneously carburized and case hardened. Further, the hammered metal was beaten into a thin strip, and later several such strips were forge welded together to shape metal of a size suitable for making a given tool. The hardness and strength of these products was mainly derived from the process of carburization, tempering, annealing and quenching.

Ever since Alexander the Great invaded India in the fourth century B.C., India has been renowned for the quality of its steel. How this steel was produced is something about which archaeology has as yet little to say. The early European travellers in South India recorded a technique employed by the ironsmiths of Mysore to produce 'wootz' steel, and, in default of any other evidence, we may conclude that this was the method employed anciently also. To make this steel, pieces of wrought iron are cut off and put in a crucible together with certain organic substances. The crucible is then sealed and fired in a furnace. The principal result of this firing is to increase the carbon content of the metal and thus produce a low-grade steel. Crucibles which may have been employed for this purpose are reported from a number of sites, but probably all are later than the period we are concerned with.

In recent times the spread of iron working in India has been linked by some writers in some unclearly defined way with various specific culture traits (particularly Painted Grey ware, black-and-red ware and megalithic graves) and even with the spread of Indo-Aryan speaking peoples. Others have argued, sometimes with inexplicable vehemence, against such links. The initial spread of iron working certainly coincided with the more or less rapid disappearance of stone or copper–bronze axes from the tool repertoire, no doubt on account of their being relatively less efficient and more expensive to make. Also, it cannot be denied, it coincided to some extent with parts of the currency of the cultural traits mentioned above, but in our view this need not imply any one-to-one relationship between them. While there are still few satisfactorily dated horizons for the early use of iron, we believe that it is premature – if not pointless – to attempt to demonstrate any single pattern of spread, either from north to south, west to east, or vice versa. Our aim, therefore, is to record the pattern as it appears regionally, in relation to broader cultural features, following our general plan of starting in the west, in Pakistan, then moving east across the Gangetic plains, and then south through Central India into the peninsula.

In following this plan we should at the outset stress that the perspective of this chapter must be much wider, in that we are here attempting to trace the onward development of those already well established regional 'cultures' which we discussed in chapters 9 and 10, into an age when historical and traditional evidence becomes increasingly important. Although India in this period is still narrowly speaking 'prehistoric' it becomes ever clearer that to treat it as such is to ignore the growing weight of available 'protohistoric' sources. The perspective therefore is of India emerging into the second, North Indian phase of urbanism, and of the spreading throughout all parts of the subcontinent of an all-Indian cultural ideal which everywhere modulates differently with the developing regional cultures. These underlying themes are dealt with only very briefly, because to do them justice demands separate and more expansive treatment.

North India and Pakistan

The Indus system and Baluchistan

The evidence for the western regions is still very slight and scarcely enough to generalize. On the western borders of the Indian subcontinent, in southern and central Baluchistan, a whole chain of cairn cemeteries has been discovered, producing, in the words of Gordon, identical pottery especially characterized by the squat, spouted flask with lugs pierced for carrying, and representing a people who had a uniform cultural level which manifested itself in horse riding, the use of iron and handmade pottery. Three-flanged arrowheads in bronze and iron come from this group of sites, as well as, in one instance, a horse's skull, suggestively reminiscent of the Gandhara graves and Iron Age burials from Nagpur. At present all these sites can only be vaguely dated: it is probable that they cover many centuries, and range from *c.* 1100 to 500 B.C. Some of the burials are certainly much later, and some writers have questioned whether any are of the antiquity we have suggested.

The excavations at Pirak, near Sibi (see also p. 233) are of considerable importance because they show that here the introduction of iron was a gradual affair, during the course of the otherwise continuous occupation. The earliest iron objects occur before the end of period II, that is before *c.* 1000 B.C., and during the succeeding period iron becomes noticeably more common (*c.* 1000–800 B.C.). During the three stages of period III the painted pottery of the earlier periods is gradually replaced by a plain grey-black pottery (Fig. 12.2). The evidence from Mundigak is less definite. The first object of iron appears in an early level of period VI, and iron becomes common in the succeeding (and final) period VII. But these periods cannot as yet be firmly dated.

In a previous chapter we discussed the graves of the Gandhara grave complex found in the valleys of the North West Frontier region. Although the majority of these graves contain only objects of copper or bronze, a small number do produce iron objects, including in one case from Timargarha, an iron cheek

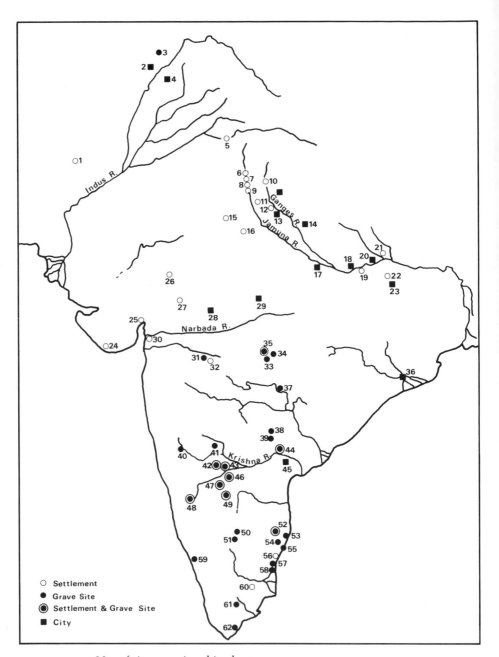

12.1 Map of sites mentioned in chapter 12

Key
1. Pirak   2. Charsada   3. Timargarha   4. Taxila   5. Rupar   6. Bhagawanpura   7. Panipat   8. Sonpat
9. Indraprastha   10. Hastinapura   11. Lalqila   12. Jakhera   13. Atranjikhera   14. Sravasti   15. Jodhpura
16. Noh   17. Kausambi   18. Rajghat   19. Prahladpur   20. Buxar   21. Chirand   22. Sonpur   23. Rajgir
24. Somnath (Prabhas Patan)   25. Nagara   26. Ahar   27. Nagda   28. Ujjain   29. Eran   30. Nagal
31. Ranjala   32. Prakash   33. Takalghat   34. Mahurjhari   35. Naikund   36. Sisupalgarh   37. Pochampad
38. Bhongir   39. Raigir   40. Terdal   41. Jevargi   42. Piklihal   43. Maski   44. Yelleshwaram
45. Nagarjunakonda   46. Tekkalakota   47. Sanganakallu   48. Hallur   49. Brahmagiri   50. Jadigenahalli
51. Savandrug   52. Kunnattur   53. Pallavaram   54. Sanur   55. Perumbair   56. Arikamedu
57. Souttoukeny   58. Mouttrapaleon   59. Porkalam   60. Alagarai   61. T. Kalluppatti   62. Adichanallur

piece for a bit, for which Central Asian parallels suggest a date in the early first millennium. The chronology of the graves, and of the early, middle and late phases proposed by Stacul, and somewhat differently by Dani, is still in need of clarification; but we are inclined to agree with Dani and place the late phase, in which it seems that the iron objects mainly occur, around the opening of the first millennium. This in no way rules out the possibility that occasional objects of iron may be found in graves assignable to the middle phase, indeed we may expect them to. The association of horse furniture and horse burials with the graves of this group has led some writers to associate them with Indo-Aryan speaking people. But if this be the case, the first such immigrants must have arrived in the valleys long before iron, and its subsequent appearance in this region need carry no such connotation.

The establishment of cities in the Gandhara region – the North West Frontier Province of Pakistan – follows a somewhat different pattern. Here it was long thought that the cities were the outcome of the extension of the Persian

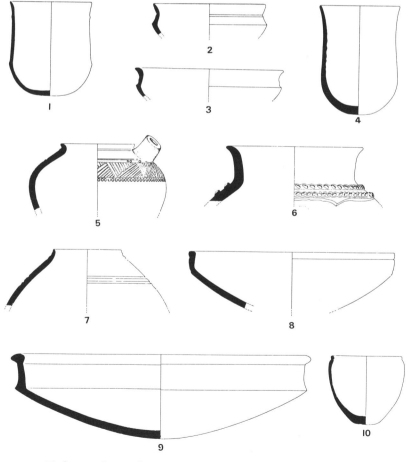

12.2 Pirak, period IIIB: plain grey-black pottery (1:6) (*after* Jarrige)

Achaemenid empire into this area by Cyrus during the sixth century B.C. In support of this view it could be pointed out that the Bhir mound at Taxila, long regarded as the first city, was probably founded around 500 B.C. However, Wheeler's excavation at the Bala Hissar mound, Charsada, revealed the presence of a red burnished pottery which suggested that this city was founded some two or more centuries earlier (Fig. 12.3). This lay below an occupation which paralleled that of the Bhir mound. Recent discoveries by the Cambridge–Pakistan team at Taxila have revealed the existence of an earlier settlement of considerable size in the Hathial area adjacent to the Bhir mound. Here the red burnished ware and accompanying materials have shown not only close correspondence with those of Charsada, but even more striking affinities with the pottery and material culture of the later phase of the Gandharan graves of Swat. Both the Taxila and Charsada red burnished wares show also some relationship with the pottery of Mundigak VI and VII. C14 dates from Hathial suggest that the period lasted from 800–400 B.C. Its beginning was probably somewhat earlier. The culture at this time has

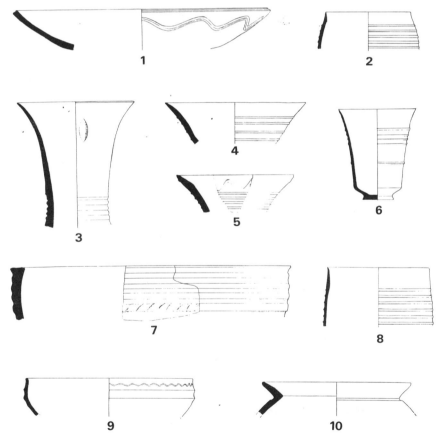

12.3 Charsada, Bala Hissar: red burnished ware: 1–2, 4, 6 Ch I, layers 50–46; 7, 9–10 Ch I layers 43–39; 3, 5 and 8 Ch III, layers 10–8 (1:6) (*after* Wheeler)

a markedly local Gandharan flavour; while that of the subsequent Bhir mound period appears to indicate the arrival of a much more urbane and widely diffused Gangetic character. From around 500 B.C. a fine grey or black burnished pottery appears, to occupy much the same role as the NBP of the Ganges region (see below, p. 323–4). It may be noted that there is not as yet any evidence that the Painted Grey ware ever gained currency in this area.

North India and the Ganges valley

When we move eastwards into what we have called the Northern Nuclear Region – the Punjab, northern Rajasthan and the Ganges–Jamuna Doab – we enter an area from which there is currently much more evidence, both archaeological and literary. This is the Indo-Aryan heartland anciently known as Brahmāvarta or Brahmarṣideśa. As we saw in the previous chapter, from around 1300 B.C., and the compilation of the Rigveda, we enter a new period which is generally referred to as 'Late Vedic'. This period culminates in the emergence of the great cities of classical India and of more or less full historical records, with the foundation of Buddhism, Jainism and the other sects which arose in reaction to the ritualism of the Vedic tradition. During these centuries we are thus in a strictly protohistoric situation, when the textual data, when once we can use them in a controlled, critical manner, can augment the archaeological evidence. One striking feature of the Late Vedic literature is the eastward expansion of its horizons. During the succeeding centuries the focus of attention of the Rigveda was the Punjab; now it shifts to the Doab of the Ganges and Jamuna rivers, the ancient Kurukshetra, the kingdom of the Kuru and Pāncāla tribes. The Punjab seems gradually to fade into the background until by the latest texts of the period, such as the *Śatapatha Brāhmana*, it is regarded even with disapproval. To the east we hear more of such tribes, or states, as Kosala (Avadh, Oudh), Kāśī – whose capital was at Banaras – and even Magadha in southern Bihar. There is another general expansion of horizons towards the south. The new and wider area thus covered was that known as the Madhyadeśa or Mid-land. Even before archaeology could supply any basis against which these data might be evaluated, it was already accepted that they referred to an eastward expansion of the Aryan tribes. A key passage in the *Śatapatha Brāhmana* tells how a certain king who formerly resided in the Punjab on the banks of the river Sarasvati carried fire (sacrificial or otherwise) eastwards to Videha (in northern Bihar) as far as the Sadānīra (modern Gandak) river. In those days, we are told, there were no Brahmans to the east of this river, but already by the time of the text the expansion had continued and Brahmans were to be found beyond it.

The later Vedic literature provides a mass of information on the life and culture of the times. A wide range of crops is mentioned, including wheat, barley, millet and rice. There are repeated references to iron, as well as to copper, bronze, lead and tin. The plough was used for cultivation, and it must be inferred that there was a progressive clearance of the flat, often swampy, forests of the Ganges plains, in preparation for their adoption for agriculture. There are indications of the growing complexity of society and of the formation of 'castes'. The old tribal groups must have disappeared as population increased and the size and number of settlements multiplied. We find considerable detail on agricultural operations – ploughing, cattle-keeping, etc. We read of numerous trades and crafts. The texts further supply information on those topics on which archaeology is most reticent, such as religious beliefs and political ideas. Thus in a very real sense, for the regions to which these texts apply, we may regard the archaeological cultures as protohistoric.

In recent years the earliest Iron Age occupation has been associated with a fine, well-fired Painted Grey ware which has hitherto been used as a hallmark of this cultural period (Fig. 12.4). This pottery was first isolated in a stratified context in 1946 in an analysis of the finds from Ahicchatra, but its full significance only became apparent in 1950–2 with B. B. Lal's excavations at Hastinapura. The distribution of the Painted Grey ware extends from the dry bed of the Ghaggar in Bahawalpur and north Rajasthan, eastwards across the watershed of the Ganges and the Indus to the Ganges–Jamuna Doab. At Rupar, in the Punjab,

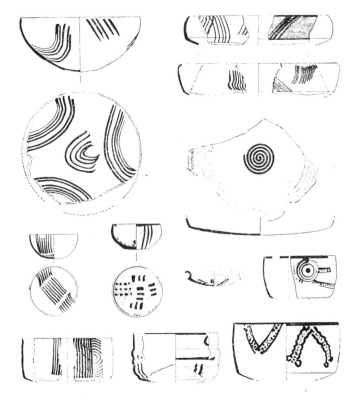

12.4 Hastinapura: Painted Grey ware pottery (1:6) (*after* B. B. Lal)

it is stratified between Harappan and Early Historic remains. In the Doab, the Kurukshetra of the Mahābhārata, it has been found in excavations or on the surface at such historically important sites as Panipat, Indraprastha (the Purana Qila mound at Delhi), Mathura, Bairat and Sonpat. Further, it has been found in excavations of the vast mounds at Atranjikhera and at Alamgirpur. Many smaller sites have also been recorded. Thus the grey ware 'culture' occupied almost the same area as that postulated for the Late Vedic settlement. Its eastern limits are at present at Sravasti, high on the northern plains of the Ganges. Nearer the river it gives way, from about the junction of the Ganges and Jamuna, to another – central Ganges – cultural zone, which we shall discuss below.

The selection of this single culture trait as possessing special significance has led to unfortunate distortions and confusions of interpretation in much of the published literature. One frequently reads of a 'Painted Grey ware period' and of 'Painted Grey ware people' as though they were entirely different from the 'Late Harappans' who occupied many of the same settlements during the preceding period, when often all that the evidence suggests is that a new fashion in pottery was growing in popularity. Above all the concentration on a single trait has diverted attention from the major cultural developments.

Broadly, the culture sequence revealed in excavations is as follows. In the second and third quarters of the second millennium, most sites produced a predominantly red ware which constitutes the last stage of pottery of Harappan or even Early Harappan tradition. This is more or less synonymous with the so-called Ochre Coloured Pottery (OCP). As far as technique is concerned, this pottery, like the majority of pottery from east of the Indus, was probably not made with a foot-wheel, and, in the early period, not even with a spun-wheel. Firing was mostly by simple pit or bonfire, while the ancillary forming techniques included the turntable, the mould or form, and dabbers and anvils. These latter are exemplified by specimens from excavations at several sites, and represent a potter's technique which diffused throughout the entire subcontinent and continues to dominate its pottery down to the present day.

This OCP is followed (though not at all sites) by a short period in which a substantial part of the pottery consists of a black-and-red burnished ware (technically related to that of Ahar, but without painted designs). The earliest fragmentary evidence of iron working comes from this period (as at Noh) with the appearance of shaft-hole tools. This method of attachment is in marked contrast to that found in the south of India, where attachment for the typical flat axes is by means of iron cross-bands. Not only do axe shapes differ between these two areas, but arrowheads in the north include, from a very early date, the three-flanged varieties which provide a link with Iran and Central Asia, but are absent in the south. The date for this second period is difficult to fix, but the evidence from Noh suggests inferentially a date of *c.* 1100–900 B.C.

This period which at some sites is characterized by black-and-red burnished ware is, in the north of the Northern Nuclear Region, followed by a period in which the distinctive Painted Grey ware becomes gradually more common alongside the coarser red ware – and the black-and-red ware, where present, decreases. This sequence is in evidence at many sites, including: in Rajasthan, Noh and Jodhpura; in Haryana, Bhagawanpura and Dadheri; in Uttar Pradesh at Atranjikhera, Lal Qila, Jakhera, etc.; and either in part or wholly at many other sites. It is currently not firmly dated. The third stage is dated by a fairly large number of radiocarbon samples from a number of sites yielding Painted Grey ware and, fairly commonly, iron. This suggests dates of c. 900–500 B.C. Any earlier occurrence of iron can as yet scarcely be recognized in this area. The single date from Atranjikhera, which when calibrated gives c. 1150 B.C. for the Painted Grey ware, seems to be divergent and must be discounted until supported by other evidence.

Most of the excavations of these sites have been exploratory and have not investigated the Iron Age occupation to any great extent as yet. Moreover, only Hastinapura has so far been fully published. Hence, when one comes to consider broader aspects of the culture, confirmation is sadly lacking. Another reason for this is that at almost every one of the sites there was subsequent continuity of settlement so that the early levels are now buried under many metres of later deposits. Enough has been recovered to make it clear that the equipment stands in marked contrast to that of all earlier periods. Comparatively little can be said of house types. At Bhagawanpura the houses of the early phase are circular huts of wood and wattle and daub; those of the later phase are more substantial houses with earth walls. At Jakhera circular huts continue throughout the whole period, but in the later part are augmented by rectangular huts as well. Plant and animal remains so far reported indicate that wheat, barley and rice were cultivated; and cattle, pig and (latterly) horse were kept. A stone-blade industry is totally absent. Iron is a fairly constant find from the earliest levels, but few illustrations of any objects have yet appeared. The most frequently reported finds are of arrowheads, both barbed and leaf-shaped, in one case with a socketed tang, and spearheads. Axes, probably shaft-hole, but this is not specified, are reported from Noh and Atranjikhera; and from the latter site a pair of iron tongs from a late level of the period. Bone points, most probably arrowheads, are frequently referred to (Fig. 12.5). From this site also comes evidence of wheat, barley and rice. Copper is less common but objects made from it include small leaf-shaped arrowheads with solid tang from Hastinapura, pins and unguent rods. Glass beads and bangles are found, as well as stone, (?) frit and terracotta discs, which are probably ear ornaments, and bone dice (which play so important a part in the Mahābhārata). The pottery is predominately wheel-thrown and shows a remarkable degree of standardization. The Painted Grey ware is dominated by bowls of two shapes, a shallow tray and a deeper bowl, often with a sharp angle between the walls and base. The range of decoration is limited, vertical, oblique or criss-cross lines, rows of dots, spiral chains, and concentric circles being common. The same forms occur again in plain and slipped red ware, along with larger water pots, showing the combination of wheel-throwing for the upper parts and beating for the lower that so typifies Indian pottery of the Early Historic period.

We have dwelt on this region – the Madhyadeśa – in some detail because it played so important a part in the formation of what we may call the second, or Gangetic civilization of India. Lal has drawn attention to the fact that many of the places mentioned in the Mahābhārata have been found to have settlements of this period. As we have seen the settlements often followed directly on even earlier settlements of the final post-Harappan phases – those associated with the red 'Ochre Coloured' and black-and-red wares. However, by the end of the period a more or less uniform culture, whose hallmark is the black lustrous pottery known as Northern Black Polished ware (or NBP), extended from the lower Ganges to the Punjab. This culture provided the milieu for the early cities of classical India, which find repeated mention in the accounts of the life of Gautama the Buddha and Mahāvīra, the founder of the Jain sect, no less than for such dynasties as the Śaiśunāgas, the Nandas and the Mauryas; and for the development of the characteristic Indian script, the *Brāhmī lipi*, and of Indian coinage.

To the east of the junction of the Ganges and Jamuna rivers lies the central region of the Ganges valley, comprising eastern Uttar Pradesh and parts of Bihar. Kausambi stands at the boundary between the two regions, sharing features of each, including the cultivation of rice. The distinctive eastern sequence, in which a black-and-red ware plays a prominent role, was first recognized in excavations at Sonepur (Sonpur) in Gaya district in 1956. The sequence at this site has now been refined by further work, and a related sequence revealed by excavations at a number of other sites, some of great historical renown, among them Rajghat (Old Banaras), Buxar, Chirand and Prahladpur. At all these sites the true Painted Grey ware is absent, although in the earliest phase a plain grey

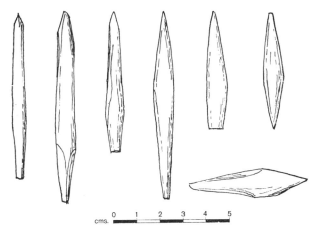

12.5 Bone and ivory points, Kausambi II and III (*after* G. R. Sharma)

ware is found, and the black-and-red gives way directly to the Northern Black
Polished ware around 500 B.C. This part of the Ganges valley, enjoying as it does
a rainfall of over 100 cm per annum, must anciently have been more densely
forested than the Doab, and for this reason, if for no other, the expansion of
settlements must probably have depended upon the availability of effective
methods of forest clearance. There is at present no indication from which
direction the first settlers came. It is possible that they moved in from the hills
and forests to the south of the Ganges; but the more likely direction seems to
have been from the west, in which event they would have moved eastwards
down the river valley before the pressure of the expanding population associated
with the iron-using Painted Grey ware culture. One possible way of charting
this expansion would be to document the occurrence of rice, for in the Ganges
valley, during both the periods of the Painted Grey, and the Northern Black
Polished wares, the build-up of population and the consequent increase in the
number of settlements appears to coincide with a great increase in the cultivation of rice and its growing dominance as a cereal source.

It is thus probable that the movement will ultimately be amenable to some
sort of documentation. The sequence revealed at these Central Ganges sites is as
follows:

1. As we have seen earlier, there are as yet but few places known in the Middle Ganges
   valley where there are settlements of the pre-iron period. Among them are Chirand,
   where period I appears to be Neolithic, and period II Chalcolithic, and Sohgaura in
   Gorakhpur district which corresponds to the latter phase. They show radiocarbon
   dates for the Chalcolithic of between 1500 and 800 B.C. The earliest occupation at
   Sonpur perhaps also goes back to this period.
2. This first period is followed by one in which the first use of iron is attested. It occurs at
   such major settlements as Rajghat IA–B; Prahladpur IA; Kausambi II, and at smaller
   settlements such as Chirand IIB and Sonpur IB. The date of the beginning of this period
   is not clearly established, but a date of c. 770 B.C. from Sonpur leads us to expect that it
   may be around c. 800 B.C. Its ceramics are mainly a black-slipped ware, black-and-red
   ware (sometimes painted) (Fig. 12.7), and coarse red ware. A small quantity of plain
   grey ware is found. This period seems also to be in evidence in the early excavations at
   Rajgir, and in the lowest levels of Tilaura Kot in the Nepal Terai, sometimes thought
   to be the site of the city of the parents of the Buddha, where a Painted Grey ware
   which, although recognizably different, is the easternmost extension of the ceramic of
   the Ganges–Jamuna Doab, occurs. Arrowheads of horn and bone are common (Fig.
   12.6). They include both tanged and socketed varieties, and one with a triangular
   cross-section, reminiscent of the triple flanged arrowheads of metal encountered on
   the western borders of Pakistan and in Central Asia. The diet, where there is evidence,
   seems always to have been based on rice.
3. Shortly after 500 B.C. at all these sites, no less than those of the Madhyadeśa, a new and
   striking pottery, the black gloss ware known as NBP ware, makes its appearance (Figs.
   12.8–9). With it the cultural unification of Gangetic India becomes apparent in the
   material record. The black ware adopted the two major forms of the Painted Grey, a
   shallow tray-bowl and a deeper, often sharply carinated bowl. The technique of the
   black gloss surface was apparently very similar to that of the Greek Black ware, both

cases depending upon the unusually fine particle size of the clay employed for the dressing.

The age that follows is one which may in all ways be regarded as a civilization. Iron now becomes commonplace, and was used for all purposes. Coins, both of cast copper and punch-marked silver, make their appearance (Fig. 12.10). Writing, although not attested by inscriptions until over two centuries later, may be inferred to have come into use early in this period. Politically the sixth century saw the emergence of Magadha as the dominant state in the Ganges valley and the break-up of the old tribal society. One of the first indications of these developments is the construction of great new mud or mud-brick ramparts as defences for the newly emerging cities. By contrast, the settlements at Hastinapura and most of the early Painted Grey ware sites are really villages rather than cities. But at Rajgir, already before the time of the Buddha, a great stone perimeter wall was constructed. At Kausambi the excavator claims for the brick defences even greater antiquity, going back to the tenth century B.C., though

12.6 Chirand, Bihar: points and arrowheads of bone, horn and ivory (3:4) (*courtesy* Director of Archaeology, Bihar)

this may need some modification when better dating is available. At Eran, as we shall see below, and at Ujjain, the first ramparts can claim comparable antiquity. Many other great cities of classical India have such ramparts, but in most cases their age has not yet been established, or appears to be somewhat later.

It is only in this period that substantial evidence is available for the house and settlement pattern of the Ganges valley, and this is largely beyond the time limits of the present book. It is possible that the vogue for burnt brick began again in the Ganges valley during the first half of the first millennium B.C. This is certainly suggested by the dates proposed for Kausambi, although mud-brick continued in general use at least until some centuries later. It is interesting to consider the constituent parts of the cities of the Ganges valley, but while their

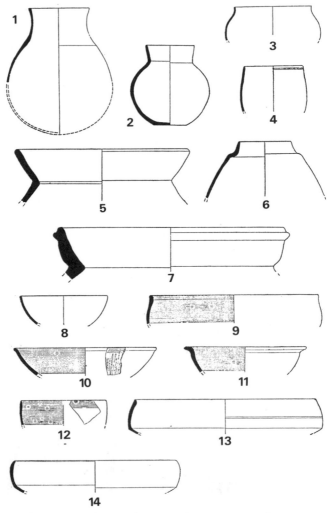

12.7 Rajghat, Banaras: pottery from period IA: 1, 2, 5–7 red ware: 3–4, 8, 13–14 black slipped ware; 9–12 black-and-red ware (1:6) (after Narain and Roy)

chronology remains so much in doubt we are hesitant to do so. From the excavations at Kausambi, Rajgir, Ujjain, Eran, etc., it would seem that the need to protect the growing cities by great brick ramparts and moats or ditches was felt from early in the first millennium, if not before, and during the next few centuries the same features are found at many of the great cities.

Before leaving our discussion of the Iron Age in the Ganges–Jamuna Doab and the Ganges valley, it is perhaps pertinent to comment further on what are arguably the finest pottery types ever to be developed in India – the Painted Grey and the Northern Black Polished wares. As suggested above, the NBP is a further refinement and development of the Painted Grey ware, but both of them demonstrably belong to a continuing craft tradition which probably goes back to the final centuries of the second millennium, when the ware first appears in the eastern Punjab and the Ganges–Jamuna Doab. The production of both wares depends upon selection of a very fine clay, which was probably further levigated. There is clear evidence that both the turntable and spun-wheel were used in forming. As mentioned, the two dominant forms were a shallow carinated tray-bowl, with a slightly rounded base, and a series of smaller, deeper bowls, some with carination. The range of painted decorations of the grey ware is quite wide. Coarser grey, buff or pink wares occur in any assemblage alongside the finer ware, which is generally less than half of the total. Already on a proportion

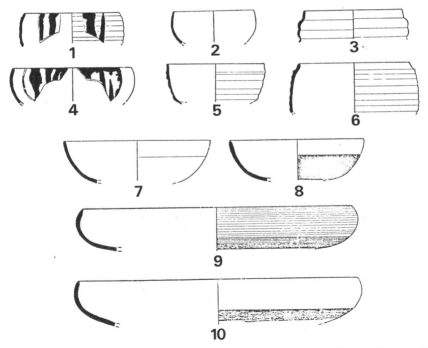

12.8 Rajghat, Banaras: pottery from period IB: 2–3, 5–7 monochrome Northern Black Polished ware; 1, 4, 8–10 bichrome Northern Black Polished ware (1:6) (*after* Narain and Roy)

of vessels of the Painted Grey ware series a plain black slip was employed, being a reduced red ochre. This provides the forerunner to the NBP, which develops around 500 B.C. To produce the glossy surface of the NBP a further coating of alkali, acting as a flux, and producing, under reducing firing conditions, a fine black gloss, was applied. The ware has recently been reproduced experimentally by Hegde, and his reconstruction of the techniques of producing it seems to be authoritative. The firing calls for accurate control of temperature and atmosphere, and must imply the use of a sophisticated kiln with a separate fire-chamber. Several special varieties are found: among them is a bichrome black and bright red ware (Fig. 12.8, 1, 4), and wares with gold and silver lustrous gloss. The NBP represents the technical skill of the early Indian potters at its best. The

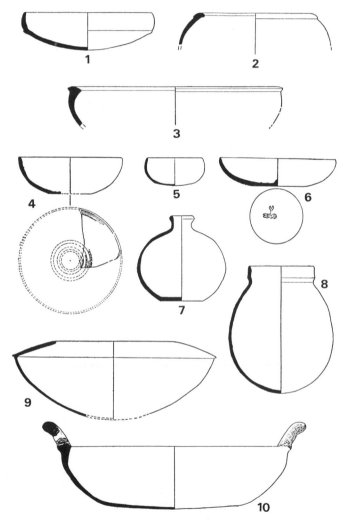

12.9 Rajghat, Banaras: pottery from period IC: 4–8 coarse Northern Black Polished grey ware; 1–3, 9–10, red ware (1:6) (*after* Narain and Roy)

black gloss ware shows a close relationship to the Greek Black ware, but there is no reason to suppose that it was derived from that source, as the Painted Grey ware already shows almost all the necessary skills to produce it.

Peninsular India

The Southern Nuclear Region

The sequence during this period in Saurashtra and south Rajasthan is not at present very well documented, and until further excavation has been carried out and better dating evidence is available it remains rather uncertain. The date of the introduction of iron in these areas is indicated, in a rather negative way, by the dates relating to the end of the preceding Chalcolithic period. Thus at Ahar a date of 1490 B.C. marks the topmost layers of period 1. As we have seen above, this period is regarded by its excavators as Chalcolithic, and as being followed by a long hiatus before the succeeding iron-using settlement, which is datable to the middle of the first millennium. However, this has recently been questioned by Sahi who points out that about a dozen iron objects, along with iron slag, were recovered in the excavations from the upper layers of period 1. This

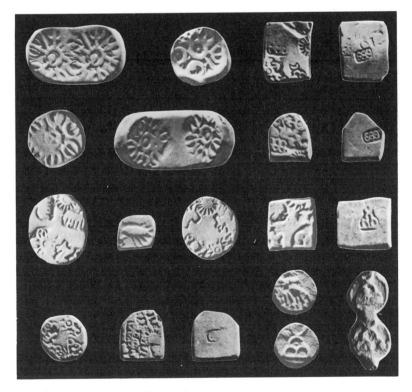

12.10 Silver bar, punch-marked silver and cast copper coins

remarkable evidence suggests that at Ahar the first introduction of iron took place around 1500 B.C. Without further excavation this conclusion must be treated very cautiously. At almost all the other sites so far excavated there appears to be a long hiatus between the end of the Chalcolithic period and the ensuing Iron Age occupation. This is considered to be the case at Somnath (Prabhas Patan), where the excavator postulates a break of some eight centuries in the sequence. In Gujarat a number of sites have yielded evidence of a comparable later phase. At Broach and Nagal, on the north and south of the Narbada estuary respectively, and at Nagara, the old Cambay, excavations have revealed a period of black-and-red ware preceding the importation of sherds of NBP. The black-and-red ware at Nagal often bears scratched graffiti or decoration, suggesting its relative earliness, and a stone-blade industry was found in association with it. Iron came from all levels except the lowest; while bone arrowheads and points, and beads of carnelian and semi-precious stones were found throughout. At Nagara the early period ends c. 300 B.C. with the appearance of the first coins and sherds of Gangetic NBP. Below there are some 7 metres of deposits which the excavator believes to date back to the sixth century B.C. They represent a single uniform cultural pattern but produced no absolute dating materials. It is possible that some of these sites may represent a considerably longer occupation, taking the sequence back at least to c. 800 B.C. But this has still to be demonstrated.

The picture from Malwa and the Central Indian sites is slightly clearer. At Nagda, period II appears to have been a direct continuation of the earlier settlement; it produced black-and-red ware, some iron objects, and a continuation of the blade industry. At the neighbouring Ujjain, period I produced black-and-red and plain red ware. At both these sites a considerable depth of occupation ensued before the importation of stray pieces of NBP. The Ujjain I assemblage is reported to have included a sherd of Painted Grey ware, along with the more common pottery. Iron arrowheads and spearheads and bone arrowheads were also found. As period II can be reasonably associated with the Mauryan occupation, its forerunner may well extend back to c. 600 B.C. The latest recorded radiocarbon date for the Chalcolithic period at Eran is c. 1170 B.C. At Eran, period IIA coincides with the appearance of black-and-red ware. A copper object is also reported, as well as the first iron, and this may be expected to follow immediately upon period I. It is noteworthy that at Eran as at Kausambi, the excavator claims that the fortifications were anterior even to the Iron Age, going back to the Chalcolithic period. Thus at these sites a similar picture prevails, still lacking clarity with regard to the date at which iron working first comes into use, and open to varying interpretations. One must express the hope that the important excavations at Eran may be more fully published.

Farther east, on the western fringes of the Ganges delta there is every sign that iron working spread to the existing areas of Chalcolithic settlement at an early date. Thus at Mahisadal, period II commences before 800 B.C. The main elements of the material culture continue from the previous period, suggesting that the arrival of iron involved no profound change in population. The pottery becomes somewhat coarser and is augmented by a grey or buff ware. Iron appears to have been plentiful and quantities of slag are reported. Whether this culture had closer links with the Central Ganges region, or with settlements in the forests to the south of the Ganges, has yet to be seen and must await further publication. The radiocarbon date is certainly close to that of Chirand IIB.

The Deccan

Turning southward into Maharashtra, the situation is no more definite. The many radiocarbon dates from Nevasa, Chandoli and above all Inamgaon indicate that the Late Jorwe Chalcolithic phase continued to c. 900–800 B.C. It might be expected that the first iron objects would occur during this period. But this has not yet been shown. At several sites there appears to have been no hiatus between this period and the succeeding Iron Age. There is still, however, a perplexing absence of radiocarbon dates relating to early Iron Age levels. At Prakash in the Tapi valley, there was a short hiatus before period II (Figs. 12.11–12). This latter was represented by some fourteen to fifteen feet of black-and-red ware deposits below the first occurrence of NBP, and therefore testifies to a fairly protracted occupation. Iron appears at the beginning of the period and continues alongside the black-and-red ware. Among iron tools we may note the flat celt-like axes, recalling the forms of copper axes of Harappan and post-Harappan times; shaft-hole axes appear at Prakash only in the subsequent period. Although the duration of the period must have been considerable, there is little apparent indication of any significant changes in the material culture throughout. At Bahal, period II produced similar evidence. At Tekwada on the opposite bank of the Girna river an important related burial site was discovered. Here M. N. Deshpande excavated three urn burials and one pit burial. The burial-pit had a floor lined with stone slabs. The pottery from these burials is a compound of elements belonging to the Jorwe phase and elements of the earliest phase of the Iron Age. Hence we are inclined to assign them to the Late Jorwe period heralding the arrival of iron. No iron was discovered, but the black-and-red ware was in some cases marked or rather scratched with owners' marks. These graffiti recall those commonly found on pots of Rangpur III, and also on black-and-red grave pottery from many sites in the south. The pit burial and pottery recall certain early Iron Age burials from Brahmagiri (to be considered below). The excavator assigned the Tekwada graves to Bahal IB, but we are inclined to place them at the junction of IB and II. Another grave site at Ranjala in West Khandesh also produced typical Iron Age black-and-red ware with scratched graffiti.

In the eastern part of Maharashtra, around Nagpur, a number of important grave sites have been excavated (to be described below) and several associated

settlements. One of the latter, Takalghat, has produced a radiocarbon date of
c. 750 B.C. from one of the middle layers. As there are around two metres of
occupation deposit below, it is reasonable to expect that the beginning of this
settlement will be found to go back a further century or more. Two more dates
have been obtained from 'megalithic' graves at a neighbouring site, Naikund.
These too have yielded dates around 750 B.C. They are thus of considerable
importance as charting the age of this important group of sites, and of the
megalithic graves in general.

In the Karnataka region the position at the settlements so far excavated is
little clearer. At Brahmagiri, Piklihal, Sanganakallu and Maski, the depth of Iron

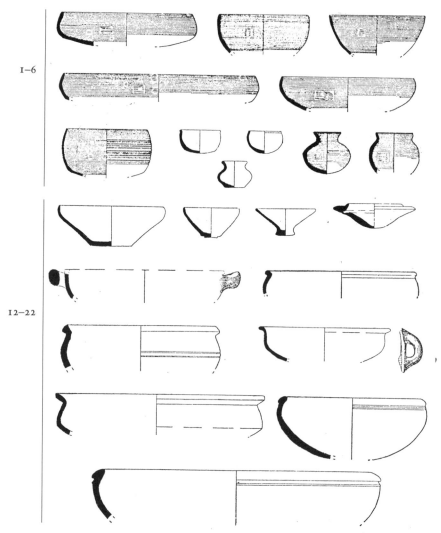

12.11 Prakash, Dhulia district, period II, pottery: 1–6, 10–11, black-and-red ware; 7–9,
12–22 other wares (1:6) (after Thapar)

Age occupation is generally less than four feet. More recent excavations at Hallur in South Dharwar district, and Paiyampalli in North Arcot district yield rather similar evidence. The introduction of iron takes place at the close of the Neolithic–Chalcolithic period. The earliest phase of the Iron Age is represented in the excavation at Piklihal and Hallur. It is probably to be identified in burial-pits with stone-slab floors excavated by Wheeler in the Iron Age burial ground at Brahmagiri, but antedating the later cist graves. These burials produced a combination of black-and-red ware, and a distinctive matt-painted buff and red ware, somewhat akin to the Jorwe ware, along with the first iron objects, therefore recalling the Tekwada burials. Another diagnostic trait which appears in the region at this time is white-painted black-and-red ware. In the settlements stone-axe and blade industries apparently continue. From the pottery of this period in Karnataka have come two examples of textile impressions, thus to a small extent filling in the gap in the history of textiles between the Mature Indus and later periods. Radiocarbon dates from Hallur suggest that the opening of the period may be as early as 1150–1030 B.C.

The succeeding phase is dominated by burnished but unpainted black-and-red ware with accompanying red or black wares. This is represented by the 'megalithic' period at Brahmagiri, Piklihal Iron Age, Sanganakallu 'overlap' and Maski II. Iron is now a fairly regular occurrence, both in graves and habitations, while copper, bronze and gold are also found. The stone-blade industry continues but on a diminished scale, and stone axes are rarely present. There are indications that this period may ultimately be amenable to some sort of further division on the basis of grave and pottery types, but more research is called for before this can be achieved. The excavations hitherto have not been very helpful, in terms of purely stratigraphic differentiation.

At Brahmagiri, Maski and Piklihal, the period is followed by one in which a

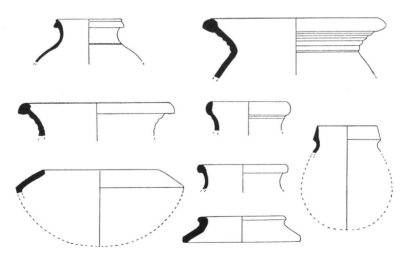

12.12 Prakash, period II: pottery of other wares (1:6) (*after* Thapar)

distinctive white-painted black-and-red or plain red ware with russet dressing (the 'Russet coated' or 'Andhra' ware) appears. With it are tray-bowls recalling North Indian forms appearing in the NBP ware, but bearing a rouletted pattern on the inside of the base. From the coincidence of this ware on the Tamil coast at Arikamedu with Roman imports, including inscribed or stamped sherds of Arretine ware, the commencement of the period as a whole cannot be much earlier than the opening of the Christian era. However, the rouletted ware pre-dated the Arretine at Arikamedu, and there is a likelihood that in the western parts of the peninsula it may be found to occur at a somewhat earlier date. As the principal form of the rouletted ware is the tray-bowl characteristic of the Ganges valley, and as this form more or less disappears from pottery in the north before the opening of the Christian era, some considerable revision of chronology may be necessary when further evidence comes to light.

The sequence of the eastern coastal plain or Tamilnad is revealed by the excavations of Wheeler and Casal at Arikamedu, and the more recent excavations at Kunnattur, Alagarai and Tirukkambuliyur in Trichinopoly district. At all these sites a period coinciding with Roman trade imports and producing a predominantly red pottery is preceded by one in which the characteristic pottery is black-and-red, similar to that of the graves. It is obviously of great interest to discover how this sequence relates to the introduction of such elements as writing, and to the flowering of the early South Indian civilization which finds its echoes in the poetry of the 'Sangam' period. In this region, as in Karnataka, there are indications of several sequential phases of the Iron Age, although as yet excavation has scarcely demonstrated this. For example, from T. Kalluppatti, about thirty miles west-south-west of Madurai, urn burials have been excavated containing (among other things) fine white-painted black-and-red ware of a kind which may well date from the very beginnings of the Iron Age and indicate a rapid movement from far to the north-west in Malwa or beyond. Certainly it demands comparison with that from Hallur in Karnataka. This type of painted decoration is comparatively rare at present. The russet dressed and painted black-and-red ware, from Coimbatore, Jadigenahalli, Tirrukambuliyur, etc., probably indicates a late phase of the Iron Age, coinciding with the centuries around the turn of the Christian era and also echoing the third phase of Karnataka, but these have not yet been dated satisfactorily.

The situation in Sri Lanka has not been clearly established but, from the reports of many typical megalithic graves with associated black-and-red pottery, one might infer that there was immigration from South India, before the arrival of the North Indian settlers in the second half of the first millennium B.C.

Burial complex of the South Indian Iron Age

From the preceding paragraphs it will have seemed that the Iron Age of the southern peninsula is in some respects curiously neglected, and indeed little understood. But there is another large body of evidence relating to it, which derives from the great complex of Iron Age burials, frequently known as 'megaliths'. The term has been rather widely interpreted and has on occasion been used for urn burials lacking the presence of small, let alone great stones! We may associate an important change from burial among the settlements to burial in separate graveyards approximately with the first appearance of iron in the south. The subsequent centuries saw an enormous proliferation of varied practices of disposing of the dead, and as modern observation has revealed a corresponding variety still in vogue in South India, it seems reasonable to infer that the burial complex has continued as a part of South Indian culture for a very long period.

The distribution of these Iron Age graves is far wider than any one culture region: they are reported in great numbers from the extreme south and coastal Sri Lanka, throughout most parts of the peninsula in which granites and gneisses are the predominant rocks, and as far north as Khandesh and Nagpur. A few isolated sites from the hills south of the Ganges valley (such as Kotia in Allahabad district) may also be regarded as outliers both in time and space.

Among the graves certain main types regularly recur, of which we note the following:

(a) Large urns, often piriform, containing collected bones previously excarnated, and buried in a small pit, marked in some cases by a stone circle or small capstone or both. The pits, and sometimes the urn itself, often contain grave goods. Urn burials of this sort are common on the eastern coastal plains, and have a wide distribution elsewhere.

12.13 Brahmagiri: cist graves, showing port-hole and grave goods (*courtesy* Archaeological Survey of India)

(b) Legged urns and legged pottery sarcophagi, the latter sometimes with an animal's head, are less frequently found but have a fairly wide distribution. Sarcophagi without legs also occur (Fig. 12.18).

(c) Pit circle graves, of which several examples were excavated at Brahmagiri, in which the body had evidently been placed on a wooden bier in a large open pit and exposed, perhaps to allow for excarnation. Grave goods are found in the pits, and a stone circle is erected round the circumference (Figs. 12.15–16).

(d) Cist graves (Figs. 12.13–14). Of these there is a great variety. The stone cists are usually of granite slabs, sometimes with port-holes, variously oriented. The cists may be deeply buried in pits, partly buried, or erected upon the bare rock surface. Some cists are compartmented and have several separate chambers: in some instances a separate slab resting on four stones suggests a bed. The capstones may be single or

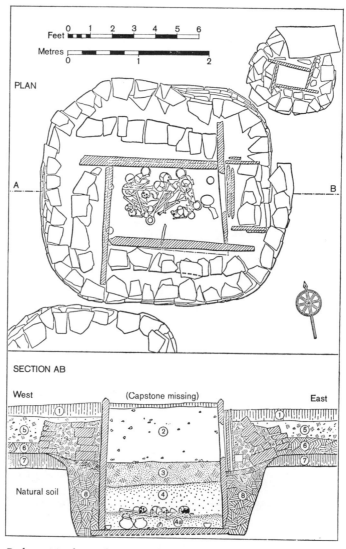

12.14 Brahmagiri: plan and section of cist grave (*after* Wheeler)

multiple. Many different arrangements of burial – both single and multiple – are found, and grave goods were placed both within and around the cists. In some cases a ramp below ground level leads down to the port-hole entrance and this has been covered by a slab door. The cist is usually marked by a stone circle or on occasion by a double or treble circle.

(e) In the Malabar coastal laterites small rock-cut chambers are found, sometimes approached by an entrance from above and covered with a capstone. Some of these chambers have vaulted roofs.

(f) One further monument associated with the graves and belonging to the Iron Age is the stone alignment, comprising carefully oriented rows of standing stones set in a square or diagonal plan. The standing stones are generally from 1.5 to 2.4 metres in height but occasionally examples of over 6 m are recorded. Small alignments have been reported with as few as three rows of three stones, four rows of four, five rows of five, etc., but large diagonal alignments with sometimes many hundreds of standing stones are reported from Gulbarga district. These monuments are so far mainly distributed in the central Deccan, in the districts to the south of Hyderabad.

A century and a half has elapsed since the first excavation of one of these burial sites, and during this period many hundreds of graves have been excavated. A recent bibliography lists more than 250 published books or articles on the subject. Among them a few outstanding examples may be mentioned: between 1851 and 1862 Colonel Meadows Taylor published accounts of his excavations in Shorapur; Alexander Rea between 1899 and 1904 excavated many urn burials at Adichanallur in Tinnevelly district; in 1916 and 1924 Dr Hunt published accounts of graves he had excavated at Raigir and Bhongir, east of Hyderabad. Since 1945 many more sites have been excavated including

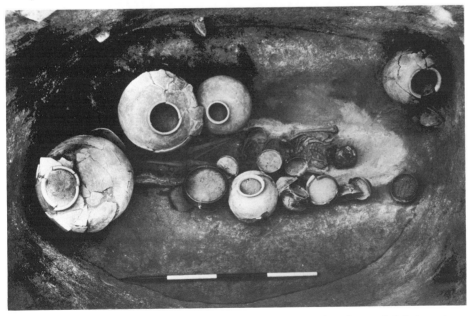

12.15 Maski, Raichur district: pit burial with grave goods and extended skeleton (*courtesy* Archaeological Survey of India)

Brahmagiri, Sanur in Chingleput district, Porkalam in Trichur district, and many graves around Nagarjunakonda and Yelleshwaram, Maski, Jadigenahalli in Karnataka, Souttoukeny and Mouttrapaleon in Pondicherry, Mahurjhari and Naikund near Nagpur.

Although there is a wide diversity of burial customs, other factors give this whole series a general uniformity. In all the graves pottery, and particularly burnished black-and-red ware, is found, often in quantity (Fig. 12.17). In almost every excavated grave some objects of iron, of surprisingly uniform types, occur (Fig. 12.19). The pottery from the graves is patently that of the Iron Age levels in the settlements, although certain special forms are found in the graves. Distinctive types include a shallow tray-bowl and a deeper bowl, both with a rounded base, conical lids with knobs or loops on the apex, pottery ring stands, larger waterpots, invariably with rounded bases, and so on. Other commonly found grave goods include etched carnelian and other beads, rare objects of copper,

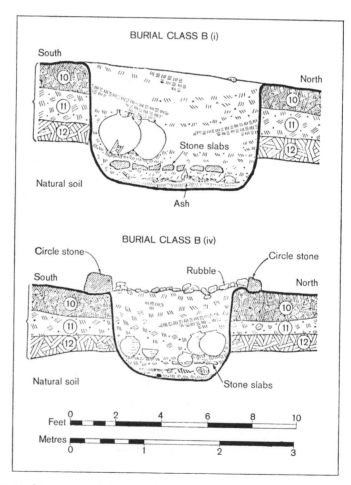

12.16 Maski: sections of pit graves (*after* Thapar)

bronze or stone and only occasional gold objects, despite the presence in the south of India of gold mines which by this time were being extensively mined. But iron is almost universal, and the range of identical tool-types, repeated many times, at sites as far apart as Nagpur and Adichanallur – some 1450 km apart – must testify to the diffusion of a fairly tightly knit group of iron workers (Fig. 12.19). Among the most common tools are flat iron axes often with crossed iron bands for hafting (Fig. 12.12(a)). The shaft-hole axe, which appears at a very early date in North India and spreads south during the first millennium A.D., to become today almost the universal axe type, is unknown in the Iron Age graves of South India. A second common type includes varieties of flanged spade, hoe, spud or pick axe, and a third includes sickles or bill-hooks. Iron wedges and

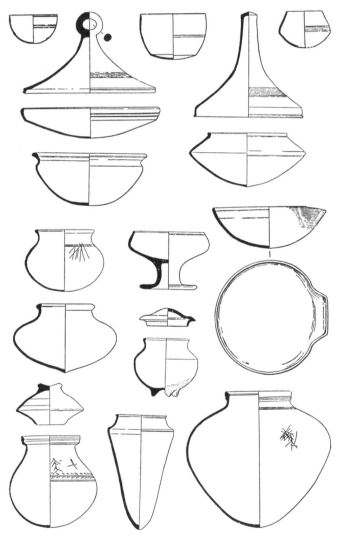

12.17 Brahmagiri: black-and-red burnished ware (1:8) (*after* Wheeler)

crowbars, or perhaps spears, of up to seven feet in length are found. A variety of knives, chisels or adzes, iron tripods or pot rests, saucer hook-lamps and many-armed lamp-pendants, are perhaps for domestic use. Daggers and swords, sometimes with ornamented bronze hilts, arrowheads and spearheads – usually with hollow sockets and ceremonial scalloped axes – are probably for military purposes. Iron tridents, in one case with a wrought iron buffalo attached to the shaft, were probably of ritual significance. Another special group of objects includes horse furniture. In several of the graves around Nagpur, Junapani, Khapa, Mahurjhari and Naikund, iron snaffle bits have been found, some with iron cheek pieces: one bit was found in the mouth of a buried horse (Fig. 12.20(b)). There were also simple bar-bits of iron with looped ends. The latter type, along with a curious bar-bit with an iron looped nosepiece or mouthpiece occurs at other widely separated sites, including Adichanallur in the extreme south and Sanur in Karnataka. Among metal objects of copper or bronze, one may mention bells, which may have served for either cattle or horses. One specimen from Raigir has a broad bronze band to fit an animal's neck. From Khapa and Mahur-jhari, near Nagpur, come remarkable head ornaments, one found on the skull of

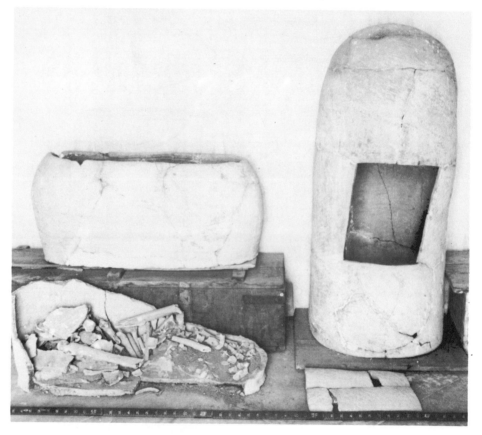

12.18 Maski: pottery sarcophagi

a horse (Fig. 12.21). These had copper additions with iron rivets and holes around the edge for sewing on to a cloth or leather mount.

At some of the South Indian burial sites there is further evidence of the use of gold. The diadems from the Adichanallur urn-burials are noteworthy. This evidence, along with that mentioned earlier in connection with such sites as Tekkalakota I, highlights the necessity for further investigation into the Karnataka mining localities. The evidence of stray finds in old workings, two radiocarbon samples from Hatti, and field investigation of settlements associated with

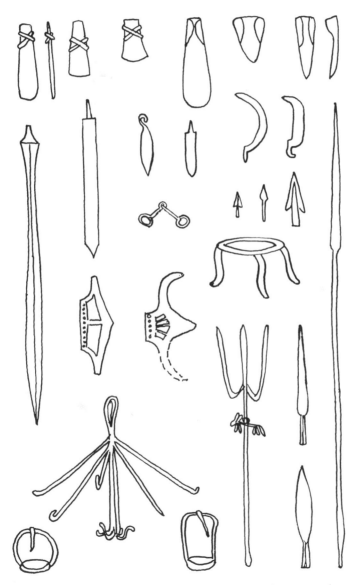

12.19 Iron objects from the South India graves (1:18 approx.)

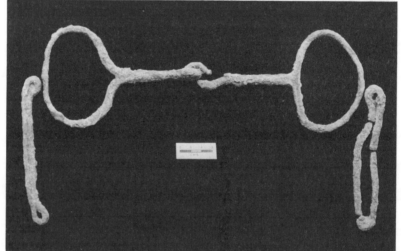

12.20 Iron objects from Nagpur graves (*c.* 6th century B.C.): (a) iron axes with cross-band hafting, Naikund (b) iron snaffle bit and cheek pieces, Mahurjhari (c) iron dagger with copper hilt, Mahurjhari (*courtesy* Deccan College, Pune)

old workings, all indicate that already by the opening of the Christian era shaft mines through the quartz veins had in cases reached a depth of over 600 feet; it is probable therefore that the beginnings of open-cast mining are very ancient. Whatever the history may have been, we may recall the vast quantities of gold-dust paid by the Indian provinces as tribute to Darius the Achaemenid at the close of our period. Fire-setting was probably also used in the gold-bearing regions of Karnataka (mentioned above) from the Iron Age onwards, in connection with the deep shafts of gold mines sunk in the quartz veins at such sites as Hatti and Kolar. The apparent similarity of the ancient gold-working methods of Karnataka to that recorded on the Red Sea coast of Egypt by Agatharcides in the second century B.C. is interesting.

The slabs of granite used in cist graves (and occasionally in other contexts, such as embankments of small surface drainage dams) in the Iron Age, and to a lesser extent in the preceding Chalcolithic, were probably obtained by the process of fire-setting. This technique is still common throughout South India, so it is possible that the ancient craft survives with little change. With the availability of iron and steel, wedges, crowbars and even cold-chisels are found, and these must have augmented fire-setting and the use of heavy hammers.

Our information concerning the religion of the peoples of the southern Iron Age is derived almost entirely from these graves. The many excavations show a baffling assortment of burial practices. In some instances simple inhumation is found; in others the unburnt bones were collected after they had been excarnated and placed in an urn or in a stone cist; in others again only fragments of bone were deposited, and often fragments of many individuals are found in a single grave; cremated bones are encountered in rare cases. It may be remarked that in modern practice burial rites vary from caste to caste, and ethnographic reports from South India can show just as great a variety as the Iron Age graves. Through the whole series runs the idea, present in the earliest Tamil literature and in modern practice, of a dual ceremony. The initial funeral leading to the exposure, burial or cremation of the corpse, is followed by a second ceremony, perhaps taking place only after many months, when the collected bones are deposited in their final resting place. Another detail which links some of the graves with modern practice is the use of lime in the infilling. The orientation of port-holes and entrances on the cist graves is frequently towards the south, although in some burial grounds it is towards another quarter, and the grounds themselves are most frequently found to be to the south of the settlements. This demands comparison with later Indian tradition where south is the quarter of Yama. Among the grave goods, iron is almost universal, and the occasional iron spears and tridents (*triśūlas*) suggest an association with the god Śiva (Fig. 12.19). The discovery in one grave of a trident with a wrought-iron buffalo fixed to the shaft is likewise suggestive, for the buffalo is also associated with Yama; and the buffalo demon was slain by the goddess Durgā, consort of Śiva, with a trident. A number of remains of structures associated with the graveyards have been reported, but none has so far been excavated. In some cases these appear to have been stone enclosures, in others more probably actual buildings or temples. So too may we mention in this connection the alignments of standing stones oriented on the cardinal points which are usually found in close association with burial grounds. What their purpose may have been, and how they relate to religious or funerary practice, is still mysterious. The picture which we obtain from this evidence, slight as it is, is suggestive of some form of worship of Śiva, but it is too early to say more.

There has been a great deal of often quite unwarranted discussion of the origin and external affinities of the Indian megalithic graves. Over a century ago Meadows Taylor wrote of them as the works of 'the great Aryan nomadic tribes

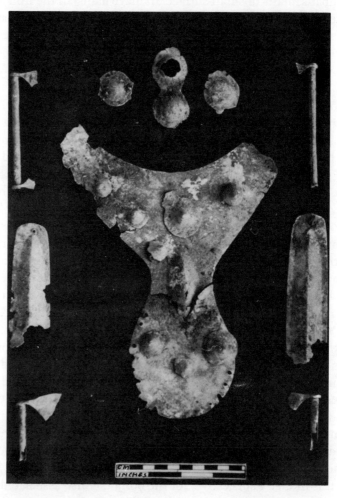

12.21 Copper horse ornaments from Nagpur graves (c. 6th century B.C.): (a) head ornament for mounting on leather base, Khapa (courtesy Deccan College, Pune)

of the Eastern Celts or Scythians', and since that time numerous other, often extravagant, claims have been made for them. In particular, Sir Elliot Smith, W. J. Perry and other Diffusionists have sought to show that the graves were traits of a great megalithic or 'Heliolithic' civilization which spread through the ancient world from its centre in Egypt.

The South Indian graves appear as a developing complex, first arising around the end of the second millennium, and lasting for many centuries, probably not less than a thousand years. Modern burial customs in many parts of South India reveal direct continuation of the tradition into modern times. How it arose is problematic, but several streams of influence appear to combine in its first development and subsequent history. First, it must be accepted that it arose in a

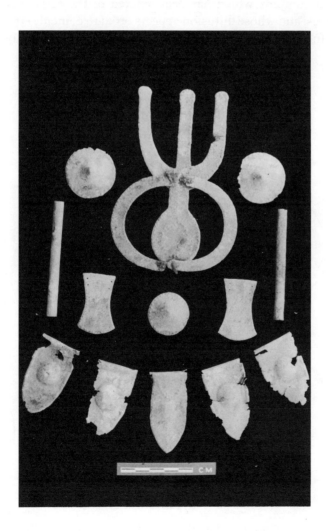

12.21(b) (?) head ornament, Mahurjhari (*courtesy* Deccan College, Pune)

culture contact situation. There was a widely spread population in the peninsula during preceding centuries, and there is sufficient evidence of its contribution. Thus some of the burials reveal what appear to be indigenous burial
customs of the Deccan during Neolithic–Chalcolithic times. The hollow legged
pottery urns of the Iron Age are already in evidence in a burial from Inamgaon
of the Later Jorwe period (c. 1000 B.C.). Other features may have developed as
local cultural innovations. It is possible that the stone alignments, with their
very local currency, form one such group. But the principal elements in the
whole burial complex suggest contact with some external source, and this, it
seems clear, must be derived from the direction of the Caucasus, Iran and
Central Asia. This complex of traits may be associated ultimately with the
'Kurgan' burial complex which has been related to the early Indo-European
speaking peoples, and whose diffusion appears often to coincide strikingly with
the spread of Indo-European languages into areas where previously they were

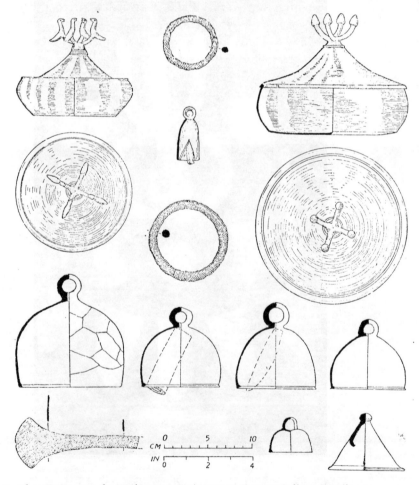

12.22 Khapa, Nagpur: objects from graves (courtesy Deccan College, Pune)

not known. Comparison of the burials of the late second millennium from the Lenkoran lowland, on the south-western shores of the Caspian, will show our meaning. Perhaps the earliest indication of this influence from the north-west can be seen in a group of graves which are pits lined with stone slabs in graveyards remote from settlements. They can be tentatively dated to the final centuries of the second millennium B.C. There is still a great need for absolute dating of individual graves and of types, so that the Indian evidence can be more firmly established in time. Only when a satisfactory framework is obtained will it become possible to consider the nature of such external contacts with greater assurance.

We now wish to discuss briefly the chronology of the South Indian megalithic grave complex. We do this because in a recent study Leshnik (1974) proposed that the graves arose as the result of an influx of Iranian speaking people in the 3rd–2nd centuries B.C. This view is surely unacceptable. We saw above that at Hallur iron and white-painted black-and-red ware occurred already before the strata giving dates of 1150–1030 B.C. Recently identical pottery has been found in pit-circle graves at a neighbouring site, Tadakanahalli, suggesting a similarly early date for the graves. Other graves suggest equally early beginnings. The radiocarbon dates from the Nagpur area, both for settlements and graves, suggest that they may well go back to an origin around the eighth century B.C. (above p. 328).

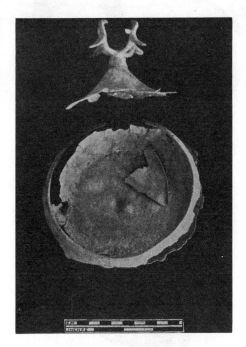 

12.23 (a) Copper dish and conical lid with bird finial, Khapa; (b) copper pot with sections riveted together with iron rivets, Naikund (*courtesy* Deccan College, Pune)

Aiyappan excavated two graves in the Perumal hills, far to the south in the Madura district, which produced jugs with long raised channel spouts, channel-spouted bowls and a small bowl-on-stand with vertical cuts in the stand. Similar vessels were found not far away in the Palni hills in graves which sometimes produced copper but no iron objects. The nearest analogue for the bowl-on-stand is from one of the earliest pit burials at Maski; beyond that one must go to the Gandhara grave complex and to Cemetery B at Sialk. Complementary evidence comes with late Jorwe-like pottery found along with black-and-red ware at Tekwada, Tekkalakota, and the 'pottery pits' (graves) which antedate the stone cist graves at Brahmagiri. The horse furniture is suggestive that the first graves belonged to horse riding immigrants who arrived in peninsular India from outside. The close similarity of the head ornament found on a horse's skull in a burial in the Nagpur graves to objects found at Djonu in Lenkoran, and of accompanying horse burials among the graves of humans here, no less than in the Gandhara graves, also point towards that direction. The dates of the Nagpur horse burials almost exactly coincide with that found at Baba Jan Tepe in

12.24 Adichanallur: bronze lids, cock and dog (*courtesy* Madras Government Museum)

western Iran. There are beyond doubt interesting parallels in the actual burial types between the graves of the north-western valleys of Kashmir and Pakistan and the South Indian graves, in spite of the many obvious differences in the material culture contained in them. That, once established, the burial custom continued for many centuries is attested by stray finds of Roman or other coins in graves. It is to be expected that there are many more graves belonging to the later centuries than to the earlier.

The cultural implications of the long duration of both the grave complex and the Iron Age itself in South India have still to be investigated. The thinness of the occupation in the settlements is perplexing and leads one to think that there was a progressive establishment of settlements in newly colonized areas, in consequence of the growth of population. One may also suppose that the influx of horses indicates that at least a part of the population were nomadic. Where the settlements continue from the preceding period there is little indication of a major change in the life-style.

The early use of iron in India

At the outset we referred to Young's division of the Iron Age in Iran into three stages. We suggested that these offered a rough pattern for comparison with the evidence from India and Pakistan. To summarize our conclusions on this point we may recapitulate our findings. First, the evidence currently available is often insufficient to permit us to decide with any degree of assurance how rare or how common iron was at any point. To do this scientifically will call for the excavation of a large sample of sites in each region. Nevertheless, there appears to be sufficient evidence for us to propose, however tentatively, a differentiation between contexts in which iron was a rare occurrence and others in which iron played a major part. The resultant picture is as follows:

Period I. 1300–1000 B.C. Iron occurs only rarely and then generally in small quantity. The earliest report is from south Rajasthan (Ahar); slightly later from the western borderlands (Pirak), and Karnataka (Hallur); and still later from the Brahmāvarta heartland (Noh).

Period II. 1000–800 B.C. Iron reported to be more common in the western borderlands and Karnataka and, slightly later, in Brahmāvarta; first occurrences in the North West Frontier valleys, Malwa and Central India, and possibly also in Maharashtra.

Period III. 800–500 B.C. First occurrence in the Middle Ganges valley and Ganges delta regions. Iron is now in general use in all the other regions, and now comes into common use. In making this suggestion we must recall that there may well have been within each of the regions pockets of iron working and other pockets where the new technology was much more slow in gaining acceptance. Thus the generalization needs to be treated with every caution.

We also mentioned the postulation that the early use of iron was associated with various other culture traits, notably black-and-red ware, painted grey ware and megalithic graves. Our survey shows that there is indeed a remarkable coincidence of the occurrence of black-and-red ware in a number of regions with that of iron. This is found in the Brahmāvarta, Saurashtra and south Rajasthan (where the black-and-red ware tradition is far older than the iron); Malwa and Central India, Maharashtra, Karnataka, and (somewhat later) the Middle Ganges valley and Deltaic Ganges region.

By comparison the association with the Painted Grey ware, or a related plain grey ware, is really only attested in the Brahmāvarta, and doubtfully in parts of the Middle Ganges. Similarly, the association of iron with the megalithic graves is apparently constant throughout all the regions in which they occur in Peninsular India. What, if anything, may be the significance of all these things we do not know, but it is striking that on present showing the earliest occurrence of iron is in the region in which the black-and-red ware was already current. It is therefore possible that these two traits spread roughly in association into other regions. We earlier remarked (1968) that a special feature of both the Painted Grey and black-and-red wares was that they were generally reserved for the service and consumption of food, and that in both there is a predominance of two forms, a shallow tray-bowl and a deeper cup-like bowl. This we felt indicated the development of a certain pattern of eating habits, and thus we suggested that their spread indicated a broad cultural unification taking place at about this time. We still believe that this is a valid point, and that it may have some bearing upon the primary and secondary extension of Indo-Aryan speaking people throughout large parts of the subcontinent.

CHAPTER 13

SUBCONTINENTAL UNITY AND REGIONAL DIVERSITY

In discussing the early cultures of the Indian subcontinent we have again and again had cause to notice how closely they relate to their physical background, and how changing emphases at different periods have caused fluctuations in the regional pattern. In retrospect the regions we have discussed fall into certain major groups which have tended to remain constant in spite of these fluctuations. The cultural patterns which emerged during the course of the period of earliest recorded settlements have in many cases continued into modern times and contribute profoundly to the character of the modern cultural and linguistic regions. We have come to think that these individual regional characters have often survived in spite of technological changes and advances, migrations of new elements of population, and political or social change. Quite why or how this should be is a matter deserving further investigation. But in our view if any single set of factors may be said to define the complex character of the Indian subcontinent, they are probably the geographical, archaeological and cultural relationships of its major regions.

Viewing the subcontinent in most general terms, the regions fall into two classes: those on the frontiers which form contact zones with the outside world and which may therefore be regarded as transitional zones; and those which lie within and whose principal contacts are with one another. In the former class are Baluchistan and the North West Frontier, the Himalayan zone, and the hilly country of Assam and Bengal. In the latter there are three major regions, a western centring upon the Indus system, a northern and eastern centring upon the Ganges system, and a southern or peninsular region. Between these three, the central hill and forest zone forms something of an internal frontier province. The three major regions have in every sense – archaeological, cultural and political – played leading roles in the history of Indian civilization. Communication between the regions has tended to take place along two major corridors, a northern and a southern. The northern corresponds approximately to the ancient *Uttarapatha* or northern route of early historic times. It leads from the North West Frontier, across the northern Punjab, the Indo-Gangetic divide and the Doab of the Ganges and Jamuna rivers – the area we have called the Northern Nuclear Region – into the Ganges valley and Bengal. The southern corridor links Sind to Gujarat, Malwa and southern Rajasthan – the area we have called the Southern Nuclear Region – and thence passes through the low rainfall regions of Maharashtra, to the southern peninsula and the Tamilnadu coast. There are several cross-links between the corridors, one of the most important being that which links the Northern Nuclear Region to the Southern.

What part the people of the Lower Palaeolithic played in forming the character of subsequent cultures we are not in a position to estimate. But in Middle Palaeolithic times we have seen that there was already a marked distinction between the stone industries of the western region and those of the east and south, and there are already indications of many kinds, notably the large factory sites of this period, that the western region was one of population mobility. With the Upper Palaeolithic and, to an increasing extent, with the Mesolithic we find ourselves dealing with a body of material which not only lends itself to a somewhat more complete reconstruction of the life of the people involved, but can in many cases be seen as the starting point of surviving entities and regional characters. Both biologically and culturally the Mesolithic population, which may have been of no mean proportions, must have contributed some of the most deep-seated and – one might almost say – the most Indian elements of the culture of later times. Certain attitudes and assumptions which are now regarded as typically Indian must have their origin in the culture of these people. The complex character of modern society, and the manner in which groups at widely different social and economic levels co-exist, often in close proximity to one another, are features to which we have already had occasion to allude. Since the end of the Pleistocene there have been repeated arrivals of new elements, from both east and west; and this continuing process has through the years built upon the indigenous foundation the complicated structure and hierarchy of Indian society. Many of these arrivals constituted new groups within the total body, all more or less self-contained, and many encapsulating features of the culture they had brought with them, together with much that they absorbed from their surroundings. Thus, throughout her prehistory and history, India has presented an increasingly rich and varied fabric, woven of many strands.

Of the frontier provinces Baluchistan is, historically, one of the more important. Through it, wave after wave of immigrants and merchants have passed travelling both to and from India proper. Baluchistan may be regarded both as an independent entity and as a transition zone between the Indus valley and the Iranian plateau. It is not surprising that the modern population still speaks Baluchi, a language of the Iranian branch of the Indo-Iranian family. The Baluchi valleys provided homes for the earliest Neolithic settlers so far known in any part of India or Pakistan, and from the sixth millennium, if not earlier, there is evidence of an enduring pattern of villages in an arid landscape, their size and growth limited by water supplies and the quantity of land fit for cultivation. The main domestic animals and crops seem to have changed little since their introduction at that time. Probably the severe restrictions of the environment were responsible for the absence of any development of city life here. From the earliest settlements of which we have evidence, domestic cattle appear to have been of the humped zebu variety, and this suggests that elements of the culture were already of Indian rather than Iranian origin. The impression is strengthened by the early appearance of cotton and such distinctly Indian motifs as the *pīpal* leaf among the predominantly abstract repertoire of Baluchi painted pottery designs. From very ancient times trade and contact with Central Asia were at least as important as those with Iran, and contact with the coastal region to the south is also in evidence.

Somewhat different is the pattern in the North West Frontier region, where the valleys penetrating deep into the northern mountain mass offer more attractive, and generally more sheltered and secure territories. These valleys seem to have had an indigenous population extending back to Middle Palaeolithic times. It is evident that groups of invaders penetrated the valleys, particularly during the second millennium, and perhaps earlier, bringing with them Dardic and Indo-Aryan languages which have survived in this sheltered area, preserving many very early words and linguistic forms. The valleys were open to contact with Central Asia and China from early times, and at the same time there has been a general tendency for people to move up from the plains to the south.

As soon as one leaves the valleys of Baluchistan and the North West Frontier, one enters one of the major cultural regions of the Indian subcontinent. The Indus plains, as we have seen, were the home of the earliest Indian civilization; and the name of the river Indus (*Sindhu*) has been extended to the subcontinent as a whole (India) and to the predominant religion of its peoples (Hinduism). In the light of the discoveries of the past decade or so, it may now be seen that the roots of this civilization (of whose absence Piggott remarked in 1950) are fairly and squarely to be found in the Indus valley and along its edges. At Mehrgarh this story begins with the deep, and as yet scarcely dated, deposits of pre-ceramic Neolithic, ending *c.* 5000 B.C. with the first appearance of pottery. Thereafter the settlement continues without break until the opening of the Mature Indus civilization. Around 3000 B.C. a new development is in evidence, extending from the central part of the valley north to the foothills of the Himalayas, west to the hills which bound the Indus plains, southwards to the Indus delta, and eastwards towards the Indo-Gangetic divide. This Early Indus stage is in every way the formative period of the civilization, when a continuing expansion of population, increase in trade and contacts of all kinds throughout the whole area, and the beginnings of a unified 'Indus' ideology began to appear. This is the so-called 'Kot Dijian' culture. What led to the emergence around 2550 B.C. of Mature Indus urbanism is not yet firmly established, but the change involved the almost simultaneous appearance of seals and inscriptions carrying a uniform script and iconography, and evidence of a new and unprecedented level of trade and communication throughout the whole Indus region. Radiocarbon dates suggest that the Mature stage lasted for some five centuries until around 2000 B.C. Thereafter the chronology is still uncertain, and there are at present few dates to clarify the situation.

The extent of our knowledge of the Indus civilization is limited, because although a number of excavations have been carried out the range of objects which has survived is considerably more restricted than in either Egypt or Mesopotamia; there is an almost total absence of pictorial representations of the life of the people, and such short inscriptions as survive, mainly on seals, are still unread. Technically, however, the Harappan civilization was not backward. As Gordon Childe so rightly pointed out, India produced a 'thoroughly individual and independent civilization of her own, technically the peer of the rest', although resting upon the same fundamental ideas, discoveries and inventions as those of Egypt and Mesopotamia. We are now in a position to add to his statement that the extent and consistency in terms of town planning, crafts and industries, of the Harappan culture, far exceeded either. The most important single advance must have been the exploitation of the Indus flood plains for agriculture, offering a vast potential production of wheat and barley. Many pieces of equipment, such as bullock-carts, provided prototypes for subsequent generations of Indian craftsmen, to spread through the whole subcontinent and survive into the twentieth century.

If, as we are inclined to believe, the Mesopotamian contacts with Meluhha, reported in the time of Sargon of Agade (2371–2316 B.C.) were indeed with the Indus region, then they may well have complemented the internal developments. The evidence of the extent of Harappan trading contacts with the outside world has recently been augmented by the remarkable discovery of what appears to be a small Harappan colony in north-west Afghanistan, evidently strategically placed for its role in the trade in lapis lazuli and copper.

The unread script makes some things still elusive. We can, however, now see the outlines of the Indus religion and mythology, and feel that it must have greatly contributed to the religious ideas and mythology of later Indian culture. We may infer, but cannot as yet prove, that the principal language of the population, and hence of the inscriptions, was almost certainly Dravidian. It is such things that point to the importance and interest of current efforts to read and transliterate the Harappan script. For there can be little doubt that the script and the religious iconography of the seals were uniformly disseminated throughout the whole Indus culture region. All in all, we may conclude that the early urbanism of the Indus civilization not only had its indigenous roots in the Indus valley, going back for many centuries, even millennia, but throughout showed its own personality; and that that personality contributed a major element to the life and culture of the Indian people long after the first cities had disappeared.

Beyond the natural frontiers of the Indus system one enters regions which have – in most general terms – an internal uniformity of their own. This uniformity coincides with a comparative absence of western, Iranian components in the cultures, and a corresponding preponderance of indigenous traits. The regions have in most instances marked local individuality. In many ways the whole of this great area appears to have been somewhat conservative, and the southern part in particular is characterized by an innate conservatism in material culture. This is already evident in Mesolithic times, when the southern peninsula shows a remarkable series of evolved Middle Palaeolithic elements in contrast to the more advanced industries of Western and Central India. As it appears in 1981, the earliest settled communities in India east of the Indus system cannot be dated to before 3000 B.C., and in many regions are considerably later than this date. One may well ask what were the causes of this apparently great disparity between the first development of sedentary agricultural settlement in the Indus system, and in India east of the Indus. We hesitate to attempt to supply an answer here, but we would point to the considerable differences of environment which led to many different patterns of economy developing and surviving in the east and south, while a more or less West Asiatic pattern of wheat and barley, cattle, sheep and goats developed in the Indus system. In considering the evidence from these regions, we followed roughly the lines of the two great corridors, starting with the northern.

As we saw, the northern corridor has its starting point in what we called the Northern Nuclear Region, the Punjab, the Indo-Gangetic divide and parts of the Doab. Here we are in a contact zone, where settlements appeared first in Early Indus times, i.e. probably around 3000 B.C. Evidence of a continuing interaction between the local cultural style and that of the Indus region continues through the third millennium and into the second. During the latter, these Late Harappan cultures, as they are frequently called, appear to have received new influences from the arrival and settling-down of Indo-Aryan speaking peoples in the area. We shall return to this subject later. Farther east, in the Middle Ganges valley, there is evidence of the survival of Mesolithic groups in the dense forests and swamps. As yet there is very scanty evidence of any settlements going back into even the third millennium here, presumably because of the difficulty of clearing the forests or draining the swamps. When evidence is found, as at Chirand in Bihar, it suggests a new and different Neolithic style, based partly on rice. Beyond, in the Ganges delta and in the Brahmaputra river system, the evidence is yet scantier. Here no settlements are attested beyond the second millennium. Yet farther east, the eastern border regions, represented by the hills of Assam and Bengal, show many profound influences from Burma and south China, and it is not surprising that the Neolithic culture known from surface collections of stone implements and from the few excavations should reflect cultural traits deriving from the same direction. These traits are also to be found, though mixed with those of India, in the surface collections of Neolithic tools from the eastern parts of the central region. It is noteworthy that their distribution in India is approximately limited to the areas in which today Tibeto-Burman or Munda languages are spoken. Here, culturally, one is on the frontiers of South-east Asia and China, just as in the far west one reaches the frontiers of Iran and Central Asia. Perhaps partly because of the difficulties of communication through the thickly forested mountains of Burma and south China, and partly because of other factors, these eastern influences do not seem to have played nearly so obvious a role as do the western in the making-up of Indian civilization. In this context one may note that Indian contacts with China, when they developed in the first millennium A.D., did so primarily via the western routes across Afghanistan and Central Asia, and by sea.

The southern corridor also had its starting point in a Southern Nuclear Region, comprising roughly southern Rajasthan, Saurashtra and Malwa. This region too is a contact zone between the Indus system and India beyond the Indus, and its history in some ways parallels that of its northern counterpart. There is evidence of local regional cultures developing during the third millennium B.C. and interacting with the Indus civilization. Just as in the north, these local cultures seem to have survived the end of the Indus civilization and to have continued to develop along their own lines. The so-called 'Banas culture' is a good example of this process. Here too we may expect that during the second millennium there was a period of contact and interaction between the existing population and newly arriving groups of Indo-Aryan speakers. As one moves towards the east into Malwa traces of the various western, Indus, or even Iranian elements become more and more attenuated.

Turning south and crossing the Narbada river, one enters Peninsular India proper. The first region encountered is Maharashtra, where the evidence from Daimabad suggests that the first agricultural settlements developed during the second half of the third millennium. The culture of this region throughout the early period shows close links with the Southern Nuclear Region to the north. This is particularly clear with the 'Malwa' phase during the opening centuries of the second millennium. During the second half of the millennium this is succeeded by the 'Jorwe' phase. It has been suggested that the place-names of Maharashtra show a substratum of Dravidian elements, and these we may expect to relate to an earlier culture phase, such as that represented by the Malwa ware or the as yet little known pre-Malwa Neolithic phase which was akin to that of the south. We may therefore postulate that the original population of agricultural settlers was Dravidian speaking, and that the changes associated with the Jorwe period coincided with the arrival in the area of immigrants from the north, speaking an Indo-Aryan language. This language must have been the ancestor of modern Marathi.

The corridor now passes southwards into Karnataka. Here the earliest settlements seem to have been associated with a group of pastoralists who appear in the area early in the third millennium B.C., although no settlements as such are known before the end of the millennium.

What is striking about the culture of the earliest settlements of the southern Deccan is their apparently independent ancestry. There is an extraordinary continuity linking even the earliest settlements with the whole subsequent pattern of life. It is still not possible to decide whether this culture arose in response to some external stimulus, and if so from what direction it came. The indications are that there was a strongly indigenous flavour from the start. It has been suggested that the Indian humped cattle were domesticated locally in the peninsula, and certainly they had already achieved a dominant economic position in the earliest settlements of the Deccan. A range of food grains was cultivated, some of them almost certainly native to the region. It is interesting to note that local variations in grain utilization at the present day are already reflected during the Neolithic–Chalcolithic period. The house patterns of the earliest settlements, and the general layout of villages can also be found as living elements in the countryside today. The conservatism of material culture continues to exert itself over long periods: thus the appearance of iron, which in the north is inferred to have coincided with the introduction of western tool types, such as the shaft-hole axe, in the peninsula witnessed the adaptation of a flat rectangular axe of a type already current in copper and bronze in the Harappan and post-Harappan periods. This type survived in the south until the opening of the Christian era.

The southern part of the peninsula is today the homeland of the Dravidian languages, and we may well enquire what – speaking in broadest terms – is likely to have been their history. It has been claimed, though on no very solid grounds, that the earliest speakers of these languages brought with them into Peninsular India both iron and the custom of making megalithic graves. In the light of archaeological evidence this appears to be extremely improbable. We now know that for at least a millennium prior to the arrival of iron there were established settlements in Karnataka, and probably also in other parts of the peninsula, and these settlements show evidence of a remarkable continuity of culture. Many modern culture traits appear to derive from them, and a substantial part of the population shows physical affinities to the Neolithic people. In the light of all this it is difficult to believe that the Dravidian languages do not owe their origin to the same people who produced the Neolithic cultures there.

There need not be any doubt that the several regional cultures which developed along the southern corridor are all reasonably closely related, that they had throughout a degree of interaction and probably originally a common language family, Dravidian. We do not really know enough about the remaining regions of the south at this early period to recognize further local cultures there, though they may well be discovered in the course of further research. However, it cannot be over-emphasized that in Karnataka, Maharashtra and the Southern Nuclear Region the settlements of the third–second millennia appear to be ancestral to those which we encounter there from the beginnings of history onwards. It must also be recalled that these developing settlements in all cases probably only represented a part of the total population of any area, the remainder being in the form of hunting and collecting tribes whose Mesolithic ancestry can still be recognized in their manufacture of stone blades and microliths.

The extreme south of the peninsula – Tamilnadu, Kerala and Sri Lanka –

forms a cultural grouping of a sort. Here land contacts with the north become relatively weaker, as lines of communication lengthen, and sea contacts develop in importance. The whole of eastern coastal India (including Sri Lanka) participates in a kind of cultural corridor around the coasts of the Bay of Bengal, and therefore has links with South-east Asia: nevertheless the overriding links and cultural contacts at all times have been with the Indian mainland and more remotely with the Ganges valley. Thus, Sri Lanka, no less than the southern peninsula, participated in the cultural unification of India during the first millennium B.C.; a fact that is witnessed still today in its population's two main languages, Tamil (a Dravidian language) and Sinhalese – an Indo-Aryan introduction of the *c.* fifth century B.C. – and of its predominant religions, Buddhism and Hinduism.

Midway between the two corridors lies the central belt of hills and forests, still to this day relatively sparsely populated. Here tribal peoples, preserving a hunting and gathering economy, lingered on into the present century. Neolithic–Chalcolithic settlements, some dating back to the beginning of the second millennium, are relatively few and appear as islands in a sea of unsettled forests. This whole central region has formed a target for small scale colonization from very early times, and in historic times, favourable areas have been settled by means of land gifts to groups of Brahmans, etc. Otherwise, it forms a nucleus around which the more important centres of civilization lie, and the cities and towns which grew up there at such places as Eran, or Tripuri, were probably staging points upon the caravan routes which linked the outer regions.

We must now return from our excursions down the two corridors to consider something which was of the highest importance for the future of Indian civilization, namely the arrival and spread of the speakers of the Indo-Aryan languages. The importance of this event, or series of events, is paramount for two reasons: first that it set in train a process of linguistic imperialism which resulted in the almost complete extinction of Dravidian, Munda and whatever other languages were previously spoken by the inhabitants of the Indo-Gangetic plains, and beyond; and secondly that it is associated with the production of the oldest surviving texts of the Indo-Aryans, the hymns of the Rigveda, which are still today recognized as the primal source for Indian tradition, even by those, such as the Buddhists, who later denounced their authority. The religious, scientific and humane thought and learning of ancient India are known to us preeminently through the medium of the developing Indo-Aryan languages, Vedic, Sanskrit and the Prakrits. Some archaeological purists have maintained that languages and their history cannot properly be related to the sort of data available to the archaeologist. To admit such a restriction would, in our view, make a nonsense of our aim of reconstructing the rise of Indian civilization, since it would rule out a large and most interesting part of the evidence. Rather, it is incumbent upon the archaeologist, we would like to insist, no less than upon the language historian, to attempt to discover the correct methods for interrelating the two sets of data, and hence to produce a satisfactory model by which we may proceed.

The interpretative model we have proposed is along the following lines. In ancient times languages did not spread except through the agency of people who already spoke them. The Indo-Aryan and Iranian branches had already divided from the parent Indo-European family on the Eurasian steppes, and had then spread southwards into Iran and thence eastwards and westwards, the Indo-Aryans entering India mainly during the second millennium B.C. The Indo-Aryan tribes were a barbarous people, keeping horses and using them to draw light war chariots with spoked wheels. They also made efficient weapons of copper and bronze. They moved into the Indus region and thence spread through various parts of the subcontinent. In many parts of the country they encountered existing populations of settled agriculturalists, nomadic pastoralists, etc. It cannot be that these existing populations were entirely exterminated, nor that they moved off to the east ahead of the invaders, because there is ample evidence that their physical types, along with much of their culture, arts, crafts and ideology survived. Therefore we must conceive of the arrival and movements of the Indo-Aryans as a dynamic process of culture contact, differing from one region to another in line with the already existing differences in the earlier population and the numbers and circumstances of the new arrivals. This process resulted in a series of cultural syntheses, so that from this time onwards we may speak of populations which are culturally Indo-Aryan. In our submission, therefore, the task of the archaeologist is not to look for the Aryans, but rather to look to the surviving material culture for evidence of this dynamic process. We gain confidence in the validity of our model when we compare it with a similar model applied strictly to linguistic evidence. The earliest Indo-Aryan text, the compiled Rigveda, shows several influences of a non-Indo-Aryan, Dravidian, element, in the form of phonetic changes, introduction of loan words and names, etc. These presuppose the co-existence of Vedic and Dravidian speaking peoples in a culture contact situation for a period, perhaps of centuries, before the compilation of the Rigveda.

We cannot say when the first Indo-Aryans entered India, but as we have seen there is even a fair possibility that it was before the end of the third millennium, and contemporary with the full Indus civilization. We feel that in all probability the main movement was somewhat later than this, perhaps around 1700 B.C., coinciding with the already post-urban, Late Harappan stage of the Indus civilization. We are inclined to look to the Indus valley and the two nuclear regions for evidence of primary Aryan settlement, and to expect to find it in the Cemetery H–Bara phase in the north and the Banas–Malwa phase in the south. The picture in the Indus valley itself is unclear, but we would expect the Jhukar culture to be contemporary with the same development. Whether the appearance of metal objects of decidely Iranian facies is direct evidence of this primary settlement, or merely coincidental with it, is perhaps not important.

Nor can we recognize with any certainty how long the movements of Indo-Aryans may have lasted. We are inclined to think that there may have been several waves and that the whole process lasted many centuries, perhaps even a thousand years. The secondary and tertiary stages are bound to have been complicated by the fact that they would have involved both newer arrivals and earlier settlers, either of whom may have from time to time moved on towards the east or the south. The archaeological chronology for these centuries is unclear because of the paucity of runs of radiocarbon dates from various key areas. The chronology based upon the linguistic and textual development of the Vedic literature is also uncertain, because of the absence of documents or absolute dating. Nevertheless, we may be reasonably certain of its broad outlines. The compilation of the Rigveda presupposes several centuries of inter-action with local populations and cultures. We are inclined to place its comple-tion between 1500 and 1300 B.C. Thereafter we enter the Late Vedic phase which saw the growth of an extensive literature, the later accretions to the Rigveda itself, the other Vedas, particularly the Yajur and Atharva Vedas, and a growing volume of exegetic texts including the voluminous Brāhmanas. It is possible to sub-divide the period further, but for our purpose this is scarcely necessary. By the end, around 600 B.C., the central geographical focus of the texts has shifted from the Brahmāvarta, the original Āryāvarta, to the Middle Ganges valley, the Madhyadeśa, and the language has developed from its Vedic stage to something close to classical Sanskrit.

Some writers have sought to find an identity between the Indo-Aryans and the first exponents of iron working to arrive in the subcontinent. Others have suggested a similar relationship between the Aryans and the introducers of the custom of building megalithic graves. Still other writers have equally hotly denied both. As we saw, iron working appeared first in several areas during the second half of the second millennium, perhaps earliest of all in the Southern Nuclear Region. By 1000 B.C. it had spread to several other regions, and after 800 B.C. we can speak of the full Iron Age in large parts of the country. This development is therefore coincidental with the secondary spread of the Indo-Aryans, but it encompassed a considerably wider area. It is indeed possible that the rapid diffusion of the new technique of iron smelting may in part have been assisted by mobile bands of horse riding Indo-Aryans, who, there is some reason to believe, reached even the extreme south by the opening centuries of the first millennium. This need in no way conflict with the indigenous population's beginning to exploit local sources of ore and to smelt their own iron. Certainly the wider diffusion of iron working is likely to have been largely in the hands of indigenous people. Both iron working and the spread of Indo-Aryan speech coincide roughly in time with the appearance of new burial traits in Peninsular India, traits which recall those of the Caucasus or northern Iran around this time, and which contribute to the development of the megalithic grave complex. Once again there is apparently a marked disparity in the geographical distribution, but as with the case of iron, there is no inherent reason why burial practices which are believed to be those of Indo-Iranian speakers in Central Asia or Iran should not also be found to belong to speakers of the same languages after they had moved into India or Pakistan. But this does not mean that all the megalithic graves are those of such speakers. Clearly they are not, and clearly the local population must have adopted the same customs from some source. These clues offer a hint that throughout the Dravidian speaking south the process of 'Aryanization' may have already begun by the opening of the first millennium B.C. Thus it would seem that contact of Indo-Aryans and Dravidians began long before the flowering of the Tamil culture of the south-eastern coastal plains during the Sangam period (in the early centuries of the Christian era). If some groups of Aryans did reach the far south it is evident that they lost their original speech and adopted the Dravidian tongues of the people they settled among. This is therefore the reverse of the situation in the north, and must indicate that their numbers were far smaller than in the areas of primary settlement.

We have seen that the primary settlements of the Indo-Aryans were in Sind and the Southern Nuclear area to the south, and in Punjab and the Northern Nuclear area to the north. What actually happened there is still largely a matter of guesswork, but it must have been a highly successful exercise in colonization from the Aryan point of view. Linguistic evidence shows that within a few centuries the settled urban and agricultural population, in spite of their background, abandoned their own languages in favour of Indo-Aryan speech. Yet archaeological evidence suggests that this must have been achieved by means other than the wholesale extermination of the existing population, since a great deal of their agricultural practice, arts and crafts, and even patterns of settlement survived, and must have been steadily absorbed by the newcomers. That we are witnessing a process of cultural interaction and synthesis may be suggested. We believe that the Rigveda must represent the same process, so that increasingly in its later parts an element of the older, pre-Aryan ideology has become absorbed into it. What all this meant in social and human terms is difficult to imagine. We would expect that for the higher strata of society it meant intermarriage at a suitable level. In this way the ideology of the earlier population would have been passed on to the newcomers. This would probably have applied to priests and leading warrior families. But for the lower strata, the agriculturalists and menial groups, such intermarriage becomes increasingly improbable, and we must envisage for the latter relegation to a lower stratum still, in which the soon to be prized boast of Aryan descent was totally excluded. This state of affairs, which provides the germ of the developing caste system can be clearly recognized in the Puruṣa Sūkta, one of the later hymns of the Rigveda (x. 90), where the Brahmans are said to have come from Puruṣa's head, the ruling class from his arms, the common people (*Viśa*, agriculturalists, traders, etc.) from his thighs and the *Śūdras* (menials) from his feet. In late Vedic texts we are repeatedly reminded that the lower two castes were to serve the upper, and the *Śūdras*, who in time came to be regarded as 'untouchables', were to serve all others.

The late Vedic period witnessed the progressive expansion of Aryan settlements down the northern corridor, first into the Doāb and then into the Middle Ganges valley. The earliest Aryan homeland in India–Pakistan (Āryāvarta or Brahmāvarta) was in the Punjab and the valleys of the Sarasvati and Drishadvati rivers in the time of the Rigveda. Thereafter it shifted into the Mid-land (Madhyadeśa), the Doāb (already regarded as the central territory in the Mahābhārata), and yet later far to the east, to eastern Uttar Pradesh and Bihar. This development must have called for extensive clearance of the forests which formerly covered the Gangetic plains and is likely to have coincided with the general adoption of iron tools for purposes of agriculture. The archaeological evidence for the expansion is to be seen in the spread of Painted Grey ware and black-and-red ware sites, and in the growth of cities. Once again we have very little idea of what was entailed in human terms, but the increasing volume of texts adds a dimension. We assume that it involved a repetition of the same formula of colonization which had already proved successful in the Northern Nuclear Region. Presumably relatively small numbers of Aryans, belonging primarily to the upper levels of society, would have moved and established military control over the existing populations. The literature provides hints of the process. In the Rigveda an earlier theme was of the triumphant progress of Indra, the Aryan warrior in divine form, against the native *dasyu* (the word later means slaves) and *panis*. We also read of battles between tribes, including Aryan tribes, and such events may well have sparked off further movements. The Mahābhārata, although in its present form the result of several major enlargements, has a core which must go back to the Late Vedic period and which tells of further such internecine battles between Aryan tribes in the Doāb. By the end of the period we learn of sixteen *janapadas*, tribal territories, which had already become established kingdoms with their own capital cities. Through the opening centuries of the first millennium these states fought with one another and were gradually absorbed into larger units, until in the end, Magadha, one of the easternmost, established an empire which embraced all the rest.

One of the most significant features of the archaeology of these developments is the emergence of cities in the Ganges valley (Fig. 13.1). At the same time outlying cities also appear in the Southern Nuclear Region and in islands in the forest zone which divided the northern and southern corridors. The cities are in most cases identifiable by their great ditch and rampart systems, and by their great size. Their archaeological study is still not far advanced, and we can rarely determine with precision when any city was founded. However, their identification is generally not in dispute, as living tradition and place-names combine

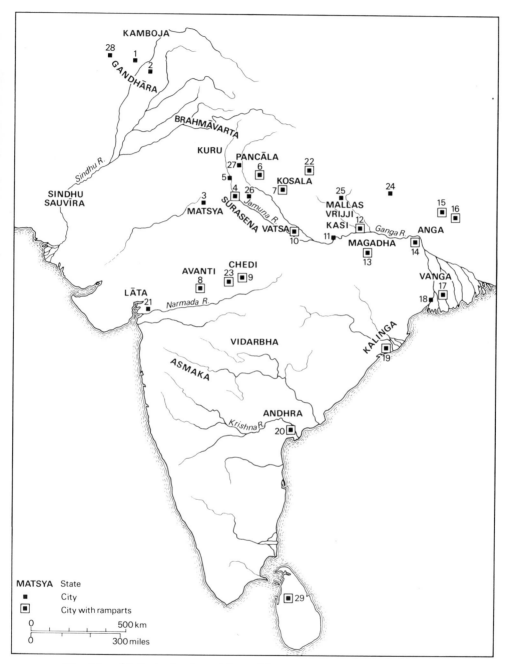

13.1 Map of India in the time of the Buddha: cities and states

1. Pushkalāvati (Chārsada)   2. Takshaśilā (Taxilā)   3. Virāta   4. Mathurā   5. Indraprastha   6. Ahicchatra
7. Śrāvasti   8. Ujjain   9. Eran   10. Kausambi   11. Vārānasī (Banāras)   12. Vaiśālī   13. Rājagriha (Rājgīr)
14. Champā   15. Bāngarh   16. Mahāsthan   17. Chandraketugarh   18. Tāmluk   19. Sisupālgarh
20. Dhanyakataka   21. Bharukaccha   22. Kapilavastu (Tilaura Kot)   23. Vidisā   24. Balirājpur
25. Sohagaurā   26. Atranjikherā   27. Hastināpura   28. Nagarahāra   29. Anurādhapura

with historical tradition and excavated inscriptions to confirm each other. Among the great cities of the Ganges plains we may mention Kausambi, capital of the Vatsa Janapada; Śrāvasti, capital of Kosala; Banāras, capital of Kasi; Rājgīr, capital of Magadha; and Vaiśāli, capital of the Vrijjian Confederacy. In the Southern Nuclear Region we may mention Ujjain, capital of Avanti; and in the intervening forests, cities such as Vidiśa and Eran. In the north-western regions, now in Pakistan, the great cities of Pushkalāvati (Chārsada) and Taxilā were probably among the earliest of the new cities.

The social, economic and intellectual concomitants of this near sudden flowering of city life are striking. The use of writing seems to have vanished with the end of the Indus cities. Now, a new Indian script, the *Brāhmī lipi*, the ancestor of all subsequent Indian scripts, was produced by grammarians in the seventh or eighth century B.C., as a result apparently of an initial borrowing from the north Semitic script. Traditionally the weights and measures of ancient India were first regulated only in the fourth or fifth century B.C. by the Nanda dynasty, but at least a part of the system involved units which had been in use since the times of the earlier Indus civilization. The earliest silver and copper coinage, marked with punched signs and hence referred to as punch-marked, appears around the fourth or fifth century B.C., perhaps as a result of Achaemenid provincial silver currency circulating in the north-west (Fig. 12.10).

The intellectual developments of these centuries are also prodigious and demand comparison with what was happening almost at the same time in Greece. Within the orthodox Vedic schools there was a growing interest in speculation relating to the meaning and symbolism of the Vedic sacrifices, the creation of the world and the nature of God and the ātman (or Self). This found its culmination in the early Upaniṣads, which combine exegetic study of the Vedas with the systematic thought which provided the basis for all subsequent orthodox Hindu thinkers. Foremost among the names of this period is that of the sage Yājñavālkya, who has been credited with the most subtle speculations upon the nature of the ātman. Next there was the development of the branches of Vedic exegesis, which laid the foundations for subsequent specialized branches of learning. These included astronomy, geometry, phonetics, grammar and etymology. One of ancient India's greatest achievements lay in the field of phonetic and grammatical analysis of language. When the greatest of the old Indian grammarians, Pāṇini, composed his Eight Chapters (Aṣṭādhyāyi) around the fifth century B.C. he could point to a long line of earlier grammarians whose work has now been lost. The period was also one of intense religious ferment. Apart from the orthodox schools there were several influential schools founded by heterodox teachers. These teachings included the fatalism of Makkhali Gosāla and the Ājīvaka sect he founded; the frank materialism of Ajita Kesakambali, the founder of the Charvaka or Lokāyata sect; and the pessimism of Mahāvīra, the founder of the Jain religion. However, the most influential of all was the teaching of Gautama, the Buddha. This appears as a brilliant reaction to the idealism and theism of the orthodox Brahmans. All these great teachers flourished around the sixth century B.C., and their works together constitute a remarkable body of original thought.

This emergence of city life in the Ganges valley marks the beginning of the classical period of Indian civilization, and we cannot fail to wonder to what extent it was also a rebirth of something which had long before flourished in the valley of the Indus. For the distinctive character of Indian thought in the classical period preserves many things which appear to have derived from this source, and which emphasize the continuity of a pattern of life which was already very old. While we have concluded that the special developments of this period took place in the Ganges valley, they were not slow to develop elsewhere. Thus begins a period in which the Ganges valley formed the dominant force in welding a new interregional Indian culture. By the time of the great lawgiver Manu (c. 2nd century B.C.) the geographical bounds of the Aryan homeland (Āryāvarta) had expanded from their original narrow limits to include all the land from the Himalayas to the ocean on the east and on the west, that is the entire subcontinent. Doubtless its growth was facilitated by the growing role of Sanskrit as an all-India culture language. At the same time the regions, with their own individual patterns of life, language and culture, continued to exist and flourish alongside the newer all-India pattern. Thus came into being one of the features of South Asian life which has lasted down to the present.

SELECT GENERAL BIBLIOGRAPHY

General works

Agrawal, D. P. *The Archaeology of India*, London and Malmo, 1982
Agrawal, D. P. and Chakrabarti, D. K., *Essays in Indian Protohistory*, Delhi, 1979 (**EIP**)
Agrawal, D. P. and Ghosh, A., *Radiocarbon and Indian Archaeology*, Bombay, 1973 (**RIA**)
Agrawal, D. P. and Kusumgar, S., *Prehistoric Chronology and Radiocarbon Dating in India*, New Delhi, 1974
Allchin, B., Goudie, A. S. and Hegde, K. T. M., *The Prehistory and Protohistory of the Great Indian Desert*, London, 1978
Allchin, F. R. and Chakrabarti, D. K., *A Source-book of Indian Archaeology*, vol. 1., New Delhi, 1979
Chakrabarti, D. K. *A History of Indian Archaeology*, New Delhi, 1988
Fairservis, W. A., *The Roots of Ancient India*, 2nd edn, London, 1971 (**RAI**)
Ghosh, A., *The City in Early Historical India*, Simla, 1973
Gupta, S. P., *Archaeology of Soviet Central Asia and the Indian Borderlands*, 2 vols., Delhi, 1979
Kosambi, D. D., *The Culture and Civilization of Ancient India in Historical Outline*, London, 1965
Lal, B. B. and Gupta, S. P. *Frontiers of the Indus Civilization*, New Delhi, 1984
Masson, V. M. and Sarianidi, V. I., *Central Asia: Turkmenia Before the Achaemenids*, London, 1972
Piggott, S., *Prehistoric India*, Harmondsworth, 1950
Possehl, G. L., *Ancient Cities of the Indus*, New Delhi, 1979
Sankalia, H. D., *Prehistory and Protohistory of India and Pakistan*, 2nd edn, Poona, 1974 (**PPIP**)
    Prehistory of India, New Delhi, 1977
Subbarao, B., *The Personality of India*, 2nd edn, Baroda, 1958
Wheeler, R. E. M., *The Indus Civilization*, 3rd edn, Cambridge, 1968

Periodicals and series

Ancient Ceylon, Journal of the Archaeological Survey Department of Ceylon, Colombo, 1, 1971–
Ancient India, Bulletin of the Archaeological Survey of India, 1, 1946– (**AI**)
Ancient Pakistan, Bulletin of the Department of Archaeology, University of Peshawar, 1, 1964– (**AP**)
Indian Archaeology 1953–5 – A Review, Archaeological Survey of India, 1954– (**IAR**)
Man and Environment, Indian Society for Prehistoric and Quaternary Studies, Ahmedabad, 1, 1977– (**ME**)
Pakistan Archaeology, Department of Archaeology, Government of Pakistan, 1, 1964– (**PA**)

Puratattva, Bulletin of the Indian Archaeological Society, **Varanasi,** 1, 1967–8– (**Pur**)
South Asian Archaeology, Papers from the International Conferences of South Asian
    Archaeologists in Western Europe, 1st Conference 1971, published London, 1973,
    etc. (**SAA** 71–)
South Asian Studies, Journal of the South Asian Society, London, 1, 1985–

Chapters 2, 3 and 4

Past environments

There is no single volume dealing with past climates and environments of the Indian
subcontinent, but there are several books that deal with various aspects of past climates
and environments of the arid and tropical regions of the world in general. These contain
much relevant material and in some cases have chapters devoted to South Asia. The
following three are recommended for further reading, and all contain extensive bibliographies: M. F. Thomas, *Tropical Geomorphology,* London, 1974; A. S. Goudie, *Environmental Change,* Oxford, 1977; C. Vita-Finzi, *Recent Earth History,* London, 1973. Papers
dealing with certain aspects of South Asian climatic history will be found in W. C.
Brice, ed., *Environmental History of the Near and Middle East,* London 1977; and
K. A. R. Kennedy and G. L. Possehl, eds., *Ecological Background of South Asian Prehistory,* Cornell, 1973, contains papers dealing with many parts of the subcontinent.

There are other books that deal with these questions in regard to specific regions, in
some cases fairly exhaustively, and in others only briefly. Western India has been more
thoroughly investigated than other parts of the subcontinent. H. de Terra and T. T.
Paterson, *Studies in the Ice Age in India and Associated Human Cultures,* Washington,
D.C., 1939, has for long been looked on as a prime source. While their study of the
Kashmir valley, and brief observations on the Narbada and the Bukkur gorge in Sind
probably still stand, the major part of their work dealing with the Potwar plateau and
Soan valley has been shown to need complete revision. This is currently in progress. The
Thar desert, Indus region and surrounding arid zone in Western India are discussed in
B. Allchin, Goudie and Hegde, 1978, and in a series of papers in D. P. Agrawal and B. M.
Pande, eds., *Ecology and Archaeology of Western India,* Delhi, 1977. Further aspects of the
geomorphology and environmental history of this region are covered by publications of the
Arid Zone Research Centre, Jodhpur. Western Central India and the western Deccan are
covered by papers and monographs published by the Deccan College, Pune, cited by H. D.
Sankalia, *PPIP,* 1974.

The Himalayan region or individual valleys within it have received a considerable
amount of attention from geomorphologists and others. Among more recent and relevant
studies are R. V. Joshi, 'Quaternary studies in the Sub-Himalayas', *Bulletin of the Deccan
College Research Institute,* 33, 1973, 101–16; S. C. Porter, 'The Quarternary glacial record
of Swat Kohistan, North-west Pakistan', *Bulletin of the Geological Society of America,* 81,
1970, 1421–46.

A limited amount of work has been done in India on palaeobotany. This has been
concerned chiefly with the Himalayan region and there is also a study of cores from saline
lakes in the arid zone. References to this work will be found in the bibliography to
chapter 5.

Physical and cultural anthropology

K. A. R. Kennedy's 'Prehistoric skeletal record of man in South Asia', *Annual Review of
Anthropology,* 1980, 9, 391–432 gives an admirable summation of evidence for all parts of
South Asia of ancient skeletal remains.

For a survey of methods and problems in India, see D. K. Sen, 'Ancient races of India and Pakistan', *AI* 20–21, 178–205.

For cultural anthropology there are many monographs dealing with specific tribes and communities. S. Fuchs, *The Aboriginal Tribes of India*, Madras, 1973, gives a most useful survey of the tribal population of all parts of India and Pakistan. The Anthropological Survey of India's Memoir 8, *Peasant Life in India*, Calcutta, 1966, is difficult to obtain, but full of useful information on aspects of material culture.

A veritable mine of reference to all kinds of anthropological and prehistoric writing is to be found in E. von Fürer-Haimendorf's monumental *Anthropological Bibliography of South Asia*, vols. 1 and 2, The Hague, 1958, 1964.

Palaeolithic and Mesolithic

Virtually all work of any significance on the Palaeolithic and Mesolithic of the Indian subcontinent, up to the time of its going to press is covered by H. D. Sankalia *PPIP*, 1974, which also contains a comprehensive bibliography. The same author's *Prehistory of India*, 1977, covers the same ground, giving a shorter and more digested account; his *Stone Age Tools: Their Techniques, Names and Probable Functions*, Poona, 1964, discusses Stone Age technology. F. Bordes, *The Old Stone Age*, London, 1968, although now somewhat out of date with regard to South Asia, gives a useful overall picture relating the subcontinent to other regions of the world.

Valuable discussion of various major problems and of regional and cultural relationships of the Asiatic and South Asian Stone Age will be found in the following: S. P. Gupta, *Archaeology of Soviet Central Asia and the Indian Borderlands*, Delhi, 1979, vol. 1; Fumiko Ikawa-Smith, ed., *Early Palaeolithic in South and East Asia*, Paris, 1978; D. P. Agrawal and A. Ghosh, eds., *RIA*, 1973, includes a number of papers dealing with Palaeolithic and Mesolithic topics.

Further papers will be found in the following Indian publications: *AI*, *IAR* (short notes only), *ME* and *Pur*. Papers have also appeared in a wide range of journals outside India. The following are among the more important: V. N. Misra, 'Bagor, Late Mesolithic settlement in North-west India', *World Archaeology*, 1973, 5, 92–110; G. R. Sharma, 'Mesolithic lake cultures of the Ganga valley', India, *PPS*, 1973, 39, 129–46; M. L. K. Murty, 'Blade and burin industries near Renigunta, on the south-west coast of India', *PPS*, 1968, 34, 83–101; R. V. Joshi, 'Acheulian succession in Central India', *Asian Perspectives*, 1964, 8; V. N. Misra, 'Middle Stone Age in Rajasthan', *La Préhistoire*, 1968, 298–302; B. Allchin, 'The discovery of Palaeolithic sites in Sind and their geographical implications', *The Geographical Journal*, 1976, 142, 471–89; A. Goudie, B. Allchin and K. T. M. Hegde, 'Former extensions of the Great Indian Sand Desert', *The Geographical Journal*, 139, 243–57; G. R. Sharma, V. D. Misra, D. Mandal, B. B. Misra and J. N. Pal, *Beginnings of Agriculture*, Allahabad, 1980.

Chapter 5

General

It is difficult to recommend any single source to provide an integrated survey of the current state of knowledge of the earliest development of settled agricultural communities in West, Central and South Asia as a whole. A short summary is provided by J. V. S. Megaw, ed., *Hunters, Gatherers and First Farmers Beyond Europe*, Leicester, 1977. J. Mellaart's *Earliest Civilizations of the Middle East*, London, 1965, and more detailed study of *The Neolithic of the Near East*, London, 1975, are useful contributions from the

Western side. The Central Asian material is briefly discussed in V. M. Masson and V. I. Sarianidi's *Central Asia: Turkmenia before the Achaemenids*, 1972, and in greater detail by S. P. Gupta in his pioneering study of the *Archaeology of Soviet Central Asia and the Indian Borderlands*, Vol. 2, 1979. But there remains a real need for a synthetic study embracing side by side the development of agriculture and settled life in all three parts of Asia.

Early agriculture in South Asia

See Vishnu-Mittre's contribution, 'Palaeobotanical evidence in India', in Sir Joseph Hutchinson, ed., *Evolutionary studies in world crops*, Cambridge, 1974; also the latter's 'India: local and introduced crops', in J. Hutchinson, G. Clark, E. M. Jope and R. Riley, eds., *The Early History of Agriculture*, London, 1977, 129–42. The evidence of Mehrgarh is obviously crucial: see J.-F. Jarrige's reports in *SAA* 77, and *SAA* 79; also important are R. Meadow's paper on 'Early animal domestication in South Asia: a first report on the faunal remains from Mehrgarh' (*ibid.*, 143–80), and L. Costantini's 'Palaeoethnobotany at Pirak' (*ibid.*, 271–8).

Baluchistan and the borderlands

J. G. Shaffer's *Prehistoric Baluchistan*, Delhi, 1978, is a pioneering work, in this still little-studied region; the same author's contribution to F. R. Allchin and N. Hammond, eds., *Archaeology of Afghanistan*, London, 1978, provides a survey of the evidence from Mundigak and elsewhere. Another useful discussion is in W. A. Fairservis, *RAI*, 2nd edn, 1971. Between them, these works give a comprehensive bibliography.

The Indus system

For the earliest settlements of the Indus system one must go to individual reports: for Mehrgarh see J. F. Jarrige and M. Lechevallier, 'Excavations at Mehrgarh' in M. Taddei, ed., *SAA* 77, 463–535, and M. Lechevallier and G. Quivron, 'The Neolithic in Baluchistan' in *SAA* 79, 71–92; for Gumla see A. H. Dani, 'The excavations in the Gomal valley', in *AP* 5; for Sarai Khola see M. A. Halim, 'Excavation at Sarai Khola', in *PA* 7 and 8; for Ghaligai see G. Stacul, 'Excavations near Ghaligai' (1968) and chronological sequence of protohistoric cultures in the Swat valley, *East and West* 19, 1969. The important excavations at Burzahom are still only published in summary form: see R. N. Kaw, 'The Neolithic culture of Kashmir', in *EIP*, 1979; and Madhu Bala, 'A survey of protohistoric investigation in Jammu and Kashmir', *The Anthropologist*, 22, 1975.

Earliest settlements east and south of the Indus system

Hitherto discussion of these topics has been largely in terms of discoveries of ground stone axes, often without proper archaeological contexts. It is now becoming possible to consider other sorts of evidence: the indications of early agriculture in Rajasthan were first pointed out by Gurdip Singh, 'The Indus valley culture seen in the context of post-glacial climatic and ecological studies in North-west India', *Archaeology and Physical Anthropology in Oceania*, 6(2), 1971, 177–89. For early sites in Central India, see G. R. Sharma *et al.*, *Beginnings of Agriculture*, Allahabad, 1980. The earliest sites recorded in South India are ash-mounds: see F. R. Allchin, *Neolithic cattle-keepers of South India*, Cambridge, 1963, and K. Paddayya, *Investigations into the Neolithic culture of the Shorapur Doab, South India*, Leiden, 1973. For other excavated sites in Peninsular India see recommended reading for chapter 9.

Chapter 6

The Early Indus period

As yet only one book has appeared devoted to the discussion of the formative period of the Indus civilization; this is M. R. Mughal's *The Early Harappan Period in the Greater Indus Valley*, 1971 (1976), Xerox University Microfilms, Michigan. Further discussion will be found in W. Fairservis's *RAI*, 2nd edn, 1971, and in the works cited in the preceding sections. For a general discussion of the Early Indus period and its place in the rise of the Indus civilization see F. R. Allchin, 'Antecedents of the Indus civilization', *Proceedings of the British Academy*, 1982. Among other relevant reports are the following:

AMRI: J.-M. Casal, *Fouilles d'Amri*, 2 vols., Paris, 1964

KOT DIJI: F. A. Khan, *PA* 2, 1965, 11–85

HARAPPA: The pre-defence pottery is published by Sir Mortimer Wheeler in *AI* 3, Calcutta, 1947, 91–7

KALIBANGAN: *IAR*, 1961, 30–1; 1961–2, 39–44; 1962–3, 20–31, etc. B. B. Lal, 'Kalibangan and the Indus civilization', in Agrawal and Chakrabarti, eds., *EIP*, 1979

JALILPUR: M. R. Mughal, 'New evidence of the early Harappan culture from Jalilpur, Pakistan', *Archaeology*, 1974, 106–13

MITATHAL: Suraj Bhan, *Excavation at Mitathal (1968) and other explorations in the Sutlej–Yamuna divide*, Kurukshetra, 1975

OTHER SITES IN SIND: N. G. Majumdar, 'Explorations in Sind', *Memoirs of the Archaeological Survey of India*, 48, Delhi, 1934

RAHMAN DHERI: F. A. Durrani, 'Rehman Dheri and the birth of civilization in Pakistan', *Bulletin of the Institute of Archaeology*, 18, 1982, 191–207

TARAKAI QILA: F. R. Allchin *et al.*, 'The Bannu Basin Project (1977–79), A preliminary report', in H. Härtel, ed., *SAA* 79, 1981, 217–50

Chapters 7 and 8

General

The best introductions to the Indus civilization are to be found in S. Piggott's *Prehistoric India*, Harmondsworth, 1950; G. Childe's *New Light on the Most Ancient East*, 4th edn, London, 1952, ch. 9; W. Fairservis, *RAI*, and the same author's short essay on *The Origin, Character and Decline of an Early Civilization*, New York, 1967; and H. T. Lambrick, *Sind Before the Muslim Conquest, History of Sind*, vol. 2, Hyderabad, 1973. An invaluable collection of more than forty relevant papers or extracts is to be found in G. L. Possehl's *Ancient Cities of the Indus*, New Delhi, 1979; and further recent articles are in Agrawal and Chakrabarti's *EIP*. A further invaluable source will be found in G. L. Possehl's *Harappan Civilization: a Contemporary Perspective*, New Delhi, 1982.

Sites

The original excavation reports are still essential reading: Sir John Marshall, *Mohenjo-daro and the Indus Civilization*, 3 vols., London, 1931; E. J. H. Mackay, *Further Excavations at Mohenjo-daro*, 2 vols., New Delhi, 1938; M. S. Vats, *Excavations at Harappa*, 2 vols., Delhi, 1941: E. J. H. Mackay, *Chanhu-daro Excavations*, New Haven, Conn., 1943. Among more recent excavations are:

AMRI: J.-M. Casal, *Fouilles d'Amri*, 2 vols., Paris, 1964

KOT DIJI: F. A. Khan, 'Excavations at Kot Diji', *PA* 2, 1965

LOTHAL: S. R. Rao, *Lothal and the Indus Civilization*, New York, 1973

Shorter reports on other sites are to be found in:

KALIBANGAN: *IAR* 1960–8; B. B. Lal, 'Kalibangan and the Indus civilization', *EIP* 65–97; B. K. Thapar, 'New traits of the Indus civilization at Kalibangan, an appraisal', *SAA* (1971), 85–104

BALAKOT: papers by Dales, Meadow and Durante, in *SAA* 77, 241–344

ALLAHDINO: W. A. Fairservis, *Excavations at Allahdino*, 1: *The seals and other inscribed material*, Papers of the Allahdino Expedition, 1, New York, 1976; J. G. Shaffer, *Allahdino and the Mature Harappan*, Cleveland, 1974; M. A. Hoffman and J. H. Cleland, *Excavations at Allahdino*, 2: *The lithic industry*, New York, 1977; W. A. Fairservis, *Excavations at Allahdino*, 3: *The graffiti*, New York, 1977 (all in typescript)

SHORTUGAI: H.-P. Francfort and M.-H. Pottier, 'Sondage préliminaire sur l'établissement protohistorique Harappéen et post-Harappéen de Shortugai', *Arts Asiatiques*, 1978, 34, 29–86

SURKOTADA: J. P. Joshi, 'Exploration in Kutch and Excavation at Surkotada', *J. Oriental Inst. Baroda*, 22, 1972, 98–144; *idem*, 'Surkotada: a chronological assessment', *Pur* 7, 1974, 34–8

Architecture and planning

A. Sarcina, 'House patterns at Moenjo-daro', *Mesopotamia* XIII–XIV, 1978–9, 155-99; M. Jansen, *Architektur in der Harappa Kultur*, Bonn, 1979; B. B. Lal, 'Some reflections on the structural remains at Kalibangan', Paper presented at a conference on the Indus Civilization held in Karachi, 1978 (typescript).

Trade and contacts with the West

S. Asthana, *History and Archaeology of India's Contacts with Other Countries*, Delhi, 1976; E.C.L. During Caspers, 'Cultural concepts in the Arabian Gulf and the Indian Ocean: transmissions in the third millennium and their significance', *Proceedings of the Seminar for Arabian Studies*, 6, 1976; *idem*, 'Harappan trade in the Arabian Gulf in the third millennium B.C.', *Proceedings of the Seminar for Arabian Studies*, 1973; G. F. Dales, 'Shifting trade patterns between the Iranian plateau and the Indus valley in the third millennium B.C.', Colloquium on 'Le plateau Iranian et l'Asia central des origines à la conquête islamique', Paris, 1976; C. C. Lamberg-Karlovsky, 'Third millennium modes of exchange and modes of production', in J. A. Sabloff and C. C. Lamberg-Karlovsky, eds., *Ancient Civilization and Trade*, Albuquerque, 1975, 341–68; D. K. Chakrabarti, 'India and West Asia – an alternative approach', *ME* 1, 1977, 25–38.

Agriculture

H. T. Lambrick, *Sind – a General Introduction*, History of Sind Series, vol. 1, Hyderabad, 1964; B. B. Lal. 'Perhaps the earliest ploughed field so far excavated anywhere in the world', *Pur* 4, 1970–1, 1–3.

Attempts to decipher the Indus script

See particularly A. Zide and K. V. Zvelebil, eds., *The Soviet decipherment of the Indus Valley script: Translation and Critique*, The Hague, 1976; K. Koskenniemi and A. Parpola, *Corpus of Texts in the Indus Script*, Helsinki, 1979; K. Koskenniemi, A. Parpola and S. Parpola, *Materials for the Study of the Indus Script*, Helsinki, 1973; I. Mahadevan, *The Indus Script, Texts, Concordance and Tables*, New Delhi, 1977.

Chronology

G. F. Dales, 'A suggested chronology for Afghanistan, Baluchistan, and the Indus valley', in R. W. Ehrich, ed., *Chronologies in Old World Archaeology*, Chicago, 1965, 257–84; on radiocarbon dating see papers by Meadow, Rao and Sankalia in D. P. Agrawal and A. Ghosh, eds., *RIA*, 1973. There is a useful section on Harappan chronology in D. P. Agrawal and S. Kusumgar's *Prehistoric Chronology and Radiocarbon Dating in India*, 1974.

On the end of the civilization

See R. L. Raikes, 'The end of the ancient cities of the Indus', *American Anthropologist*, 66, 1964, 284–99, and *idem*, 'The Mohenjo-daro floods', *Antiquity*, 39, 1965, 196–203; G. F. Dales, 'New investigations at Mohenjo-daro', *Archaeology*, 18, 1965, 145–50; G. L. Possehl, 'The Mohenjo-daro floods, a reply', *American Anthropologist*, 69, 1967, 32–40; H. T. Lambrick, 'The Indus floodplain', *Geographical Journal*, 133, 1967, 483–94; J.-F. Jarrige, 'La fin de la civilisation Harappéene', *Paléorient*, 1973, 263–85.

Chapter 9

There is now so great a list of excavated sites, at least summarily published, that it is not possible to list more than a few major examples. For other synthetic views of the period and for greater detail and large bibliography see Sankalia *PPIP*, 2nd edn, 1974; Sankalia, *Prehistory of India*, 1977; Fairservis, *The Roots of Ancient India*, 2nd edn, 1971. For the geographical concept of the two Nuclear Regions and corridors compare W. Kirk, 'The role of India in the diffusion of early cultures', *Journal of the Royal Geographical Society*, 141, 1975, 19–34.

Baluchistan and Sind

J.-F. Jarrige, *Fouilles de Pirak*, 2 vols., Paris, 1979.

Gandhara graves

G. Stacul, 'Preliminary report on the pre-Buddhist necropolises in Swat', *East and West*, 16, 1966, 37–79; C. Silvi Antonini and G. Stacul, *The Proto-historic Graveyards of Swāt*, 2 vols. Rome, 1972; A. H. Dani *et al.*, 'Timargarha and the Gandhara grave culture', *AP* 3, 1967, 1–407.

Saurashtra and Cutch

Sites in this area are described in detail by Sankalia, *PPIP*, 1974; see also relevant papers in

Agrawal and Chakrabarti, *EIP*, 1979. G. Possehl, *Indus civilization in Saurashtra*, Delhi, 1980, contains an interesting discussion of the post-urban phase.

Punjab and the Northern Nuclear Region

Suraj Bhan, *Excavation at Mitathal and other explorations in the Sutlej–Yamuna divide*, Kurukshetra, 1975; articles in Agrawal and Chakrabarti, *EIP*, 1979; R. C. Agrawala, 'Recent explorations in Rajasthan', *ME* 5, 1981, 59–63.

Copper hoards

A useful discussion is to be found in D. P. Agrawal, *The Copper Bronze Age in India*, Delhi, 1971, and in Sankalia, *PPIP*, 1974.

Bihar and Bengal

B. S. Verma, 'Excavations at Chirand', *Pur* 4, 1971, 19–23.

Chapter 10

Almost all the major sites referred to in this chapter have been published in the appropriate years of *Indian Archaeology – A Review*, and are discussed in Sankalia, *PPIP*, 1974, with rich bibliographical detail. We shall therefore notice relatively few references to key publications.

Southern Nuclear Region

H. D. Sankalia *et al.*, *Excavations at Ahar*, Poona, 1969; Z. D. Ansari and M. K. Dhavalikar, *Excavations at Kayatha*, Pune, 1975; H. D. Sankalia, S. B. Deo and Z. D. Ansari, *Chalcolithic Navdatoli*, Poona, 1971; M. K. Dhavalikar, 'Early farming communities of Central India', in Agrawal and Chakrabarti, *EIP*, 1979.

Maharashtra

H. D. Sankalia *et al.*, *From History to Prehistory at Nevasa*, Poona, 1960; B. K. Thapar, 'Prakash, 1955', *AI* 20 and 21, 1964/5, 5–167; M. K. Dhavalikar and G. Possehl, 'Subsistence patterns of an early farming community of Western India', *Pur* 7, 1974, 39–46; H. D. Sankalia *et al.*, 'An early farming village in Central India', *Expedition*, 17, 1975, 2–11; M. K. Dhavalikar, 'Early farming cultures of Deccan', in Agrawal and Chakrabarti, *EIP*, 1979; *idem*, 'Settlement archaeology of Inamgaon', *Pur* 8, 1975–6, 44–54; Vishnu-Mittre and R. Savithri, 'Ancient plant economy at Inamgaon', *Pur* 8, 1975–6, 55–62; and papers from the Inamgaon seminar in *ME* 1, 1977.

Karnataka and Andhra

F. R. Allchin, *Piklihal Excavations*, Hyderabad, 1961; M. S. Nagaraja Rao, *Protohistoric cultures of Tungabhadra valley*, Dharwar, 1971; Z. D. Ansari and M. S. Nagaraja Rao, *Excavations at Sanganakallu*, Poona, 1969; M. S. Nagaraja Rao, *The Stone Age hill dwellers of Tekkalakota*, Poona, 1965.

Chapter 11

Indo-Iranian language history

A short and lucid account of modern thinking on the Indian and Iranian languages and their relationship is provided by R. E. Emmerick's article, 'Indo-Iranian languages' in the current *Encyclopaedia Britannica*, 9, 438–57. For the early Indo-Aryan branch in particular see T. Burrow, *The Sanskrit Language*, London, 1955. Sir George Grierson's paper on *The Languages of India*, Calcutta, 1903, was later incorporated into vol. 1 of the *Linguistic Survey of India*, Calcutta, 1927. See also T. Burrow, 'The Proto-Indo-Aryans', *JRAS*, 2, 1973, 123–40, and A. Parpola, 'On the protohistory of the Indian languages in the light of archaeological, linguistic and religious evidence: an attempt at integration', in van Lohuizen, ed., *SAA 73*, Leiden, 1974.

Archaeological

For a general discussion of the archaeological problems of interpreting linguistic data see C. Renfrew, 'Problems in the general correlation of archaeological and linguistic strata in prehistoric Greece: the model of autochthonous origin', in R. A. Crossland and A. Birchall, eds., *Bronze Age Migrations in the Aegean*, London, 1974, 263–79. Two important recent volumes are G. Cardona, H. M. Hoenigswald and A. Senn, eds., *Indo-European and Indo-Europeans*, Philadelphia, 1970, containing a variety of papers on linguistic and archaeological topics, among them M. Gimbutas's 'Proto-Indo-European cultures'; and M. S. Asimov, B. A. Litvinsky, L. I. Miroshnikov and D. S. Rayevsky, eds., *Ethnic Problems in the History of Central Asia in the Early Period (second millennium B.C.)*, Moscow, 1981, with many relevant papers. On the Iranian perspectives see R. Cuyler Young, 'The Iranian migration into the Zagros', *Iran: Journal of the British Institute of Persian Studies*, 5, 1967, 11–34, and R. Ghirshman, *L'Iran et la migration des Indo-Aryans et des Iraniens*, Leiden, 1977.

On the Kalibangan evidence see B. K. Thapar, 'Kalibangan: a Harappan metropolis beyond the Indus valley', *Expedition*, 17, 1975; the same author's 'New traits of the Indus civilization at Kalibangan: a re-appraisal', in N. Hammond, ed., *SAA* (1971), 1973, 85–104; and B. B. Lal, 'Kalibangan and the Indus civilization', in Agrawal and Chakrabarti, *EIP*, 1979, 65–97.

Protohistoric evidence

R. C. Majumdar, ed., *History and Culture of the Indian People*, vol. 1, *The Vedic Age*, Bombay, 1950, contains a series of excellent chapters dealing with different aspects of the early literary evidence and its contents. See also Jan Gonda, *Vedic Literature*, in *A History of Indian Literature*, vol. 1.1, Wiesbaden, 1975, for detailed discussion of the Vedic and Late Vedic evidence.

Chapter 12

The beginnings of iron working in South Asia

For recent studies see D. K. Chakrabarti, 'The beginnings of iron in India', *Antiquity*, 50, 1976, 114–24; R. Pleiner, 'The problem of the beginning of Iron Age in India', *Acta Praehistorica et Archaeologica*, 2, 1971, 5–36; N. R. Banerjee, 'The Iron Age in India', in Mishra and Mate, eds., *Indian Prehistory: 1964*, Poona, 1965, 177–218. For the comparable period in Iran see Cuyler Young, article cited in previous chapter. For early metal technology see K. T. M. Hegde, 'A model for understanding ancient Indian iron metallurgy', *Man*, 8, 1973, 416–21.

The Indus System and Baluchistan

References to Pirak and the Gandhara graves are cited in previous chapters. For Wheeler's excavations at Charsada, see Mortimer Wheeler, *Charsada, a Metropolis of the North-West Frontier*, Oxford, 1962. For the Taxila evidence see F. R. Allchin, 'How old is the city of Taxila?', *Antiquity*, 1982. See also D. K. Chakrabarti, 'Early Iron Age in the Indian North-west', in Agrawal and Chakrabarti, *EIP*, 347–64.

North India and the Ganges valley

See N. R. Banerjee's *The Iron Age in India*, Delhi, 1965, and V. Tripathi, *The Painted Grey Ware: an Iron Age Culture of Northern India*, 1976; also papers in Agrawal and Chakrabarti, *EIP*. On the so-called Ochre Coloured Pottery (OCP) and Northern Black Polished ware (NBP) see Proceedings of the Seminar on OCP and NBP, *Pur* 5, 1971–2, and B. P. Sinha, ed., *Potteries in ancient India*, Patna, n.d. For the technology of the NBP the most important contribution to date is K. T. M. Hegde, 'Analysis of ancient Indian Deluxe wares', *Archaeo-Physika*, 10, 1978, 141–55. On the early Ganges urbanism see A. Ghosh, *The City in Early Historical India*, Simla, 1973.

The Southern Nuclear Region and the Peninsula

See papers in Agrawal and Chakrabarti, *EIP*, particularly M. D. N. Sahi, 'Iron at Ahar'; Thapar's report on Prakash has already been cited in chapter 10; on Takalghat and Khapa see S. B. Deo, *Excavations at Takalghat and Khapa*, Nagpur, 1970.

South Indian burial complex

The megalithic graves have received an almost undue share of attention. A full *Bibliography on Indian Megaliths* has been prepared by K. S. Ramachandran, Tamilnadu, 1971. L. Leshnik has published a comprehensive study, *South Indian 'Megalithic' Burials*, Wiesbaden, 1974, marred by its somewhat arbitrary chronology; B. K. Gururaja Rao, *Megalithic Culture in South India*, Mysore, 1972; A. K. Sundara, *The Early Chamber Tombs of South India*, Delhi, 1975; B. Narasimhaiah, *Neolithic and Megalithic Cultures in Tamilnadu*, Delhi, 1980; A. Parpola, *South Indian Megaliths*, Tamilnadu, 1973; A. K. Narain, ed., *Seminar Papers on the Problem of Megaliths in India*, Varanasi, 1969. Among recent monographs S. B. Deo, *Mahurjhari Excavation*, Nagpur, 1973, is of particular interest. On the physical types of the megalith builders, see K. A. R. Kennedy, *The Physical Anthropology of the Megalith-builders of South India and Sri Lanka*, Canberra, 1975.

INDEX

Principal references are in **bold** type